Joshua Oppenheimer is a filmmaker
London. Combining fiction with docu
ultra-right-wing cells, pretends to be abducted by aliens, and 'joins' Christian cults which try to cure gays and lesbians. His films have played in festivals in the US and Europe. He has written for *Theatre Magazine* and *Seagull Theatre Quarterly.* Active in ACT UP and OutRage!, he co-ordinated a street theatre project in Calcutta's Kalighat Red Light District and a needle exchange program in Boston.

Helena Reckitt has been a commissioning editor for Routledge and is currently Deputy Director of Talks at the Institute of Contemporary Arts in London. At the ICA she has organised events including Big Thinkers, Addressing Dressing, Preaching to the Perverted, and the Acting on AIDS conference. She is compiling a sourcebook on Feminist Art for Phaidon Press.

acting on AIDS

sex, drugs & politics

edited by Joshua Oppenheimer
& Helena Reckitt

Library of Congress Catalog Card Number: 96–69725

A catalogue record for this book is available from the British Library on request

First published in 1997 by
Serpent's Tail, 4 Blackstock Mews, London N4 and
180 Varick Street, 10th floor, New York, NY 10014

website: www.serpentstail.com

Phototypeset in 10½pt Plantin by Intype London Ltd
Printed in Great Britain by Mackays of Chatham

contents

voices from the front

For Sarah and to the memory of John Harelkin

acknowledgements

It would be impossible to name everyone who offered the support, encouragement, and ideas which made this collection possible. Several people deserve special thanks. At Serpent's Tail, Laurence O'Toole gave us the initial impetus for the book, and Pete Ayrton's dry wit and friendly guidance made a pleasure of the publishing process. Simon Watney opened his famous address book for us early on and offered advice at all stages. For the Acting on AIDS conference, Dorothy Mukasa's ideas on speakers and issues relating to African Communities were invaluable. At the Terrence Higgins Trust, Robin Gorna offered welcome support, Shaun Whelan provided constant assistance and morale boosting, and Andrew Moffatt secured funding for the conference. At the Institute of Contemporary Arts, Alan Read's enthusiasm and energy for the project sustained us. Keith Rudkin worked tirelessly to realize the conference and activist report. Thanks to everyone at the ICA who worked on conference web-site, publicity, and technical staging: Lars Drinklow, Dionne King, Shelley Malcom, Caroline Miller, and Sholto Ramsay, and to Sian Cook and art2go for their work on the leaflet. Liz Gibbs' invaluable work in the Talks Department enabled Helena Reckitt to focus on this book during a three-month sabbatical.

The volume would have little of its dynamism were it not for the many who spoke at the Acting on AIDS conference, who could not contribute to this anthology. Each of these cultural and political activists has contributed to the way we respond to the epidemic.

For Joshua Oppenheimer, several people deserve special thanks. In the United States, Kwame Anthony Appiah, Michael Bronski, Christine Cynn, and Sarah Oppenheimer offered both friendship and scholarly advice. In England,

Ray Harvey-Amer, Robin Baker, Kellan Farshea, and Susan Winter Hall gave love and inspiration.

For Helena Reckitt, the love of family, friends, and girlfriend, the memories of friends lost to AIDS, and the inspiration of all those committed to the fight against the epidemic, have been a vital source of strength.

Grants from Education for Action at Radcliffe College and the Weissman International Fellowship at Harvard University enabled Joshua Oppenheimer to work on this book.

Our biggest debt is to the writers who worked to very tight deadlines to make this book possible.

The conference was generously supported by the Cooperative Bank and the Health Education Authority.

Versions of some essays have appeared elsewhere and we are grateful to the publishers for permission to reprint them here.

A version of 'Queer Peregrinations' by Cindy Patton originally appeared in *Challenging Boundaries*, Michael Shapiro and Hayward R. Alker (eds), University of Minnesota Press, 1996.

Eve Kosofsky Sedgwick's essay, 'Gary Fisher In Your Pocket', is taken from *Gary Fisher In Your Pocket: Stories and Notebooks of Gary Fisher*, Duke University Press, 1996, which she edited.

A longer version of 'How To Read A Condom: Lessons from the AIDS Epidemic' by Paula Treichler appears as 'How to Use a Condom: Bedtime Stories for the Transcendental Signifier' in Cary Nelson and Dilip P. Gaonkar (eds), *Disciplinarity and Dissent in Cultural Studies*, New York, Routledge, 1996, chapter 16.

An amended version of 'The Nature of AIDS-related Discrimination' by Jonathan Grimshaw was originally prepared in December 1995 for a Working Group on Legal Services for Discrimination in AIDS and HIV cases funded by the European Union.

introduction

Joshua Oppenheimer and
Helena Reckitt

In 1981, the *New York Times* announced the mysterious outbreak of a rare cancer called Karposi's sarcoma among gay men living in New York and San Francisco. Unsure of the outbreak's cause or future course, nobody could have known that this ominous rash of illness was the beginning of one of the most devastating health crises of our time. Fifteen years later, 27.9 million people have been infected with HIV worldwide. Of these, 21.8 million are still alive. Close to 19 million adults and children (86 per cent of the world total) living with HIV or AIDS are in sub-Saharan Africa, and in South and South East Asia. Of the adults, 58 per cent are men, and 42 per cent are women.[1]

In the United States, almost three quarters of a million people have died of AIDS. Roughly half the gay men living in New York and San Francisco are HIV-positive. In America's neglected inner cities – where poverty and violence are rife – uncontrolled HIV epidemics have claimed the lives of hundreds of thousands of injecting drug users and their partners. In the United Kingdom, roughly 17,000 gay men are HIV-positive, and in certain communities of African immigrants, refugees, and asylum seekers, HIV seroprevalence hovers between 5 and 25 per cent.

AIDS is at once a medical and a political crisis. It was a grim irony that this terminal syndrome would wreak most of its havoc on communities already subject to persecution.

Not only were gay men, injecting drug users, commercial sex workers, Africans, and African refugees confronted with wave upon wave of death and illness; they were subject to intense discrimination and stigmatization. The fact that AIDS disproportionately affected 'undesirables' did little to move politicians and public health officials to admonish intolerance and to make saving those at greatest risk their top priority. Instead, it became an excuse for inaction. It was thus wholly justifiable when in the mid-1980s, desperate that something be done to fight the epidemic, AIDS activists began to assert that 'AIDS affects everybody.' And for once, this warning did not fall on deaf ears. Many governments scurried to prevent HIV from leaking into the general population. They spent millions producing generalized 'AIDS awareness' campaigns which taught nothing to nobody in particular. These campaigns effectively reinscribed boundaries of the various western national communities – white nuclear families were on the inside, while those actually affected by AIDS were positioned on the outside. Meanwhile, the authorities continued to do nothing to empower those at real risk to actually prevent transmission of the virus.

Given the emerging hegemony of a diffuse and untargeted AIDS awareness, it is no surprise that by the late 1980s, the common-sense, progressive understanding of AIDS began to speak in terms of a single, global pandemic. Indeed, the rhetoric of pandemic fosters a liberal tolerance for the diversity of people with AIDS, a broad commitment to offering resources to fight AIDS in the poorer countries, and a diffuse resolve to get on with bringing the epidemic under control. But the idea of a single, global epidemic is profoundly unhelpful to those who are interested in implementing prevention, treatment, and care programmes designed to minimize the harm caused by AIDS to actual communities.

If they have one thing in common, the essays in this collection understand AIDS in its specificity, as a series of many different epidemics, each situated at the intersection of local and global politics, culture and demographics. Virtually all contributions insist that attention needs to be directed to those populations most affected by the virus.

While some of the essays were commissioned specifically for this volume, many of the contributors initially spoke at the three-day Acting on AIDS conference (London, 1996) organized by the Institute of Contemporary Arts and the Terrence Higgins Trust. The event brought together activists, cultural critics, artists and policy-makers from the UK, US, Africa, and Europe to build alliances, reinvigorate strategy, and set new goals in the community response to AIDS. It was held in a non-professional, non-specificalist environment – an arts centre – within the context of a regular public programme of critical dialogues and debates. The conference was unusual in the UK for bringing gay men, African communities, commercial sex workers, and drug use researchers together on the same platform to exchange experiences and to build a broader coalition dedicated to the urgent business of stopping AIDS.

The Acting on AIDS conference made one thing more clear now than ever: fifteen years into the epidemic, there is no progressive consensus about which issues are most urgent, or on how best to strategize HIV prevention and treatment. Reflecting this diversity of opinion, and somewhat unlike earlier collections concerning the cultural politics of AIDS, Acting on AIDS does not offer any one 'party line'. From their multiple, sometimes conflicting positions, and across a vast array of disciplines and discourses, contributors are in dialogue and counterpoint with each other.

The collection does not privilege any particular method or mode of analysis over any other. While the whole volume is accessible to the lay reader (and does not include any technical essays), it is committed to the idea that a politics of health can be forged only through an understanding of the epidemic's multiple contexts: epidemiological, medical, social, sexual, racial, global, economic, and psychological. As Robin Gorna puts it in her essay, 'AIDS brings the most personal, intimate elements of human existence into the political arena, and demonstrates how political decisions invade personal lives.' The stigmas, prejudices, and taboos which have been aggravated by AIDS are at the same time an important part of the epidemic's reality. Without them, the crisis would be – as this collection's essays on AIDS prevention reveal – far less deadly.

In July 1996, shortly after the Acting on AIDS conference, scientists at the Eleventh International Conference on AIDS in Vancouver announced powerful new antiviral treatments which show far more promise than anything available to date. The possibility that someday, perhaps in the near future, AIDS will become a treatable, chronic condition means that this collection is offered in a rare moment of hope and cautious optimism. However, even as newspapers tout the end of AIDS, there is little doubt that the combination therapies will never be available to the vast majority of those infected: the 19 million HIV-positive residents of sub-Saharan Africa and South and South East Asia. In a particularly barbaric twist to economic injustice, poverty becomes for many a sentence to a potentially preventable death.

In the context of these significant shifts in what we know about HIV, the first section of this book, Science and Safety, highlights the interface of medical research and HIV prevention. Edward King opens the section with an explanation of the new combination therapies, and their implications for HIV prevention. Paula Treichler offers a brief history of the condom in popular culture and the popular imagination, exploring its role in American debates about safety and morality. She examines the gay community's swift appropriation of the condom, and she calls for new scientific research to provide more effective and empowering alternatives. Tim Rhodes critiques the ways epidemiology understands risk among injecting drug users. He challenges objective models of risk, and stresses that until prevention campaigns discuss the risks of injection in terms with which drug users themselves identify there is no possibility of effective health promotion for drug injectors. Simon Watney continues with the theme of epidemiology, but turns his attention to an analysis of the politics of statistics, in the light of debates about the re-gaying of AIDS. Watney stresses the need for epidemiologists and statisticians to face the political and ethical implications of their work.

The book's second section, Prevention: New Directions, raises hard questions about the roles of beauty, identity and honesty in safer sex messages. By providing a forum for the most cutting-edge debates in HIV prevention, we seek to suggest possible solutions to AIDS education's most disturbing aporia: why do people continue to put themselves at risk when they know what they need to do to protect themselves?

Sander Gilman opens the section with a critique of safer sex campaigns' reliance on stereotypical constructions of beauty, and their inability to deploy imaginative representations of human frailty. Michael Bronski levels these concerns at the gay community. By suggesting that gay men still have unsafe sex because of low self-esteem, he stresses the relationships between health, beauty, and consumerism. Articulating the dangers of the inevitable translation of an HIV-negative test into a seemingly immutable HIV-negative identity, Bronski argues that safer sex campaigns must not rely on rigid differentiation between the HIV-positive and the HIV-negative. Walt Odets also begins with the argument that unsafe sex can be explained, if only in part, by low self-esteem, but he sharply disagrees with Bronski by calling for primary prevention which accommodates the knowledge of people's own HIV status. He argues that until prevention specifically addresses its target community – HIV-negative gay men and those who do not know their status – it will never be effective. Robin Gorna explores the relationships between women, AIDS, and feminism. She exposes the multiple ways in which concern for paediatric AIDS and antenatal infection has both displaced attention from the prevention needs of adult women, and limited women's autonomy in making decisions about their own maternity and sexual health. Jonathan G Silin closes the section with a discussion of AIDS education for children. He questions established notions of childhood, development and innocence, and argues for an AIDS education which understands HIV as part of children's broader experience, as inseparable from other issues of social and economic injustice.

The volume's third section, Diaspora and Globalization, explores issues at the junction of cultural and racial contexts and differences, and globalizing institutions and discourses. Dorothy Mukasa assesses the needs of African communities affected by HIV in Britain. She describes how a culturally insensitive social service system has neglected these needs, and argues that Africans themselves should be empowered and supported to spearhead the response to AIDS in their own communities. Building on Mukasa's implicit claim that resources need to be directed to empower those really affected by AIDS, Chetan Bhatt and Robert Lee argue that an uncritical endorsement of a liberal model of multiculturalism has led to a cultural relativism within the HIV service sector. They argue that funds are distributed not on the basis of epidemiological need, but rather according to a model by which every community may deserve equal resources, according to political agendas which are often inappropriate or ill-judged. Meurig Horton turns the debate to issues of globalism, arguing that the global response to AIDS has rendered invisible the millions of homosexually active men in the third world. Finally Cindy Patton contrasts two master discourses which have shaped the way we think about AIDS in a global context. By examining the implications and legacies of tropical medicine and epidemiology, Patton shows how discourses have a direct impact on policy and, in turn, on those affected by the epidemic.

The fourth section, Traditions of Activism, both questions the changing roles of different activist strategies and provides grassroots counter-memories of the epidemic in relation to social change. The essays in this section ask which structures of community and identity foster activism, and which do not. They understand AIDS activism as the collective effort – within the confines of given medical knowledge – to minimize the epidemic's impact and to prevent the preventable. Though there may be cause for optimism about new treatments, now is no time for complacency. As many first-generation AIDS activists leave the struggle because of exhaustion, pressures of professionalism, despair, and, tragically, death, new activist energies are urgently needed to fight censorship of safer sex material, to demand that resources be distributed to those in most need, and to pressure drug companies and governments to make new treatments accessible to all.

Mark Harrington opens this section with a history of AIDS treatment activism in the US. He stresses the failures as well as the successes of treatment activism, and he warns against an uncritical commitment to ACT UP's strategy of direct action. Joshua Oppenheimer assesses the decline in grassroots gay and AIDS activism in the United States. He argues that with the commercialization of gay communities, professional lobbies have replaced grassroots forums, and writing contribution cheques has replaced protest. He questions the interests these changes serve. Like Oppenheimer, Scott is concerned with the obstacles which discourage gay men from becoming AIDS activists. In his account of gay men's AIDS activism and the re-gaying of AIDS, he describes the consistent exclusion of gay men's work – which has revolutionized HIV prevention – from official histories of the British epidemic. Cheryl Overs gives a first-hand account of the sex workers' rights movement in relation to AIDS, describing the creation of a sex workers' identity politics at odds with orthodox socialist feminism. She suggests that the emergence of a queer sensibility in sex workers' organizations was a vital step in the development of a viable political response to AIDS. Building on analyses of the role of identity and community in the articulation of activism, Edmund White and Larys Frogier discuss the lack of a strong sense of gay community and identity in France. They argue that French resistance to identity politics has obstructed efforts to target HIV prevention work to those at greatest risk of infection. Frogier points to ACT UP/Paris as a new and much-needed force which articulates a gay identity politics in relation to the epidemic. Alexander García Düttmann's concise interruption, 'Wait a Minute', questions the relationship between thought and dissent, philosophy and activism. In his own words: 'Activism must try to recognize and to seize occasions which by definition escape coordination. [Activism is] the very moment thought is carried away by its own movement and activity.'

The collection closes with Voices from the Front. These essays articulate the complex realities of AIDS as they are lived every day. They meditate on banality and redemption, fear and resolve, anger and mourning, opportunism and bravery. Michael Bronski offers a bitter and moving litany, a re-working of the founding catechism for Catholic education. Sarah Schulman exposes homophobia in the growing Viatical industry, and indicts niche marketing to people with AIDS. Jonathan Grimshaw documents the widespread discrimination against the HIV-positive. Juan Vicente Aliaga discusses artistic and political responses to AIDS in Spain. Eve Kosofsky Sedgwick contributes a memorial to a writer and friend, Gary Fisher. Ron Athey writes the apocalypse in *Deliverance*, a lacerating account of redemption and ritual, of bodies on the brink. Lastly, Edmund White closes the volume with a tribute to the last photograph taken of his lover, Hubert Sorin.

The essays in this section remind us that there is nothing noble about suffering, nothing fashionable about the epidemic. These are pieces about dying and about survival, about finding oneself alone after one's friends and lovers have died, about suffering and devastation, and about the terror of death. If their vision is bleak, this should be understood as an act of dissent, a source of quiet but persistent hope for a more humane future. In this hope, articulated in the face of loss, lies the impetus to take action, to act on AIDS.

notes

1. 'The Status and Trends of the Global HIV/AIDS Pandemic: Final Report at the Eleventh International Conference on AIDS', United Nations Joint Programme on AIDS, Vancouver, 1996.

science and safety

HIV prevention and the new virology

how new understandings of AIDS pathogenesis and improvements in antiviral treatments will impact on HIV primary prevention

Edward King

Since January 1995, developments in HIV basic science and clinical research have come thick and fast. Important advances have been made in understanding the natural history of HIV within the infected person's body and in developing anti-HIV treatments whose effectiveness is orders of magnitude greater than those previously available. Already the medical arena is being transformed, as many clinicians feel increasingly confident that their interventions can have a dramatic impact on the quality and quantity of life of people with HIV.

However, there has been little consideration of the ways in which the new virology will affect HIV prevention policies and practice. This paper argues that it will inevitably result in unprecedented upheavals. Even if the effectiveness of today's therapies is still insufficient to bring to fruition the more optimistic aims, such as totally halting disease progression or even curing infected people, the fact that these possibilities are now openly discussed in medical circles itself has implications for HIV prevention work. In the UK treatment issues have usually been ignored or overlooked by the AIDS voluntary sector.[1] Now more than ever it is essential that HIV prevention workers understand the significance of recent medical advances and prepare for the impact on their own work.

the new virology

New insights into the relationship between HIV and the human immune system have been central to the latest developments. Until recently, it was widely believed that shortly after infection with HIV the body mounts a strong immune response that drives the virus into latency, and that the virus remains relatively inactive throughout the asymptomatic period. Only as the disease advanced was HIV thought to be re-activated by some unknown trigger and to start replicating at high levels.

In January 1995 two American research teams produced evidence that this was not the case.[2,3] Their studies relied on two new tools – viral load tests and protease inhibitors – and an understanding of the process of drug resistance.

There are several different viral load tests – or quantitative HIV RNA assays, to give them their precise technical name – but they all measure the same thing. Using a variety of amplification techniques, they 'count' the number of pieces of HIV RNA in a sample, usually blood plasma. RNA is the form in which HIV particles (and other retroviruses) normally carry their genetic material. When HIV infects a cell, it converts its RNA to DNA (the same form as the genetic code of human cells) and merges with the host cell's genes. HIV RNA assays therefore measure the number of HIV particles that are present in the sample, as opposed to the number of HIV-infected cells.[4]

Protease inhibitors are the newest class of anti-HIV drugs to be developed.[5] Three protease inhibitors have advanced to the clinic – saquinavir (Invirase) manufactured by Roche, Abbott's ritonavir (Norvir) and Merck's indinavir (Crixivan). As a class, protease inhibitors have substantially greater anti-HIV effects than earlier drugs such as the nucleoside analogue family that includes AZT, 3TC, ddI and ddC.

However, when exposed to ritonavir or indinavir as single drug treatments (monotherapy), HIV strains that are resistant to the effect of the drugs rapidly evolve. Resistance is thought to occur primarily through a process of Darwinian selection – 'survival of the fittest'. HIV replication is a relatively error-prone process, so each new HIV particle produced from an infected cell contains subtle genetic variations from the parent virus. Some of these naturally occurring mutants may, by chance, be inherently less susceptible (or resistant) to the effects of anti-HIV drugs than others. When HIV reproduces within the body of someone taking a drug, any susceptible viruses that are produced are likely to be eradicated by the drug, but resistant viruses are more likely to survive to infect new cells and themselves reproduce. Over time, this 'selective pressure' may mean that an initially drug-susceptible virus population evolves into a predominantly drug-resistant population.[6]

The American research teams examined the short-term impact of a protease inhibitor on levels of HIV in the blood of infected people. They found that plasma viral load rapidly declined within hours of starting treatment. Protease inhibitors only block HIV replication within HIV-infected cells; they do not kill free-floating HIV particles. The fact that the number of virus particles in the blood fell so rapidly once the production of new viruses from infected cells was stopped by the drug thus indicated that the 'life expectancy' of a free-floating virus particle in the blood must itself be very short.

Substantial numbers of virus particles can be measured even in the blood of healthy, untreated, symptom-free HIV-positive people. Because the life-span of such particles is short, their presence proves that high levels of HIV reproduction must be taking place during the period in which HIV was previously thought to be primarily latent.

Throughout this asymptomatic period, though, people with HIV tend to have relatively stable CD4 cell counts. CD4 cells, or T-helper cells, are the primary immune cell infected by HIV and destroyed either by the virus or by other immune cells that recognize infected CD4 cells. The only way that the CD4 count could remain stable even though a large number of HIV particles is being produced every day is if the immune system is producing new CD4 cells at about the same rate as they are destroyed.

Thus, a picture emerges of the virus and the immune system engaged in an ongoing, high-level battle throughout the asymptomatic period. Every day billions of HIV particles are produced, and just as quickly as these viruses destroy CD4 cells, the immune system valiantly produces more CD4 cells to replace them. The apparent stability of the CD4 count and viral load over periods of many months belies the true level of viral and immune activity; it is like trench warfare viewed from the air, in which the battlelines barely move but both sides constantly suffer massive casualties and must marshal a steady stream of reinforcements.[7]

Within a few months of infection, an individual's viral load has reached this state of equilibrium with the immune system; the level of the viral load at this point is called the 'set-point', and it is thought to remain relatively stable until significant disease progression occurs. The viral set-point has been shown to be strongly correlated with the rate at which an individual's CD4 cell count subsequently declines and with their medium- to long-term risk of developing AIDS and dying. In a study of stored blood samples from over 1,600 gay men in the Multicenter AIDS Cohort Study in the USA, people with the lowest viral load (below 3,000 copies/ml) soon after infection took an average of over ten years to develop AIDS, while those with the highest viral load (over 30,000 copies/ml) took an average of only 2.8 years to develop AIDS.[8]

therapeutic advances

Since a low viral load is associated with a good prognosis among untreated people, many researchers argue that reducing a high viral load with anti-HIV drugs (either before the set-point is established or at any subsequent stage in the course of infection) should be expected to improve prognosis. This concept has not been definitively proven, but is supported by the recent results of several trials studying the effects of drug combinations on HIV-related symptoms and life expectancy. These have consistently indicated that the regimen that leads to the greatest reduction in viral load within the first one to two months of therapy is also the most effective at reducing disease progression and prolonging life in the long-term.[9] With two or three-drug combinations, dramatic falls in viral load can be achieved. In some studies the majority of treated people have had their viral load reduced to levels that are undetectable with even the most advanced viral load assays. This does not necessarily mean that there is no virus present at all – just that virus levels are below the limit of detection. Even if no virus is present in the blood, it is possible that HIV is persisting in 'sanctuary sites' in parts of the body to which the drugs may not penetrate as well, such as the brain, spinal cord and testes, and will re-emerge if treatment is stopped or multi-drug resistant HIV strains develop.

A rebound in plasma viral load has indeed been observed in every case to date in which someone whose viral load had been reduced below the level of detection has elected to stop treatment.[10] In one case reported at the Eleventh International Conference on AIDS in July 1996, a man who had had no detectable HIV in his blood or lymph nodes for eighteen months decided to stop treatment – and the virus promptly reappeared.[11] Nevertheless, the more optimistic researchers argue that treatment with the most powerful drug regimens available might theoretically eliminate HIV from the body altogether, although it would probably take three years or more for some of the longer-lived cell types infected by HIV, such as macrophages, to die and be replaced by uninfected cells.

Experiments designed specifically to test the ability of three and four drug combinations to cure newly infected people are underway in New York. The researchers argue that people who have been infected for only a few months are the best candidates in whom to try to eradicate the virus, for three reasons: because HIV may not have had a chance to spread widely throughout their body tissues; because relatively few HIV life-cycles will have taken place, limiting the number of potentially drug-resistant mutants that are likely to be present; and because these individuals are unlikely yet to have suffered irreversible damage to their immune systems.[12]

It will take many years for these studies to reach a conclusion. However, even if early aggressive treatment does not cure newly infected people, many researchers argue that it may still dramatically alter the long-term course of infection. As noted earlier, among untreated people, those with a low viral load a few months after infection are much less likely to develop AIDS during the next ten years than those with a higher viral load. Researchers hope that reducing the set-point of viral load through the prompt use of anti-HIV drugs at or soon after seroconversion will also improve long-term prognosis, although this remains unproven.

implications for prevention

Treatment information providers have responded quickly to the urgent need to inform people with HIV, their doctors and those responsible for funding treatment and care services about these advances. Yet the implications extend far more widely than this.

Three major issues for HIV prevention workers can already be identified. First, how will improvements in the treatment of HIV affect the willingness of people who may have been at risk of infection to take the HIV antibody test? Secondly, what is the significance of evidence that prompt treatment soon after exposure to HIV can reduce the chance of becoming infected? Thirdly, what does the new virology have to tell us about the infectiousness of people with HIV, and ways in which it may be reduced by drug therapy?

testing

The lack of anti-viral treatment options that might delay the onset of AIDS has been a strong disincentive against taking the HIV antibody test. Many individuals and HIV advisors have argued that there is little point in finding out whether one is HIV-positive if there is nothing that can be done to delay the development of symptoms. In fact, there are medical interventions that can benefit asymptomatic people with HIV, such as the use of antibiotics to prevent PCP pneumonia among people with CD4 counts below 200, but in the UK at least these have never received much attention as an argument in favour of testing.

Just as doctors report that a growing proportion of people already diagnosed with HIV are choosing to take anti-HIV drugs, so awareness of the availability of combination therapy regimens that can delay AIDS and prolong life when started before symptoms occur is likely to encourage a growing proportion of previously untested people to find out their status. The ability of viral load testing to predict an individual's likelihood of disease progression (especially when used in combination with the CD4 count) may provide a further incentive for testing among symptom-free people, who in the past might have concluded that testing HIV-positive would introduce more doubts and uncertainties than if they remained untested.

There is also likely to be a new concern to identify recently infected people and offer them aggressive anti-HIV therapy during the period known as 'primary' or 'acute' infection. As discussed earlier, the set-point at which an individual's viral load settles three to six months after infection is a good predictor of their long-term prognosis, with a low set-point clearly associated with a reduced risk of disease progression. Several studies suggest that using combination therapy in recently infected people can reduce viral load to undetectable levels in a high proportion of treated people, raising the hope that this will also dramatically improve their prognosis. Although many questions remain unanswered – for instance, is a viral load that has been lowered with drugs as good a prognostic marker as a viral load that is low without treatment? Will viral load rebound if treatment is stopped? – already some American AIDS groups are initiating campaigns to raise awareness of the symptoms of HIV primary infection and encourage affected people to access medical services.

People who have previously tested HIV-negative may start to take repeat tests every few months, so that if they do become infected they are diagnosed promptly. A less frequent form of repeat testing is already commonplace among American gay men, not least on account of the requirement that federally funded prevention campaigns include a testing component[13], but on the whole community educators have insisted that testing is significant, in Simon Watney's words, 'as a means of access to treatment and care, rather than as a form of primary HIV prevention'.[14] During the 1990s, this separation of testing and prevention was challenged by the recognition of the complex strategies employed by many gay men to reduce their risk of HIV infection, such as the 'negotiated safety' approach in which men in relationships use the test to establish that they share the same serostatus, then only use condoms during sex outside the relationship.[15] This trend towards the wider acceptance of HIV antibody testing as a useful component of HIV prevention strategies can only accelerate if the test is recognized as the means of access to new biomedical forms of HIV risk reduction such as post-exposure prophylaxis, discussed below.

This pressure towards early diagnosis may require the introduction of new tests in the clinic. The one-to-three month 'window period' between infection and the production of HIV antibodies means that conventional HIV antibody tests are not a useful tool for definitively diagnosing recent HIV infection. Alternative approaches include the use of direct viral assays that measure HIV RNA (viral load tests) or the presence of p24, an HIV protein that can be detected in the blood of many infected people.

post-exposure prophylaxis

In recent months there has been renewed interest in the use of anti-HIV drugs not to treat established HIV infection, but to try to prevent the virus from gaining a foothold in the body of, for example, a health care worker exposed to HIV through an accident such as a needle-stick injury. While debate on this subject currently focuses on the medical profession, post-exposure prophylaxis (PEP) may also be important for people exposed to HIV through sexual or drug-using behaviours.

Post-exposure prophylaxis has previously been controversial because of the limited evidence that it works. The average risk of infection from an occupational injury involving HIV-infected needles or other sharp instruments has been estimated at one in 300, or 0.3 per cent[16], making it very difficult to show whether the prompt use of anti-HIV drugs can reduce this very small risk still further, and the only attempt at a controlled trial failed to enrol enough participants.[17] Nevertheless, in 1992, 40 per cent of health care workers who suffered occupational exposure to HIV chose to use PEP.[18] In 1996 the US Centers for Disease Control and Prevention issued new recommendations following a pooled analysis of cases involving health care workers in the USA and Europe, which concluded that PEP with AZT monotherapy reduced the risk of HIV seroconversion by 79 per cent.[19] As multi-drug combinations have been demonstrated to be more effective than AZT monotherapy in treating people with HIV[20], the new guidelines suggest that combinations should also be considered for PEP in the hope of increasing its effectiveness.

The CDC now advocates four weeks' treatment using regimens of varying intensity, depending on the severity of the exposure. For example, towards the lower end of the spectrum of risk, workers who suffer exposure of a mucous membrane to a potentially infectious fluid such as semen or vaginal secretions (in which cases the average risk of infection is estimated at 0.1 per cent[21]) should be offered

AZT perhaps with the addition of 3TC. In more serious exposures, such as those involving contact between mucous membranes and blood, or when the skin is broken by a bloodied instrument, or when the blood may be suspected to contain high levels of HIV (as in cases involving newly infected people or people with advanced AIDS), treatment with the triple combination of AZT, 3TC and indinavir may be recommended. The guidelines note that in cases where the HIV status of the 'source patient' is unknown, 'initiating PEP should be decided on a case-by-case basis, based on the exposure risk and the likelihood of HIV infection in known or possible source patients'.[22]

At a session discussing PEP during the Eleventh International Conference on AIDS in Vancouver in July 1996, physicians voiced their sense of unease at limiting PEP to health care workers.[23] If PEP works, ethically it should be made available to individuals who are placed at significant risk of infection through other exposure routes. For example, if the condom breaks while an HIV-positive man is fucking an HIV-negative partner, the receptive partner is arguably placed at a risk of infection that is at least as high as in many cases of occupational exposure in which PEP is now recommended.

Use of PEP in non-occupational settings has only previously been considered for survivors of sexual assault. The American Society of Law, Medicine and Ethics convened an interdisciplinary Working Group on HIV Testing, Counselling, and Prophylaxis After Sexual Assault, which published its recommendations in 1994. At that time the efficacy of PEP was less clearly established, but nevertheless the group concluded that survivors should be provided with information about the availability of PEP to enable them to decide whether or not to use it, 'based on a risk assessment of the exposure. The risk assessment should consider available information on the serostatus of the assailant, the type of exposure (anal, vaginal, or oral penetration and ejaculation), the nature of the physical injuries, and the number of assaults', as well as the potential for drug side-effects.[24]

When viewed alongside the growing acceptance of treatment during or soon after seroconversion, the case for offering PEP to anyone recently at significant risk of infection becomes quite compelling. It will certainly be difficult to define the boundary between cases of sexual risk which are high enough to justify offering PEP, and those in which the risk of infection is sufficiently low that the financial cost of PEP and the risk of drug side-effects is felt to be unjustifiable. For instance, the CDC guidelines indicate that combination therapy may be reasonable for health care workers who experience mucosal exposure to semen even where there are only grounds for suspicion, rather than certainty, that the source patient is HIV-positive. How does this differ from the situation of any gay man who gets fucked without a condom in a large city in the UK?

When used, PEP must be initiated promptly; the CDC guidelines note that animal research suggests that PEP may be ineffective if started later than twenty-four to thirty-six hours after exposure, although starting even one to two weeks post-exposure may be justified in cases of the highest risk. The protocol used at San Francisco General Hospital notes that 'after an exposure, most health care workers are upset and find that decisions about treatment are very hard to make. We recommend that the exposed person start therapy. Therapy can be stopped later, after the exposed person has had a chance to talk with their clinician and loved ones. Once the immediate crisis has passed, it is usually easier to make the best decision.'[25] If PEP is ever to become a practical option for non-occupational exposure, a new system of 'rapid response' clinic services may be required to provide prompt access to treatment.

infectiousness

The development of potent anti-HIV regimens that can have a dramatic effect on HIV viral load has coincided with increased interest in whether the infectiousness of HIV-positive people varies over time. If there is a relationship between viral load and infectiousness, the benefits of drugs that lower viral load might be two-fold – benefit to the individual in terms of improved quality and quantity of life, and benefit to society in terms of a reduced risk of transmission to others. Thus, use of anti-HIV drugs might constitute both primary and secondary HIV prevention.

Several research teams have proposed that periods of high viral load in the blood may also be periods of high infectiousness. On the basis of complex mathematical models, Jerome Koopman, Professor of Epidemiology at the University of Michigan, has concluded that the vast majority of cases of HIV transmission may occur during the 'primary infection' stage when the transmitter is himself only recently infected and has very high viral load.[26] By analyzing data from cohorts of gay men, this team has estimated that the probability of HIV transmission during a single act of anal intercourse is 0.1 to 0.3 (from one in ten to about one in three) during primary infection – which, incidentally, is comparable to the average risk in cases of occupational exposure to blood in which PEP is recommended. At other stages of infection they estimated the risk to be considerably lower: 0.001 to 0.0001 (between one in a thousand and one in ten thousand) during the long asymptomatic period, and 0.01 to 0.001 (between one in a hundred and one in a thousand) once symptoms have developed.[27]

If correct, Koopman's theory has wide-reaching implications. Behaviours that carry at most a modest risk of HIV transmission when undertaken with a partner with established infection, such as oral sex[28], might plausibly be efficient modes of infection when undertaken with a partner during primary infection. The theory would also lend weight to the importance of early diagnosis of seroconverters. By the time most infected people test positive with an HIV antibody test and thus receive advice or reinforcement of the importance of safer behaviours, the period during which they were most likely to infect others may already have passed. The challenge for HIV prevention campaigns would be to reduce the likelihood of a person who has unprotected sex on one occasion (the source of infection) from having unprotected sex again within the following days or weeks (the high risk period for transmission). However, the only epidemiological study specifically to examine this issue in the real world found no indication of an increased rate of transmission in serodiscordant heterosexual couples during the primary infection period.[29] No similar studies to assess the significance (or otherwise) of primary infection among gay men have yet been reported. Nevertheless, even if primary infection is not the sole period of concern, other research has supported a link between viral load and transmission. Some researchers have found a correlation between the level of HIV in the blood and the level of HIV in semen[30], although others disagree.[31] Among HIV-positive pregnant women, those with higher viral load are more likely to pass on the virus to their unborn child.[32] Finally, epidemiological studies have consistently found that unprotected sex with a person with advanced HIV infection, when viral load tends to be higher, carries a greater risk of infection than unprotected sex with an asymptomatic partner.[33]

Thus it remains plausible that reducing viral load with anti-HIV therapy may in turn reduce infectiousness. For sexual transmission, this assumes that drugs that reduce viral load in the blood will have a similar effect on virus load in semen and vaginal fluids – an assumption supported by some[34,35], but not all[36], of the limited number of studies looking at the effect of anti-HIV drugs on the amount of HIV in semen. In a placebo-controlled study among HIV-positive pregnant women, the rate of transmission of HIV to their unborn children was indeed reduced from 25 per cent to

8.3 per cent by treatment with AZT during pregnancy, delivery and the infants' first weeks of life. The mechanism of action is thought to be a combination of a reduction in the woman's viral load, and pre- and post-exposure prophylaxis in the child.[37]

In 1991 Professor Roy Anderson of Imperial College London and his colleagues provoked a brief controversy by arguing that treatment which lengthens the lives of people with HIV could be against the interests of the community as a whole, since by prolonging the period during which HIV-positive people were infectious it could lead to an increased rate of spread of the virus and ultimately a higher total of AIDS deaths.[38] However, this model pessimistically assumed that treatments which prolonged life would not also reduce infectiousness. If in fact wider uptake of today's potent anti-HIV regimens would lead to a decrease in the rate of HIV spread, it could be considered that both the individual and the public health would be best served by encouraging HIV testing and early treatment.

motivation for safer behaviour

As the new mood of scientific optimism filters into the public domain, health educators will need to consider carefully the likely effects on individuals' motivation to sustain safer behaviours.

To take an extreme scenario, a well-informed gay man could formulate the following multi-level rationalization for unprotected sex with a partner whose HIV status he did not know, in which each step is factually correct:

1. it is statistically probable that my new partner is HIV-negative because even in the most sexually active sections of the British gay community, only a minority of men are infected
2. if he is infected, the risk of transmission in a single act of unprotected sex is statistically tiny

3. if he is taking anti-HIV drugs, his infectiousness may well be decreased still further
4. even if he does pass on the virus, it is possible that prompt testing and treatment will act as post-exposure prophylaxis, preventing the infection from becoming established in my body
5. even if I do become infected, treatment during seroconversion may dramatically improve my long-term prognosis
6. even if treatment at seroconversion does not affect long-term outcome, using different combinations of the powerful new anti-HIV drugs may mean that I may still be able to look forward to a very long or perhaps indefinite delay in disease progression.

Clearly there are powerful counter-arguments to such a rationalization. Many of the more optimistic predictions of the possible effects of treatment remain unsubstantiated. The multi-drug regimens are hard to take, potentially involving twenty or more pills a day which have to be taken according to a strict dosing schedule, some with food and some on an empty stomach, to maximize their benefits and minimize the chances of resistance. They may cause a significant level of side-effects, and treatment may have to be sustained for at least several years, if not indefinitely. A growing number of people may experience new forms of psychological distress as they anxiously follow trends in their CD4 count and viral load to try to assess whether drug therapy is working. These negative factors are likely to impact most forcefully on asymptomatic people, who might otherwise enjoy a normal lifestyle. It will be important to communicate these harsh realities of the new virology, not just the potential rewards. Other implications of the medical advances should actively reinforce the importance of avoiding infection with HIV. For example, it is clear that AZT-resistant strains of HIV are transmissible, and that these strains account for a growing proportion of new infections.[39]

It is reasonable to assume that people infected with AZT-resistant HIV will be less able to benefit from treatment regimens containing AZT. They could also have an inherently worse prognosis; several studies have found that the emergence of AZT-resistant strains among people taking the drug is associated with an increased risk of disease progression and death even if they change treatment to ddI.[40,41]

If medical progress leads to an increase in the number of people with HIV who are on treatment, the proportion of new infections that involves single- or multi-drug resistant HIV strains may rise. Thus, individuals who abandon safer sex because of optimism over the availability of treatments might in practice find themselves unable to benefit fully from those treatments.

Increasingly, HIV prevention campaigns will need to take account of these factors in exploring the reasons why risky behaviours persist, and in devising interventions to encourage and support safer sex.

conclusion

It is arguable that there have been few significant developments in HIV prevention approaches since the mid 1980s. The standardized nature of safer sex messages is reflected in the existence of almost formulaic elements in prevention materials – familiar statements fossilized for a decade, such as 'In the absence of a vaccine or cure, safer sex is our only protection against HIV'.

Recent developments must force a re-examination of these assertions and the orthodoxy that lies behind them, which too often denies the complexity of the contexts in which decisions about safer sex and other forms of HIV risk reduction are made. The potential contribution of the psychological and social sciences to HIV prevention has long been acknowledged; now, more than ever, it is essential also to recognize the role of medical sciences in illuminating prevention strategies and debates.

To date, HIV prevention has been understood – or at least implemented – exclusively in terms of individual or community-wide behaviour change. The potential role of a biomedical 'safety net' has been recognized in principle in the recent prioritization of research into microbicides, which could not only provide a woman-controlled means of HIV prevention when used vaginally, but also expand the prevention possibilities for gay men if used anally.[42] The use of anti-HIV drugs to manipulate viral load and infectiousness may offer a further biomedical approach to HIV prevention, as an alternative or adjunct to conventional behaviour change strategies. Likewise, the old separation between HIV antibody testing and HIV prevention strategies, already seriously challenged by 'negotiated safety' strategies, can only be undermined further as individuals decide to test as a means of access to post-exposure prophylaxis and/or early treatment.

In the USA, treatment education has long been accepted as a crucial service for people with HIV. Many AIDS service organizations have departments devoted to secondary prevention, alongside other care and support provision and primary prevention work.[43] These organizations should be well-placed to assimilate the potential significance of medical advances for primary HIV prevention.

In the UK and much of Europe, however, treatment information has been relatively neglected. In the vast majority of instances, organizations have devoted little or no staff time to any aspect of secondary HIV prevention work, leaving them in the dark about the likely impact of progress in AIDS research on all aspects of their work.[44]

Take another look at that statement: 'In the absence of a vaccine or cure, safer sex is our only protection against HIV'. What does it therefore mean for safer sex if the prospect of a cure has moved into the realms of the possible?

notes

1. See E. King, 'Bridging the Gap Between Science and AIDS Service Provision', in L. Sherr, J. Catalan & B. Hedge (eds), *The Impacts of AIDS: Psychological and Social Aspects of* HIV *Infection*; London, Harwood, in press; available on the Internet a http://www.users.dircon.co.uk/-eking/.
2. D.D. Ho et al., 'Rapid turnover of plasma virions and CD4 lymphocytes in HIV-1 infection', *Nature*, 1995, 373:123–6.
3. X. Wei et al., 'Viral Dynamics in Human Immunodeficiency Virus Type 1 Infection', *Nature*, 1995, 373:117–22.
4. For a more detailed lay explanation, see E. King, 'What Role for Viral Load?' *AIDS Treatment Update*, 1996:39, 1–3, London, NAM Publications, and E. King, 'Update on Viral Load', *AIDS Treatment Update*, 1996, 44:4–5. London, NAM Publications, both available on the Internet at nttp://www.nam.org.uk/nam/.
5. G. Moyle, B. Gazzard, 'Current Knowledge and Future Prospects for the Use of HIV Protease Inhibitors', *Drugs*, 1996, 51(5):701–12.
6. G. Moyle, 'Resistance to Antiretroviral Compounds: Implications for the Clinical Management of HIV Infection', *Immunology and Infectious Disease*, 1995, 5:170–82. For a lay overview of resistance, see E. King, 'Preventing resistance', *AIDS Treatment Update*, 1996, 44:6–7, NAM Publications, London, available on the Internet at http://www.nam.org.uk/nam/.
7. I believe this simile was originally coined by Peter Aldhous in HIV's war of attrition, *New Scientist*, 1977, 146:36, 13 March 1995.
8. J.W. Mellors et al., 'Prognostic Value of Plasma HIV-1 RNA Quantification in Seropositive Adult Men.' Eleventh International Conference on AIDS, Vancouver, abstract We.B.410, July 1996, available on the Internet at http://sis.nlm.nih.gov/aidsabs.htm.
9. Reviewed in E. King, 'Update on Viral Load', op.cit.
10. Reviewed in K. Alcorn, 'Eradicating HIV?' *AIDS Treatment Update*, 1996, 44:2–3, available on the Internet at http://www.nam.org.uk/nam/.
11. B.M. Saget et al., 'Dramatic Suppression of HIV-1 Plasma RNA Using a Combination of Zidovudine, Didanosine, Zalcitabine, Epivir, and Interferon-alpha in Subjects with Recent HIV-1 Infection.' Eleventh International Conference on AIDS, Vancouver, abstract We.B.533, July 1996, available on the Internet at http://sis.nlm.nih.gov/aidsabs.htm.
12. ibid.
13. See C. Patton, 'Media, Testing and Safe Sex Education', in *Inventing AIDS*, New York, Routledge, pp.25–49, 1990. See also *Fatal Advice: How Safe-Sex Education Went Wrong*, Duke University Press, Durham N.C., pp.30–3, 1996, in which Patton reviews how community-based groups

found themselves having to counter the conflation of testing and prevention in government funded safer sex campaigns.

14. S. Watney, 'Muddling Through; The UK responses to AIDS', in *Practices of Freedom*, London, Rivers Oram, p.249, 1994. This is not to say that discovering one's HIV status may not affect one's behaviour, although any such change may be more a product of the counselling that may accompany the test, rather than of the revelation that one is HIV-positive or HIV-negative.

15. Early papers formally documenting such strategies include (in the UK) E.C.I. Hickson et al., 'Maintenance of Open Gay Relationships: Some Strategies for Protection Against HIV', *AIDS Care*, 1992, 4(4), pp.409–19; (in Australia) S. Kippax et al., 'Sustaining Safe Sex: A Longitudinal Study of a Sample of Homosexual Men', *AIDS*, 1993, 7(2):257–63. However, Community groups such as London Lesbian and Gay Switchboard recognised the existence of such strategies from the mid-1980s, and advice on ways of reducing risk while continuing to practise unprotected anal sex with some partners was contained even in early editions of information publications such as the UK National AIDS Manual (P. Scott, personal Communication.)

16. J.I. Tokars et al., 'Surveillance of HIV Infection and Zidovudine Use among Health Care Workers After Occupational Exposure to HIV-Infected Blood', *Annals of Internal Medicine*, 1993, 118:913–19.

17. S.W. LaFon et al., 'A Double-blind, Placebo-controlled Study of the Safety and Efficacy of Retrovir (Zidovudine, ZDV) as a Chemoprophylactic Agent in Health Care Workers', Thirtieth Interscience Conference on Antimicrobial Agents and Chemotherapy, Atlanta, abstract 489, October 1990.

18. J.I. Tokars et al., 'Surveillance of HIV Infection and Zidovudine Use among Health Care Workers After Occupational Exposure to HIV-infected Blood: The CDC Cooperative Needlestick Surveillance Group', *Annals of Internal Medicine*, 1993, 118:913–19.

19. CDC. Case-control study of AIDS seroconversion in health care workers after percutaneous exposure to HIV-infected blood – France, United Kingdom, and United States, January 1988-August 1994. Morbidity & Mortality Weekly Report 44:929–33, 22 December 1995. An electronic version of this document (in Adobe Acrobat format) can be downloaded from the internet at ftp://ftp.cdc.gov/pub/publications/mmwr/wk/mm4450.pdf.

20. See, for example, the results of the Delta trial. Delta Coordinating Committee. 'Delta: a randomized double-blind controlled trial comparing combinations of zidovudine plus didanosine or zalcitabine with zidovudine alone in HIV-infected individuals'. *Lancet* 1996,

348:283–91, or its American equivalent ACTG 175, (S. Hammer et al., 'Nucleoside monotherapy (MT) vs. combination therapy' (CT) in HIV infected adults: a randomized, double-blind, placebo controlled trial in persons with CD4 cell counts 200–500/mm^3', Thirty-fifth Interscience Conference on Antimicrobial Agents and Chemotherapy, San Francisco, abstract LB1, September 1995).

21. J.L. Gerbending, 'Management of Occupational Exposure to blood-borne Viruses', *New England Journal of Medicine*, 1995, 332:444–51.

22. DC. Update: Provisional Public Health Service recommendations for chemoprophylaxis after occupational exposure to HIV. Morbidity & Mortality Weekly Report 45:468–72, 7 June 1996. An electronic version of this document (in Adobe Acrobat format) can be downloaded from the Internet at ftp://ftp.cdc.gov/pub/Publications/mmwr/wk/mm4522.pdf.

23. Issues in post-exposure prophylaxis and treatment of primary infection. Eleventh International Conference on AIDS, Vancouver, roundtable session B3, July 1996.

24. L.O. Gostin et al., 'HIV Testing, Counseling, and Prophylaxis After Sexual Assault', *Journal of the American Medical Association*, 1994, 271(18):436–44.

25. San Francisco General Hospital Epi-Center. Post-exposure prophylaxis for occupational HIV exposures. July 1996. Available on the Internet at http://epi-center.ucsf.edu.

26. J.S. Koopman et al., 'Core groups cause primary infection to dominate HIV transmission even when more than 90% of virus is excreted during later stages of infection', Eleventh International Conference on AIDS, Vancouver, abstract Mo.C.570, July 1996, available on the Internet at http://sis.nlm.nih.gov/aidsabs.htm.

27. J.A. Jacquez et al., 'Role of the Primary Infection in Epidemics of HIV Infection in Gay Cohorts', *Journal of Acquired Immune Deficiency Syndromes*, 1994, 7:1169–84.

28. For a thorough analysis of the HIV transmission risk involved in oral sex, see E. King, *Safety in Numbers: Safer Sex and Gay Men* London, Cassell, 1996, pp.99–114. Available on the Internet at http://www.users.dircon.co.uk/-eking/.

29. A. Dueer et al., 'Risk of HIV transmission during the seroconversion versus the post-seroconversion period'. Eleventh International Conference on AIDS, Vancouver, abstract Mo.C.571, July 1996, available on the Internet at http://sis.nlm.nih.gov/aidsabs.htm.

30. R.W. Coombs et al., 'Association between cultivable virus in semen and HIV-1 RNA level in seminal plasma', Eleventh International Conference on AIDS, Vancouver, abstract We.B.3383, July 1996, available on the Internet at http://sis.nlm.nih.gov/aidsabs.htm.

31. S. Jurriaans et al., 'HIV-1 viral load in semen versus blood plasma', Eleventh International Conference on AIDS, Vancouver, abstract Th.A.4036, July 1996, available on the Internet at http://sis.nlm.nih.gov/aidsabs.htm.

32. R.S. Sperling et al., 'Maternal plasma HIV-1 RNA and the success of zidovudine (ZDV) in the prevention of mother-child transmission', Third Conference on Retroviruses and Opportunistic Infections, Washington, late-breaker abstract, January 1996.

33. T.D. Mastro et al., 'Probabilities of Sexual HIV-1 Transmission', *AIDS* 1996, 10 (suppl A): S75–S82.

34. B.L. Gilliam et al., 'Effects of reverse transcriptase inhibitor therapy on HIV-1 viral burden in semen', Eleventh International Conference on AIDS, Vancouver, abstract Mo.A.1083, July 1996, available on the Internet at http://sis.nlm.nih.gov/aidsabs.htm.

35. D.J. Anderson et al., 'Effects of Disease Stage and Zidovudine Therapy on the Detection of Human Immunodeficiency Virus Type 1 in Semen', *Journal of the American Medical Association*, 1992, 267:2769–74.

36. J.N. Krieger et al., 'Seminal Shedding of Human Immunodeficiency Virus Type 1 and Human Cytomegalovirus: Evidence for Different Immunologic Controls', *Journal of Infectious Diseases*, 1995, 171(4):1018–22.

37. R.S. Sperling, et al., op.cit.

38. R.M. Anderson et al., 'Potential of Community-wide Chemotherapy or Immunotherapy to Control the Spread of HIV-1', *Nature*, 1991, 350:356–59.

39. D.L. Mayers et al., 'Prevalence and clinical impact of seroconversion with AZT-resistant HIV-1 between 1988 and 1994', Second National Conference on Human Retroviruses and Related Infections, Washington, abstract 385, January 1995.

40. R.T. D'Aquila et al., 'Zidovudine Resistance and HIV-1 Disease Progression During Antiretroviral Therapy', *Annals of Internal Medicine*, 1995, 122:401–8.

41. A.J. Japour et al., 'Prevalence and Clinical Significance of Zidovudine Resistance Mutations in Human Immunodeficiency Virus Isolated from Long-term Zidovudine Therapy', *Journal of Infectious Diseases*, 1995, 171:1172–79.

42. R. Gorna, *Vamps, Virgins and Victim: How Can Women Fight AIDS?* London, Cassell, 1996, pp.303–9.

43. S. Watney, 'The Politics of AIDS Treatment Information Activism', in P. Bywaters & E. McLeod (eds), *Working for Equality in Health*, London, Routledge, 1996.

44. E. King, op.cit.

how to use a condom

lessons from the AIDS epidemic

Paula A. Treichler

> A guy goes into a drugstore and says to the druggist, 'I'll have a dozen condoms, please.' Then he leans forward and whispers, ('And a package of Marlboros').

> A duck goes into a drugstore to buy a condom. The druggist says, 'That'll be a dollar. Shall I put it on your bill?' The duck says 'No thanks, I'm not that kind of a duck.'

In her analysis of the 1832 Anatomy Act in England, which enabled the bodies of the poor to be used for medical dissection, historian Ruth Richardson calls it 'a gift for anyone interested in attitudes towards the body, the dead, death, grief, and beliefs in the afterlife'. Richardson argues, in part, that the Anatomy Act was in some sense the revenge of the rich on the poor as payback for the Poor Laws which had earlier authorized taxing the upper classes to pay for charity.[1] In this essay, I argue that the condom is a gift for anyone interested in the history, culture, and discourse surrounding sex, gender, and sexually transmitted disease. First, I use examples from contemporary 'condom discourses' to document the condom's pre-AIDS history, its extraordinary cultural and political makeover within gay, lesbian, and activist communities, and its continuing deployment across multiple cultural domains, including those in which condoms are resisted or reviled. I argue that while the condom provides extraordinarily cheap, efficient, and versatile protection against both disease and conception, it also serves – like the 1832 Anatomy Act – as a form of revenge: the moralists' revenge on all forms of pleasurable or transgressive sexuality. By demonizing the condom, and by extension the subset of 'homosexual penises' that inhabit it, a small core of the immoderate and ideological right has proved adept at sustaining an aggressively phallocentric discourse, preventing study and development of real and potential alternatives. In turn, by fighting – as we must – to maintain the right to use the word 'condom' in public discourse and to institutionalize the product itself in AIDS education and intervention, we abet the condom's emergence by default as the alpha and omega of protected sex in the age of AIDS. Finally, I suggest that the condom's leading role, which molds a whole universe of possibilities into a phallic shape, is not inevitable: by identifying not only the strengths and strategies of contemporary discourses but also what is absent from them, we can more creatively conceptualize new and alternative approaches for the future.[2]

For many decades, in the United States and elsewhere, the condom occupied a special place in the sexual imaginary of teenage boys, a place captured nicely in the 1971 film *Summer of '42*, itself an adult remembrance of adolescence during World War II. In one scene, Hermie, the fifteen-year-old protagonist, is being tutored for a date by his more sophisticated pal Oskie, their text an abstruse sex manual swiped from Oskie's parents. Having worked his way through the manual's step-by-step instructions, Hermie (with misplaced optimism) spots a problem:

HERMIE:	Look, Oskie, if I follow these 12 points, she just might have a kid – and I tell you I can't afford a kid at this stage of my life. So the whole thing's off.
OSKIE:	I really can't believe it, Hermie. You are really

dumb!

HERMIE: I may be dumb but I'm not gonna be a father. Two wrongs don't make a right.

OSKIE: You use protection. You use a rubber. Haven't you ever heard of a rubber?

Oskie shows Hermie the treasured condom bequeathed him when his older brother went off to war. Armed with this talismanic authority, Oskie tells Hermie he will have to brave the drugstore to acquire his own.

HERMIE: Oh, no, I'm not gonna risk it. I happen to be underage. And, for your information, Oskie, women shop in drugstores.

OSKIE: OK, so where do you wanna get it? A sporting goods store?

HERMIE: Well, if you were a really good friend, you'd lend me *yours*.

OSKIE: WHAT?

HERMIE: I'll return it to you.

OSKIE: Hermie, I'm beginning to think you must be a homo! . . . You don't know *anything*. A rubber is to be used once and only once. And only by one party. Not even the best of friends can go halvsies on a rubber.

The drugstore scene depicts a rite of passage often recounted in twentieth-century literature. With Oskie supervising through the pharmacy window, Hermie loiters miserably as long as he can, then finally gets up the courage to approach the druggist and order: an ice cream cone. Stalling his way through three scoops, sprinkles, and a napkin, he's finally out of excuses:

DRUGGIST: All right – anything else?

HERMIE: How about some rubbers?

DRUGGIST: Pardon?

HERMIE: I understand that you carry them.

DRUGGIST: Carry what?

HERMIE: Aw, come on – you know what!

DRUGGIST: Contraceptives?

HERMIE: Yeah, right.

The druggist tortures Hermie:

DRUGGIST:	What brand?
HERMIE:	Brand?
DRUGGIST:	Brand and style?
HERMIE:	The usual.
DRUGGIST:	Well [setting samples on counter] there's a number to choose from. Which is your usual?
HERMIE:	The blue ones.
DRUGGIST:	All right – how many would you like?
HERMIE:	Ohhh . . . 3 dozen.
DRUGGIST:	Planning a big night?

The *Summer of '42* encapsulates many features of 'condom discourse' that existed in pre-1980s cultural memory: a masculine oral tradition passed along from older to younger brother, veteran to rookie; a symbol of sexual knowledge and index of sexual prowess – make that heterosexual prowess, for as Oskie disdainfully charges, 'homos' know nothing about rubbers. Indeed, the condom's historical non-relevance within homosexual subcultures was a major challenge gay men faced in pioneering safer sex campaigns for their community; there was no cultural tradition to build on. What's absent from the film is any implication that the condom will lessen the pleasure of the sexual experience. Rather, the condom invokes a world of adult male knowledge and practices, a world that both acknowledges and provisionally evades the entailments of a heterosexual society; to purchase a condom pits the would-be transgressor against adult professional authority. To pass successfully through this public Checkpoint Charlie, he must speak the right language, naming out loud the commodity that the conspiracy of silence has long forbidden and withheld – a conspiracy that has been, for most of its history, almost universally male.

The condom has been called the 'perfect anticonceptual remedy',[3] a characterization both literally and metaphorically germane: for the condom is not only an effective birth control device, it is also an 'anticonceptual' technology, so mundane and simple that anyone can make it work, anywhere in the world. (Indeed a whole series of condom jokes turn on the idea that you don't have to be a rocket scientist to use a condom. For instance: A guy walks into a drugstore and asks for a dozen condoms. The druggist says, 'That'll be 5 dollars plus tax.' The guy says, 'The hell with the tacks, I'll use glue.') For all its simplicity, however, the condom has led a complicated double life throughout its history as a preventative of pregnancy and of disease, the two foremost constraints on unchecked sexual freedom. Put another way, by simultaneously preventing pregnancy and disease, the condom threatens – or challenges – civilized life as we know it and thus becomes an object of fear, anxiety, and promise.

Like other technologies, the condom has evolved in the context of specific social, cultural, economic, and political realities, and it continues to play its own part on that larger stage: a detailed chronology would be needed to track the condom's complicated historical evolution as word, medical device, technology, and commodity. But I can at least summarize the features of this history most germane to my concerns here.[4] First, the birth and recent fortunes of the modern condom industry in the US is a story fraught with gaps, contradictions, and ironies – which is to say, a peculiarly American story in which medicine and public health intersect densely and inextricably with morality, culture, politics, patriotism, and the market. Second, the condom was a prime victim of the 1878 Comstock Laws and other puritanical measures that designated contraceptives obscene and prohibited their sale and distribution. It took an unusually astute businessman (Merle Youngs, who developed Trojans), the economic hardships of the Great Depression, a crusade by medical and public health professionals, and the military priorities of two world wars to bring condoms out of the closet. Third, despite steady improvement over the postwar period in quality, accessibility, reliability, and social acceptability, three concurrent developments were helping transform cultural attitudes and practices toward sexual activity and its consequences. The discovery of penicillin gradually reversed the perception of venereal disease as devastating and long-lasting; recognition of a worldwide population explosion created the first major impetus for research on reproductive phenomena, with philanthropists and pharmaceutical companies putting significant resources into the development of contraceptive technologies; and women began to be encouraged to enjoy sex – their enjoyment enhanced by the culture of the 1960s and the development of antibiotics and contraceptive alternatives. Fourth, these changes affected not only traditional heterosexual customs but courtship and sexual practices in the growing women's liberation and gay liberation cultures: between the early 1960s and the early 1980s, the most sexually active generation in modern history – including women and gay men – attained sexual maturity without using or even thinking about condoms. By the late 1970s, the condom industry seemed to be going nowhere, and had developed a reputation for being insular, close-mouthed, and paranoid. The condom, thanks to the three p's – penicillin, population, and the pill – was still disreputable and now, in addition, perceived as increasingly obsolete: 'a distasteful relic,' as one commentator wrote, 'of more primitive times'.[5] Finally, as sales fell, and the condom became a product not even its stockholders could love, its significant remaining use was in international family planning programs; and this outlet, too, was about to be severely undercut by the Reagan administration's policy of withdrawing foreign aid to projects that advocated any form of birth control.

This was the context in which the AIDS epidemic arrived, a context that makes the resurrection of the condom by the gay community even more remarkable. How did this come about? In 1983, driven by a growing sense of crisis and tragedy, a small group of gay physicians and patients produced and distributed the pamphlet *How to Have Sex in an Epidemic*.[5] Though a virus had not yet been established as the cause of AIDS, they reasoned that the devastating effects of AIDS (whatever it was) might be prevented or lessened by preventing other sexually transmitted diseases. Placing AIDS within the broader context of gay STDs and general health, *How to Have Sex* provided recommendations for reducing disease transmission without giving up sex. The pamphlet's respect for both sexual pleasure and cultural identity became a hallmark of 'safer sex' campaigns within the gay community. Not an end in itself, the condom was inscribed as one mechanism for preserving significant features of gay practices and politics. As Douglas Crimp and Simon Watney have written, the condom also signalled the adoption of a communal ethic of universal protection (i.e. wear a condom with every partner, as if both you and your partner were infected).[7] These gay education efforts at once borrowed the condom from the legacy of straight culture and challenged that legacy by advocating the preservation of sexual life for people with or at risk from AIDS. These were radical moves – so radical they have never been securely incorporated into the larger realm of de-gayed AIDS discourse, where the only sexually-active person with AIDS is a figure of demonization and blame (the sexually addicted homosexual, the deceitful bisexual who continues to prey on and infect others). Within gay discourses, then, the condom to some extent functioned as an unauthorized device, a transgression against patriarchal expectations. This did not mean it was accepted automatically by gay men. One gay activist, describing the development of gay safer sex programs, commented that until AIDS arrived, 'gay men had as much interest in condoms as Eskimos do in air conditioning'.

As the AIDS epidemic gathered strength and came to be perceived as both a medical and a cultural crisis, the condom came to be widely hailed as the single best hope in the battle against AIDS. Our only weapon, the mantra went, is prevention. 'It was an odd turn in the story of this dying product,' wrote Colin Leinster in *Fortune* in 1986, 'when a horrific disease revived it.'[8] Today, in consequence, 'condom discourse' is significantly different. It is varied and voluminous. The condom has become the mirror – or receptacle, if you will – for broad debates about disease and sin, technology and nature, transgression and desire; and it appears to have opened debates on these matters irrevocably. The condom's growing social presence and acceptability has been one consistent cultural theme since the advent of AIDS. A 1986 ad for Trojans played on the change between the condom's bad old *Summer of '42* drugstore days and its new incarnation as a high tech product. Messages about condoms designed by AIDS activists and gay community projects stress a number of themes, including sexiness, politics, and responsible community ethics. Gay Men's Health Crisis, notably, produced and distributed a series of 8-page bibles; created by graphic artists working pro-bono and discussed at length by Douglas Crimp,[9] these publications are striking in their skill at advocating safer sex practices without sacrificing the cocky exuberance of their unrepentantly seedy genre. In contrast, the ads and posters that came later – those produced by public health agencies, for example, were largely de-sexed, almost always de-gayed, and constructed around some unifying metaphor or phrase (Australia's Grim Reaper figure, the gravestones of the UK campaign, the CDC's 'You can't get AIDS from [handshake, toilet seat, etc.]' posters, and so on). As condom campaigns became increasingly ubiquitous, authorizing the condom as vehicle of health and responsibility, irony and dark humor became the antidote to earnestness.[10]

Condoms are now both gendered and global. The Mentor campaign illustrates how a male condom can be marketed for the woman consumer. The white female narrator of a 1987 Mentor ad stresses responsibility, not pleasure, and claims that Mentor offers women 'smart sex' for the 1980s. 'Smart sex' is right: the Mentor comes with lengthy, complicated instructions in print so tiny it should come with a magnifying glass, like the compact *Oxford English Dictionary*, or at least a cell phone for calling the emergency 800 number included with the instructions. 'And how about some new nicknames for the old standbys?' writes Mimi Coucher, 'Love skins. Slicks. Wet suits. Silk stockings.

Eight-by-two glossies.' Her 'Girl's Guide to Condoms'[11], like the best of the safer sex guidelines for women but unlike the Mentor ad, preserves the notion that there's some fun in all of this.[12] The same can't be said of Channing Bete Inc.'s *About Women and AIDS*, a scriptographic pamphlet whose generic cartoon figures ponder the merits of condoms as if they were Tupperware. Not that there's anything wrong with that: Channing Bete could do a really interesting pamphlet about the safe sex parties, mainly by and for women, modelled in fact on Tupperware parties where participants share concerns and suggestions on everything from condoms to communication to sex toys.[13] Condoms for women are now on the market, though for a lot more money and a lot less convenience than one might wish. The Reality condom press kit includes a video demo; the Women's Choice condom is called by a feminized noun form – *condomme*. And the artist Masami Teroaka has incorporated the female condom into his universe of intricate watercolors on AIDS.

As condoms go global, diverse cultural spins are placed on 'How to Use a Condom,' messages, cautionary posters, commercial competition, and social marketing campaigns. In some cases, a generic message is made culturally specific – its new format eerily echoing other times and places. A public service announcement in Brazil, for example, plays on longstanding cultural stereotypes about women as secret reservoirs of infection; coupled with the image of a beautiful woman, its word – 'Those who see the face cannot see AIDS' – are almost identical to those World War II VD posters that associated women with venereal disease.[14] There are class dimensions to condoms too. One involves the relatively broad access to condoms in contrast to other methods of protection; though men in the US had to cope with decades of 'druggist only' laws, condoms did not require access to a personal physician or a prescription. Class is an element of marketing and sales around the world. For example, India experienced a nasty class battle between the upscale, sexy, and new Kama Sutra condom and the workaday government-sponsored and subsidized Nirodh, called 'the khadhi condom' after the no-frills cotton cloth called *khadhi*.[15] Barcelona's *goma* shops are said to carry as many as fifty condom varieties with names that play on male self-images and fantasies – Conquistador, El Cid, Brave Bull.[16] Advertisers, too, are trying to change the condom's low concept image by going high concept and high tech: Lifestyles' Nuda brand has been praised as 'the Porsche of condoms', and Adam Glickman, a 1980s Tufts graduate who founded the Condomania chain of specialty stores, says that names aside, the Japanese and the Germans make the best condoms – just like cars – or planes, if the Stealth condom is an example. Both names and styles have proliferated in the 1980s and 1990s, with careful attention to markets and marketing, and today condom makers offer many new lines. Among them are Excita (including the textured Excita Extra and Excita Fiesta, in colors), Lifestyles (Lifestyles Conture, Stimula, Nuda, Nuda Plus, Extra Strength), Personal, Prime, Protex (Protext Man-Form Plus, Protex Contracept Plus, ultrathin Protex Secure and Protex Touch, Protex Sunrise in colors, textured Protex Arouse, and for women Protex Scentuals and Lady Protex).

Just as these other issues are simultaneously global and local, so is language associated with condom use. Like debates in the US and UK about such terms as 'safe sex' or 'monogamous sexual relationship', several African prevention campaigns have provoked controversy over the wording of messages designed to promote monogamy, marital faithfulness, and/or condom use. In early 1988, for example, Zambia's campaign to slow the spread of AID and HIV infection featured a full-page advertisement in local newspapers. Sponsored by the Family Life Movement of Zambia, FLMZ, the ad urged readers to 'stay on the ground' rather than chance flying on 'Pleasure Airways' and 'crash-landing' with 'parachutes' that weren't safe. The *News and Features Bulletin* of the All Africa Press Service APSNFB cited the ad as an example of the 'humor and innovation' of the anti-AIDS campaign in Zambia, and praised especially the way that a serious message about sexual behavior was cleverly communicated through metaphor.[17] The bulletin noted that Zambia's extensive screening and education campaign includes establishing thirty-two screening centers throughout the country, widely distributing a booklet called *AIDS Information for Schools*, and enlisting Zambian journalists in an effort to combat western propaganda about AIDS in Africa, in particular the claim that African governments were 'doing nothing' about the epidemic. By the following month, however, the Zambian government was under fire from the Christian church, which argued that the information booklet would encourage promiscuity among the young and called on the FLMZ 'to deal with AIDS advertisements in a more appropriate manner'.[18] The *Times of Zambia*, owned by the government, countered by asserting that 'the campaign against AIDS should . . . not fail because of crazy clerics'.[19] In other central African countries the clash between church and state took a variety of forms. In Uganda, a planning survey had determined that 96% of Uganda's population were regular churchgoers, so from the beginning the government health ministry sought cooperation from the church in designing AIDS education programs: hence when 20,000 bibles were distributed to school children with AIDS information inserted, the first page answered medical questions about AIDS and prevention; the second page cited scriptural passages to answer spiritual questions about sex and marriage.[20] But the church opposed the import of three million condoms donated by the United States on the grounds that the condoms represented a distraction from ongoing health priorities, especially minor and curable diseases.[21]

The condom thus makes visible details of a global arena often left unexamined. Indeed, the differing views over condoms and sex education in Zambia and Uganda challenge the portrait of unrelieved devastation in a monolithic 'third world' and provide a useful corrective to the notion, still widespread in western media, that no fruitful discussion is occurring within Africa by Africans. These internal debates suggest rather that controversies in African countries over AIDS parallel those that have marked the unfolding of AIDS as a complex narrative in the developed world. They also suggest, perhaps, that debates over condoms will always be shaped by the politics, unique internal structuring, and pre-existing priorities of groups and interests within any given country or region. Likewise, resistance to condoms is not unique to the church or Zambia or Uganda and does not necessarily signal unfounded opposition to scientific public health measures. A pervasive theme of discourse in many developing countries, however – particularly in postcolonial Africa – is that the 'AIDS crisis' with its corollary condom campaigns is merely the latest in a series of previously unsuccessful first world strategies to curtail population growth in formerly colonized territories (i.e., among people of color). Just as the 'Pleasure Airlines' metaphor drew both praise and criticism, the phrase 'Love faithfully', a warning against promiscuity, advocates strict monogamy and is preferred by church groups; but secular sponsors favor more flexible recommendations: 'Love carefully', an instruction to use condoms, and 'graze at home', an instruction to reduce the number of sexual partners and specifically, for men in multiple marriages, to confine sexual contact to the household. Some programs have creatively introduced condoms into monogamous marriages as well: Brooke Grundfest Schoepf[22] describes discussions between the CONAISSIDA Project and village elders in Zaire; other programs have sought to draw on women elders to incorporate condom instruction into marital preparation sessions. A calendar from Tanzania, designed as a source of revenue for AIDS education, shows a village training session in which condoms are one of several of the lessons. Some publications create special materials to promote condom use. A fairly detailed illustrated booklet from Tanzania is made to fold up to pocket size, while a booklet from the Central African Republic works to make its instructions and pictures meaningful, showing the condom being discarded in a culturally specific latrine. Many of these campaigns have made efforts to adapt western science to local cultural priorities. In Zimbabwe, the Women's Action Group's AIDS illustrated book *Let's Fight It Together*, attempts to put AIDS in the context of broad social change, uses ordinary characters and ordinary language both to identify the hardships produced by AIDS and to model desirable responses. Tension between church and state is reflected in a poster from Zimbabwe: a picture of a condom is captioned, 'The bible may save your soul, but this will save your life.'

Research on sexuality and condom use may also serve to transform how AIDS is understood as well as challenge entrenched stereotypes about sexual practices in other cultures. Discussions in the US of HIV and AIDS in Africa, widely influenced by Daniel Hrdy's 1987 review of cultural practices in Africa contributing to HIV transmission, typically assume that sexual promiscuity is the most important factor.[23] Jane Bertrand et al., however, studying condom use in coital frequency among 1,000 men and 1,000 women in urban and rural Zaire found little evidence of 'promiscuity' or of the anecdotal notion that African men need 'sex every day'. The survey, administered in four national languages, was supplemented by interviews with focus groups.[24]

One of our central Illinois congressional representatives said a few years ago that he never dreamed that in his lifetime condoms would become a topic not only mentionable in public but discussed at his own family dinner table. A women's rap group called TLC is very explicit about this aim. Convinced that AIDS is 'killing too many people and it's killing us (Black women) at an alarmingly fast rate', they set out to make condoms popular, integrating condoms and safer sex messages into every aspect of their performance. 'Our thing is: if you're having sex, you should have safe sex. We show condoms because we're trying to make it hip.'[25] An ACT UP campaign initiated in 1988 was aimed primarily at straight men; its most striking graphic, by Gran Fury, was titled 'SEXISM REARS ITS UNPROTECTED HEAD'; a dramatically erect penis, rendered in glorious photographic detail, stood beside the textual imperative 'MEN: USE CONDOMS OR BEAT IT.' A 1991 news story from Dar es Salaam in the *Kenya Daily Nation* reported that a twenty-four-year-old Tanzanian woman murdered her husband when she found condoms in his pocket and he bragged about using them with his mistress.[26] In 1994, the *New England Journal of Medicine* cautioned that counselling women to insist their male partners wear condoms may, by raising the possibility of infidelity in the relationship, put them at greater risk of violence or death than HIV does. In 1996, oceanographic scientists discover a vast floating 'reef' in the South Pacific formed from some portion of the world's used condoms (millions per year); the mass is almost two miles long, an eighth of a mile wide, and in places up to sixty feet deep.

But even as condom discourse proliferates worldwide, so do efforts to constrain it. Given the long tradition of puritanism in the US, we can see these strategies of constraint with particular clarity in a Congressional hearing on AIDS and condom advertising, called in February 1987 by the tireless Henry Waxman, Los Angeles Congressman and then Chair of the House Subcommittee on Health and the Environment. Immediate background for the hearing included the publication in late 1986 – well into the Reagan presidency – of several authoritative scientific reports on AIDS which unanimously charged the federal government with neglecting the epidemic and argued for the effectiveness of condoms in preventing HIV transmission; at the same time, successful conservative efforts had blocked anti-AIDS funding and policy initiatives and forged regressive legislation, notably the so-called Helms amendment, which barred 'the use of federal funds for educational projects or materials that promote or encourage, directly or indirectly, homosexual sexual activity' (language comparable, of course, to that adopted in Canada, the UK, and elsewhere).[27]

In his opening statement, Congressman Waxman was characteristically blunt about the AIDS epidemic and HIV transmission, arguing that once impractical and idealistic alternatives are set aside, condoms are the only method of prevention we have.[28] Noting that condoms may be the world's oldest medical device, have cut down disease transmission for centuries, and are now advocated by virtually every AIDS expert and public health group in the country, the Congressman went on to blame the television networks for refusing to use their great power of communication to educate the population about condoms:

> While portraying thousands of sexual encounters each year in programming and while marketing thousands of products using sex appeal, television is unwilling to give the life-saving information about safe sex and condoms. We cannot afford such selective prudishness. Television networks cannot continue to pretend that this public health crisis is limited and that their viewers do not need to know about preventive measures. If doctors had withheld penicillin from syphilis patients because they might have encouraged extramarital sex, we would have recognized that as medical malpractice. In the same fashion, the networks' continued refusal to allow condom advertising is media malpractice. At this point, information is our only defense in the war on AIDS. Television has a responsibility to help fight this war. Without all assistance, the nation faces a larger epidemic with more cases and more death.

Through his parallel between medicine and television and equation of 'medical malpractice' with 'media malpractice', Mr Waxman suggested that television has the same kind of responsibility to fight this war that doctors had when they gave penicillin to patients with syphilis. (The history of US VD and birth control policies and practices is not as unambiguous as he suggested, however. The provision of antibiotics, in fact, *was* criticized for its role in fostering imprudent or promiscuous behavior, and doctors were urged to withhold it.)

But California congressman William Dannemeyer, a stalwart author of conservative AIDS legislation, countered Waxman's statement by citing evidence, in the form of anecdotes, published articles, and news reports claiming that 'casual contact' and 'horizontal transmission' (by mosquitoes, shared living quarters, and so on) are both significant factors in the spread of AIDS – thereby undermining claims for condoms' effectiveness in controlling the epidemic. Like many conservative champions of American individualism, individual moral responsibility, and sexual self-control, Dannemeyer advocates mandatory testing and contact tracing – that is, the use of strong centralized authority and punitive powers to impose that control from above. In doing so, though, he claimed to be advancing medical as well as moral arguments. Finally, Dannemeyer took issue with public health service materials promoted by US Surgeon General C. Everett Koop that advocated abstinence or a 'mutually faithful monogamous sexual relationship'; he expressed distress at this phrase, arguing that it should have specified a *heterosexual* sexual relationship, for this 'is the foundation of our civilization'. This is but one example of the vigilance with which the Surgeon General's AIDS discourse was being policed by the Right.

Dr Koop was the first expert witness to testify. A strong conservative himself, Koop's strong advocacy of condoms had shocked the Reagan administration as much as it delighted the nation's political cartoonists. He succinctly summarized the advantages of latex condoms, noting that laboratory studies demonstrate that when used properly they 'prevent both semen deposition and contact with urethral discharge and/or mucous membranes' Hearing, 4; clinical studies to date support this conclusion, he stated, with more under way. Agreeing that condom advertising 'would have a positive public health benefit', Koop identified two crucial tasks it could accomplish: broadcast verbal and visual messages specifically aimed at black and Hispanic groups; and emphasize that condoms function to prevent disease, including HIV transmission, as well as to prevent conception. 'It appears that many people do not understand how to use condoms to prevent AIDS'(6). He concluded his testimony with a final opinion: 'You cannot educate about AIDS unless you educate about sex.' (Hearing, 7).

At several points in his testimony, Dr Koop referred to his October 1986 *Surgeon General's Report on AIDS*, an admirably straightforward document that showed little of the contradictory rhetoric that marked *Understanding AIDS*, the pamphlet sent to American households in early 1988 as part of the continuing America Responds to AIDS campaign. Reports that Dr Koop made the 1986 document public without administrative approval ensured that the 1988 pamphlet would be carefully vetted. Asked whether in advocating condoms he was not treating abstinence as an afterthought, Koop, the longstanding conservative, was ready with his defense:

> If you will read my report to the American people, you will find that before we talk about condoms, there are 13 moral statements that have to do with abstinence, with mutually faithful monogamous relationships, and with advice to teenagers. The way I stated it was only for the purpose of being told to present testimony in a short period of time.

He added, echoing the sentiment Dannemeyer had earlier approved but shifting its meaning to support condoms and sex education, that 'with AIDS, if you walk down the scientific path toward containment of this epidemic, the moral path parallels that, and not many public health problems can say that.'

A condom is not simply a technological device. It has come to embody, the world over, a range of additional meanings, material interests, and comprehensive 'safer sex' campaigns. It has come to stand in for, indeed literally to substitute for, its own alternatives in the form of perfected technologies, pharmaceutical preventions and cures, equitable economic arrangements, social and political justice, improved health care resources and treatment facilities, and mandated communication about sex and sexuality. One might even conclude that the condom has come to be the one sayable thing in a sea of silence, the one do-able intervention in a world of apparent impotence. Because they can be counted, condoms operate synecdochically to measure the effectiveness of AIDS prevention programs. 'We sent 3 million condoms to Uganda,' claimed USAID in 1988. 'We gave away more than 250 condoms at the gay bar last night,' claim community AIDS projects. Counting is so important an activity that researchers' attempts to gain more accurate measures have entailed some unenviable fieldwork: morning-after scavenging yields estimates of the incidence of condom use within the population that frequents Lovers Lanes, while strained sewage permits them to recover and estimate the extent of condom use in a given geographical area over a given period of time.

The condom is not the villain of this piece: the wide world over it has fulfilled myriad tasks and demonstrated multiple talents in sex education, fertility control, anti-AIDS campaigns, and many other kinds of important cultural work. But the condom cannot continue to stand alone. So what general lessons does the AIDS epidemic offer?

1. High quality latex condoms, used correctly and consistently, are highly effective in preventing HIV transmission. The condom is therefore a partial but concrete solution to an intractable problem; it is a place to start, reinforcing the value and reasonableness of a harm reduction model – a model, that is, of probabilities and possibilities, of partial successes and incremental behavioral change. It holds promise for a range of interventions at the level of individuals, communities, and larger social and cultural units.

2. While the condom functions as an extraordinarily efficient barrier to both disease and conception, it has also come to function as the moralists' revenge on all forms of pleasurable or transgressive sexuality, made to function with equal efficiency as a barrier to more imaginative, technically sophisticated, and erotically

charged alternatives. Put another way, the condom has become for the AIDS epidemic the primary measure of all that can be said and done about sex. Its current stardom is, perhaps, well deserved after decades – even centuries – of obscure disreputability; but it is a high price to pay for the entry of sex into the universe of mainstream public discourse.

3. The condom forces notoriously difficult questions and potentially exciting solutions into a single and, as it happens, phallic shape. But this does not just happen. Another lesson from the AIDS epidemic is that conservatives like Jesse Helms know exactly how to use a condom: like meat thrown off a speeding sleigh, they throw out the condom for moderate and progressive folks to fight over; by the time we look up, they are miles ahead of us. By fixating on, obsessing over every detail and statistic of condom use, which should be the taken-for-granted starting point of any rational public health effort, the right continues to hold the entire US Congress – and the country for which it stands – hostage. While thousands of acts of unprotected sex and many more thousands of acts of violence reach television audiences unimpeded, and while people continue to get infected with HIV and die, this tiny criminal band debates whether these same audiences can withstand the shock of seeing, or hearing about, or in any way encountering the terrible satanic device that dare not speak its name: the lowly condom.

4. In a world made wiser by AIDS, a world in which condoms can be routinely talked about in dinner conversation, it is time to move beyond the condom as the alpha and omega of sustainable sexuality. We are at a historical point in which sophisticated and desirable protective technology has never been more urgent, nor more technically achievable, nor more socially justifiable. Where might the condom take us if we let its historical, metaphorical, and cultural associations work to reveal rather than suppress alternative possibilities? Writing, research, personal experimentation, literature and art of the AIDS epidemic provide cultural experience sufficient to propose several desiderata for the prevention of disease and conception in the twenty-first century (or sooner) – ideas, products, approaches, metaphors, semiotic strategies, values, features, incentives, and coalitions. Because alternatives are so rarely conceptualized in AIDS prevention and intervention discussions even this incomplete inventory constitutes an ambitious agenda of possibilities to be explored.

Desiderata in sexual protection would

- include technologies, devices, concepts, and projects
- capitalize on fantasy, transgression, and sentiments that challenge authority
- include a range of high tech simulations, for example condoms designed to look, feel, smell, and taste like a penis. (Such a product was under development in the late 1980s; I do not know its current status.)
- include a range of products for women
- be easy and convenient to use
- enable women to control their own protection
- be discreet and virtually invisible
- function simultaneously to prevent disease and conception *or* to be used for one or the other
- include a special line of condoms that would enable Catholics, with the Vatican's blessing, to use those color coded for disease prevention *only*
- be free of side effects
- be available in the form of a temporary suppository or spray-on sealant (like Pam for frying pans), with different flavors and consistencies for different orifices and with reliable sealant properties for at least forty-five minutes, after which it could be peeled off like rubber cement, allowed to harden into a secure impenetrable sphere, and thrown away

- merge latex with computer technology, embedding in a condom or other protective device a programmable vibrating chip to enhance sensation (it would have dual control programming, like a king-size electric blanket).

An agenda for the future, therefore, should begin with the condom but simultaneously move beyond it to encompass other possibilities – imaginative safer sex projects, comprehensive research programs, incentives for technological innovations, initiatives across cultures, and discussion of alternatives we have not yet thought of. Forget birth control; forget disease control: what the Right wants is sex control. To open up alternatives means undertaking a multi-dimensional struggle on many fronts, using as many strategies and constituencies and arguments as we can think of, drawing on knowledge and resources from many disciplines, addressing both short-term and long-term goals as well as individual, community, and social concerns – in short, contribute whatever strategies, technological politics, and theoretical insights the AIDS epidemic has furnished and move on. This is how you, and all of us, can use a condom.

notes

1. Ruth Richardson, *Death, Dissection and the Destitute*, London, Penguin, 1988, p.xvii.

2. A longer version of this essay appears as 'How to Use a Condom: Bedtime Stories for the Transcendental Signifier', in Cary Nelson and Dilip P. Gaonkar, (eds), *Disciplinarity and Dissent in Cultural Studies*, New York, Routledge, 1996, chapter 16'. See also my book *How to Have Theory in an Epidemic: Cultural Chronicles of AIDS*, Duke University Press.

3. Linda Gordon, *Woman's Body, Woman's Right: A Social History of Birth Control in America*, New York, Grossman Publishers, 1976.

4 Himes, Norman E. (1963) *Medical History of Contraception.* New York: Gamut Press, Inc.
Hilts, Philip J. (1990) 'Birth Control Backlash.' *New York Times Magazine* (December 16): 41.

Hochman, David (1992) 'A Safe Sex Product in Need of a Marketing Plan.' *New York Times*, September 29.
Johnson, Anne M. (1994) 'Condoms and HIV Transmission.' *New England Journal of Medicine* 331:6 (August 11): 391–92.
King, Edward (1993) *Safety in Numbers: Safer Sex and Gay Men*. New York: Routledge.
Legman, G. (1968) *Rationale of the Dirty Joke: An Analysis of Sexual Humor.* First Series. New York: Grove Press.
—— (1975) *Rationale of the Dirty Joke: An Analysis of Sexual Humor.* Second Series. Wharton NY: Breaking Point.
Englade, Ken (1992) 'The Age of Condoms.' *New York Times Magazine*, vol. 141 (Feb 16 1992) 12, 57
Murphy, James S. (1992) *The Condom Industry in the United States.* Jefferson NC: McFarland & Co.
Weller, S.C. (1993) 'A Meta-Analysis of Condom Effectiveness in Reducing Sexually Transmitted HIV.' *Social Science and Medicine* 36: 1635–1644.
'Woman kills husband over condom packet' (1991) *Kenya Daily Nation* November 9, p.8.

5. Colin Leinster, 'The Rubber Barons', *Fortune*, vol. 114 no. 12, 24 November 1988, p.105–18.

6. Richard Berkowitz, Michael Callen and Richard Dworkin, *How to Have Sex in an Epidemic*, News from the Front Publications, New York, 1983.

7. Douglas Crimp, 'How to Have Promiscuity in an Epidemic' in Douglas Crimp (ed.), *AIDS: Cultural Analysis, Cultural Activism*, Cambridge, MIT Press, 1988. Simon Watney, *Practices of Freedom: Selected Writings on HIV/AIDS*, Durham NC: Duke University Press, 1994.
See also Aggleton, Peter et al., (1989) *Educating about AIDS: Exercises and Materials for Adult Education about HIV Infection and AIDS.* Edinburgh: Churchill Livingstone.

8. Colin Leinster, op. cit.

9. Douglas Crimp, op. cit.

10. See David Feinberg, *Eighty-Sixed*, New York, Penguin, 1989; Rolf Konig, *The Killer Condom*, Trans. from the German by J.D. Steakley, New York, Catalan Communications, Written and illustrated by Rolf Konig, 1988; and the periodical *Diseased Pariah News.*

11. Mimi Coucher, 'A Girl's Guide to Condoms', *Whole Earth Review* 62, Spring 1989, p.137.

12. In an early example, see Cindy Patton, & Janis Kelly, *Making It: A Woman's Guide to Sex in the Age of AIDS*, Boston, Firebrand, 1987.

13. Susan Diesenhouse, 'AIDS Lessons Replace Tupperware at Parties', *New York Times*, 12 February, 1989.

14. Allan M. Brandt, *No Magic Bullet: A Social History of Venereal Disease in the United States Since 1880*, New York, Oxford University Press, 1987.

15. Jug Suraiya, 'The Pleasure Principle', *Far Eastern Economic Review*, vol. 155 no. 1, 9 January 1992, p.25.

16. Richard Symanski, *The Immoral Landscape: Female Prostitution in Western Societies*, Toronto, Butterworth, 1981, p.40. At my request, Manuel Martinez Nicolas, a colleague at the University of Barcelona, sought to update this report and could find no such shops nor such a variety of condoms. I would be glad to receive further information.

17. APSNFB, 22 February 1988, p.7.

18. ibid., 19 April 1988, p.4.

19. ibid., 9 May 1988, p.2.

20. ibid., 11 July 1988, p.3.

21. ibid., 25 July 1988, p.4.

22. Schoepf, Brooke Grundfest (1992) 'Women at Risk: Studies from Zaire.' *The Time of AIDS: Social Analysis, Theory, and Method.* Ed. Gilbert H. Herdt and Shirley Lindenbaum. Newbury Park, CA: Sage Publications.

23. Daniel B. Hrdy, 'Cultural Practices Contributing to the Transmission of Human Immunodeficiency Virus in Africa', *Review of Infectious Diseases* 9, 1987, p.1109–19.

24. Jane T. Bertrand, Bakutuvwidi Makani, Balowa Djunghu, and Kinavwidi L. Niwenbo, 'Sexual Behavior and Condom Use in 10 Sites of Zaire', *Journal of Sex Research* 28:3, August 1991, pp.347–64.

25. Kierna Mayo, 'TLC: Demanding Respect', *The Source*, June 1992, pp.46–9, p.61.

26. 'Woman Kills Husband', *Kenya Daily Nation*, 1991.

27. An early attempt in Australia to ban explicit AIDS education for gay men created such an outcry that a national campaign was organized before that of other countries. Despite the limitations of the Grim Reaper campaign, it captured the attention of the general population and represented, as well, considerable cooperation among diverse groups at risk. Though an attempt to create a Helms-like ban on projects failed in Canada, existing regulations have been used to seize materials at the border (see Gary Kinsman, *The Regulation of Desire: Sexuality in Canada*, Montreal, Black Rose Books, 1987). Clause 28, passed in the UK parliament, succeeded in creating Helms-like prohibitions on projects and materials. The Helms amendment was subsequently found unconstitutional in a federal court of appeals.

28. Condom Advertising and AIDS. Hearing before Subcommittee on Health and the Environment of the Committee of Energy and Commerce. US

House of Representatives. February 10, 1987. Serial no. 100–1. Washington: US Government Printing Office, 1987. Hereafter documented internally as 'Hearing,' by page number.

risk, injecting drug use and the myth of an objective social science

Tim Rhodes

There are only perceptions of risk. Our understandings of risk and risk behaviour are not based on objectively determined 'truths' about these phenomena but on how they are presented to us.[1] There are multiple and competing constructions of what the realities of risk and injecting drug use are. It is therefore important to question what we are told.

This essay explores social scientific understandings of risk related to injecting drug use. Three main points are made. First, that epidemiological knowledge about risk tells us as much about moral danger as it does biological danger. Second, that the vision of injecting drug use constructed by epidemiology is myopic in scope, and cannot capture the social dimensions of drug use and risk behaviours. And third, that ethnographic and sociological work shows that risk knowledges, perceptions and behaviours are socially organized. Bringing these points together, we need to question social scientific constructions of risk knowledge related to injecting drug use with the aim of producing counter knowledges based on drug users' own risk perceptions and lived experiences.

Of all people most affected by HIV infection in the UK, it is arguably drug injectors who are the most invisible and who lack the power or infrastructures to respond, or disagree, with what the knowledge experts say about HIV and

AIDS. Not only is it necessary to find ways of protecting the diminishing resources invested in HIV services for people who inject drugs, it is of paramount importance that debates on the politics as the of AIDS better represent the views and experiences of injecting drug users.

risk epidemiology and moral danger

Accepted facts are the essence of science. It is what we depend on scientists for, especially in times of great uncertainty. But scientific conceptions of risk tell us as much about the meaning and status of certain behaviours and populations as the threat of blood-borne viruses. This demands the need for reflexivity in the knowledge we have and the knowledge we produce. With different social and scientific organizations competing for the means of knowledge production, this task takes on a political dimension. The uneven distribution of power invested in different sciences and knowledge producers has direct consequences for how risk and health are understood, and crucially, for how risk is introduced and managed among populations without the power to compete. As producers of knowledge about 'risk behaviour', it is important that social scientists are reflexive about what they know and the expertise they have.[2]

Certain discourses representing risk acquire, by virtue of their own claims to objectivity as well as their institutional self-legitimation, more currency and symbolic power than others. Since HIV infection has been constituted both an *epidemic* and a *behavioural* disease, it appears only 'natural' that epidemiology and behavioural science have the commanding role as knowledge producers about risk behaviour. Yet it is important to challenge the myth of objectivity and certainty invested in conventional biomedical interpretations. AIDS is simultaneously a 'social' and medical disease. Every epidemiological or medical 'fact' is inscribed within a context of moral and political conflict and judgment. The presumed and self-claimed objectivity of the 'epidemic sciences' – the epitome of which is epidemiology – obscures the process by which scientific AIDS knowledge is socially organized while stamping on the feet of competing sources of interpretation and expertise.

It is the symbolic meanings of AIDS, rather than the size or content of the 'epidemic', which account for its contemporary significance. And it is this which highlights the power manifest in the epidemic and social scientists when they go about their business of defining and measuring risk behaviour. For the ways in which risk is categorized are loaded with meaning. Far from being a space of statistical associations among variables bereft of normative judgements, expert understandings of risk not only serve, for scientists, the discovery of objective dangers, but for others, the assertion that some ways of life are better than others:

> When an epidemiologist notes that the incidence of AIDS correlates with numbers of sexual contacts, he may be speaking in terms of likelihoods; to many of his fellow Americans he is speaking of guilt and deserved punishment.[3]

The identification and management of particular dangers function to sustain mainstream boundaries of morality and acceptability.[4] The risk of HIV transmission is a potent symbol of threat to 'centre community' boundaries where AIDS is articulated as the danger of 'living outside the norms'.[5] This process 'defines the normal [and] establishes the boundaries of health behaviour and appropriate social relationships' in line with the dominant practices and ideologies of the time.[6]

Public discourses on risk assert, reinforce and justify particular outlooks of life. And so do scientific discourses on risk behaviour. Ever since epidemiology condensed the diverse cases of unusual opportunistic infections associated with immuno-deficiency on to the terms 'GRID' (Gay Related Immuno-Deficiency Syndrome), 'immuno-overload' and 'risk groups', HIV infection has been constituted as both a moral and biological danger. While national media campaigns warned the British general public 'Don't Inject AIDS', early estimates in Edinburgh put HIV prevalence among drug injectors at over 50 per cent, and epidemiologists declared that the 'real heterosexual epidemic' had begun.[7] As a 'source of infection' into the heterosexual 'community', injecting drug users – along with bisexual men and prostitute women – were articulated as key viral leakage points in the prevention policy of containment. The permeability of moral and biological boundaries meant that the real danger was not so much the 'other', or even the other masquerading as the self-same, but the bodies in between.

What we know about injecting drug use not only has symbolic function in communicating meaning about drug use behaviours, it also communicates judgments about the *people* who engage in such activities. The accepted commonsensical facts of risk epidemiology must be questioned not only for their accuracy in depicting individuals' lifestyles, but also for what they imply about risk acceptability, normality and morality.

science, rationality and risk behaviour

Not only might epidemiology – as generally practised – implicitly lend credibility to the idea that certain populations are morally dangerous; it is questionable whether epidemiology is capable of understanding the determinants of risk behaviour. Much more serious for epidemiologists, modern epidemiology appears to be caught in a methodological paradox where it cannot answer the questions it poses.

objectivity, biology and individualism

Modern epidemiology may have shifted from the specific-cause etiology of germ theory to the movement of epidemics among populations, but the unit of analysis and etiologic theory remains trapped at the interface of biology and individuals.[8] On the one hand, this biomedical reductionism cannot account for the ways in which social and contextual factors influence risk behaviours. On the other, the abstracted universalism with which epidemiological facts are presented assumes certainty. The consequence is that modern epidemiology is 'ill-equipped to address epidemic control'[9] but nonetheless offers objective measures of risk. It has been said that epidemiology 'measures' and does not 'understand',[10] but it could just as easily be said that it does not understand what it measures.

This 'poor fit of universalism with human reality'[11] gives rise to two problems in risk knowledge production. First, epidemiology is unable to grasp the socially situated nature of risk behaviours. Second, being unable to allow for competing subjective interpretations of what risk is, it cannot grasp the situated nature of the knowledge it produces.

Epidemiology reduces social interactions into probabilistic calculations of biological likelihood. Take, for example, social scientific constructions of injecting drug use. In the time of AIDS, heroin use has been reduced to the act of injecting. If 'Silence=Death' is viewed as an icon for AIDS activism, then 'Injection=Infection' might reflect popular representations of heroin use. When we are told by national media campaigns 'Don't Inject AIDS', we are reminded that 'it just takes one prick to give you AIDS'. Reduced to a series of AIDS injections, the social world of injecting drug use – in the epidemiological imagination – is a very dangerous place to be.

This myopic vision gives an unrealistic picture of how risk is perceived by people who inject drugs, and of where the risk of HIV fits in.[12] The selective emphasis on AIDS dangers and injection blur the social meanings of drug injecting as understood by drug users, offer a conception of 'lifestyle' reduced to HIV-relevant behaviours alone, and narrowly define 'risk' and 'health' in terms of HIV disease. Nowhere in the epidemiological imagination is there space for an alternative objectivity or a more complex understanding of drug injecting based on the lived experiences and expertise of those who actually inject drugs.

rationality and human nature

Scientific understandings of risk behaviour are culture-bound. They draw on prevailing commonsensical beliefs about human nature. Two popularly held views represent risk in almost diametrical opposition. On the one hand, it is thought to be in our nature to protect ourselves. We are supposedly risk averse, acting in ways so as to avoid self-danger. Only heroes and villains deliberately take risks. For the rest of us, risk avoidance is represented as an instinctive response which ensures the quality and presence of our lives. On the other hand, it is thought that certain types of people – if not viewed as villains, seen as fatalists – persistently harm themselves and others. In the time before AIDS it was not uncommon for 'addicts' and 'junkies' to be represented in these terms:

> There was widespread acceptance of the folk myth that most injectors are incorrigible addicts, impelled down a pipeline leading to high morbidity and premature mortality, and caring for little but their next injection[13]

AIDS to some extent, has helped change beliefs that injecting drug users are no more than 'incorrigible addicts'. Such beliefs become difficult in the face of evidence indicating behaviour change and the effectiveness of harm reduction initiatives. Yet dominant scientific theories of risk behaviour, which draw on psychological ideas of 'rational decision-making' and 'reasoned action' view risk avoidance behaviours – often termed 'healthy choices' – to be synonymous with 'rational' or 'reasoned' actions. Psychological theory assumes rational individuals to be 'risk averse'. This singular criterion of 'rationality' relegates risk behaviour (or 'risk acceptance') to the realm of individual mistakes, irrational thinking and self-destructive behaviour. As noted by Mary Douglas:

> We are said to be risk-averse, but, alas, so inefficient in handling information that we are unintentional risk-takers; basically we are fools . . . I do not doubt that danger is with us, and very real, but for heaven's sake, how could we have survived on this planet if our thinking is so inherently flawed?[14]

Viewed as risk-averse rational actors, individuals can be blamed for making dangerous choices. Injecting drug use is at once biologically risky and morally questionable, as are the individuals and populations who 'choose' to partake in such activities. Psycho-social risk theorizing colludes with a commonsense rationality which does not understand the pursuance of behaviours deemed epidemiologically risky as 'rational'. Such theory fails to acknowledge that a plurality of rationalities and risk perceptions exist.

This has encouraged moves towards 'situated rationality' theories of risk.[15, 16] Since rationalities are shaped by surrounding systems of knowledge, and since individual actions are contingent on the actions of others and the situations in which these occur, risk is best viewed as the outcome of 'situated actions'. Giving room to multiple perceptions of risk in different contexts, these theories acknowledge that epidemiological predictions based on the assumption that all individuals are risk averse is scientifically naive.

It is misguided to base theories of risk wholesale upon a notion of individual rationality and choice, situated or in vacuo. The idea of individual choice is a fallacy; one person's choice is another's constraint. Risk actions are rarely systematically 'calculated' by individuals as most social science theories presume, but are invariably the outcome of negotiated or habituated actions. Risk behaviours are 'social actions', shaped through social interactions and contexts. Any theory which takes the individual as the sole unit of analysis mistakingly obliterates the social context in which interaction – and individuation itself – takes place.

ethnography and the lived experience of risk

If epidemiology reduces risk to 'objective' estimates of likelihood, then by contrast sociology and anthropology are concerned with describing people's lived experiences of risk. Ethnographic research aims to understand how risk is socially organized. First, it describes the social meanings attached by drug injectors to behaviours deemed risky. Second, it describes the social processes by which these meanings become attached to particular behaviours.

Viewing risk as a perceived reality puts the drug user back in the driving seat. For ethnographers documenting drug users' experiences of risk, it is drug users – rather than scientists – who are the experts. We know enough about what researchers call 'risk behaviour'. We need to know more about what risk means for the people who partake in injecting drug use. Rather than measures of 'relative risk' in the mathematical sense, ethnography seeks to view risk as 'part of a probabilistic system of social relations'.[17]

The ethnographer of risk makes two simple discoveries. First, drug use can mean very different things for drug injectors and epidemiologists. Injecting drug use is not synonymous with 'risk behaviour' or 'HIV transmission' but carries with it a host of other, often more mundane, social meanings. Second, injecting drug use may be associated with risks and dangers other than HIV transmission, which to drug injectors may be more important. Four lessons from ethnographic work on risk and drug use are that: all risks are relative; risk behaviours communicate social meanings; social meanings and behaviours are context dependent; and risk reduction requires social change. The implications of these lessons are the focus of the rest of this essay.

relative risks and everyday injecting drug use

Epidemiological science is often blind to what drug injectors perceive as risk. Heroin injectors often cite overdose as their main health concern.[18] It is not 'irrational' for British drug injectors to give greater priority to overdose than HIV transmission. Home Office statistics indicate that the likelihood of deaths from heroin overdose far outweigh those from HIV disease. In London, 23 per cent of injectors say they have overdosed and 41 per cent of these have overdosed in the last year.[19] Nevertheless, and betraying the unacknowledged political and moral influences on their allegedly objective preoccupations, social scientists have rarely discussed overdose in their assessments of risk behaviour.

An equally incisive example is hepatitis. Not only is hepatitis C on the increase (estimates suggest 60 per cent prevalence in London), over half of drug injectors are positive to hepatitis B virus.[20] Despite the availability of a hepatitis B vaccine, and surveys which indicate that the majority of drug injectors want vaccinations, few British drug agencies offer immunization as part of their prevention services. It is difficult to imagine a similar scenario if a vaccine against HIV existed.

The selection and management of drug use dangers reflect broader social and political concerns. With indications that drug use and related deaths are on the increase, and voiced concerns that a 'liberal' drug policy in the time of AIDS has done little to combat drug taking, we are witnessing the emergence of 'back to basics' drug policy. There is little emphasis on 'harm reduction' in the recent government White Paper, 'Tackling Drugs Together' (1995), and the dangers of drugs have been re-articulated to signify crime. Concern for drug users' health takes second place in this re-articulation of risk associated with drug use.

Reports to government prepared by the Advisory Council on the Misuse of Drugs have shifted from the assertion that 'HIV is a greater danger to individual and public health than drug misuse' (1988) to 'greater efforts are now needed to reduce the extent of drug misuse itself' (1993). We are now told that the challenge is to recognize the 'twin epidemics' of AIDS and injecting drug use. In conceptualizing drug use itself as a kind of chronic epidemic disease, new dangers are found to protect the public good and centre community boundaries.

sex and sharing: symbolic actions, social meanings

Behaviours communicate social meanings. Not only is sharing injecting equipment influenced by immediate material contexts (such as availability and affordability), it may function as a symbolic act. The shared use of injecting equipment may not be viewed as anything unusual, or even risky, and may not be understood as 'sharing' as epidemiologically defined.[21] Sharing is more than pragmatic, it communicates social meanings, such as reciprocity and trust, in people's social interactions.[22] Such behaviours are not simply taken to mean 'biological risk' but function at a symbolic level to maintain the social and interactional order of relationships.

Similar observations have been made about the sharing of drug solutions prepared for injection. While epidemiological studies note the potential HIV transmission risks of 'frontloading' and 'backloading' they fail to capture the social dimensions of these practices.[23] 'Indirect sharing', including the related activities of sharing cotton filters, spoons and rinse water, are everyday and unspectacular, but they are nonetheless based on situated pragmatics and social values. These range from the trust and assurance gained from the equal sharing of drug solutions (as with front/backloading) to the giving and receiving of 'gifts' (as with the borrowing of used filters containing a residue of drug solution). Sharing drug solutions may come to be collectively viewed as symbolic displays of trust and reciprocity and not simply as pragmatic ways to divide up drugs.

People similarly attach symbolic meanings to protected and unprotected sex. Unprotected sex can be taken as communicating trust, commitment and love, and this may seem to outweigh the potential dangers of STD transmission.[24]

One brief example from our own research illustrates this point. This concerns 'unsafe protected sex' or 'UPS'.[25] Defined as the practice where condoms are used unsafely, two similar forms of UPS identified in our ethnographic work with drug users were: using condoms for ejaculation only; and using condoms after limited unprotected penetration had taken place. In the context of perceived social norms seen to legitimate unprotected sex as a normal feature of most drug users' heterosexual relationships, *some* condom use may be rationalized as better than *no* condom use. But UPS may also be a one stage transition from condom use to non-condom use in relationships. As a symbolic act, the presence of UPS can make 'permissible' a certain amount of unprotected sex, which in turn can make a transition towards no condom use easier to justify and negotiate.

galleries and relationships: social contexts, social relations

The social meanings of risk behaviours are context dependent. The ethnographic studies of Larry Ouellet and Wayne Wiebel reveal, for instance, how different Chicago shooting galleries have different rules for renting out injecting equipment.[26] In 'cash galleries', the sale or rental of syringes is run like a business, where gallery operators establish a formal set of rules and enforce compliance. In 'taste galleries', which usually operate from an injector's house, reciprocity is less formalized, and the operator is normally given a small portion, or a taste, of the drugs in exchange for a safe place to inject. In 'free galleries', such as in abandoned buildings, there is no cash or drug exchange for borrowed equipment.

Different gallery structures influence risk behaviour in different ways. In free galleries, for example, running water is rarely available. This means that injectors leave containers of water for mixing, shooting and rinsing at gallery sites. There is, as a consequence, an associated risk of HIV transmission through the sharing of contaminated water.

Whereas cash galleries are often receptive to HIV prevention initiatives, and may provide bleach, clean water and containers for syringe disposal, many taste galleries are closed operations inaccessible to health outreach workers.

Just as shooting galleries structure risk, particular social relationships fashion risk perception and behaviour norms. Studies repeatedly show, for example, that drug injectors are more likely to use condoms in casual rather than primary relationships, and that this relates to the social meanings attached to protected and unprotected sex in heterosexual primary and casual encounters.[27] In 'primary' sexual relationships, in particular, the perceived benefits of unprotected sex are often seen to outweigh the potential risks, and making a transition from condom use to non-condom use in long-term or 'serious' relationships is viewed by most heterosexual drug users to be 'normal'.[28] Breaking a precedence of condom use may provide symbolic displays that relationships have indeed become 'primary' or 'serious'. Condom use – and its dissociable other, no condom use – become definitional of given relationships. The social contexts of drug use environments and sexual relationships thus mediate social meanings of risk behaviours.

networks and communities: risk reduction, social change

Over the past five years there has been considerable effort to encourage community-based changes in HIV transmission behaviour. Established examples of group-mediated change interventions among drug injectors include: the Indigenous Leader Outreach Model in Chicago,[29] the Peer Driven Intervention Model in Connecticut,[30] the collective organizing strategies in Williamsburg, New York,[31] and the social network interventions in Arizona.[32] These interventions aim to change the social relationships which structure individual risk behaviours by encouraging collective or 'community' changes in social and behavioural norms.

Based less on epidemiological expertise than ethnographic appreciation of how risk is socially organized, these efforts target not only the individual and self-perceptions; they target social relationships and their systemic norms, rules and rituals. The basis for change rests upon the assumption that risk perception is a group-mediated activity, and that it is 'social networks' and 'social interactions' that are responsible for a 'large part of the perceptual coding on risks'.[33]

Yet the burgeoning literature on the need for group-mediated change hides the potential limits of community initiatives among drug injectors. It is unclear how effective 'social diffusion' interventions have been in actually bringing about 'group-mediated' and 'community' change. This is especially evident in the context of drug users' sexual behaviour where doubts exist about the chances of changing sexual safety norms. Many individuals deviate from group norms and will have unsafe sex even in contexts where safer sex is perceived to be the norm. Indeed, 'rule breaking' norms may legitimate deviation from public and community safety norms when in the context of private sexual encounters, where a 'slip-up' culture permits a certain amount of unsafe sexual behaviour.[34]

The 'change experts' have constructed a limited understanding of 'community' and 'community change' as it relates to injecting drug use. The political meanings and use of the term community function as part of wider discourses on community action and political activism. Yet the ideals of community action and the notion of there existing drug injecting 'communities' may be more imagined than real. Individuals within drug using networks connect largely as a function of their drug use. This functionality often works against the idea of community or community identity in the ideological sense associated with identity politics.[35]

The impersonal, and ostensibly pragmatic, nature of many drug 'acquaintanceships' are often more characteristic of a culture of individualistic survival than they are of a collective reciprocity. The claim that among drug injectors there is a universal subcultural code – as opposed to a negotiated and unspoken arrangement between individuals – of 'sharing', 'collectivity' and 'community' may be more romantic fallacy than social reality. The uplifting language of community change adopted by activists serves a clear political objective but it may often lack credence as lived experience. If community-organized social changes are to become possible among drug injectors, it is important that we are not simply convinced by the commonsense appeal of our favoured theories of community change, but that we also know something about the chances of their success and how to apply them.

conclusion: situating risk knowledge

Social scientific constructions of risk reify and reflect public discourses of morality and danger. Expert knowledge about HIV disease not only communicates certainty about the relative biological dangers of viral transmission, it also says much about the perceived threat or danger consituted by certain behaviours and populations. The classification of risk behaviours not only preserves the health of the public through epidemic control, it protects the 'good' of the public by symbolizing the right and wrong ways to behave. In times where epidemics precipitate moral panic, it is difficult to separate scientific categorizations of biological risk from the social management of moral dangers. The self-proclaimed 'objective' risk knowledge produced by the epidemic sciences is situated within a particular cultural and political milieu.

If we understand science's portfolio of fact as inseparable from broader social values and attitudes, we begin to understand the unacknowledged and dangerous complicities between 'objective' social science and discourses of intolerance, stigmatization and censure. This is particularly important, as HIV infection has proved, in times of epidemic uncertainty and anxiety, and where there happens to be a congruence between affected populations and stigmatized behaviour.

Modern epidemiology is backed by more symbolic – and financial – capital than competing schools of thought, principally because epidemiology touts its own objectivity. The essence of orthodox science is objectivity and certainty. And this is what is urgently demanded from social science in times of a new epidemic. The sciences most adept at investigating epidemics are also those most 'epidemic' in our society.[36] Yet it is these 'epidemic sciences' – and especially epidemiology – which are most methodologically and theoretically ill equipped to understand human behaviour. Modern epidemiology appears caught in a methodological paradox where it has to provide universal objective truths about risk probability whilst being unable to understand the interplay of factors which cause risk behaviour. Whilst claiming objectivity, it cannot see the subjective nature of the truths it offers.

Competing social sciences, such as sociology and anthropology, view risk differently. Asserting that all risk is relative, risk is viewed as emanating from the social meanings and contexts in which interactions and risk encounters take place. The risk knowledges produced by ethnography are not taken as objective or accepted fact but are given as interpreted reflections of how actors themselves perceive and live risk. As we have seen with the example of injecting drug use, this gives alternative versions of risk and danger, and permits the possibility for multiple rationalities of risk action to exist. These counter knowledges point to how dominant scientific constructions of risk and injecting drug use are inadequate in describing how risk is actually lived and perceived.

Ethnography describes risk as a product of drug users' perceived realities, and thus offers a *situated* knowledge of expertise on risk behaviour. This is pragmatic because it encourages HIV prevention efforts which make sense to drug users and not simply to epidemiologists. Any system of knowledge production on the subject of drug use and HIV infection demands grounding in the expertise of those it wishes to serve. It is not only necessary to question the taken-for-granted certainty of scientific knowledge, but it is important to understand how the knowledges of science have impact and meaning for people's lived experiences. This should be the starting point of any understanding or intervention related to risk and injecting drug use.

Of all people most affected by HIV infection in the UK, it is arguably drug injectors who are the most invisible and who lack the platform or infrastructures to challenge 'expert' opinions about HIV and AIDS. This is a very precarious situation, especially when the politics of HIV funding and planning is so fierce. While ethnography may provide some opportunity for describing the social relations of risk among drug users, it is no substitute for protecting the ever decreasing resources invested in HIV treatment and prevention services for drug injectors. It is rare that injecting drug users are represented amongst those acting on AIDS or among those party to decisions made about HIV service planning and funding. Activists who share a belief in the ideals of community organizing cannot ignore the lack of investment in community development work among people who inject drugs.

notes

1. P. Treichler, 'AIDS, HIV and the Cultural Construction of Reality', in G. Herdt, and S. Lindenbaum, (eds), *The Time of AIDS: Social Analysis, Theory and Method*, London, Sage, 1992.
2. C. Patton, *Inventing AIDS*, London, Routledge, 1990.
3. C.E. Rosenberg, 'Disease and Social Order in America: Perceptions and Expectations', in E. Fee, and D.M. Fox, (eds), *AIDS: The Burdens of History*, London, University of California Press, 1988.
4. M. Douglas, *Risk and Blame: Essays in Cultural Theory*, London, Routledge, 1992.
5. J. Weeks, 'Post-Modern AIDS?', in S. Gupta, and T. Boffin, (eds), *Ecstatic*

Antibodies: Resisting the AIDS Mythology, London, Rivers Oram Press, 1990.

6. D. Nelkin, and S.L. Gilman, 'Placing Blame for Devastating Disease', in A. Mack, (ed.), *In Time of Plague*, New York, New York University Press, 1991.
7. A. Moss, 'AIDS and Intravenous Drug Use: the Real Heterosexual Epidemic', *British Medical Journal*, 1987, 294, pp.389–90.
8. M. Susser, and E. Susser, 'Choosing a Future for Epidemiology: From Black Box Chinese Boxes and Eco-Epidemiology', *American Journal of Public Health*, 1996, 86, pp.674–77.
9. ibid.
10. N. Pearce, 'Traditional Epidemiology, Modern Epidemiology and Public Health', *American Journal of Public Health*, 1996, 86, pp.678–83.
11. M. and E. Susser, op.cit.
12. T. Rhodes, 'Theorising and Researching "Risk": Notes on the Social Relations of Risk in Heroin Users' Lifestyles', in P. Aggleton, P. Davies, and G. Hart, (eds), *AIDS: Sexuality, Safety and Risk*, London, Taylor and Francis, 1995.
13. G.V. Stimson, 'AIDS and Injecting Drug Use in the United Kingdom, 1987–1993: the Policy Response and the Prevention of the Epidemic', *Social Science and Medicine*, 41(5), pp.699–716.
14. M. Douglas, op.cit.
15. M. Bloor, *The Sociology of HIV Transmission*, London, Sage, 1995.
16. T. Rhodes, 'Risk Theory in Epidemic Times: Sex, Drugs and the Social Organisation of Risk Behaviour, *Sociology of Health and Illness*, 1997, 19, pp. 208–27.
17. M. Douglas, op.cit.
18. T. Rhodes, 1995, op.cit.
19. M. Gossop, P. Griffiths, B. Powis, S. William, and J. Strang, 'Frequency of non-fatal heroin overdose', *British Medical Journal*, 1996, 313, p.402.
20. T. Rhodes, G.M. Hunter, G.V. Stimson et al., 'Prevalence of Markers for Hepatitis B Virus and HIV-1 Among Drug Injectors in London: Injecting Careers, Positivity and Risk Behaviour, *Addiction*, 1996, 91, pp.1465–75.
21. T. Rhodes, and A. Quirk, 'Heroin, Risk and Sexual Safety: Some Problems for Interventions Encouraging Community Change', in T. Rhodes, and R. Hartnoll, (eds), *AIDS, Drugs and Prevention: Perspectives on Individual and Community Action*, London, Routledge, 1996.
22. W.A. Zule, 'Risk and Reciprocity: HIV and the Injection Drug User', *Journal of Psychoactive Drugs*, 1992, 24, pp.243–9.

23. S. Koester, 'The Process of Drug Injection: Applying Ethnography to the Study of HIV Risk Among IDUs', in T. Rhodes, and R. Hartnoll, (eds), *AIDS, Drugs and Prevention: Perspectives on Individual and Community Action*, London, Routledge, 1996.

24. B. Sibthorpe, 'The Social Construction of Sexual Relationships as a Determinant of HIV Risk Perception and Condom Use Among Injection Drug Users', *Medical Anthropology Quarterly*, 1992, 6, pp.255–70.

25. A. Quirk, T. Rhodes, and G.V. Stimson, 'Unsafe Protected Sex: Qualitative Insights on Measures of Sexual Risk', *AIDS Care*, 8, in press.

26. L. Ouellet, A. Jimenez, and W. Johnson, 'Shooting Galleries and HIV Disease: Variations in Places for Injecting Illicit Drugs', *Crime and Delinquency*, 1991, 37, pp.64–85.

27. B. Sibthorpe, op.cit.

28. T. Rhodes and A. Quirk, op.cit.

29. W. Wiebel, 'Ethnographic Contributions to AIDS Intervention Strategies', in T. Rhodes, and R. Hartnoll, (eds), *AIDS, Drugs and Prevention: Perspectives on Individual and Community Action* London, Routledge, 1996.

30. R.S. Broadhead, and D.D. Heckathorn, 'AIDS Prevention Outreach Among Injection Drug Users: Agency Problems and New Approaches', *Social Problems*, 1994, 41, pp.473–95.

31. S.R. Friedman, A. Neaigus, D.C. Des Jarlais, et al., 'Social Intervention Against AIDS Among Injecting Drug Users, *British Journal of Addiction*, 1992, 87, pp.393–404.

32. R.T. Trotter, J. Potter, and A.M. Bowen, 'Networks and Ethnography: Group-Based HIV Prevention for Small Town and Rural Drug Users, Unpublished manuscript, Department of Anthropology, Northern Arizona University, 1993.

33. M. Douglas, *Risk Acceptability According to the Social Sciences*, London, Routledge and Kegan Paul, 1986.

34. R. Gold, 'Why We Need to Rethink AIDS Education for Gay Men', *AIDS Care*, 1995, 71, S11–S19.

35. T. Rhodes, 'Outreach, Community Change and Community Empowerment: Contradictions for Public Health and Health Promotion', in P. Aggleton, P. Davies, and G. Hart, (eds), *AIDS: Foundations for the Future*, London, Taylor and Francis, 1994.

36. P. Strong, 'Epidemic psychology: a model', *Sociology of Health and Illness*, 1990, 12, pp.249–59.

the political significance of statistics in the AIDS crisis

epidemiology, representation and re-gaying

Simon Watney

summary

I begin this essay by considering ways in which HIV and AIDS statistics have been gathered and presented by epidemiologists in official tables and charts. I examine how journalists and others have frequently based misleading accounts of the epidemic on selective reporting of statistics, which in turn reflect other forms of bias. I propose that epidemiology should be understood as a primary system of representation, mediating between the lived experience of the consequences of HIV infection and wider social beliefs, attitudes and behaviour, including public policies. In conclusion, I look at some of the ways in which targeted HIV/AIDS education for those at greatest risk has been widely neglected, whilst the needs of those at least risk have consistently drawn the most attention and resources. Throughout the AIDS crisis, the field of epidemiology has been the site of several complex biopolitical struggles in relation to a wide range of issues, from questions concerning the aims and methods of medical research (including clinical trials), to questions of social service provision and prevention strategies. These struggles demonstrate the importance of recognizing that statistics should be public rather than governmental property, and that epidemiologists have ethical responsibilities as social scientists to make the significance of their findings widely and accessibly available. Nor should the methods or reporting of national epidemiological research be subject to partisan political pressures from government or government agencies.

introduction

Much attention has been paid in the history of the AIDS crisis to the roles played by language and visual imagery, from photography to feature films, in mediating and representing the epidemic.[1] Indeed, sometimes it has seemed as if the goal of changing and improving the words and images generated in response to HIV/AIDS has had a higher priority than concrete issues of social and medical policy and the provision of care and services. Yet the primary purpose for a cultural critique of the uses of language and imagery in relation to HIV/AIDS should always be immediate questions of social policy. Social policy, in turn, is a site of conflicting demands, based on different and opposing values. For example, a vocal lobby has long campaigned for sweeping cuts in government funding for all aspects of the epidemic, on the grounds that HIV is a 'self-inflicted' illness, and that it has received 'disproportionately' high resources in relation to other medical conditions such as heart disease or cancer.[2]

It is important to understand that such opinions express deeply held beliefs and prejudices, which are deployed by academics, journalists, and lobbyists in order to directly influence public policies. When such views prevail, real harm may result. The fight against such prejudice is not simply an abstract battle for 'truth', but a politically necessary struggle for specific goals. Furthermore, many of the controversies surrounding almost all aspects of the epidemic are in one way or another related to statistically based claims and counter-claims. In this respect, the ways in which HIV and AIDS statistics are gathered and published take on special significance, since they provide us with the most scientifically accurate pictures of the epidemic. Statistics such as numbers of newly reported cases of HIV infection, average life-expectancy and mortality rates provide the key data from which we build our understanding of the epidemic and its progress. Understanding the role of statistics is particularly important in relation to the introduction in the 1990s of a form of market economy within the British National Health Service (NHS). Whilst the enforced competition for funds from NHS 'purchasers' of services, such as health authorities, for 'providers' of services, such as charities, may be seen as harmful, the system must, for the time being at least, be made to work as well as it can. Epidemiology provides vital information on the basis of which projects competing for scarce funds may be evaluated by professional purchasers. It is on the grounds of statistics, and their interpretation, that actual policies are funded and put into practice, in a wider social climate of considerable public confusion and misunderstanding concerning HIV and AIDS. Whilst health care systems differ in different countries, it is nevertheless significant that the British experience is typical rather than an international exception, especially in the provision of prevention resources to those at least risk from HIV, rather than to those at demonstrably greater risk.

facts and figures

British epidemiological surveillance of AIDS began at the Public Health Laboratory Service (PHLS) and the Scottish Centre for Infection and Environmental Health (SCIEH) in 1982. Epidemiological surveillance of HIV began two years later, after the introduction of blood tests for the recently discovered retrovirus. Summaries of statistics are published monthly, with a *News Release* every six months, and detailed *aids/hiv Quarterly Surveillance Tables*, which are distributed to leading state agencies including the Health Education Authority and the Medical Research Council. Unfortunately these statistics are not distributed to HIV/AIDS charities who are equally involved in the national management of the epidemic. Throughout the developed world, government agencies provide similar services, whilst wider regional and global statistics are produced by agencies including the European Centre for the Epidemiological Monitoring of AIDS, UN AIDS, and the World Health Organization. American HIV/AIDS statistics are published by the Centers for Disease Control and Prevention (CDCP), in Atlanta, Georgia.

It is on the basis of changing patterns of infection and illness that epidemiologists are able to make mathematical projections concerning the likely course of the epidemic. Statistics are gathered in relation to factors of age, class, gender, sexuality, ethnicity, and mode of HIV transmission. Such statistics do not transparently disclose the changing mathematical 'truth' of the epidemic. Attention, in most official epidemiological reporting, is given in accordance with contingent social factors and institutional pressures (such as entrenched prejudice). Thus, of the thirty-two sets of tables in the most recent British *AIDS/HIV Quarterly Surveillance Tables* (N. 13, to March 1996), there are eight which consider heterosexual transmission from different perspectives. Only two tables consider specific aspects of male-to-male transmission, although these constitute 69 per cent of new AIDS cases in the first quarter of 1996. Simply put, epidemiology focuses in greater or lesser detail on its social targets according to determining factors which are best understood as biopolitical. In the accompanying notes published with the *AIDS/HIV Quarterly Surveillance Tables* the reader is informed that:

> For the UK, the proportion of AIDS cases attributable to sexual intercourse between men has consistently declined, from 95 per cent of those reported by the end of 1985, to 69 per cent of those reported in the first quarter of 1996. Over the same period, the proportion of cases attributed to heterosexual exposure has risen from 4 per cent to 23 per cent.[3]

The intended meaning could hardly be more clear: AIDS amongst gay men is on the decline and AIDS amongst heterosexuals is on the increase. This has been the editorial tendency of the PHLS publications for many years. Yet a closer look at the actual figures reveals any such conclusion as extremely misleading if left without further qualification. Initially, we should examine the difference between HIV statistics and AIDS statistics. AIDS statistics are extremely useful for the planning and costing of services, including hospital treatment, but they tell us nothing about the state of current HIV infections. Hence the importance of making the careful distinction between HIV and AIDS statistics, recognizing that they look at different aspects of an epidemic which essentially moves in very slow motion. Unfortunately, the separate publication of Scottish statistics from those from the rest of the UK does not facilitate our understanding of over-all patterns of infection and illness. Taken together however, figures for newly reported cases of AIDS in Britain in 1995 show 1,248 cases resulting from male-to-male transmission, and 408 cases resulting from heterosexual transmission (202 men and 206 women). However, of these cases of heterosexual transmission, only 18 had resulted from exposure in Britain from a partner with no obvious risk factor.[4]

Turning to HIV statistics, the picture is depressingly similar. There were 2,709 newly reported cases of HIV in Britain in 1995, of which 1,540 resulted from male-to-male transmission, and 777 from heterosexual transmission, of which 523 occurred abroad. This hardly supports the widely assumed view that HIV and AIDS are somehow less of a problem for gay men than for heterosexuals. Yet it is precisely this view which has dominated prevention and education campaigns in the UK. We thus see that blanket comparisons between percentage increases in cases of HIV or AIDS resulting from male-to-male and heterosexual transmission are likely to be highly misleading. A relatively small increase in cases amongst heterosexuals may result in a percentage increase which is then contrasted to the more or less steady rate of male-to-male cases, as if the former were larger and more in need of intervention than the latter. In reality, nothing could be further from the truth. It's clear that if some trends are emphasized to the exclusion of others, a false picture of the real epidemic is manufactured and promoted. Moreover, male-to-male cases are not given a fraction of the ancillary detail provided for cases of heterosexual transmission, according to a wide variety of ascertainable risk factors.

Knowledge of these could help in the design of targeted health promotion interventions. In the last few years, new tables have been published concerning younger gay men, but much less data is provided about the risk factors involved in male-to-male transmission than is routinely provided in relation to heterosexual transmission. Far more information is available about the 669 cases of HIV in children than about the 16,542 cases amongst gay men. This is not to argue that too much information is provided about paediatric HIV and AIDS, but merely to underscore how little is provided about the social group most devastated by illness and death. If the types of data one might reasonably expect to be provided as the basis for prevention work amongst those at demonstrably greatest risk is not collected, one can only assume that this is because they are not thought to be sufficiently important. The implication of such selective data gathering and reporting is that all gay men are the same, without significant variant risk factors in relation to patterns of infection. This, in turn, suggests that nothing could be known about how we become infected, an assumption which would never be acceptable in relation to heterosexuals, especially if they were experiencing a devastating epidemic in their midst.

Data are collected in relation to heterosexual transmission of HIV as if this reflected a major epidemic, whilst the absence of data concerning gay men implies that HIV is somehow no longer a catastrophe for us. Such largely unconscious attitudes also explain the way in which the PHLS has frequently advanced the highly misleading notion of a 'plateau effect' in relation to HIV/AIDS amongst gay and bisexual men. Whilst comparative rates of increase may have shifted, this should not be allowed to mask the actual figures from which such statistical artefacts are derived, which demonstrate only too clearly the vastly disproportionate impact of AIDS and HIV on gay men in Britain, as in many other developed countries. I do not want to belittle heterosexual or other modes of HIV transmission, but I do want to call for a more sophisticated (and accessible) articulation of the ways in which different constituencies are affected by HIV in the UK.

Similar problems of omission sadly afflict the reporting of HIV and AIDS statistics which reference race and ethnicity. In the only table which deals with these issues, HIV and AIDS statistics are conflated, and detailed annual statistics are not provided. Instead, cumulative totals of cases are published in such a way that it is impossible to see whether or not there have been changes in rates of HIV transmission within different British ethnic groups, in relation to different modes of transmission. The available statistics are thus unusable for prevention and education campaigns, which should be their *raison d'être.* Official epidemiologists may recognize the role their own statistics might play in relation to the needs of prevention workers on the front-line of the crisis. Why else should detailed statistics be gathered, if not to help target resources to sites of greatest demonstrable need? Yet in Britain they are prevented by departmental directives from gathering just the kind of information relating to factors of race and ethnicity which would be of most practical use.

All too often, state agencies such as the CDCP provide summaries of statistics about the epidemic which amount to strategic misinformation in so far as they only provide AIDS figures with an absence of the more important HIV figures. These summaries are usually accompanied by sensationalizing generalizations which tend to obscure more than they reveal, as in the conclusion that: 'AIDS is the leading cause of death among all men between the ages of 25 and 34 in New York City, Newark, Los Angeles and San Francisco'.[5]

This sounds dramatic, but tells us nothing about the things we most need to know: who is getting sick and how they were infected. In this manner the direct effects of homophobic evasion obliterate the real epidemic, which is replaced by statistical abstractions based only on cumulative totals of AIDS cases. Without regularly updated information about patterns of HIV transmission, effective prevention work cannot easily be designed and undertaken. Yet ironically it is precisely these detailed statistics which in most countries are hardest to obtain.

statistics into stories: reporting HIV/AIDS

A useful and fascinating book could be written about the ways in which journalists have translated epidemiological data concerning HIV/AIDS into newspaper features, editorials, and stories. Certain clear trends may be retrospectively observed over time, and thus clarified.

In British journalism, HIV and AIDS affect only 'people' or 'individuals', never gay men or African immigrants and refugees. Thus, in 1986, *The Times'* science editor noted: 'Current estimates indicate that more than 20,000 individuals in the UK are believed to be infected'.[6] In 1987, Andrew Veitch reported in *The Guardian* that 'another 22 people died from AIDS last month',[7] whilst in 1988, *The Independent's* Health Service correspondent informed readers that 'a further 32 people died of AIDS last month'.[8] Summary statements such as the ones cited are sometimes qualified with more detailed information, but none the less there is a noticeable tendency towards statistical generalizations, with misleading emphasis placed on percentage increases in the rate of heterosexual transmission, which is thus exaggerated out of all proportion to other modes of transmission.[9] There are literally thousands of examples of this type of journalism.

Uncertainty about the future course of heterosexual transmission was entirely understandable in the 1980s, before it became overwhelmingly clear from many years of statistics that an epidemic amongst heterosexuals was not going to take place. This uncertainty was made all the more confusing as a direct result of the taking up of rival 'positions' about AIDS on the part of rival newspapers seeking to capture readership with deliberate breaches in objectivity. Thus, throughout the 1980s and early 1990s some papers would routinely exaggerate the risks of heterosexual transmission, whilst others denied that HIV could be heterosexually transmitted at all. This uncertainty and confusion has caused much real harm.

I am not aware of any straight newspaper journalist in the UK in the 1980s who reported HIV and AIDS statistics reliably, without disguising their underlying significance: the deaths of thousands of gay men. This was often justified on the grounds of avoiding 'scapegoating', as if this made it legitimate to entirely ignore the human centre of the UK epidemic, colluding with the contingent political tendency to refuse funding for gay men's health education throughout the 1980s. All of this was reported in the national British gay papers, but the dailies were unimpressed.

Conspiracy theories have always played a part in AIDS journalism, escalating in ambition at a time when there was genuine medical uncertainty, but subsequently remaining impervious to scientific evidence. For example, in the summer of 1996, *The Sunday Times* is still seemingly committed to its former policy of denying any clinical association between HIV and AIDS, and denying that there is or ever has been an AIDS epidemic anywhere in Africa. There have been, however, several other types of conspiracy theories which have flourished in the tabloids and beyond. The first concerned the origins of the epidemic, and blamed anything from the KGB to the CIA to meteors. Subsequently there were medical conspiracy theories, usually of a highly sensationalist kind. For example, for many years doctors with HIV ('AIDS Doctors') were subjected to extensive media witch hunts, and were deemed to be intrinsically dangerous, and therefore beyond the protection of professional confidentiality. These in turn melded with stories about how the key doctors, together with medical researchers, and frequently community activists (the 'AIDS establishment') were harassing and intimidating those who denied any clinical association between HIV and AIDS ('AIDS dissidents'). These 'dissidents' claimed that doctors were deliberately killing or harming their patients with bogus treatments. This type of conspiracy theory feeds back directly into earlier beliefs that AIDS is a form of genocidal warfare against particular population groups, as has been argued by some black radicals in the United States (including Spike Hughes).[10] For some, there simply is no epidemic. For others, HIV remains a 'self-inflicted illness'. As recently as 1993, *The Guardian's* weekly Pass Notes column recorded of AIDS: 'One early theory had it that it originated in US or Soviet laboratories specialising in biological warfare. Isn't that a bit far-fetched? No more so than HIV-AIDS'.[11] Yet by 1993, it was already overwhelmingly clear from epidemiological evidence that the clinical association between HIV and AIDS was scientifically verified. Moreover, besides Robert Gallo, the scientist who discovered HIV, I am not aware of a single leading HIV/AIDS research scientist who has ever claimed that HIV explains all the many variations of illness experienced by most of the infected.

It is plain that epidemiology has not been well reported in the national British press. Journalists cannot be held entirely responsible for this, since epidemiologists themselves have rarely entered into public debate about the nature of the epidemic and the effectiveness of policies. Ironically, it is the very newspapers which themselves in the 1980s vastly exaggerated the potential threat of HIV to heterosexuals in Britain, which now claim that it was gay men who exaggerated the risk of heterosexual transmission, in order to obtain government funding. Furthermore, newspapers maintain that these same (always un-named) gay men somehow determined official Cabinet Committee policies leading up to and beyond the national 1986 mixed-media AIDS education campaign, based around images of icebergs and tumbling tombstones, and accompanied by a leaflet-drop to every household in the land. It may, however, be fairly said that some lesbians and gay men within AIDS service organizations actively colluded with the de-gaying of AIDS education, just as they refused to provide treatment information services (see Edward King, 'HIV Prevention and the New Virology' in this volume). It is worth recalling the cautionary note in *New Scientist* in 1993, which quietly pointed out that epidemiological predictions from 1989 and 1990

> were astonishingly close to the numbers now emerging. In 1992 there were 1,573 cases in Britain. The last prediction by government scientists . . . predicted 1,600 cases for 1992, with upper and lower ranges of 950 and 2,800 . . . All we know is that this epidemic is unstable, unpredictable from place to place and dangerous. Caution is the only rational response – which means drawing a fine line between doom-mongering and idiotic complacency. Newspapers may not think this makes for good copy, but they must get their facts right.[12]

Sadly, nothing suggests that this much-needed fine line has yet emerged, let alone widened into the established 'common sense' of journalistic understanding of the epidemic.

re-gaying AIDS I

Writing in a letter to *The Independent*, Edward King sets out most cogently the rationale behind the 're-gaying' of AIDS:

> By all means report that heterosexuals can and do become infected with HIV. But is it too much to ask that some sense of perspective is maintained between the hysterical extremes of those who believe that 'everyone is equally at risk' and those who believe that 'straight sex is safe'? Gay and bisexual

> men are far more at risk of HIV than anyone else, now and for the foreseeable future. It is only right and proper that this indisputable fact should be taken into account both by those who allocate scarce education resources, and by those who aim to record the reality of the epidemic in Britain today.[13]

Little reliable statistical evidence was available in the mid and late 1980s and at the same time there was abundant evidence of the possibility of heterosexual transmission. This possibility threatened to turn into a widespread probability if AIDS continued to be treated only as a 'gay plague', affecting only members of 'high risk groups'. In the mid and late 1980s, the 'straight sex is safe' line was widely promoted in several national newspapers. I and others[14] criticized the category of 'high risk groups' in an attempt to explain the realities of the epidemic in terms of specific high risk behaviours. We could not have predicted that this would prove a blessing to the lobby which proclaimed that 'everyone is equally at risk'. HIV was presented by them as a general, abstract peril, and for this position to be credible it was necessary to ignore the actual epidemiology.

It is still not widely understood, even amongst British gay men, that only a tiny fraction of available resources for HIV/AIDS education in the UK was ever made available to projects for gay men. The great difficulties experienced by many of us attempting to develop safer sex education in the voluntary sector in the late 1980s obliged us to contrast our experience of the epidemic with the ways it was routinely portrayed in the mass media. Whilst Cindy Patton introduced the notion of the 'de-gaying' of AIDS as early as 1986, this had referred to the refusal of American health care professionals to acknowledge the pioneering work of gay and lesbian activists in the earliest years of the epidemic. This was not posed as an epidemiological argument, as it was later by myself, Edward King, Peter Scott, and others. This work was subsequently institutionalized in a series of major research projects in the early 1990s, documenting in great detail the neglect of gay men's needs.[15] King, together with Michael Rooney and Peter Scott, revealed in a widely influential 1992 Report that two thirds of public agencies undertaking safer sex work were providing nothing whatsoever for gay and bisexual men.[16]

In reality, re-gaying has involved repeated and patient explanation of the predictable human and economic costs of policies which continue to neglect education for those most demonstrably vulnerable to HIV. Epidemiological arguments thus lay at the heart of re-gaying, described by Edward King as 'applied epidemiology'.[17] As I observed in 1991, 'The perception is that AIDS has, as it were, "moved on" from gay men. Nothing could be further from the truth, as the most recent statistics demonstrate only too clearly'.[18]

The emergence of 'AIDS prevention activism' in the UK, in organizations such as Gay Men Fighting AIDS (GMFA), was the institutional embodiment of the principles informing the re-gaying of AIDS. Such institutions were needed to undertake sometimes controversial research and health promotion interventions, from which the older AIDS charities at that time distanced themselves. The arguments involved were widely reported in the gay press by Keith Alcorn, Edward King, Peter Scott, myself and others, but never permeated through to the straight press, which was still vainly disputing inaccurate 'positions' amongst themselves, without any interest at all in the crisis confronting gay men. Re-gaying was directed primarily in relation to the agencies and public institutions managing the course of the epidemic from the top. Ironically, it was the introduction of some degree of market choice in the field of health promotion which permitted the re-gaying of AIDS where it most matters – in public policy and resourcing. A 1996 report, prepared by two experienced HIV/AIDS administrators from the statutory sector, notes that 'Being explicit about the epidemiology behind targeting allows providers to understand clearly the types of bid that will be welcome, and enables commissioners and providers to engage in strategic debate'.[19]

Some gay commentators have criticized the re-gaying of AIDS on the grounds that it somehow leads to the neglect of heterosexuals in other countries.[20] Such objections fail to understand the sheer scale of official refusal to provide resources for gay men's work in countries where gay men have all along made up the majority of cases, as well as in countries where we constitute a disproportionately affected minority. There is no single, universal, educational answer to the challenges of HIV/AIDS prevention, and demands for simple transcultural solutions are themselves symptoms of a naive globalism which has its political roots elsewhere in contemporary Leftist theory. Hence the continuing importance of repeating that there is no single, unified, global epidemic. Rather, as has long been apparent to those working in this field, there are distinctly different epidemics within any given country, moving at different speeds within different sections of the population, in relation to different modes of transmission, and different degrees and types of prevention work.[21] For example, where injecting drug use is aggressively policed, and clean injecting equipment is not readily available, HIV transmission is likely to spread rapidly amongst injecting drug users who have effectively been obliged to share needles. If needle-exchanges are introduced, rates of infection fall incrementally. Similarly, where gay men's needs are neglected, rates either stay stable, or even rise, as was scandalously the case until recently in Scotland. Yet as Keith Alcorn pointed out in *Capital Gay* in 1993, none of this is widely understood because

> The whole UK debate about AIDS continues to be dominated by a phantom – a heterosexual epidemic running out of control – which is summoned up whenever anyone questions the accepted wisdom. It dominates the debate to such an extent that epidemiologists find it impossible to acknowledge the importance of targeting gay men except as a means of preventing the heterosexual epidemic.[22]

The success of re-gaying in Britain has been entirely pragmatic. It has been a remarkable achievement on the part of determined campaigners and activists working within and between the statutory and voluntary sectors, who were able to mobilize epidemiology as the primary justification for their intended changes in official policy. That this should have been necessary is one measure of the extent to which British responses to the epidemic were deflected by influential currents of moralism, bigotry and prejudice in the 1980s. The response that 'AIDS affects everyone equally', which was widely held in professional HIV/AIDS circles until very recently, ended up addressing nobody in particular, and least of all those at greatest risk.

re-gaying AIDS II: media reactions and misunderstandings

The consequences of not acknowledging the communities most affected by HIV/AIDS is not widely understood amongst British journalists. Recently, Tom Wilkie reported in *The Independent* that 'globally, in 1996, AIDS is a disease of heterosexuals'.[23]

In a bizarre new twist to the journalistic spectre of a phantom heterosexual epidemic running out of control, Wilkie proposes that although

> gay men remain the most affected group in Western countries and the death toll amongst them is terrible . . . if there is any consolation or comfort to be gained from this tragic waste of human life, these men did not die in vain, in so far as their deaths have acted as a global early-warning signal. A touching analogy is with the delicate canaries that coal-miners used to take with them down the pit, because these fragile birds were more exquisitely sensitive to danger than the miners themselves.[24]

Quite how the deaths of hundreds of thousands of gay men in Europe and North America is supposed to help heterosexuals in the developing world is not vouchsafed. Besides, only someone far and safely away from the direct, long-term realities of the epidemic as it is experienced by gay men could expect it to provide any kind of consolation or comfort, whilst the analogy to canaries is as absurd as it is distasteful and insensitive.

Similarly disturbing are the comments of cultural critics such as Jenny Gilbert, dance critic of the *Independent on Sunday*, who recently complained of a fund-raiser for AIDS at Covent Garden:

> Why AIDS? Why not multiple sclerosis? The reason is that we have a strong gay lobby, and a large gay presence in the arts. No wonder people complain that the arts serve their own interest.[25]

Perhaps Ms Gilbert is aware of another incurable epidemic, currently prevalent in Britain? As soon as gay men are seen to organize on our own behalf, we are dismissed as self-serving conspirators. Behind such modish contemporary attitudes lies a total ignorance of the real HIV/AIDS situation. In an epidemic, such an ignorance reveals an indifference to our deaths which is a reliable indicator of attitudes towards our lives.

More subtle, but equally unpleasant, were the comments of the *Independent On Sunday's* television critic, Lucy Ellmann, in response to the December 1995 broadcast of the very first programme made to document the tragic consequences of the de-gaying of AIDS in Britain, and to explain the agenda of re-gaying. As far as Ellmann was concerned, the programme merely:

> made the newly fashionable point that, at least in Britain, AIDS is still a gay disease, and the government's 'Iceberg' campaign was misleading and ineffective. So my 10 years of abstinence was all for naught. And I'm rapidly tiring of those twee red ribbons, which look like fashionably crossed legs. They seem to signify the latest method of AIDS prevention: cross your legs and think about fund-raising.[26]

'Newly fashionable'! I wonder where? Thus she casually dismisses a major political struggle waged by a handful of gay men with very few social or political allies, in a period of widely sanctioned homophobia, with almost no support or interest from the liberal intelligentsia or the British Left.

I point this out to underscore the point that the most significant democratic political dimensions of the AIDS crisis have taken place in institutional and discursive arenas with which few on the traditional Left are at all familiar – including the field of epidemiology. What is so typical, and insufferable, about Ellmann's comments, is the way she instinctively turns the subject of AIDS to herself, as if her experience were what the epidemic is all about: poor old Lucy! She used those nasty condoms all those years, or perhaps was even frightened into celibacy. How one's heart breaks for her noble self-sacrifice. Lucy is furious, but unlike us, she is not furious about the scale of stupidity and injustice manifested in public policy throughout the history of British HIV/AIDS education, with predictably tragic consequences amongst gay men. She's furious with the annoying little red symbols which irritate her so much. Gay men's lives, my dear? An entire programme? How passé, how boring! This, apparently, is the way in which significant swathes of British public opinion respond to AIDS. It seems to be connected to a strong sense amongst some heterosexuals that they were deliberately misled into unfounded anxieties about AIDS, which indeed became a symbolic site for a wide range of sexual concerns in the 1980s.

Back in 1987, the now sadly defunct *London Daily News* advertised 'a fascinating new survey' of how 'AIDS has altered Londoners' sex lives', with an enormous bold-type headline, underlined in the original: 'No Sex Please We're Scared To Death'.[27] To me this serves to underline the vast empirical gulf between most heterosexuals' experience of the epidemic, and the experience of gay men. From the earliest days of the epidemic, gay community-based AIDS educators have struggled, with almost no resources until very recently, to develop health promotion strategies for gay men which were the very opposite to the messages beamed at heterosexuals. Government campaigns presented HIV as a threat to isolated individuals from dangerous strangers. Preposterous goals of lifelong monogamy, or celibacy, were widely advocated, alongside condom use. For gay men, such strategies would have been catastrophically misguided, not least because the sheer prevalence of HIV in our midst means that monogamy wouldn't constitute meaningful prevention. Community-based AIDS education in Britain was based on the clear principles of achievable risk reduction, whilst 'AIDS awareness' campaigns for heterosexuals were based on the incitement of fear, and aimed at total risk elimination.

Yes, we were there in the private statistics, but rarely in the public reporting of them, or subsequent commentary or consideration. Those few of us who pointed out from the late 1980s that gay men's health education was being disastrously and scandalously neglected, were heard with indifference, disbelief, or embarrassed silence. Nor was there ever support for re-gaying from within the institutional vanguard of lesbian and gay politics, or the British civil rights movement, or any party political position. We set pragmatic, well-reasoned, achievable goals, targeted to the various public and private institutions in whose power the direction of resources for health promotion lay, and for years and years we slogged away, until we were successful. This was a long, drawn-out process. It was, of course, a process which should never have had to take place at all, if public policy had followed available epidemiological evidence, rather than the more powerful pressures of ideology, politics, and prejudice. We will never know how many gay lives were lost because no relevant campaigns reached them. But we can be sure that had resourcing for targeted education been allocated in a manner proportionate to major demonstrable epidemiological trends in Britain, France, the United States, and numerous other countries, many lives would have been saved.

conclusion

Epidemiology is not a unified science. It comprises many schools of thought, following different lines of emphasis. In post-war Britain, epidemiology has tended to be sensitive to statistical associations between factors of class, region, and occupation, in relation to long-term patterns of health, illness, and life expectancy rates.[28] In this respect British epidemiology has reflected the prevailing ethos of socialized medicine in an industrial, class-based society. Sadly, in comparison with its recognition of gender as a major factor in public health, British epidemiology has not been sensitive to sexuality. In an important recent article, Professor Ronald Frankenberg noted that:

> Classical British epidemiology . . . is devised, in contrast to that of the United States, by physicians (together with the occasional biological convert) and for physicians. The considerable power and effectiveness of its arguments come neither from its verbal rhetoric nor, unlike that of neighbouring France, from its biological base, but from the clarity of definition of its variables and their irrefutable mathematics.[29]

Frankenberg is critical of the way in which 'pure' statistical epidemiology lacks any immediate connection to notions of application, and that even more interventionist forms of epidemiological description can only imagine people via unwieldy abstractions such as 'lifestyle', which are understood as totally individual and voluntary. Hence in the dominant academic literature of HIV/AIDS epidemiology, the only practical goal is to tell people to hurry up and change their 'lifestyles'. 'Failure' to do so is interpreted as a personal fault, with much attendant talk of 'recidivism' and 'relapse', and a reliance on simple and quantifiable explanations, such as drug use, for complex human behaviour.[30] Neither classic nor interventionist epidemiology shows any understanding of human sexuality or sexual desire, which are simply treated like any other 'behaviours'.

The consistently low quality of levels of journalistic reporting of HIV/AIDS statistics, with little or no recognition of the significant differences between HIV and AIDS figures, strongly suggests that the system of public epidemiological press releases is not effective. This is not to say that epidemiologists have a responsibility to advocate specific types of prevention programmes. However, like other scientists, social and otherwise, epidemiologists do have an ethical responsibility to ensure as far as is reasonably possible that their findings are initially reported to the public in ways that cannot easily be sensationalized or misinterpreted. This requires that epidemiologists should not be subjected to government pressure either in the aims of their work, their methods, or the conclusions they reach.

Throughout the AIDS crisis there has been a degree of dialogue between state epidemiological agencies, and community-based prevention workers. Categories of reporting have, as a result of such dialogue, grown more sensitive to factors to which educators have drawn attention. Furthermore, epidemiologists have been hampered in their work by direct and indirect government interference concerning issues which are held to be politically sensitive. In this way, necessary long-term scientific research may be sacrificed to short-term political expediency. Epidemiologists have followed methods which might be relevant to short-term epidemics of infectious disease, but which are woefully inadequate to long-term epidemics, in which risk factors change over time, in the lives of vulnerable individuals and whole groups. Whilst the concept of 'risk group' may indeed imply a spurious cohesion of all members, responses to HIV/AIDS should alert us to the fact that the term continues to play a vital nominative role in situations where those at real risk of harm are already pariahs of one kind or another. Paradoxically, in Britain, humane post-war policies towards injecting drug users had provided them with an identifiable place on the social map, as far as epidemiologists were concerned. The introduction of needle-exchanges around the UK since 1986 (with a resulting steady, detectable decline in new drugs-related HIV infections) is an excellent example of 'applied epidemiology'.[31]

Unfamiliar with gay men as a social constituency, epidemiologists have often been unable to imagine the situation facing community-based education and prevention workers.

This difficulty has been compounded by the new gulf between biomedical administration within the National Health Service, and those who implement strategies 'on the ground'. When the directions and resources for primary prevention are controlled by politicians, as was the case with HIV/AIDS education in Britain throughout the 1980s, there are serious grounds for alarm. Historians will doubtless debate why it was the case that Thatcherism responded comparatively well to the needs of injecting drug users in the UK, and so badly to African women resident in the UK and to gay men. In the meantime, the least we may expect is that epidemiologists will find collective means of ensuring that their voice is unambiguously heard when government policies that are ostensibly intended to alleviate or reduce harm, are demonstrably misguided and actually working to increase harm. The expansion from a social epidemiology of class and gender to a social epidemiology sensitive to the full range of sexual and other primary social identities in Britain is long overdue. Its absence has already contributed to public misunderstanding and mismanagement of HIV/AIDS education in the UK.

notes

1. See Simon Watney, *Policing Desire, Pornography, AIDS & The Media*, London, Cassell, 1987/Minneapolis, University of Minnesota Press, 1996.
2. See Simon Watney, 'Figure Skating', *Gay Times*, London, October 1994, p.38.
3. PHLS AIDS Centre – Communicable Disease Surveillance Centre, and Scottish Centre for Infection & Environmental Health. Unpublished Surveillance Tables No. 31 March 1996, Notes to Tables 10–12.
4. PHLS AIDS Centre, *Six Monthly AIDS And HIV Figures*, July 1996, Table 1.
5. *Safetynet*, Current Statistics November 1993, Centers for Disease Control and Prevention, Atlanta, Georgia, USA.
6. Science Editor, 'AIDS cases in Britain double in 10 months', *The Times*, London, Saturday 14 June 1986, n.p.

7. Andrew Veitch, 'Forecast of 4,000 deaths as AIDS kills 22 more', *The Guardian*, London, 10 March 1987, n.p.
8. Nicholas Timmins, 'Recorded cases of AIDS double', *The Independent*, London, Tuesday 12 January 1988, p.3
9. Peter Wilsher and Neville Hodgkinson, 'At Risk', *The Sunday Times*, London, 2 November 1986, p.25
10. Simon Watney, 'Conspiracy Theories', *Gay Times*, London, March 1993, p.14. See also Nat Hentoff, 'Conspiracy Theories: J Edgar Hoover to Spike Lee', *The Village Voice*, New York, 22 January 1993, n.p.
11. 'Pass Notes No. 295: AIDS', *The Guardian*, London, 30 November 1993, p.2.2.
12. 'The numbers game', *New Scientist*, 29 April 1993, n.p.
13. Edward King, 'Predicting an epidemic of heterosexual AIDS', *The Independent*, London, Tuesday 25 May 1993, p.17
14. Simon Watney, 1987, op. cit. See also Simon Watney, 'Preface: My Project', *Practices of Freedom: Selected Writings on HIV/AIDS*, London, Rivers Oram Press/Durham, Duke University Press, N.C., 1994.
15. For example, Michael Rooney and Peter Scott, 'Working where the risks are: Health promotion interventions for gay men and other men who have sex with men in the second decade of the HIV epidemic', in B. Evans, S. Sandberg & S. Watson (eds) *Working Where The Risks Are: Issues in HIV prevention*, London, Health Education Authority, pp.13–65: Edward King, Michael Rooney and Peter Scott, *HIV Prevention For Gay Men: A survey of initiatives in the UK*, London, North West Thames Regional Health Authority, 1992; Edward King, *Safety In Numbers: Safer sex and gay men*, London, Cassell, 1993; New York, Routledge, 1994; Peter Scott, *Purchasing HIV Prevention: A No-nonsense guide for use with gay men and bisexual men*, London, Health Education Authority, 1995.
16. Edward King, Michael Rooney and Peter Scott 1992, op. cit.
17. Edward King, 'Fucking boyfriends', *Fact Sheet* No. 4a, 1994, Gay Men Fighting AIDS, London, January/February 1994. See also Edward King, 'Bridging the gap between science and AIDS service provision', in L. Sherr, P. Catalan & B. Hedge (eds), *The Impact of AIDS: Psychological and Social Aspects of HIV Infection*, London, Harwood, 1996.
18. Simon Watney, 'State of Emergency', *Gay Times*, April 1991; reprinted in Simon Watney, 1994, op. cit., pp.187–90.
19. Andrew Ridley and Stephen Jones, *Criteria for prioritizing HIV prevention services*, The HIV Project, London, HIV Seminar Notes, No. 5, December 1995, p.4.

20. For example, Toby Manning, 'Media hype', *Positive Times*, London, Issue 18, August 1996, p.13.

21. See Simon Watney, 'Signifying AIDS', in P. Buchler and N. Papastergiadis (eds) *Random Access: On Crisis and its metaphors*, London, Rivers Oram Press, 1995, pp.193–210.

22. Keith Alcorn, 'Fighting the real epidemic, not the phantom one', *Capital Gay*, No. 595, 21 May 1993, London, p.14.

23. Tom Wilkie, 'Beware false comfort for heterosexuals', *The Independent*, London, Friday 21 June 1996, p.19.

24. ibid.

25. Jenny Gilbert, 'Dancing with tears in their eyes', *Independent on Sunday*, London, 11 February 1996, p.15.

26. Lucy Ellmann, 'He's been tangoed!', *Independent on Sunday*, London, 10 December 1995, p.14. Referring to Nigel Evans' film, *The End of Innocence*, broadcast earlier that week on BBC2.

27. Advertisement, *The Guardian*, London, 6 May 1987, n.p.

28. See D.J.P. Barker and G. Rose, *Epidemiology For the Uninitiated*, British Medical Association, London, 1992.

29. Ronald Frankenberg, 'The Impact of HIV/AIDS On Concepts Relating To Risk And Culture Within British Community Epidemiology: Candidates Or Targets For Prevention', *Soc. Sci. Med.*, Vol. 38, No. 10, p.1327, 1994.

30. See Simon Watney, 'AIDS and Social Science: Taking the scenic route through an emergency', *NYQ*, New York, Nos. 11 and 12, 12 and 19 January, 1991: reprinted in Simon Watney, *Practices of Freedom*, op. cit., pp.221–7.

31. Edward King's book, *Safety In Numbers*, op. cit., is the *locus classicus* of this whole debate. It is a book that every thoughtful gay man should read.

prevention: new directions

AIDS and stigma

Sander Gilman

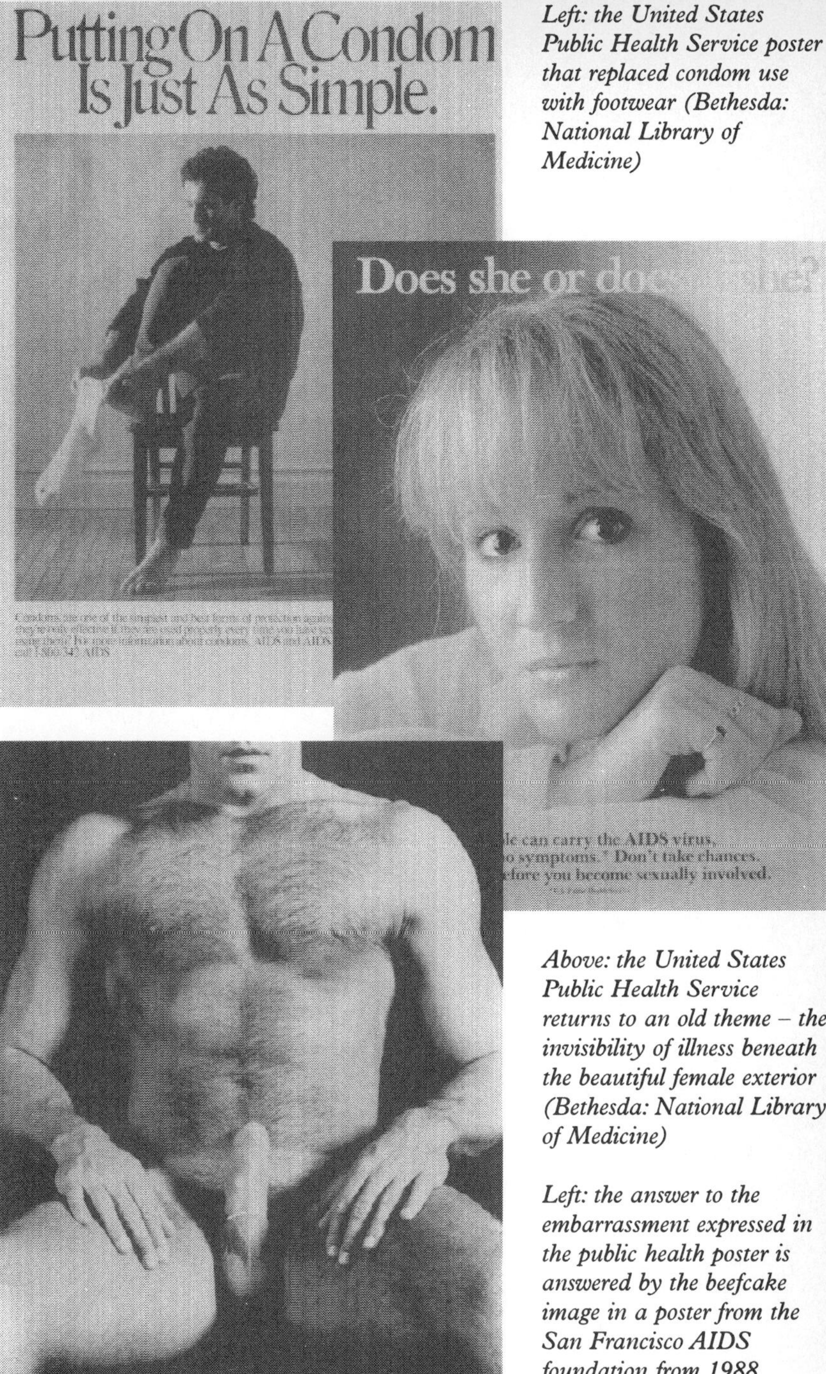

Left: the United States Public Health Service poster that replaced condom use with footwear (Bethesda: National Library of Medicine)

Above: the United States Public Health Service returns to an old theme – the invisibility of illness beneath the beautiful female exterior (Bethesda: National Library of Medicine)

Left: the answer to the embarrassment expressed in the public health poster is answered by the beefcake image in a poster from the San Francisco AIDS foundation from 1988 (Bethesda: National Library of Medicine)

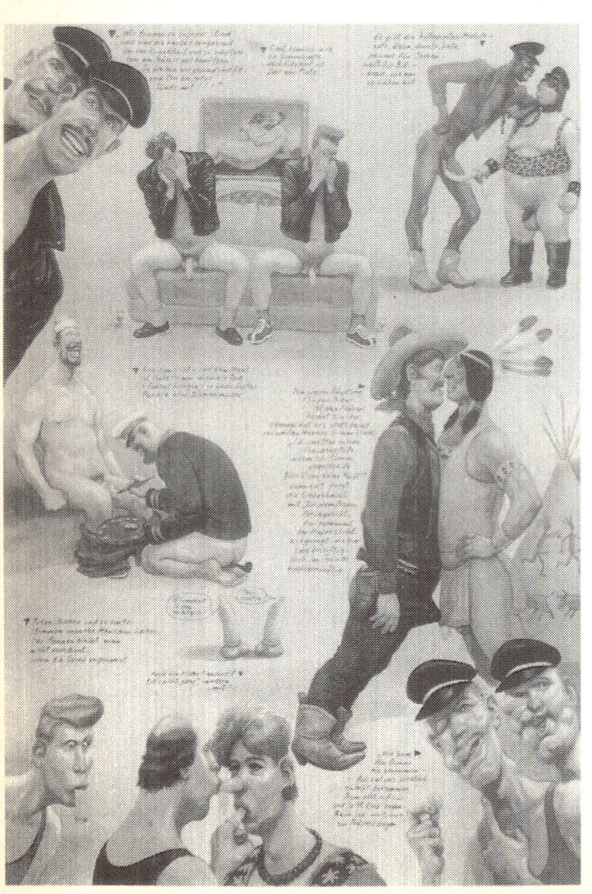

Above: a narrative poster from the Commonwealth Department of Community Services and Health for the Aboriginal Health Workers of Queensland (Australia) (Bethesda: National Library of Medicine)

Left: a narrative poster from the Austrian AIDS-Hilfe (Bethesda: National Library of Medicine)

AIDS and Stigma

'Being sick' is a two-edged phrase. On one level we have all and are all going to be sick. Illness is an integral part of the human experience. Yet 'being sick' also carries (at least in American English) the sense of being perverted, odd, unhealthy in a metaphoric sense. In the representation of people with AIDS (PWAS) the merging of these two images is seamless. The PWA is the scapegoat for all of the collective's anxiety about all of our fragility. And this anxiety has been frozen in the cultural representations of illness. The stigmatization of AIDS and the PWA has had two major turns in the recent past: 1) the creation of the image of the beautiful body with AIDS in public health advertising and 2) the stigmatization of the HIV negative gay body in gay culture. The response to negative stigma is often the valorization of that which is attacked. The history of images associated with AIDS illustrates how the PWA has become an idealized type in left-liberal culture in response to homophobic attacks on PWAS. The culture of AIDS has shifted over the past five years and the idea of stigma has taken on quite different meaning. Simon Watney, in 1987, described AIDS as presenting 'a crisis of representation itself, a crisis over the entire framing of knowledge about the human body and its capacities for sexual pleasure'.[1] Today, we can perhaps begin to understand the complex queer cultural response to internalizing this crisis of representation.

What immediately strikes a viewer coming to the 'mass' world of the public health poster from the 'high art' world of 'AIDS art' is the virtual absence of images of the diseased body. The posters represent, when they represent human beings at all, three categories. There are numerous images of people at risk as well as people who are HIV-positive, and some very few representations of death as an abstraction. The expectation that the ill body will be visually marked as ugly makes it striking that these posters represent the body at risk and even the ill body as beautiful, even erotic. Death certainly threatens, but dying itself is absent. The image of the body at risk and the ill body in public health posters parallel one another in the limited context in which even the symbolic representation of the mask of death is evoked. Only rarely is the visually compromised body portrayed.

The rationale for this avoidance seems clear. The classic model of 'healthy/beauty' and 'illness/ugliness' is part of the cultural baggage that accompanies any representation of the ill or healthy body. Associated with that model is its moral dimension. The historical context of the meaning of AIDS and its powerful association with homosexuality must be added as a sub-text. The healthy in this model cannot be the homosexual, who has been medicalized as pathological since at least the middle of the nineteenth century. Indeed, the gay liberation movement to depathologize homosexuality that began in the 1960s needed to create an image where the homosexual is not only not 'ill' but 'healthy', is not 'ugly' but 'beautiful'. The image of the homosexual, especially in the light of the association of AIDS and homosexuality, is eroticized to counter the association of homosexuality with deviancy and disease. The collective in this case is no longer the 'general culture' (self-defined) but the world of the homosexual, that must be preserved and seen as healthy. This is the antithesis of the older, popular image of homosexuality transmitted in the general culture by the Western media.

The anxiety about illness as a danger is repressed in a continuation of the older model of 'healthy/beauty' and 'illness/ugliness'. The person at risk of but uninfected by HIV is 'healthy' and therefore beautiful, and poses no danger to the collective's continuity. The person with an HIV infection, however, is the focus of anxiety about individual as well as collective death and decay. This person is a reminder of the necessary presence of death even in a seemingly healthy world. Such an image becomes the locus of 'sympathy' and 'identification' as a means of combating the anxiety that this category evokes. Everyone will die, the argument goes, and the only way we can deal with death is by constructing categories that deny dying – such as 'beauty/health'. Thus the PWAs in these images are both dying and not really dying. Anxiety about death can be thus bounded.

A corollary seems true of this corpus of images – even the infected body, the body that overtly signifies its potential for death and therefore provokes our anxiety about dying, must be so constructed that it denies the potential of dying. For if the body at risk is the healthy body (by definition), the infected body should be the ill body and should be ugly and diseased, if not in its present then in its future state, to show that it is not beautiful and healthy. This would continue the older, general model of deviancy and disease associated with the homoerotic and by extension with other 'groups' defined as risk groups. The argument that everyone is part of a risk group is one means of countering this. Each body that constitutes this 'everyone' must be 'beautiful/healthy'. The answer is to see the potentially ill body only in terms of the iconography of the healthy body at risk. This is not to highlight the potential for illness but to link this category with that of the healthy body, the body that does not endanger the collective. This denies the older association of the homoerotic body that was seemingly 'beautiful/healthy' on the surface yet was understood to contain within it the seeds of its own corruption and death.

The ill body with its visual pointers to the disease process (defined as ugly) is missing from this iconography. But the dead body is present. The dead body is the antithesis of 'healthy/beauty'; it is 'illness/ugliness'. It is not only non-erotic but presents an anti-body, a body completely separate from the erotic, living body. The reduction of the body to the skeleton is the reduction to the overtly symbolic. Here we see echoes of the medieval tradition of the memento mori or the early modern one of *Et in arcadia ego*: Even in Arcadia, there am I (spoken by death) is evoked to separate the 'erotic/beautiful/healthy' with its commitment to the continuity of the group from the terminated/grotesque/dead body.[2] This is not the eroticized corpse one finds in male fantasies about the female body.[3] The erotic body, no matter what its actual status, remains associated with the healthy, not with the dead or dying. Dying is excluded, as it forms a transition between the 'infected' category and the iconography of death. Death, represented by the icon of the skeletal body, is separate from the categories of life and of the perpetuation of the group. For here the evocation of death using the iconography of the dead/ugly is clear. The vocabulary of images found in this material is shaped by the older view of the antithesis of 'healthy/beauty' and 'illness/ugliness'. And yet this model restructures death so that it is applicable to new social images and cultural belief systems.

The body at risk is clearly the eroticized body.[4] It is a youthful body. It is the beautiful body of the advertising agency or health promotion department selling a new product – safe sex. But the eroticization of the body, especially the male body, seems always to be tinged with a sense of anxiety or guilt. The locus classicus for this in the public health poster is the widely circulated United States Public Health Service image of the young man pulling a sock on his foot. This rather self-embarrassed poster presents a photograph, placed slightly off centre, of a fully clothed, slightly built, seated male putting on a sock with the motto 'Putting on a Condom is Just as Simple'. [A27955*] (illus. 1) A series of associations is made in a highly censored and rather fetishistic vocabulary – the foot replaces the penis, the sock the condom, the clothed body, the naked (but not nude) body. The very angle of the photograph throws our gaze on the image of a second chair upon which rests the second sock. The reference is opaque, even if the intent is clear. The second sock represents a second condom – the offstage presence of a male partner. This poster (and the parallel television advertisements) quickly became the brunt of jokes on national television, reflecting the innate prudery of the representation.[5]

An answer to this type of symbolic representation of the individual at risk in the images of safe sex has been to 'eroticize the condom', rather than to symbolize it. A photographic image from the San Francisco AIDS Foundation from 1988 represents a nude (not naked) male with an erect penis sheathed in a condom. [A29366] (illus. 2) The body alone is presented, the head (except for the mouth) is masked by the frame so as to emphasize the muscular, healthy, erotic body. This is a very different body to that of the sock advertisement. It sits at the centre of the frame, it is muscular and dominant, rather than bowed and subservient. The eroticized male body is directed at a male gaze, drawing on the conventions of the soft-porn or erotic photography of the male body in Western gay culture. No partner is represented, as the viewer is the implied partner.

A sexualized, nude body does not need a head as long as it has a mouth; the erotic pose emphasizes the relationship between mouth and penis. The anonymity of the eroticized male body in a beefcake pose evokes sexuality but also presents danger. A British poster presents a photograph of an exposed male torso labeled 'AIDS is in Town – don't pass it on'. [25265] Here, too, the eroticized position of the subject, torso exposed, undershirt pulled up over the pectorals, thumbs hooked in the pockets of tight jeans, evokes the male viewer. But the phrase 'AIDS is in Town' literally replaces the head of the image. If the San Francisco poster places its message between the legs of the male to deliver its message about safe sex, then the British poster uses it as a cartoon balloon, presenting the presumed thoughts of the sexualized torso. Indeed, even in the

African-American community the evocation of this masculinity at risk uses the beefcake approach, although desiring to evoke older images of enslavement and powerlessness. [A22784] A poster by the South Carolina Coalition of Black Church Leaders uses the drawing of a muscular slave in chains (in a tobacco field), upper torso bare, dressed in torn-off pants, to stress that one should not be 'Bound by the Chains of Ignorance – learn About AIDS'. The evocation of the slave, so permanent a part of the African-American historical vocabulary, returns to older, familiar associations of risk and the African-American male.

All these images, in their varied contexts, represent healthy if not beautiful bodies. Condom education is likewise tied to the image of the healthy male body in a state of partial undress. One poster from the Health Education Resource Organization in Maryland (USA) represents two males, one partially removing his undershirt in a photograph with the motto 'You won't believe what we like to wear in bed'. [25231] Likewise, the British 'Play Safe this Summer' poster features a drawing of two beefcake males caressing, stripped to the waist before a giant safety pin. [25416] The informal 'pickup' in a train in a Swedish poster presents a photograph of two clothed men with the warning 'You get all of his experiences'. [27397] Being clothed (wearing a condom) evokes the notion of being safe from danger. A parallel Norwegian image of two smiling, nude males, placed front to back, with the motto 'joy is caring', cuts them off well above the waist. [27919] The image of the partially clothed male, whether clothed in jeans or a condom or without socks, comes to represent safe sex, sex with condoms.[6] The eroticization of the body is intended to carry over into the eroticization of the act of safe sex. Again the viewer is 'told' that being partially clothed is better than being unclothed, which is the not so subtle message of beefcake images anyway. That which is hidden is that which is eroticized.[7]

Not only the homoerotic is sensualized in AIDS public health advertising. Posters depicting heterosexuality employ the same tropes of clothing and eroticizing the body. In a poster from the Danish National Board of Health, a photograph of a scene of heterosexual sexuality, elegantly backlit, carries the motto 'Sex is Beautiful'. The female is nude, but the male is clothed in jeans. [25097] Here the male's body as the protected/ing partner is equivalent to his penis. In the heterosexual images in a French poster, the male is actually reduced to a condom. 'He' as a disembodied voice (represented by a rolled condom) complains to 'her' about wearing a condom and 'she', a photo of a beautiful woman, responds by laughing at his complaint. The motto is that today a condom prevents everything even ridicule. [25272] The 'Elle' and the 'Lui' evoke the imagery of chic upscale magazines with those names and the labels are placed in a way that presents the images as magazine covers. An Italian-Swiss public health poster reduces the male to a brightly painted Peter Max-style condom, shielding a missing, but clearly erect penis. [45315] The male in these images is reduced to his parts, but these parts remain invisible. Yet even this 'invisible' body, by its very imagined presence, is healthy and joyful – an on-going theme in representing the body at risk. Sexuality is enjoyment but, says the subtext, risk-taking too. The infected body, the ill but unmarked body, is displaced on to the image of the condom as a sign of illness. A poster from the German AIDS-Hilfe presents the naked feet of a male and a female shot from above with the label 'active condoms'. [25282] This effects the same displacement as the socks in the poster discussed earlier. Here the uncovered feet are a sign of the erotic (and the beautiful) but also of the potential for infection.[8,9]

It is not that fully nude bodies are missing from public health posters. The nude bodies of lesbians, for example, can be eroticized too. In a poster from the Terrence Higgins Trust in London two beautiful female bodies are intertwined with the motto 'Wet your appetite for safe sex'. [57790] The Austrian AIDS organization presents a series of 'art' posters representing heterosexual and homosexual partners as aesthetic Others under the motto: 'Protect Out of Love'. [S 25319–24] Love, defined as caring and protecting, is the 'natural' extension of sexuality. The hidden message is that using condoms is a sign of caring and removes sexuality from its brutal, coarse, ugly, and destructive mode of representation. 'Sex', in these erotic presentations, is sublimated into other categories such as 'love', because the visual language employed comes from the erotic vocabulary of mass advertising. One 'loves' one's partner, says the erotic image, just as one 'loves' one's jeans. The posters refuse to treat sex as sex, just as advertising refuses to treat commodities as commodities.[10]

These images of holding and touching commodify the closeness of 'love' to justify the use of condoms. One does not hurt the thing one loves, to reverse Oscar Wilde's dictum. And one is keyed to buy the product so presented. 'Love', here represented by the unclothed body, is the eroticized body. In these images the one at risk is the partner; the risk to the self is minimal. The beautiful Other who can be corrupted by the agency of the self, seems to stand apart from the observer. But of course, this is intended quite differently. The beautiful, youthful people at risk are projections of the idealized self, eternally healthy and youthful and safe. In reality, say the posters, you are healthy, you are beautiful, and you want to stay that way, so you are going to make sure that your partner uses a condom.

Risk is represented in the broadest way. Thus the image of the healthy, beautiful family is central to AIDS education. The German AIDS-Hilfe presents a gender-balanced family (father, mother, one male and one female child) with the motto: 'Because I Love You.' [25182] It resonates with the theme that 'Anyone can get AIDS' which forms the basis of an American poster figuring photographs of a wide range of individuals of various ages, social classes, and genders. [25500] The figures in both of these posters are clothed, for this is not the place to evoke the erotic. They are also 'beautiful' – no signs of any illness or 'disability'.

Determining the source of infection is vital, according to

these campaigns. If everyone is at risk, at least all the beautiful people, where does the danger lie?[11] You cannot tell where danger lies, these images suggest, but it is clearly beyond the self. 'Does she or doesn't she?' [27827] (illus. 3) asks the poster of the viewer looking at the portrait of a beautiful, white woman. This uncertainty echoes earlier images of the 'beautiful woman' as in the 1944 American poster with the motto 'She may look clean – but pick-ups, "good" time girls, prostitutes spread syphilis and gonorrhea. You can't beat the Axis if you get VD.' The audience for the VD poster was clearly the American armed services, who were understood as male. The audience for the AIDS poster, which employs the same rhetoric and the photographic image for realism, has quite a different audience, or does it? Each of the photographs is of a beautiful female – but the VD poster employs a visual vocabulary implying innocence in the viewer which is lacking from the AIDS poster.

The image of the 'positive' body or the body with AIDS is strictly controlled in the public health poster. Nowhere is an image of the 'ugly' or diseased body evoked directly, for any such evocation would refer back to the sense of AIDS as a 'gay' disease and the powerful effect which this has had to re-pathologize homosexuality. *Mens non sana in corpore insano* [A sick mind in a sick body] can not be the motto. For representing the ill body as a dying body is not possible. Such a body would point to 'deviance from the norm' in the form of illness. This association with homosexuality and addiction labeled as illness must be suppressed. The 'beautiful' remains the transnational sign for the healthy and the 'ugly' is banished. Yet hidden within images of the beautiful is the potential for death. Death comes to be limited as the beautiful body moves to its antithesis without the processes of dying. Death itself becomes aestheticized. These images are not of education, but of control. They seek to present worlds which are as static as the images themselves. The dynamic reality of dying as part of the life cycle and its real, concrete, frightening presence for those with AIDS is denied and repressed. When we view these posters, we are educated in the potential for action – which is what advertising does best, but little else. The chimerical world of picturing beauty and health at the close of the twentieth century provides as little access to the complex images demanded of our society as do the images of the last fin de siècle. However, in their overwhelming simplicity, these images form the stuff for an understanding of the implications of the study of public health images, both 'state' and 'private', for health education.

A proof-text for our various models of reading can be found in two 'narrative' posters which represent the entire course of AIDS in one person. The first was developed by the Commonwealth Department of Community Services and Health for the Aboriginal Health Workers of Queensland. Queensland is the Australian state where the tensions between the 'white' and 'aboriginal' inhabitants are the most strained. [A25509] (illus. 4) Headed 'You don't have to be a Queenie to Get AIDS: An AIDS Story', this comic strip poster uses the image of the beautiful male, represented here by the sports hero, who has sex with 'someone who has AIDS', represented as a prostitute in a bar, and who returns home and infects his pregnant wife. Here an unsafe person, the prostitute, in an unsafe place, the bar, marks the origin of the illness. Heterosexual transmission occurs even in someone who is marked as robust. Transmission to the pregnant wife is implied by her melancholic expression as well as her bowed head, her hand on her abdomen. Here the infection of the extended group is implied with the caption: 'They All Get Very, Very Sick.' For the 'all' implies not only the individuals but the clan, visualized in the hospital ward. Thus the destruction of the aboriginal people is the result of their inability to measure their own risk. It has little to do with the introduction of a wide range of illnesses, such as tuberculosis and AIDS, into their world.

The aboriginal male on the ward is represented as dying of AIDS, his face clearly marked by the disease as he lies in bed with an IV tube in his arm. His dying is the death of an entire people, as a result of the actions of even the best of them. The final panel shows the graveyard with the crosses marked with the letters A I D S. Between the crosses are the ritual aboriginal clubs associated with masculine status. Here the attempt to distance the disease from connotations of gay identity employs the 'healthy' trope (here meaning beautiful and heterosexual).

The second poster is from Vienna. [A25276] (illus. 5) Unlike the Australian poster it uses visual 'irony' to stress the course of illness. Here the tradition of the 'beefcake' image of the male at risk is linked expressly with images of race and images of the outcome of illness. The poster employs a series of images otherwise completely taboo in the tradition of the public health poster. The beefcake images on the left side of the poster, with all of its versions of safe sex, are paralleled by two interracial couples on the right. The stress on the extraordinary long penis of the African (wearing a white condom) and contrasted with the small member of his partner (wearing a black condom) as well as the visible member of the Native American evokes the myths of the hypersexuality of the Other. A parallel with the Australian poster is evident. True danger lies in the exotic. The poster not only works on a left-right opposition, but even more strikingly underwrites this dichotomy of the place danger in terms of the upper left and lower right corners of the poster. The upper right corner represents two males who use condoms; the lower left, in clear association with the images of race, two highly disfigured males who don't use them! The passage from beauty to ugliness via the world of racial images underlines the danger, not of homosexuality, but of crossing specific cultural borders without correct defensive measures. Just as masculinity is shown to be at risk, so is male beauty.

In these two posters the marked body is present. The marked body places the blame, which is what the other public health posters we have examined have refused to do. The marked body localizes the blame within the victim, which is, of course, precisely the rhetoric that has been applied to AIDS in the general culture – people with AIDS 'brought it upon themselves'. But the marked body also associates this blame with images of racial difference and highlights the question of the narratives imposed upon those who are represented as different.

Can we understand the power or the powerlessness of the images we use and those of advertising? Advertising is aimed at individuals who are to be 'educated' through the use of visual traditions which appeal to a subliminal or visceral level of response. The effects and implications of the visual and political codes described above on the lives of people and communities affected by AIDS is evident in the mixed messages found in these images. What is flawed in all of these campaigns is the reliance on a set of visual images which are understood to be universal but are actually taken from the vocabulary of Western advertising. The absence of visual traditions which are separate from the sexualized vocabulary used to sell jeans and soft drinks means that these images are read as a continuation of a cultural preoccupation with a notion of 'beauty' (and health) and their antithesis: ugliness and illness.

HIV prevention must move beyond or self-consciously refigure these codes in order to reach its target audience. Health promotion must separate itself from the vocabulary of contemporary advertising since that vocabulary (especially in selling medicine) denies the true power and presence of illness in our world. 'Being sick' should not be limited to the PWA; we are all fragile and that fragility must be acknowledged. In this present volume, Peter Scott and Jonathan Silin, for example, have argued that health promotion's reliance on images per se is circular and limiting, and that discussion groups amongst affected individuals and groups (rather on the model of feminist consciousness-raising) would be a more effective way forward. Certainly human interaction, with an awareness of human fragility, would be a powerful replacement for the glitz of the image. But even the representation of this awareness in the use of images which reflect the true complexity of illness, including images of death and dying which do not replicate the antithesis between 'beauty/health' and 'ugliness/illness', would be a valuable antidote to the 'sickness' of the present day slickness of public health images of AIDS.

notes

* All of these plate references are to the call numbers at the National Library of Medicine, Bethesda.

1. Simon Watney, *Policing Desire: Pornography, AIDS and the Media* Minneapolis, 1987, p.9.
2. Julia Kristeva, in her *Black Sun: Depression and Melancholia*, tr. by Leon S. Roudiez, New York, Columbia University Press, 1989, describes Holbein's painting of the dead Christ as sort of the first modern image of death: completely alien as medieval death is not.
3. Elisabeth Bronfen, *Over Her Dead Body: Death, Femininity and the Aesthetic*, New York and Manchester University Press, 1992.
4. Lee Edelman, 'The Plague of Discourse: Politics, Literary Theory, and AIDS', *South Atlantic Quarterly* LXXXVIII, 1989:, 302–17
5. As in the images collected in Allen Ellenzweig, (ed.), *The Homoerotic Photograph: Male Images from Durieu/Delacroix to Mapplethorpe*, New York, 1992.
6. Martti Grönfors and Olli Stålström, 'Power, Prestige, Profit: AIDS and the Oppression of Homosexual People', *Acta Sociologica* XXX, 1987: 53–66 and Martin Eide, 'Dodskysset: Den Ney Nyheten om den Nye Pest', *Samtidem* XCVIII, 1989:, 6–12.
7. David L. Kirp and Ronald Bayer, eds., *AIDS in the Industrialized Democracies: Passions, Politics, and Policies*, New Brunswick, N.J.: Rutgers University Press, 1992.
8. Theodor Nasemann, *AIDS: Entwicklung einer Krankheit in Amerika und in Deutschland*, Stuttgart, 1987.
9. Compare Michael Pollak, *The Second Plague of Europe: AIDS Prevention and Sexual Transmission among Men in Western Europe*, New York, 1993.
10. Compare Diane Richardson, *Women and the AIDS* Crisis, London, 1989.
11. Dorothy Nelkin and Sander L. Gilman, 'Placing the Blame for Devastating Disease', Arien Mack (ed.), *In Time of Plague: The History and Social Consequences of Lethal Epidemic Disease*, New York, 1991, pp.39–56.

why gay men still have unsafe sex

beauty, self-esteem and the myth of HIV-negativity

Michael Bronski

The word has been out for almost two years now: more and more gay men are having unsafe sex. Studies from San Francisco show a two to three per cent rise in seroconversion-conversion among the city's young HIV-negative men; recent studies from other US cities have pointed in the same direction. Articles in *The New York Times*, medical journals, and the gay press have spread the word that AIDS prevention campaigns have been less than successful. In the December 1994 issue of *Out*, columnist Michelangelo Signorile shocked readers with the news that he had engaged in unprotected anal sex. He did this in spite of his wealth of information about HIV transmission, his articulated commitment to having safer sex, and his (presumed) desire to remain HIV negative. The bottom line is that after more than a decade of safer sex education, years of theorizing about educational and support strategies, and living through the devastation of AIDS, gay men are still – perhaps even more than several years ago – engaging in unsafe sex. What is going on?

This is a question subject to enormous speculation. Despair: eight years ago many thought the end of the epidemic was in sight, this is not the case now. Depression: cumulative death has created an atmosphere so without hope that some gay men see little reason to continue to act safely. Survivor guilt: how is it possible to reconcile the complete lack of logic that grants men with similar sexual histories differing HIV and health statuses? Denial: arguments ranging from 'If I haven't gotten AIDS by now, I won't' to 'If he wants to fuck me without a condom he must be negative' allow gay men the luxury of not discussing or articulating their complicated feelings and conflicts about sexual activity.

Each of these ideas contains elements of truth, but at the root of each is the notion that self-esteem is the motivating force behind the desire and ability to continue to engage in safer sex. Some of the newer, and most persuasive, prevention studies argue that without self-esteem, gay men often fail to make logical, thoughtful and informed decisions about their sexual practices. This idea is resonant, but raises larger questions about gay male and popular culture.

Perhaps the most profound question raised about gay male self-esteem and AIDS is how do any of us – gay or straight, male or female – maintain a sense of self-worth in a society that continually tells us that we are lacking? Consumer culture is predicated on explicating the ways in which we are deficient and what we can buy to make us less so. From an early age we are told that there is always a better car, a better brand of soft drink, a better vacation place, a better way to look, a better way to smell, a better way to dress, a better way to have sex, a better way to enjoy life. This has a profound effect both on our self-images and on our views of sexuality, romance, and relationships. The problems consumerism creates for self-esteem is magnified for gay men who live in a culture that continually tells gay people that they are worthless.

Self-esteem is innately tied to our ideals and presumptions of beauty. This is as true of the heterosexual world as it is for gay male culture. Whether it be *Honcho* magazine or ads for Club Med, the idealized body has signified both health and happiness. While this may be a constant in Western societies, the mythically beautiful body occupies a particular place in contemporary gay male life. Because the idealized male body has come to symbolize sexual desire in gay male culture, its use in AIDS prevention work has become problematic. For gay men it is not simply a matter of the idealized male image engendering a lack of self-esteem, but the idea that an even more perfect body is somewhere to be found and purchased: the commodification of sex.

From the early days of AIDS prevention, campaigns have used the idealized male image to encourage gay men to have safer sex. These images – on posters and pamphlets – featured traditionally beautiful, healthy-looking men who represented not only the ideal of masculine beauty but the very possibility of enjoyable, safer sex. The message was: beautiful men = safer sex. The problem was, of course, that any man who felt that he fell short of this standard of beauty could feel excluded from the message of the poster. The idealized images themselves would contribute to a lack of self-esteem in gay men and thus perpetuate feelings of inadequacy that have been singled out as responsible for causing risky behaviour in the first place. If men feel that they can never measure up to the physical (and ethical) ideal of safer sex, they may feel like failures and have an even more difficult time acting safely when engaging in sexual activity.

But there is another problem as well. From the beginning of the safer sex education movement, a great deal of prevention work has used traditional advertising techniques and hired large advertising agencies to convey their messages. Typical is the classic safer sex campaign used across the US that touted the fact that 'Safe Sex is Hot Sex'. Recently, campaigns such as these have come under attack as ineffective because they do not address the actual concerns and realities that inform how people make safer sex decisions. By simply promoting safer sex as 'better' or 'hotter' they are offering it as a simple-minded, more enjoyable alternative. The idea of promoting one kind of sex as 'hot' is yet another spin on the consumer mentality: Coke is better then Pepsi, BMWs are better than Toyotas, safer sex is hotter than unsafe sex. The problem is that conclusions produced and encouraged by advertising don't necessarily endure over an extended period. Indeed, they're formally not designed to.

Advertising is predicated on convincing the viewer – for the moment – that they will be happier by simply choosing one product, one option, over another. We all understand that the techniques of advertising are essentially lies and that they don't make a lasting impression on us. We cannot take that chance with safer sex education.

More importantly, however, promoting safer sex as a more 'fun' alternative to unsafe sex plays upon the same underlying erosion of self-worth present in all advertising. We are being told that we are worthless, and matter less if we don't listen to the message of the advertisement, whether it be Coke, Toyota, or safer sex. This chipping away at self-esteem merely replicates the original problem that lack of self-worth hinders gay men from making safer sex decisions.

The cult of the beautiful body and consumerism shape other gay male community responses to the epidemic. In the US, there has emerged the phenomenon of private safer sex parties. These are usually for-profit endeavours, and provide a space for safer group sex. They also provide condoms, lube, towels, and atmospheric inducements such as music, porn videos, and snacks. The most notable of these are the O-Boys! safer sex parties in Los Angeles, but they also occur in many other US cities as well. Demanding a safe-sex policy, they see themselves as promoting a pro-active, community based ideal of safer sex and responsibility. Yet they also have a fairly strict 'cuteness' policy that restricts access to 'hot' men. There is a pre-screening process that determines whether or not any one man fits into this category. Marshall OBoy! and his partner Alan Grossman have defended their policy in such diverse forums as the National Gay and Lesbian Task Force's annual Creating Change Conference and the now-defunct sex magazine, *Steam*. The 'cuteness' policy is controversial but has been defended by such community luminaries as the late Michael Callen, popular gay entertainer and AIDS activist, who declared at the 1992 Creating Change Conference that '[t]here is a hierarchy of beauty [and] it is foolish to think that everyone has to be included in the aristocracy'. Callen concluded his defence of the O-Boys! exclusion policies by claiming that sexual desire 'should be placed in a natural preserve' like 'wetlands that are filled with bugs and harsh conditions but have a certain integrity all the same. This place ought to be off limits to charges of political correctness.' Alan Grossman was a little more succinct in his defence of the O-Boys! policy in *Steam*, where he claimed that there were plenty of other safer sex groups and 'unless you are a 660-pound Methuselah with visible festering sores, you can probably find a space that will welcome you'.

However, such exclusion policies reinforce a cultural standard that penalizes everyone who does not fit into the 'idealized' category, generally defined as late-twenty-something, buffed, gym-toned, and bearing a fashionable haircut and slightly larger-than-normal cock. By relying on the most traditional cultural norms, 'cuteness' policies simply reinforce the messages that many gay men – men whose bodies are less toned or in other ways seen as less-than-perfect, men who are differently abled, or simply have average or small cocks – hear every day: that they are deficient, worth less than other men who are more 'perfect'. While the private safer sex parties claim to be a responsible community response to the epidemic, their exclusive policies give enormous support to a cultural system that promotes the idea that some men, by nature of who they are and what they look like, are worth less. This, in turn, contributes to the low-self esteem that causes men to engage in unsafe sexual activity in the first place.

But 'cuteness' policies bear consequences beyond low self-esteem in HIV-negative men. It is important to imagine, and ask, how men with HIV – symptomatic and unsymptomatic – feel about such an aristocracy of beauty and the ensuing door policies. In a culture that prioritizes good looks – and equates them with good health – people with

AIDS (or any physical aliment or disability) are automatically outcast.

The construction and continual reinforcement of traditional standards of beauty and apparent health have to be re-examined in the light of HIV, not only because they undermine the very efforts which are intended to stop the epidemic, but because they stigmatize and discriminate against people living with AIDS. This is true not only in the realm of 'cuteness' codes for safer sex parties, but in how we think about and deal with everyone in our community with differing health statuses. Is there any other way to read Marshall OBoy!'s claim that only a 'Methuselah with festering sores' could not find an accommodating sex club, except as a clear warning that people with visible signs of AIDS are simply unwelcome? If we argue against discrimination against people with AIDS in the workplace, can we tolerate discrimination against them in the sexual or social realm?

The stigmatization of people with visible signs of AIDS also plays a role in why gay men continue to have unsafe sex. In our anti-gay and AIDS-phobic culture, all gay men, HIV-positive and HIV-negative, are associated with AIDS. The stigmatization of HIV-positive men – particularly if they manifest signs of AIDS-related illnesses – affects all gay men because it feeds into an endemic cultural fear and loathing of gay males that, in turn, plays into broader scenarios of mistrust and denial among gay men attempting to make safer sex decisions. More specifically, the stigmatization of gay men with AIDS designates them as a pariah class.

This stigmatization of people with AIDS creates problems for primary prevention, because primary prevention messages stress that safe encounters with positive men are, well, safe. Thus emerges a cognitive dissonance between the popular designation of positive men as 'deadly' and health promotion's representation of them as potential partners in 'hot, safe, sex'. Ironically, safer sex campaigns which avoided depicting bodies with visible signs of AIDS did so, in part, to avoid stigmatizing people with AIDS, to present positive and negative alike as beautiful. But by re-enforcing myths of beauty, such campaigns also suggest that safer sex is hotter sex *so long as both partners are 'hot'*. Safer sex with people with any visible sign of AIDS isn't what's being advertised at all. Therefore, safer sex campaigns which portray both partners as traditionally beautiful and healthy, and which exclude and subtly stigmatize people with progressed AIDS, implicitly contradict their own messages. Let there be no mistake: this cognitive dissonance surely renders safer sex campaigns' message less effective, if only because targeted gay men are less likely to pay attention to something rife with contradiction.

Even if the healthy bodies portrayed in safer sex campaigns are not necessarily HIV-negative, the inextricability of HIV and identity, and thus misinformed prejudices about health and beauty, was inevitable. In the mid-1980s, the invention of a test for HIV antibodies led to personal identities based upon the results of that test. If you test HIV-positive, it means that you are carrying the HIV virus and will, at some point, come down with AIDS-related illnesses. This means that you may also identify as 'positive'. If you test HIV-negative, it means that you do not have the HIV virus and may identify as 'negative'. But the reality is that the status of HIV-negative is essentially the absence of being HIV-positive.

The problem with this is that an HIV-negative test result quickly becomes an HIV-negative identity and this identity, in turn, becomes, for many people, a stable, unfluctuating status. With the persistent stigmatization of people with AIDS – in the workplace, socially, and sexually – is it any wonder that men hold on to their easily changed, and often quite dubious, HIV-negative status. The reality is that an HIV-negative status changes, that all positives would have been negative had they been tested prior to infection. HIV-negative identity is semi-mythical. Because there is a three to six month window between transmission and the presence of anti-bodies it is possible that, without re-testing, an

HIV-negative test result could fail to indicate the presence of the virus.

For prevention work and safer sex education the concept of an HIV-negative identity presents many problems. Most importantly a social, emotional, and physical identity based upon an HIV-negative status creates a defined category of wellness that simply may not exist. For many men, negotiating safer sex is a complex and confusing process involving awareness of transmission possibilities, complicated choices of mediating sexual desire and physical action, and honesty (often unspoken) between parties. Since the advent of an accurate HIV test, all negotiations about safer sex includes knowing (or not knowing) one's HIV status. With the ELISA test, men began to form unfluctuating HIV-negative identities, which may or may not reflect their actual HIV status. Negotiating safer sex, then, became increasingly problematic. Men began making what seemed to be informed decisions based on knowledge that was inaccurate, but which they did not want to question. The intense desire to hold on to an HIV-negative identity affects all aspects of gay male life and is at the root of obstacles to effective AIDS prevention efforts. It is as much a problem for men in 'monogamous' relationships – in which both partners are supposedly HIV-negative, but no permission is granted for discussion of extra-relationship sexual activity – as it is for men who have casual sex.

An immutable HIV-negative identity becomes even more problematic in AIDS prevention work when viewed in conjunction with those cultural processes that conflate beauty and apparent health. The irrational paradigm that emerges from this conflation (i.e. that beautiful people are healthy people) is so commonly accepted in both gay and straight culture that it often goes completely unexamined. Isn't a fantasy in gay male porn videos that the beautiful, well-built men are healthy – even though there are many porn stars who have died of AIDS, and many more who are HIV-positive? Isn't the subliminal (or not so subliminal) message of the O-Boys! parties that the body beautiful is the body healthy? Doesn't this conflation of the beautiful body into the healthy body carry over into AIDS prevention work as well, with posters of gorgeous men urging us to have safer sex and stay HIV-negative?

Of course, the beautiful body isn't necessarily the healthy body and safer sex decisions based on these presumptions are misinformed. When this confusion is re-enacted within the mythos of an unfluctuating HIV-negative status, it even further muddies the decision-making process. The cultural myths of beauty, health, and presumed HIV status consistently thwart our efforts to make informed and safe decisions about sexual activity.

Recently, a friend and AIDS educator told me of a safer sex crisis he had experienced. He'd gone into a public men's room to cruise and was standing at the urinal jerking off when a man came in and stood two spots down from him. Glancing sideways, he noted the man's dick, his good build, and his striking, bearded face. As he was about to make his move and go down on the man – things have to happen quickly in a public bathroom patrolled by the police – he saw that the man's face was covered with KS lesions. My friend hesitated, but within seconds he acknowledged that his qualms were purely a knee-jerk reaction to the man's obvious status as a person with AIDS. After all, my friend believed that sucking cock without ejaculation is a safe activity and he regularly goes down on strangers, in a variety of venues, without worrying about it. Of course, he realizes that many of these men may have AIDS; they might even have KS lesions not visible to the glancing eye. Why should he hesitate to go down on someone with visible KS when he has probably, unknowingly, gone down on men with similar conditions?

As he was contemplating this a third man came into the rest room and immediately went down on my friend's prospective trick. My friend's reaction? Well, first, annoyance that he had lost a trick, and then worry that this new man had not noticed the KS lesions. My friend realized that the physical presence of an AIDS-related illness made him question his own, well-thought out standards and decisions, and then question the ability of others to make those same decisions.

The ability to make safe and sane decisions about sexual activity is not a simple process or one that follows set rules. We are all autonomous individuals capable of making informed choices. We are also citizens in a world that overloads us with endlessly confusing and conflicting images, desires, and needs. Our attitudes about health, beauty and HIV-negative identity all conspire to make our lives and our decisions seem easier: beautiful people are healthy people; healthy people always look healthy; people who test HIV-negative always stay negative. These are seductive ideas even when we know they are not true. They are confusing ideas when we are attempting to make informed, complicated decisions that effect our egos, sex lives, and health. They are deadly ideas when confusion leads to seroconversion.

They are also ideas that draw sharp distinctions between people living with AIDS and those who are not; they separate the well from the unwell, thc healthy from the unhealthy. But the reality is that 'well' and 'healthy' are only temporary categories: If we don't get sick and die of AIDS we will die of something else.

We are not very good at dealing with death and illness. AIDS has brought illness, unwellness, and death into our lives in such a visceral, resistant and undeniable way that we struggle daily to cope without despair. But if we continue to construct false dichotomies – the sick and the well, the HIV-positive and the HIV-negative, the beautiful and the unacceptable – we do so not only at our own risk, but at the risk of everyone.

why we do not do primary prevention for gay men

Walt Odets

From the perspectives of 1996, we have failed very badly at doing good and useful prevention for gay men in the US. Fifty per cent of gay men in American urban centres are infected with HIV – about *five times* the seroprevalence among gay men in the majority of other large cities around the world. On our current course, *one-third* of gay twenty-year-olds will be infected with HIV or dead before they are thirty, and *more than half* these twenty-year-olds will contract HIV in their lifetimes. This situation is partly the consequence of the compelling nature of human sexuality and the difficulty public health has always had in changing even the simplest, least psychologically complicated behaviors. But in gay communities, our prevention results are also a product of the peculiar, powerful, and destructive ways that AIDS has engaged gay communities.[1] This engagement is experienced in myriad ways by gay men themselves, and by prevention theorists and practitioners around the world in our persistent consternation about how to construct prevention within a stigmatized minority community which seeks psychological, social, and political unity, even as it is divided by an important fact centrally pertinent to prevention: a good number of us (in the US, half of us) are infected with a communicable, largely fatal virus, and the rest of us are not.

To make matters very much worse, this virus is contracted

by gay men almost exclusively through the very behaviour that has most characterized us in the public mind for centuries, the very behaviour that is most distinctive about homosexual sex, and the very behaviour about which we feel the most shame, humiliation and guilt. This is, of course, 'getting fucked' (having a man put his penis, and often leaving his semen, in one's rectum). This act and all that it means and communicates is of profound human importance for many gay men. But at our tiny moment in history, the simple coincidence between the evolutionary whim of microbes and the importance of this often magical human behaviour has brought us a devastating epidemic among gay men.

The conflict, shame, humiliation, guilt (and often, the unmitigated self-hatred) that so many gay men feel about being homosexual and about this fundamental human need for anal sex are all feelings that have become seamlessly woven into too many gay men's feeling about the epidemic. Referring to his parents' confused contempt for his sexuality *and* his illness, a politically active, openly gay psychotherapy patient with AIDS described this process to me succinctly:

> I got AIDS by doing something important, something I believe in. Getting fucked is important, even if my mother can't bear to think about it. If avoiding HIV meant giving it all up, I'd do it again. I'd *have* to. But every now and then, this feeling just comes up, something I don't really believe: 'You're a fag, you got fucked, and now you've got exactly what you deserve.' That's the feeling that comes up in me, regardless of what I want to think, or sometimes think I feel. And that's the feeling my mother expressed to me when I first told her I was positive: 'If you live in a cesspool, you should expect to be covered by the slime.' And I know she's wrong, but I also know what it's like to feel that way, because I've had the feelings myself.

There is no hour of our lives in the epidemic that is untouched by such confusions. Guilt, shame, humiliation, or self-hatred, now consciously (and often unconsciously) pervade too many gay men's experience of being infected, of being homosexual and *not* being infected, and of being identified with a community which is now perhaps more commonly characterized in the public mind by the epidemic than by the act of anal sex.

One important consequence of these confused and entangled feelings is that quite aside from all the good, human reasons for protecting from stigmatization those dealing with HIV infection in their own bodies, we have found ourselves in the peculiar position of feeling that we have to defend HIV infection itself. The sometimes conscious, usually unconscious cycle of feelings goes: *Being queer doesn't* feel *OK, and we got* HIV *because we're queer. But we want being queer to be OK, and we* say *it's OK, so having* HIV *must be OK, and we should say* HIV *is OK, because otherwise being queer will feel even* less *OK.*

As a consequence of such 'psychological politics', we have constructed a very strange, largely unspoken protocol within gay communities. This protocol is driven by our own, individual self-hatred, uninfected and infected alike, and it is born out of the cycle of feelings just cited, as well as elaborations of the feelings expressed by the HIV-positive psychotherapy patient quoted earlier: *He's a fag too, and if anyone deserves* HIV, he *deserves it as much as* I *deserve it, so how dare he experience me differently simply because I have* HIV, *because he could have it too, and probably will.* Or, from the uninfected man's unconscious: *I'm a fag, I* could *have* HIV, *I probably* deserve HIV, *I don't know why I* don't *have* HIV, *and I don't want anything to do with people who* do *have* HIV *because it reminds me that I'm going to get it or already have it.* And of course, the absolute emotional and political unacceptability of such feelings then hatches the public protocol: *I am living and thriving with* AIDS, *and I am proud of that.* And from the uninfected man: *When I date a man, it makes no difference to me whatsoever if he's HIV-positive or not.*

Such protocol within gay communities is erected against truths which are too harsh, too painful, or too disruptive of social life. The protocol arising out of our psychological politics not only obscures the whole truth, it obstructs any effort to reveal that truth and thus help clarify what is really paining us deeply. Psychological politics within gay communities have prevented us from saying out loud that there are some real differences between positive and negative men in many psychological, interpersonal, and social issues and needs. In the shadow of the undeniably pressing needs of infected men, we have been largely unable to acknowledge that uninfected men have any needs at all. When a handful of uninfected men here and there have tried to assert needs, the response from others in the community has been badly distorted by both our psychological politics and their expression in social protocol. An HIV-positive AIDS activist was recently quoted in a San Francisco gay paper:

> I think it's very important for HIV-negative folks to have a forum where they can share their concerns, but there's a difference between creating forums of communication . . . and creating the perception of an exclusive entity that says to HIV-positive people, 'You can't come here; you don't belong; *you're not good enough*' [italics added].[2]

A decade and a half into an epidemic that has infected or killed half their community in San Francisco, HIV-negative men have pressing needs to talk among themselves about many feelings and issues which they cannot considerately or humanely discuss in the presence of positive men. That these needs, including the need to discuss them away from positive men, might be construed as saying to positive men that positive men are being excluded *because they are not good enough* brings us right back to the psychological roots of our dilemma: *I'm a fag, I got fucked, I got exactly what I deserved, and you (who do not have* HIV*) may not imply that I'm not good enough*. The assertion of these psychological politics in print or in protocol obfuscates what both negative and positive men are really feeling about the epidemic, themselves, those of the 'other group', and their social and intimate relations with each other. Unfortunately, these are the very things we must talk about if we are to survive the epidemic not only as biological organisms, but as human beings.

Aside from helping destroy many authentic, intimate, fully-lived lives, the psychological politics of our communities and their expression in protocol have had another tragic consequence. Since April 1985 when the ELISA first became available and we discovered that there were ‘positive’ and ‘negative’ gay men (and who they were, which is to say ourselves, our lovers, our best friends, or neighbours) we have been almost completely unable to do AIDS *primary* prevention: prevention to keep uninfected men uninfected. Instead, we initiated and sustain to this day a kind of ‘undifferentiated’ prevention that has insisted upon denying that there are any differences between positive and negative men which might be pertinent to prevention itself. Undifferentiated prevention has thus persisted in doing prevention roughly as we did it before the ELISA. This denial flies in the face of what men who know their antibody statuses (and those who *could* know their statuses, but do not) are really experiencing. As the epidemic has endured and deepened, positive men, negative men, and men who do not know have developed distinct social and psychological identities, and thus distinct needs, concerns, and issues, many of which are centrally pertinent to prevention. In ignoring these differences, undifferentiated prevention has almost entirely failed to address anyone’s needs and concerns, and has failed badly in helping accomplish the sole purpose of primary prevention: *keeping uninfected men uninfected.*

Undifferentiated prevention is now so familiar to most of us that the idea requires some clarification. Most simply put, undifferentiated prevention is doing AIDS prevention for ‘gay men’. As one example, it is exhorting men to Stay Healthy, without saying if we mean uninfected or asymptomatic, rather than saying the obvious, Stay Uninfected. It is, in another notorious expression, A Condom Every Time. A Condom Every Time was a sensible instruction (indeed, the only *possible* instruction) before the ELISA. But in the current age, when many men know if they are infected or not, and many others would know, if prevention provided reasons to know, it is an instruction that ignores or denies an obvious fact. Infected and uninfected men practise (or do not practise) protected sex where it would be prudent to do so for very different reasons. After all, the potential consequences of not using a condom and the potential benefits of using one are entirely different for the two groups. In 1996, the task of prevention is no longer simply to tell men who are not using condoms to use them, but rather to help them understand why they are *not* using them when there is risk of transmitting or contracting HIV. If we are to do that, rather than uselessly persevere in telling men to do what they are not in fact doing, we must know to whom we speak and about what. We simply deny the obvious in asserting that infected and uninfected men act out of the same feelings and motivations with regard to their sexual behaviors.

A detailed example of undifferentiated prevention at work is seen in a brochure from San Francisco's STOP AIDS Project (one of the world's most widely copied primary prevention programmes). A 1995 brochure inviting men to its small, peer-led meetings tells us that,

> [STOP AIDS offers] a one-shot evening with other gay and bisexual men like yourself who want to explore what good sex (safe and satisfying sex) is all about. A lecture? No way! Everybody talks. Everybody listens. After all, everyone's experience is different. It turns out we all have a great deal to learn from each other about dealing with fear and frustration. And a great deal to teach one another about what getting close really means . . . You'll hear the latest facts about the risks of different sexual practices and how you can stay safe. You'll have a chance to talk about how AIDS has changed more than our sex lives (it shapes our friendships, our community, our personal sense of the future) . . . You can even find out where to follow up or get help for a friend. To talk about what it means to be positive or negative . . . Best of all, the evening is a time for all of us to renew our commitment to protect ourselves and care for others in the ways that mean the most.[3]

The language of this very typical piece simply begs the issues of primary prevention. The purpose of the meeting (to help keep uninfected men uninfected) is hedged from the beginning by the specious idea that men are only getting together to 'explore what good sex (safe and satisfying sex) is all about'. And the hedging continues throughout. Are the other men in the group really 'like yourself', or might HIV status have something to do with that in the context of prevention concerns? Could differences in the ways men experience sex and the epidemic have anything to do with HIV status? Might HIV status contribute, in a number of ways, to problems with 'getting really close?' Are the risks of 'different sexual practices' and 'staying safe' unrelated to HIV status? Could the nature of men's 'fears and frustrations' have anything to do with HIV status? Might HIV status have something to do with the ways that AIDS has changed '*our* sex lives, *our* friendships, *our* community, or *our* personal sense of the future?' And, finally, *who* is renewing his commitment to protect *whom* from *what* and *whom* 'in the ways that mean the most?' In this very typical presentation, differences between positive and negative men are deliberately blurred on the most obvious issues, and nowhere is it simply stated that the meeting (funded to do primary prevention) is intended to help keep uninfected men uninfected.

By intentionally obfuscating the outcome population for primary prevention, uninfected men, STOP AIDS eliminates any possibility of addressing this population's specific issues and needs. Nor can STOP AIDS address the unique issues of infected men which might help them contribute to keeping uninfected men uninfected. By its very nature, undifferentiated prevention is able to talk only about issues that can be presented equivocally. As soon as prevention speaks to the purpose of staying uninfected, those who are already infected are excluded. And this, of course, is precisely where our psychological politics first reveal themselves. Undifferentiated prevention is what it is, in part, because we cannot bear to exclude positive men, cannot bear the possibility of making them feel that they *do not belong* or *are not good enough* (even when the subject is, or ought to be, keeping uninfected men uninfected).

Feelings about excluding or stigmatizing positive men are usually voiced publicly as concerns about 'dividing' the community. Divisiveness is felt to be created, most commonly, by offering forums and services exclusively for HIV-negative men and their issues. That such feelings are truly about the exclusion or stigmatization of positive men, rather than about divisiveness, is apparent in the commonplace forums and services exclusively for positive men, which are not perceived as excluding, stigmatizing, or divisive. As late as 1993, one of San Francisco's important gay papers, *The Sentinel*, characterized support groups for HIV-negative men with distress about the epidemic as an attempt at 'viral apartheid', and thereafter refused to carry public services announcements for anything identified as services explicitly for HIV-negative men. The paper carried innumerable announcements for HIV-positive services. In 1994, Chuck Frutchey, former director of education at the San Francisco AIDS foundation and board member of the STOP AIDS Project publicly asserted that local psychotherapists who spoke publicly about the problems of uninfected men were 'nail-biting Chicken Littles . . . and victim wannabes . . . [who lack] a more balanced and reality-based notion of the difficulties of coping with AIDS . . . HIV-negative gay men . . . share most of [their issues] with HIV-positive gay men.'[4] A letter from officers of STOP AIDS in defence of another primary prevention campaign of the agency also addresses the issue of community 'unity': 'It is vital to acknowledge the difficulty we face in recognizing differences among our constituents without creating a polarization between men of different serostatus.'[5]

This humanely rooted, if ill-clarified concern for the potential disenfranchisement of positive men is revealed in an obvious, but startling, observation about how we do primary prevention for negative men. Although we still address the undifferentiated group of 'gay men' that we spoke to before the ELISA, we have stopped explicitly encouraging them to stay uninfected, and we have entirely stopped talking about the horrors of HIV infection that might serve as one incentive. We have reduced prevention to a set of concrete, universal instructions that never speaks (that cannot speak) of motivation, purposes, or outcome.

If undifferentiated prevention cannot speak to negative men about getting infected (or, as another approach to primary prevention, to positive men about infecting others) how has primary prevention attempted to address its purpose at all? The answer is that undifferentiated prevention has relied entirely on the paradoxical instruction developed in pre-ELISA days, an instruction best exemplified by the idea of telling 'gay men' to 'use a condom every time'. The paradox in the instruction is that for purposes of protecting himself, every man must assume himself *un*infected and all others infected. And for purposes of protecting others, he must assume himself *infected*, and all others *un*infected. In other words, undifferentiated prevention has every gay man both coming and going regardless of what he knows, does not know, thinks he knows but does not know, or thinks he does not know but knows. While this paradox was a necessity before the ELISA, we now have at least the possibility of knowing antibody status. Unfortunately, the paradox has increasingly separated gay men from knowledge of their antibody statuses and isolated them from prevention itself.

The paradox is responsible for separating gay men from what, in the US at least, has been offered as the very backbone of prevention – HIV testing. Testing is certainly not prevention *per se*, and the role of testing in US prevention education has been inadequately understood and badly implemented. Nevertheless, antibody status has become an important component of every gay man's psychological (and often, social and interpersonal) identity, whether that aspect of identity is based on fact or misinformation. HIV testing can distinguish fact from misinformation, and in doing so it provides the HIV-negative man with the single most important component of prevention: the reasonable knowledge that he has something to protect.

In denying that antibody status is a component of gay men's experiences of themselves and others, that the reality of antibody status can be known with reasonable certainty, and that antibody status might be expressed in sexual practice, the paradoxical instruction prescribes a single behavioural code, a condom every time. Given this instruction, the very best that a gay man can hope for from an HIV test is to find he is uninfected, but is expected to stay that way by acting as if he and his partners were actually infected for the rest of their lives. The consequence is not only that there is little incentive for testing (and little sexual benefit for being and staying uninfected) but that a 'cognitive dissonance' is created. The uninfected couple must wrestle with feelings that either some prevention instructions are wrong and unnecessary *or* that one or both is not really HIV-negative. This is very much like instructing a man to walk with a cane 'just in case' he has a leg fracture. He soon comes to feel that either the prescription is unnecessary, wrong, and implies an untruth (or that perhaps he *has* a fracture after all). Neither resolution of the dissonance supports prevention objectives. Too many men now simply dismiss the pertinent messages of prevention because prevention feels irrelevant to their circumstances, and too many others lose prevention incentive because they feel that infection has somehow already occurred or surely will. AIDS prevention, over the long term, cannot be founded on supporting or encouraging men's doubt about their HIV status, the denial of the importance of HIV-status as a component of identity, or a denial of the behavioural realities that informed or misinformed conceptions of one's HIV-status might support or discourage.

With all its unclarity and confusion, undifferentiated prevention does, in fact, accurately express the public health prevention model that has become standard for gay men in the United States. The undifferentiated model and its indiscriminate, paradoxical instructions are usually justified with the obvious assertion that many gay men (in the US, probably one third) have never tested for HIV, that other men's tests are outdated by intervening behaviour, and that still others may unknowingly or intentionally misrepresent status. But this justification of the undifferentiated model is a rationalization for a prevention approach which does not truly respect the human importance of gay sex and is thus willing to predicate itself on the acceptability of all gay men acting for lifetimes as if they *cannot* know their own or their partner's status simply because many do not, or misrepresent what they do know. It is a justification which asserts that because 'being HIV-negative' is often merely a psychological or social identity, it cannot also be a biological reality that can be beneficially acted upon.

The unknown extent to which gay men maintain mistaken HIV-negative identities is, ironically, partly a product of very undifferentiated prevention which cites the potential discrepancy between identity and fact to validate its approaches. A man who believes he is HIV-negative (and that he can probably stay that way) will test to confirm his negative status and thus gain confidence that he does indeed have something to protect. Among psychotherapy patients who decide to test after long periods of indecision, I have fairly consistently seen behavioural changes in only a single group. These are men who believed, felt, or feared they were HIV-positive and then actually tested negative. These men often dramatically lower their potential exposure to HIV because they suddenly feel that they do, after all, have something to protect. Men who have never tested or have not tested with reasonable currency only rarely change behaviour spontaneously, and in 1996 only rarely do so in response to prevention education.[6]

Undifferentiated prevention in the US thus purports to rely on testing, laments the limitations imposed by so much ignorance of true antibody status, and simultaneously discourages testing by not letting men take the results seriously in the form of benefits for HIV-negative results. Undifferentiated prevention, which suggests or insists that all gay men experience themselves as 'positives' and 'unknowns', needlessly exacerbates the feelings of plausibility or inevitability about having HIV that so many gay men experience anyway simply because they are gay and the gay identity has become psychologically and socially entangled in HIV and AIDS. Such entanglement, supported by paradoxical, undifferentiated prevention, clearly contributes to new infections by making infection feel plausible or inevitable and thus not worth trying to avoid. Particularly when oral sex is added into the 'condom every time' message, undifferentiated prevention has further exacerbated feelings of plausibility or inevitability by positing a task that is experienced by too many men as monolithic and impossible.[7] The paradoxical instruction was crafted early in the epidemic when it was the only possible instruction, and at a time when we expected the epidemic to be over in a few years. But in 1996, we are asking twenty-year-olds to somehow envision success in using a condom every single time they have sex for the next half century, and we explicitly forbid latitude for knowledge of antibody status, context, or partner. If that task feels impossible (and perhaps a majority of young men today have never even dreamed it possible) contracting HIV simply feels like one's fate as a gay man, and there are many powerful incentives to accept it, throw in the towel, and get it over with *now.* 'When I told my mother I was moving to California,' a twenty-four-year-old psychotherapy patient told me,

> she said, 'If you do that you're going to get AIDS.' What she really meant was, 'You're going out there so you can be gay.' For her, being gay means having AIDS. And now that I've been here for two years, I'm beginning to think she's right. I mean, if you aren't at least positive, you're sort of a nobody in San Francisco. And anyway, if I keep having sex with guys I probably *am* going to get it sooner or later, and I guess the question isn't *if* but *when*. I'd be afraid to tell her because you know what she's going to say: 'I told you so.'

The factual reality hidden behind the paradoxical, discouraging monolith experienced by this twenty-four-year-old and his mother is that an HIV-negative ELISA taken six months after the last potential exposure to HIV by unprotected, receptive anal sex, followed by the avoidance of unprotected receptive anal sex with partners of unknown or HIV-positive status, provides a very high level of probability that one is uninfected.[8] It is difficult to quantify the exact level of probability thus derived, but it is certainly comparable to, or in excess of, many probabilities of safe passage that we accept on ordinary daily risks such as automobile travel. If gay men or their educators are unable to sustain reasonable confidence in an HIV-negative status under these circumstances (and allow some of the possibilities that status might offer) we must look to other than biological issues.[9]

The paradoxical instruction isolates gay men from prevention in another way that ought to be obvious. The very form of the message (that it must adhere to the cardinal rule of speaking 'equitably' and indistinguishably to all gay men about presumably universal issues) does not allow us to address any of the particular issues of negative and positive men, and thus bring simple *relevance* to prevention. Contrary to the assertions of many AIDS educators, gay men have not grown 'complacent' in the epidemic; they have simply become acclimated to the personal irrelevance of prevention's 'universal' messages.

While our psychological politics as reflected in undifferentiated prevention are very leery of excluding or stigmatizing positive men by speaking explicitly to negative men, there is a second, important reason why we have kept prevention messages universal. If we do the obvious and speak specifically to the outcome population for primary prevention (HIV-negative men) we simultaneously open the possibility of speaking explicitly to positive men. We have almost completely avoided doing this, for we fear stigmatizing positive men not only by excluding them, but by placing an inordinate burden of responsibility for the transmission of HIV on them. I believe there are many important human, as well as simple, pragmatic reasons *not* to use primary prevention to burden positive men with exclusive or inordinate responsibility for HIV transmission. But it is curious (and an anomaly in the history of public health) that we have constructed a prevention approach for gay men that treats public health's traditional 'carrier' and its 'public-to-be-protected' with absolute equity of responsibility for avoiding transmission, even when the infected man is aware of his infection. It is almost certain that *all* new infections do *not* occur accidentally or unknowingly on the part of the infected partner. And while in 1996, the HIV-negative gay man ought to know that he may be risking contracting HIV in an act of receptive anal sex with an unknown partner or partner of unknown status, the knowingly infected partner has certainty that this is a possibility. These observations suggest that positive men may have a clear and explicit role in primary prevention as a target, as opposed to outcome, population. Any authentic primary prevention will have to address this possibility with respect and cognizance of the psychological and social issues facing gay men and their communities, and thus without further stigmatizing or 'criminalizing' positive men.

In sum, undifferentiated prevention offers gay communities a constellation of troubling instructions and results: paradoxes, a denial of obvious incentives, apparent untruths, persistent doubt about really being uninfected, irrelevance, and feelings of uncertainty or hopelessness about the possibility of being gay and staying uninfected. Given these shortcomings, why have we persisted in (indeed, usually *insisted* upon) such an approach? Part of the answer is that our authentic and humane politics quite rightly demand that we defend the lives of those with HIV, and our psychological politics have embroiled that task in the defence of HIV infection itself. If we are all gay and all deserve what we *already* got, *might* have gotten if we hadn't been lucky, or *will* get when our luck runs out, it feels threatening and unacceptable to assert that there might be any differences at all in the experience, hopes, or futures of infected and uninfected men. If we explicitly assert that it is much better to remain uninfected, are we not implying that there is something 'wrong' with the lives of infected men? If a large segment of our community speaks openly about plans to survive the epidemic (and how, and what for) are we not abandoning those for whom such hopes seem futile? Dare the uninfected man, who is a fag too, risk pushing his luck by hoping for a future and thus tempt a fate of which he half feels deserving? Can the 'fortunate' among us hope for things that are impossible for those whom we cannot bear to acknowledge are in some regards unfortunate? In other words, can we really assert that it is better to be thriving *without* AIDS than *with* it, and not feel as if we are selling ourselves, our brothers, our community, and homosexuality itself down the river?

Such feelings, the protocol within gay communities that obscures them, and the undifferentiated prevention that reflects them are hindering us from recognizing, clarifying, and addressing obvious, often differing, realities in the lives of infected and uninfected gay men, including realities that play central roles in the ongoing toll of new infections. Among these are the realities that 'safer sex' is not a condom every time, but *any* sex that does not transmit HIV; that HIV infection cannot occur between two uninfected men; that *all* gay men need not, and cannot, bear the burden of living lifetimes as if they or their partners were infected; that there may be possibilities in the lives of uninfected men that do *not* exist for men already infected; that uninfected men who are hoping to stay uninfected *are* hoping for futures that most infected men cannot have, and that we must nurture those hopes in order to help men stay uninfected; that if 'being healthy' in gay communities has come to mean 'HIV-positive but asymptomatic', being 'healthiest' means being completely free of HIV; that we have complex, often troubled feelings about ourselves and each other, and these feelings motivate some men to knowingly transmit HIV, and others to knowingly expose themselves; that we are often guilty about each other, often frightened of each other, and that we hurt each other because of how we feel about *ourselves*;

that we *are already* deeply divided because we misrepresent and deny our differences rather than confront, clarify, and negotiate them; and, most importantly, that if our need to authentically feel acceptance of our lives as gay men cannot be disentangled from compensatory, false 'pride', including pride about having HIV, then we will lose even more to the epidemic than we have already.

Unless the uninfected gay man's hope to survive without infection *per se* is experienced as betrayal, primary prevention unfettered by the psychological politics of our communities need not betray, abandon, or accuse those with HIV. Authentic and explicit primary prevention *can* acknowledge the differences between infected and uninfected men without implying that one is 'not good enough' or is culpable. And authentic primary prevention *can* respect the desire for a humane unity among gay men without denying the truths of our lives. If the feelings that mislead us on these truths cannot be examined and clarified, we will not be able to make a decision to *do* primary prevention, or *not* do it because it is too humanly destructive and painful for those already infected. Our misrepresentations and lies have accomplished little good, and today, the epidemic in gay communities is already the product of a decision, if an unconscious one, *to not do primary prevention*. This is much too important a decision to have made unconsciously.

notes

1. I have written in some detail about the psychology of gay men and the epidemic in *In the Shadow of the Epidemic: Being HIV-Negative in the Age of AIDS*, Durham N.C., Duke University Press, 1995 and London, Cassell, 1995.
2. 'Is HIV Tearing Us Apart?', Tim Pfaff, *San Francisco Frontiers Newsmagazine*, vol. 14, no. 22, pp.24–25. The man being quoted is Bill Hershon, who is cited as a law student who also serves as the consumer advocate on the San Francisco Mayor's HIV Planning Council.
3. *You're right. A Small Group of Powerful People Can Stop the Spread of AIDS*, the STOP AIDS Project, no publication date. The brochure is funded by the California Department of Health Services, Office of AIDS.

4. 'Negatives Being Negative,' *The San Francisco Sentinel*, 26 October, 1994.

5. The letter is dated August 22, 1994 from Alan Hayes, President, and Bruce Hinton, Secretary, Board of Directors, STOP AIDS Project of San Francisco to Michael Colbruno, Editor, *The Sentinel*.

6. Prevention's inconsistent and inaccurate implication of oral sex in HIV transmission at levels warranting the routine use of condoms has created a serious prevention problem in the US. This misinformation makes important contributions to the doubt many men feel about the possibility that they are still HIV-negative and can stay that way. At San Francisco HIV test cites, the practice of unprotected oral sex is, by far, the most common reason cited for doubt about HIV status and purpose of testing. These men, however, *state no intention of changing behavior with regard to oral sex* (personal communication, 1996, Edward Wolf and Susan Thompson, San Francisco Department of Public Health, Test Center One). See also Notes 7 and 8.

7. This is particularly true in the US because oral sex is treated as such a prominent transmission issue. See Notes 6 and 8 for further discussion of oral sex and its role in prevention.

8. Doubt about HIV status and a sense of inevitability about eventually seroconverting have been badly exacerbated in the US by a persistent misrepresentation of the known facts about HIV transmission, particularly with regard to oral sex. Despite an overwhelming body of evidence suggesting that receptive anal sex with an infected partner accounts for almost all new infections among gay men, American educators continue to discuss oral sex and insertive anal sex as 'risk behaviors.' One example of the substantial data contradicting concern about any behaviors other than receptive anal sex is from the California Office of AIDS. In a sample of 8,046 gay and bisexual men, oral sex tied for last place with insertive vaginal sex among 23 risk factors for HIV transmission, and was shown to be slightly 'protective' against HIV infection. This means that those who practiced more oral sex were less likely to become infected than those who practiced less oral sex, presumably because the latter were practicing more of other kinds of sex, including anal sex. Insertive anal sex was a risk factor only because of its statistical association with receptive anal sex (as revealed in multivariate analysis). (*California HIV testing and Counseling Quarterly Report, July – September 1994*, Department of Health Services Office of AIDS HIV Counseling and Testing Section). In personal communications, Steven Truax and John Forquera of the Office of AIDS reported that this quarter's data (the most recent published as of this writing) is typical of all data collected over the last year and a half on more than 40,000 gay and bisexual men in California.

While there seems no doubt that HIV transmission by other than receptive anal sex is possible and has actually occurred, it appears to be very rare. In addition to the large, consistent body of literature on the relative safety of oral sex, it is noteworthy that there is virtually no literature supporting the idea of HIV transmission through insertive anal sex. Pertinent literature on these subjects includes: Jay Levy. 'The Transmission of HIV and Factors Influencing Progression to AIDS,' *The American Journal of Medicine*, vol. 95, July 1993; 'The San Francisco Men's Health Study, Sexual Practices and Risk of Infection by the Human Immunodeficiency Virus', *Journal of the American Medical Association*, vol. 257, no. 3, 16 January 1987; David Ostrow, et al., 'Behavioral Factors Associated with HIV-1 Seroconversion Among Members of the Chicago MACS/Coping & Change Study Cohort, 1984–1992', Personal verbal and written communication, David Ostrow, 1994 and 1995, in press with the *American Journal of Epidemiology*. Some of this data was presented at the 1994 Brighton Conference; Carlos F. Caceres, 'Male Homosexual Transmission of HIV-1', *AIDS*, 8, pp.1051–61, 1994.

9. Among the possibilities for mutually HIV-negative couples (and perhaps mutually HIV-positive couples) is the practice of 'negotiated safety', which many proponents of undifferentiated prevention have preferred to call 'negotiated danger' (see, for example, 'Safer Sex Among Gay Men: What is the Ultimate Goal', Maria Ekstrand, Ron Stall, Susan Kegeles, Robert Hays, Michael DeMayo, and Thomas Coates, *AIDS*, 1993, 7, 281–2.) There is no doubt that the negotiation of safety against HIV through agreement rather than physical barriers is a complex matter demanding communication skills and some psychological clarification of issues affecting couples. But negotiated safety is an obvious, possible, and often desirable approach to a relationship as amply demonstrated by the number of couples who are attempting it. While the results to date seem to have been mixed on the whole (one generally hears about negotiated safety only when it fails), undifferentiated prevention must take some responsibility for failures. In prohibiting the very possibility (a condom every time, *regardless*), undifferentiated prevention demands silence on the subject, and thus discourages, rather than assists, development of the very skills that might make negotiated safety work. Gay men have been forced to practice negotiated safety in secrecy, and without the support and clarification that could help make it work: support and clarification that are routinely provided US heterosexuals, for whom negotiated safety is routinely offered as the prevention method of choice (see Pamela DeCarlo, 'Do Condoms Work?', *HIV Prevention: Looking Back, Looking Ahead*, Center for AIDS Prevention Studies, University of California, San Francisco and the Harvard AIDS Institute, 1995). Are we to use gay men's results with negotiated safety to date to forecast the results of a prevention approach that acknowledged and assisted with this obvious and desirable possibility?

dangerous vessels

feminism and the AIDS crisis

Robin Gorna

This essay considers the failure of AIDS treatment and HIV prevention to acknowledge the agency, autonomy, and integrity of women with HIV (and those at risk of infection). It discusses how women have often been seen solely in terms of their childbearing potential. The impacts of AIDS on women (both the infected and uninfected) are complex, and under-studied from a feminist perspective. Women have been used to 'push' certain messages about AIDS (that anyone can get it), to prevent new HIV infections (among infants) and to study the spread of the disease (through screening programmes), but tragically little attention has been paid to the needs of adult women to preserve their health when infected, or to avoid infection when they are at risk. The continual foregrounding of the (actual or potential) foetus in considerations of women and AIDS has the dangerous effect of masking the adult woman.

Women affected by HIV and AIDS inevitably have different needs from men, yet applying a feminist analysis to AIDS is problematic. Gender cannot easily be the key interpretative framework for understanding the effects of AIDS. AIDS was first detected among men, connected by the fact that they were gay, and men continue to be impacted in disproportionate numbers. In this essay I refer principally to the UK and other countries in the industrialized first world, where women constitute a minority of those affected by

AIDS and HIV. At a global level, HIV infects the genders equally, but there is no one pandemic. AIDS is experienced locally, and any analysis needs to respond to that specificity. The effects of AIDS are never equal, and those discourses which attempt to smooth out diversity with a crass rhetoric of equality render the realities of AIDS invisible. Discourses of equality are frequently the framework within which the practical implications of feminism are interpreted, yet in the AIDS context, this is one of the most inappropriate frameworks for analysis. One of the functions of feminism is to redress inequity, to make women's perspective visible, to put women first. Yet this approach is limited in relation to AIDS because this redressing is seen as a minority concern, which can be misused to conceal the underlying inequities of AIDS.

In the UK, women are 'under-represented' in the AIDS epidemic, and only a tiny proportion of the overall female population is infected. By the end of June 1996, 4,032 omen had been diagnosed with HIV infection, and 1,268 had developed AIDS. 27,088 people had tested positive for HIV, and 12,976 had been diagnosed with AIDS. 669 children are known to be infected with HIV and 247 have developed AIDS.[1] While in total only 15 per cent of British HIV (and 10 per cent of AIDS) cases are in women – and respectively 1 per cent and 1.5 per cent are among children infected from their mothers – the rate of increase paints a different picture. Over the twelve months to June 1996, 20 per cent of new HIV diagnoses were women. While these shifts in the epidemiology are worrying, they should not detract from the terrible regularity with which, in the UK, 1,600 gay men and bisexual men newly acquire HIV every year.[2]

An additional impediment to understanding the impact of AIDS on women in the UK is the rates of HIV testing. The majority of women who have HIV are not aware of their high risk of infection (one study of HIV-positive women in London found that only 24 per cent were aware of their risk when they became infected[3]). Among gay men who have HIV it is estimated that 67 per cent have tested and know that they are HIV-positive. However, among HIV infected pregnant women, it is reported that only 12 per cent know of their HIV status.[4] This suggests that the reported HIV statistics for gay men are relatively accurate, whereas for women there is a significant under-estimation of the levels of infection (as these are based on named tests). Despite these caveats, it remains the case that the absolute numbers of women with HIV are far lower than the numbers of gay men, and are likely to remain that way in the immediate future. Policies and programmes addressing women have developed within this minority context. Any feminist response to AIDS in the West must understand the context and scale of the contemporary epidemic, rather than being dazzled by the predictions of what could come to pass, or the horror of 'foreign AIDS'.

First World and Third World AIDS are miles and continents apart. Even within continents the scale and nature of the impact of AIDS upon women differs and the women living with the virus vary. In Spain, for example, HIV-positive women often have a history of drug use, infected because they have no access to clean injecting equipment. In the US, this is also the case, complicated by the fact that the majority of women with AIDS are African-American or Hispanic, and their experiences of HIV are combined with the poverty and racism of urban life. In Uganda, most HIV-positive women are young and infected in marriage, sometimes with little consent in their sexual relationships. In India, and many other South East Asian countries, HIV is reported to be spreading at a dramatic rate and infecting large numbers of young women, especially those 'sold' to city prostitution from the poverty of village life. What is less commonly reported is the vulnerability women face consequent to the highly prevalent bisexual behaviour of their husbands and lovers – behaviour which is simultaneously accepted as part of the cultural norm, and vehemently concealed in public discourse.

In the UK, women with AIDS are predominantly infected from sex with a man (only 18 per cent of women with

AIDS were infected from shared injecting equipment). The majority of new cases occur among women from African countries – either seeking asylum from dangerous pasts, or being infected within close knit communities struggling against institutional racism, fear and hatred of refugees. The level of HIV prevalence in this sub-population of women may even exceed that among British gay men (13.3 per cent of African women in England and Wales who have tested for HIV are positive, compared with 8.3 per cent of gay men).[5] Among HIV-infected women not connected with the African continent, or with a history of injecting drug use, there are hardly any similarities of experience, let alone prior connections. They are defined by their very diversity. It is this diversity which leads so often to a strong sense of isolation, and invisibility for many women. In media representations of women with HIV this diversity is rarely visible. The stock image of a woman with HIV is a young, white European, heterosexual, infected by one of her (very few) boyfriends. HIV-positive women attending support groups are forcibly aware of the cultural, racial, religious, regional and lifestyle variations among themselves, yet this reality is studiously kept out of public view.

AIDS is simultaneously a highly visible condition (it has fed excessive column inches and broadcast time) and an invisible disease (visible symptoms are unlikely in the first ten years after infection, and when they occur, they may be mistaken for illnesses associated with other conditions). It is the most despised condition (the junkie/gay plague) and the object of serious concern (so much so that it is smeared with 'politically correct' status). AIDS asks hard questions about life, love, sex, death, degenerating illness among the young, the outcast, the pleasure seekers. It requires a local response and a global concern; it brings the most personal, intimate elements of human existence into the political arena, and demonstrates how political decisions invade personal lives.

Surely such a pre-eminent twentieth-century condition ought to be a major feminist concern. Yet despite the AIDS activism of many feminists, 'mainstream' feminists (with some fine exceptions[6]) have shied away from applying their analyses to the crisis of AIDS. AIDS is about sex, and as such it is an awkward and discomforting battle for feminists battered by the sex wars of the early 1980s.[7] For feminists who are 'anti-porn', the need for sexually explicit discourse and materials to promote sexual pleasure which avoids HIV transmission may be proof of the anti-women, oppressive nature of the response to AIDS. For example, radical feminist Sheila Jeffreys has reacted particularly violently – accusing Sue O'Sullivan and myself of conspiring with gay men to foist abusive patriarchal pornography on women.[8] By contrast, for 'anti-censorship' feminists the emphasis on educating women and girls to refuse sex, and to be alert to the potential juxtaposition of sex and death, may seem to turn back hard-won, recent 'pro-sex' gains.

Despite the contradictory reactions, and overwhelming silence, of the feminist movement, there have always been feminists involved in the fight against AIDS, although our numbers have been disproportionate to the impact AIDS has had, directly, on the lives of feminists. Most tellingly, the majority of feminists engaged in the fight against AIDS are lesbian. Consequently, the ratio of lesbian feminists working in AIDS with those infected with HIV is extremely unbalanced, and bears witness to the pre-AIDS political organizing and 'solidarity' between lesbians and gay men, rather than to the existence of a large number of HIV-infected lesbians.[9] There is a significant, and growing, body of evidence linking 'empowerment' with women's ability to protect themselves from HIV, resisting coercive or unsafe sex, asserting sexual options and desire and insisting upon condom use.[10] Whilst it would be going too far to suggest that 'feminists don't get AIDS' (and it's certainly not true that 'women with AIDS don't get feminism'), some might conclude that feminism is a protective strategy. Interestingly, in the UK, rates of HIV infection among women working in commercial sex industries are extremely low – despite many people's expectations (probably) based on reports from other countries.

This apparently reflects working women's pre-existing concerns to protect their health and safety at work, and the high degree of negotiating power women have within a 'contracted' sexual encounter.[11]

Approaches to protecting women at risk of HIV remain under-developed. Most of women's responses to AIDS which receive attention are not, however, those involving the difficulties of safer sex, but rather those concerned with the needs for care and support for people living with HIV and AIDS. While there are important local specificities to the AIDS epidemics, there are also global similarities shared by women responding to AIDS. As the traditional caregivers – within the informality of the family, or in the formality of the hospital ward – women often take the brunt of the suffering of others on every continent. Women's response has generally been marked by the altruism of the carer, supporting and accompanying people through their daily struggle. Indeed one remarkable, and under-stated, feature of most AIDS services is the disproportionate number of women providing care and support. For example, 56 per cent of staff and 51 per cent of volunteers at the Terrence Higgins Trust are women (a fact that has led one male manager to complain that women are over-represented in the organization). It is unclear whether this bears witness to extraordinary levels of compassion from women who have for so long worked in the caring professions, or whether it reflects 'care fatigue' among gay men and the brutalizing effect of AIDS on gay communities. Certainly some non-AIDS activist feminists have observed this phenomena and complained that women are exhausting their energies by taking care of men. Compared to breast cancer AIDS is a remarkably male disease in the West. So why should feminists get fired up by such a rare women's health issue?

AIDS is more than simply a health condition. The human rights issues, the stigma, prejudice and marginalization which accompany this life-threatening, sexually transmissible condition define it as a critical concern for feminist agendas. AIDS complicates existing political struggles. It complicates sex and women's independence. There is nothing within a woman's absolute control to enable her to avoid acquiring HIV: male condoms require men's compliance; female condoms require male consent; refusing sex has never been straightforward; and mutual monogamy is a matter of extreme trust (80 per cent of women with AIDS worldwide were infected in their sole sexual relationships which they believed to be monogamous).[12]

AIDS complicates women's self-agency and autonomy. Women vulnerable to acquiring HIV infection are rarely defined as women in their own right, but rather by the men they fuck.[13] This creates a terrible dilemma: feminists have struggled hard for women to be defined as individuals, and yet there is no practical way of defining most women's HIV risk without reference to men. With the exception of women who inject drugs with HIV-infected syringes, women become infected because they have unprotected vaginal or anal sex with a man who is HIV-infected. Most women who have unsafe sex with a man will not get HIV, because most of the men having sex with women are not infected. There is a significant minority of men who are infected, yet there is no common uniting feature to describe the groups of women who have sex with these men – except for the subgroup of women who come from high HIV prevalence countries themselves. The only honest way to identify most women at immediate risk of acquiring HIV is to emphasize the behavioural (past) of the men they are having sex with: Is he from a high HIV prevalence country? Has he injected drugs? Has he had sex with men? Did he receive HIV-infected Factor Eight to treat haemophilia? Ideally, social scientists would map women having sex with 'high risk' men and identify common features to enable targeting of HIV prevention programmes to these sub-groups of women. And yet no one has yet developed this kind of research.

It is far easier to identify men vulnerable to HIV because it is their own behaviour that places them at higher risk. In the late 1980s there was a shift to emphasizing risk behaviours, not risk groups. Yet in reality, HIV risk is the overlapping of both behaviour and group. Unprotected anal or vaginal sex is a risky behaviour when it is engaged in with someone from a risk group. For example, men who have unprotected anal sex with other men are quite likely to get HIV, because a significant proportion of those men *are* infected. From 1992, the UK has seen a clear strategic shift to targeting HIV prevention work to those communities at identifiable risk of infection, and this has created conflicts for work with women. In the 1980s it was customary to promote the idea that AIDS is 'Everyone's Business'. HIV is an 'Equal Opportunities Virus' was the familiar slogan, and posters proclaimed that 'AIDS does not discriminate'. And the proof? An alarmist interpretation of statistics about the possible growth of the epidemic, made flesh in the body of a woman with HIV being dragged out to tell her tale. In doing so AIDS was 'normalized', making it 'safe' and heterosexual. For example, in *Cosmopolitan* magazine in 1991, Denise Hathaway told her story of living with HIV, 'I feel I have an important role to play in breaking down stereotypes and prejudices,' she told Irma Kurtz, 'I'm doing it right now, by talking to you and coming out and saying it can happen to anyone. I mean *anyone*.' (Her emphasis).[14]

Such (mis)use of women may explain some of the fiercely anti-women and anti-feminist reactions of some gay male AIDS commentators to a continued emphasis on women's needs surrounding AIDS. They appear to fear that any attention given to women will reverse the hard-won shift to targeting HIV prevention to those at demonstrable risk. This, they fear, will jettison the needs of gay men, and will smooth out the epidemic's complexities. This is not wholly irrational paranoia, given the increasing levels of competition for funds for AIDS work. Whatever the underlying reasons for perceiving competition between women and gay men are, all AIDS organizations are increasingly pitted against each other as the statutory budgets for this work dwindle. This competition may be characterized in terms of different mixes of provision, quality of services, or of the target groups under consideration.

From women's perspectives, one of the consequences of targeting is that women adopt (in discourse at least) the 'high risk' identity of the men they fuck. Targeting can emphasize a binary way of thinking about AIDS. At a facile level a focus on gay men suggests that AIDS is either homosexual or heterosexual. If AIDS is not 'Everyone's Business' or 'heterosexual', then women with HIV must be 'queer' (if not literally homosexual). AIDS aligns women with or vulnerable to the virus with a queer sensibility that may be entirely distant from their personal reality. A middle-aged, white, suburban housewife with AIDS develops a 'queer' persona in public discourse because she has that gay/black/junkie disease. Despite the attempts of the late 1980s, no one was fooled: AIDS is not a 'normal' disease, and consequently anyone with AIDS is not normal – they become 'queer' because in public discourse the disease is represented as queer.

Woman is traditionally seen as 'other', she is defined as 'not-man', and this is particularly clear in the context of AIDS. The body becomes the contested territory of AIDS, and for women, the ever-corporal sex, the body overwhelms the individual. Male HIV risk is based upon behaviour, what he does with his body; by contrast for woman it is who she is, not what she does. She is a dangerous body, defined by her gynaecology: the womb and the vagina.[15] This bodily difference from men is fundamental to symbolic roles. Focus on her vagina and the woman becomes a dangerous whore, a vamp, the ever-menacing spectacle of the *vagina dentata* (one fuck and you're dead). This is a common feature of Safer Sex advertising.[16]

Since HIV can be transmitted during pregnancy, birth and breastfeeding, the womb and its fruits overpower representations of the woman, replacing her actual personhood. Increasingly, it is the more respectable womb that gains attention rather than the dangerous vagina. Motherhood is imagined as an innocent, virginal condition, as opposed to sexuality, as if there were no connection between the two. A newspaper advertisement campaign run in February 1990 by the government's National Health Education Authority reproduces the thoughts of two experts. Catherine Peckham, Professor of Paediatric Epidemiology, proclaims: 'As the number of women with HIV increases, this results in more babies being born who are infected. We don't want HIV infection to be a problem in the child population – we must think of the future.' She is followed by the (then) Chief Medical Officer, Sir Donald Acheson, stating, 'It may not seem very serious now but if we don't act it could have a disastrous effect on the future of our children and our grandchildren.' The woman (and her vulnerability to HIV) is a pitstop en route to a more vital population: the innocents, the children.

Women are invisible, or malevolent, players in a discourse which sees the (presumed) needs of children as superior to those of adults. Newspaper article headlines scream, 'Doctors Failing to Prevent AIDS Babies' (because pregnant women are not being tested for HIV) and 'A Million Children in AIDS Nightmare' (which reports that 14 million adults are HIV-infected, but relegates all of them to a clear second priority).[17] Whenever children enter the picture, women are sanitized (and de-humanized) as 'Moms'. In many AIDS policies, women are conceived of as constantly on the verge of conception. This limits the access HIV-positive women have to clinical trials of promising new treatments (no entry without definitive contraception – usually the pill – irrespective of need). It often informs appeals made to women: HIV tests are pushed during pregnancy, and women are inculcated with the fear of HIV transmission to their babies before they are pregnant. The first phrase on one 'Women and AIDS' leaflet is 'Protect Our Species'.[18] It may be necessary to appeal to the needs of future generations, but the denial of current life is startling. It is rare for HIV leaflets aimed at men to even mention the implications for parenting.

In the context of AIDS, the womb overwhelms the woman. This not only reflects a widespread subordination of women to their reproductive organs, but also shows how HIV-positive pregnant women and mothers are depicted as incapable of nurturing. AIDS makes women dangerous to their children – the evil 'queer' woman endangers innocents through her recklessness (of bringing new life to the world). The HIV-infected woman is a menace to embryos, and must be identified and subsequently 'encouraged' to do the right thing (as defined by scientific thinking – currently, take AZT, opt for a Caesarean-section, and don't breastfeed). It is by no means unreasonable to want to protect infants (and embryos) from HIV infection, and most parents are extremely concerned that their offspring should be as healthy as possible. What is alarming is the focus on maternity almost to the exclusion of women's own risk of acquiring HIV, or of the traumas she may experience living with the condition.

The most influential reduction of women to their wombs is not in media representation (where the categories of 'vamp' and 'hopeless victim' are almost as popular), but in the emphasis on antenatal screening for HIV. The antenatal clinic is the only health care setting where women are proactively encouraged to discover if they have antibodies for HIV. While most programmes claim to exist for the woman and her (potential) child, in practice they are clearly concerned with reducing the possibilities of HIV transmission to the foetus or newborn. Indeed, one screening programme calculates that one paediatric infection can be prevented for every 20,000 pregnant women who are offered HIV testing.[19] Whatever the rhetoric, antenatal screening is about infant HIV prevention, not preventing adult women from getting HIV, or even supporting them with access to meaningful information about their HIV status.

There have been no strategic attempts to develop general women-specific services for the prevention of HIV. If the interest was to detect HIV-infected women, a more logical site for voluntary named HIV testing would be abortion clinics, not clinics where women are pursuing their pregnancy. The 1995 anonymous HIV screening programme found (and ignored) that 0.49 per cent of women having terminations in London were HIV-infected, compared to just 0.18 per cent of pregnant women.[20] This is consistent with common sense: as a group, women who terminate a pregnancy may take fewer steps to pre-plan their sexual health. Other studies have shown this same high risk among women who terminate their pregnancies. In France, a comparison of women who took their pregnancy to term with those who aborted found that the women who aborted had double the HIV high risk factors: 38.9 per cent of women who terminated, to 17.7 per cent of the women who gave birth.[21]

Abortion clinics appear to be well-used by women who are at high risk of HIV infection. However, they may be a troubled site for proactive offering of HIV testing, given the emotional vulnerability of the majority of women ending a pregnancy. What, then, about the role of family planning clinics? Even if the principal concern remains the foetus, then testing of women (and men) who use contraception and plan their pregnancies is likely to reduce rates of HIV transmission far more effectively. Testing women for HIV in order to prevent foetuses from becoming infected is surely happening too late if the woman has already conceived and is in touch with antenatal services. At a family planning clinic – a service well used by many women – HIV infection could be determined at an emotionally neutral time of life. The majority of women will test HIV-negative, and this sex-friendly environment could provide an optimal situation to discuss broad sexual health concerns, including strategies to avoid HIV in the future. For the minority who test HIV-positive, appropriate support and advice could enable individuals and couples to have the time and emotional space to make complicated decisions about how to manage any future pregnancy. This scenario – where the locus of interest is the unborn child – may well reduce the rate of HIV transmission to children. It should be apparent that it also works well for most women, i.e. the non-pregnant.

The non-pregnant, and those not intending to conceive in the immediate future, are rarely a focus of HIV prevention and care. Instead, public health officials in most countries have developed recommendations for the (so-called) voluntary testing of pregnant women. A glance at the documentation suggests that in practice these programmes are mandatory in all but name. The US Public Health Service recommends that 'Health care providers should ensure that all pregnant women are *routinely* counselled and *encouraged to be tested* for HIV infection . . . for their own health and for reducing the risk of HIV transmission to their infants and others.'[22] Recalcitrant women who refuse HIV testing will not get away with their decision easily. Health care workers are advised: 'If the mother refuses testing for herself, she should be informed of the importance of knowing her child's infection status for the child's health and encouraged to allow the child to be tested.'[23] How would the worker then react if a woman responded by deciding not to know her HIV status, to bottle feed (just in case she is infected), and then watch her child's health hawkishly during the early years? The constant 'encouragement' seems at odds with a truly voluntary approach.

Although pregnancy is not an illness, there are good reasons for pregnant women to have health checks. It is routine to screen pregnant women for other conditions, notably syphilis, which can be treated so that the infant need not be exposed to infection in the womb, or subject to treatment after delivery. With HIV, there is no effective treatment, nor are there uncontroversial, fully efficient approaches to preventing the child from acquiring the virus. However, there are interventions which have been shown to reduce the rates of HIV transmission from a woman to her child (during pregnancy, childbirth and breastfeeding), and there is a clear hope from HIV-positive women and the scientific communities that a method of blocking HIV transmission will be discovered. When such methods are proven and accessible, it will be important for routine HIV screening to be put in place. But what is the role and meaning of antenatal screening until such a time?

Although she has fewer options than the HIV-positive woman who wants to conceive, the woman who is identified as HIV-positive during her pregnancy will be faced with many choices. It may be particularly hard for her to make such major decisions in the midst of the turmoil of pregnancy and the shock of her diagnosis. Should she terminate the pregnancy? HIV will not be transmitted to the foetus if she does this, but there is also an 86 per cent likelihood that the foetus would remain uninfected anyway. A snap decision to abort solely on the basis of HIV would be ill advised. Several reports show that women who abort under the pressure of a positive HIV diagnosis often go on to conceive again shortly afterwards. Despite most professionals' assumptions that HIV-positive women will terminate their pregnancy, over 90 per cent of women do not, and many choose to conceive again.[24] In the London survey of HIV-positive women, nearly half said that they had been pressured either not to become pregnant or to have an abortion.[25]

Should she have a Caesarean section? Some studies suggest that this may halve the risk, but the data is unclear and women may face other complications with such a major operation. In some areas she may experience difficulties finding a doctor willing to carry out this operation on a woman known to be HIV-infected. Should she breastfeed? Bottlefeeding can halve the risk of transmission, and she will be under strong pressure not to breastfeed. This pressure can cause intense distress, especially for women who perceive major emotional and cultural advantages from this method of feeding.

Probably the most fraught decision for women will be whether to take AZT. In 1994, an American trial known as ACTG 076[26] reported that pregnant women who took AZT pills from the fourteenth week of pregnancy, in infusion during delivery, and gave their babies AZT syrup during the first six weeks of life, reduced the risk of HIV transmission to their babies by two-thirds. This was immediately hailed throughout the medical profession as a major breakthrough – and not only by health care workers and scientitsts concerned with HIV-positive pregnant women. 076 provided additional steam to the heady demands for antenatal HIV screening. It was the first trial to confirm what seemed biologically plausible: if you attack the virus directly you can improve the health of someone with HIV, and also render the person less infectious. This can be described as the TB paradigm: treatment = prevention.

Unfortunately the use of AZT in pregnancy is not straightforward. The trial was statistically significant, but the numbers were low. A total of 53 HIV-infected infants were born (of a total of 421 babies), and 13 of these were born to women following the AZT regimen. The rates of HIV transmission were abnormally high among the women not taking AZT, compared with the usual likelihood of HIV transmission in Europe. Many women are concerned about the potential for AZT-associated toxicities – to the babies born with and without HIV. It is counter-intuitive for women to take drugs during pregnancy when all other advice opposes taking chemicals out of fear for the child: why then take AZT which is known to be toxic? Some have worried that babies could receive strains of HIV that are resistant to AZT (so that the child cannot benefit from future treatment), and this has been reported in at least one study.[27] There is also the major concern that women's future treatment options will be limited by AZT (damaging the babies' lives by reducing their mother's lifespans). All of the promising trials of double and triple combinations of drugs have found a more powerful effect when the adult first receives a cocktail of two or more anti-HIV drugs. Although there are still good results, the effects of the drugs are seriously weakened if an individual has already used one drug alone, especially AZT. The standard guidelines now recommend that treating someone with monotherapy (i.e. just one drug) is suboptimal treatment.[28] The use of double or triple combinations during pregnancy is a highly plausible approach but it has not been trialled. Consequently, doctors revert to traditional warnings against using any medications during pregnancy and will not recommend using these effective therapies. Yet there has been no trial assessing the long-term treatment implications of using AZT monotherapy for five or six months during pregnancy.

A pregnant HIV-positive woman is left to balance various biological possibilities, and her pre-existing perceptions of the merits of the drug. She is likely to receive forceful opinions from her doctor influencing this complex personal decision. In my book I raised the spectre of 'non-compliant' pregnant women being forced to undergo Caesarean sections for other conditions, at the expense of the mother's choice and well-being.[29] In the ensuing twelve months, the passion for antenatal screening and interventions for HIV-infected women has grown. Clinicians with impressive track records of care for HIV-positive women now worry in public that there may be a Child Protection Issue if their 'Moms' don't eat AZT. The doctors motives' are not bad. They are desperately concerned for the well-being of the child – and this can rarely be disentangled from the well-being of the mother. Some report (possibly apocryphal) cases of mothers of HIV-infected babies who assumed that they had been tested in pregnancy, and now say that they would have managed the pregnancy differently had they known they were HIV-positive. After fifteen years of gloomy medical responses to AIDS, with a sense that nothing can be done, doctors may also be over-awed by the possibility that at least this intervention can do something, that they can use medicine to save lives. Strangely, these same doctors have not responded with so much enthusiasm to the trial showing that HIV-positive women will be less likely to transmit the virus to their partners if they are not using hormonal contraception (the pill, or injectables such as Depo Provera).[30]

The encouragement of HIV tests for pregnant women is a curious human rights dilemma. Mandatory HIV testing has been condemned around the world, and is firmly opposed by the World Health Organization. Yet with this adult population, despite no definitive effective interventions to block HIV transmission or to treat the infected, mandatory testing (in all but name) is promoted. The lack of attention to the negative elements of antenatal HIV screening programmes, and of medicalized interventions during pregnancy, reflects the de-humanizing of women. When she is pregnant, the woman is pregnant first, a walking 'bump', before she is ever an adult sexual human being.[31] She is the bearer of the precious innocent, and her wellbeing and health may be willingly sacrificed to reduce the risks of her child acquiring HIV by one or two extra per cent. For the woman who is not on the verge of conception or birth, the situation is as bleak. HIV information and testing is rarely offered until she attains some maternal status.

It is not the case that all adult women are immediately vulnerable to acquiring HIV, nor that all pregnant women need to be tested to protect their foetuses. Yet without a feminist analysis those women who are at risk of HIV will be unlikely to be targeted by HIV prevention initiatives, women living with HIV are unlikely to be offered appropriate support, and women in general will receive inaccurate and misplaced AIDS information. Even where they are in the minority of HIV cases, many women are profoundly affected by the AIDS epidemic. In the absence of an evolving feminist analysis and practice in the fight against AIDS, women with and without HIV infection – and especially those at greatest risk of becoming infected – cannot receive the attention and focus they deserve. The response to AIDS will be enhanced by a feminist view, and feminism in its turn has much to learn from activism responding to the complexities of AIDS.

notes

1. A further 258 are awaiting confirmation of their HIV status. All infants born to HIV-infected women have their *mother's* HIV antibodies, so that an antibody test on a newborn will only detect maternal HIV status. It may take up to eighteen months for the child to develop its own immune system, when the HIV antibody test can detect whether the child has developed antibodies to its own virus. Increasingly, specialist centres are able to test for the virus itself, which provides a mechanism for slipping beneath the masking effect of maternal antibodies.
2. Statistics based upon PHLS AIDS Centre – Communicable Disease

Surveillance Centre, and Scottish Centre for Infection and Environmental Health. Unpublished Quarterly Surveillance Tables No. 32 June 1996, Tables 1, 17, 18, 19.

3. *Women Like Us*, Positively Women, London, 1994.
4. E. Rubery et al., *Unlinked Anonymous HIV Prevalence Monitoring Programme in England and Wales*. Department of Health, London, January 1995.

   The most referenced data on HIV infection in women is based on samples gathered during pregnancy, because pregnant women are such an easy access population, who are giving blood anyway. The women in this screening programme are not informed of their test results; these can only be given with named HIV testing programmes, described below.

   It may be that a significant proportion of the eighty-eight per cent do know that they are HIV-positive but have not reported this fact to their health care providers – perhaps out of fear of being treated differently. Even if this is the case, it still appears that the majority of HIV-infected pregnant women do not know that they have the virus.
5. PHLS AIDS Centre, Table 27, op cit.
6. For example, L. Segal, 'Lessons from the Past' in E. Carter & S. Watney '*Taking Liberties*', Serpent's Tail, London, 1989; S. O'Sullivan, 'What do you think about AIDS', *Spare Rib*, London, February 1987.
7. The critical text chronicling these debates is C. S. Vance (*ed*), *Pleasure and Danger: Exploring Female Sexuality*, London, Pandora, 1992. The implications of these debates for HIV prevention are discussed in R. Gorna, *Vamps, Virgins and Victims: How Can Women Fight AIDS?*, London, Cassell, 1996, pp. 260–93.
8. S. Jeffreys, *Lesbian Heresy*, Women's Press, London, 1994. op. cit.
9. I explore some of the implications of this imbalance in R. Gorna, op. cit. pp.337–81.
10. See, for example, studies cited in R. Gorna, ibid., pp.327–31.
11. ibid., pp.264–72.
12. Professor Anke Ehrhardt, 'Gender Risk Behavior Intervention Programs for Women', plenary talk at 'AIDS' Impact: the second International Conference on the Biopsychosocial Aspect of HIV Infection, Brighton, 8 July 1994. See R. Gorna, ibid., pp.45–7, 221–23
13. The Terrence Higgins Trust Health Promotion Strategy – which I developed – defines one of the key vulnerable groups as 'Women who may have male sexual partners from one of the core groups' (the core groups being: people living with HIV and AIDS, gay men, bisexual men, people from high prevalence areas in particular sub-Saharan Africa).
14. 'My name is Denise . . . I'm HIV positive', *Cosmopolitan*, January 1991,

p.68f; cited in R. Gorna, op cit, p.11; pp.1–71 provides a full review of how women are used to mediate the normality and queerness of the epidemic. I am not suggesting that Denise's story is unimportant. It is, of course, critical for women's words to be heard, yet this tale is all too familiar and sustains a biased minority view of HIV-positive women.

15. Some will notice that she also has a clitoris, but it is rare to find any mention of the clitoris in safer sex materials for women.

16. In 1988 the HEA produced a newspaper advertisement spread across two pages which demonstrated how HIV is an invisible virus. The image showed a stylish attractive woman, suggesting she was a dangerous fuck because men wouldn't be able to read that she was HIV-infected. See R. Gorna, op cit., pp.61f.

17. *The Times*, 14 May 1993; *Mail on Sunday*, 16 January 1994.

18. Highland AIDS Resource Centre, Scotland, 1991.

19. Dr Frank Johnstone, personal communication.

20. E. Rubery et al., op cit.

21. D. Rey et al., *Differences in HIV testing, knowledge and attitudes in pregnant women who deliver and those who terminate: Prevagest 1992 – France, AIDS Care*, 1995, Vol 7, Supplement 1, pp.S39–46.

22. *US Public Health Service Recommendations for HIV Counselling and Testing for Pregnant Women*, Draft, p.9, 23 February 1995.

23. ibid. p.10.

24. See L. Sherr, *HIV and AIDS in Mothers and Babies*, Oxford, Blackwell Scientific Publications, 1991; A. Sunderland et al., 'The Impact of HIV serostatus on reproductive decisions of women', *Obstetrics and Gynecology*, Vol. 79, No. 6, June 1992, pp.1027–31.

25. *Women Like Us*, Positively Women, pp.22f.

26. E.M. Conner et al., 'Reduction of maternal-infant transmission of human immunodeficiency virus type 1 with zidovudine treatment', *New England Journal of Medicine*, 1994, 331, pp.1173–80.

27. At the International AIDS Conference in Vancouver, a small study by Anthony Japour found that a third of HIV-infected infants, whose mothers followed the 076 protocol, had AZT-resistant virus. Abstract Tu.C.2606.

28. BHIVA anitiviral treatment guidelines in press, TAT Standard of Care, October 1996.

29. Based on (non HIV-related) reports in S. Faludi, *Backlash*, London, Vintage, 1991, p.463–91.

30. S. Mostad, Abstract We.C.333, Vancouver International AIDS Conference, R. Gorna, reported in *AIDS Care*, Volume 9, Number 1, February 1997.

31. At a recent pan-London consensus meeting on antenatal HIV screening, no one would discuss a proposal that women testing HIV-negative should be encouraged to consider ongoing risk and to use condoms if their partner's status is unknown and he is at high HIV risk. Debbie Vowles, personal communication.

AIDS education for democratic citizenship

Jonathan G. Silin

Young children's questions call to us from across the years. We are moved by their naiveté and by their profundity: If someone has AIDS and someone gives them soup, will they still have AIDS? Can you die from AIDS? Why did they invent drugs, beer, and cigarettes when everybody knows they're dangerous? These questions emerged during conversations with seven-year-olds in East Harlem, an American community especially hard hit by HIV.[1] They express hope in a simple cure for physical illness and concern for the health of the social body. They also reflect a range of children's thinking from an immediate, practical search for solutions to more abstract, philosophical reflection on the meaning of human behaviour. Children's questions ask us as caring adults to take responsibility for a world we neither have made nor approve of.

From the beginning of the AIDS pandemic educators have been more likely to offer quick answers to teenagers than listen to the difficult questions of young children. In this essay I argue that it is as important to attend to the queries of pre-adolescents as to the specific prevention needs of their older siblings. Then, when the press for risk reduction becomes more immediate, they will be better able to use the language of AIDS, knowledgeable about its structure and content.

Despite what many prefer to think, children already know

about HIV/AIDS. They were born into a world where the disease is well into its second decade. Even if a vaccine is developed tomorrow, they will never have known a world without AIDS. In New York City, where I work, 70,000 children will lose one or both parents to AIDS during the next few years. Tens of thousands of others have a close relative or friend who is HIV-positive. Worldwide, of the 8,500 new infections each day, 1,000 are children whose brothers and sisters, cousins and playmates, will soon learn of their illness.

Other essays in this volume deal with the challenges posed by HIV prevention in the media, public spaces, and venues where specific population – gay/bisexual men, injection drug users, sex workers – congregate. Time is of the essence in these situations, a few images often forced to carry more meanings than they can adequately sustain. In classrooms discussions take place over many months, within an ongoing student-teacher relationship and among peers who have shared interests and questions. The possibility of offering multiple representations and sustained investigations permits a complexity that belies the simplistic reductions of fifteen-second television commercials, billboards caught out of the corner of the eye, pamphlets and educational comic books perused in clinic waiting rooms.

Talking about HIV/AIDS in schools has its own challenges including legislation that prohibits the 'promotion' of homosexuality, distribution of condoms, or sex education that goes beyond pregnancy prevention through abstinence. Even as social conservatives seek to narrow the curriculum to academic skills, social critics such as Michel Foucault suggest the subtle forms of surveillance and control that occur when a broader curriculum is permitted. With respect to children, these challenges are augmented through literary and popular images of childhood innocence. Unfortunately, innocence is inevitably linked to ignorance, affirming a desire not to know what children may already have learned on the street, from peers, or through the media. These assumptions about children have been sustained by the science of child development that affirms children's inability to understand complex social issues.

Schools offer unique opportunities to do HIV/AIDS education. We cannot afford to surrender them to conservative social forces, scientifically rationalized beliefs about childhood innocence or our own desires to protect children from the world in which they live. Nor can we afford to limit ourselves to narrow forms of HIV prevention that focus on changing or sustaining particular behaviours. For AIDS education more broadly conceived promotes exploration of stereotypes and biases, fosters compassion for people in need, and examines how social and political institutions shape the epidemic.

I do not minimize the struggles faced by activists and community-based educators. Nevertheless, I want to clarify and expand what we seek to achieve through our work. My aim is to place the battle for better school-based HIV/AIDS education within the context of ongoing discussions within the field of education and to relate it to other issues presently excluded from classrooms. This is to assert both an epistemological position about the connected ways that children experience their worlds and a political strategy for linking AIDS advocates to school reform movements.

Conceptions of childhood have changed over time, differ among cultures and are marked by gender, class, race, geography, ethnicity, and religion. Although this essay reflects my work in a variety of American schools, it draws heavily on what I have learned about inner city neighbourhoods where HIV is primarily transmitted through injection drug use and where the long-term effects of racism and poverty make survival precarious for young children. It also reflects my experiences as an early childhood educator, community-based AIDS educator and gay man enduring the long years of loss and anger that have become an inevitable part of our life in the last decade of the twentieth century.

the curriculum in place

Even while a vocal minority committed to conserving an idealized past tries to limit the role of the school, the majority are asking it to address an increasingly broad social agenda. In a world that offers fewer and fewer support systems for children, parents turn toward the school to find assistance in meeting the hurdles of contemporary life. Schools often manage the pressure to do more and to do it better by reducing complex subjects such as HIV/AIDS or human sexuality to simplified fragments of information. Such management strategies function to police acceptable topics of study and mask social inequities. Teaching methods that focus on measurable, behavioural outcomes define children as 'learners', the sum of their intellectual capacities. Alternatively, children might be viewed as multi-faceted human beings whose socio-emotional growth and participation in community life are as highly valued as their cognitive achievements. Education might then be understood to foster activist citizens with the ethical and political determination to create a more just society.

In America, although AIDS education is mandated in the majority of states, compliance is irregular. This is especially true with respect to the early grades where prejudices about what children can understand predominate and HIV/AIDS is often submerged in generalized health promotion curricula. In the New York City Public School's *HIV/AIDS Curriculum*, for example, learning objectives for five to eight-year-olds include differences between infectious and non-infectious diseases, the availability of community resources for information, help and counselling, the practice of good health habits. Lessons for ten to twelve-year-olds include explicit information about transmission and prevention. A special note at the beginning of the curriculum informs teachers that abstinence must be stressed and given 'substantially more time' than other modes of prevention.

There are two assumptions supporting this and many other curriculum materials that bear careful scrutiny. The first is that children's minds are compartmentalized and able to deal with HIV/AIDS information in a logical, sequential order. Formal lesson plans assume, for example, that children can discuss how HIV is *not* transmitted while holding in abeyance for several lessons and/or years how it *is* transmitted – and how to prevent its spread. Little attempt is made to assess what knowledge children come to school with or the kinds of questions their personal experiences may have generated. The child is read as a tabula rasa with respect to HIV/AIDS. It seems only fair to ask for the voices of the children in the curriculum. But who is listening? Who has the time?

Although there are few formal studies of children's knowledge, I have heard the uncensored comments and watched the play of children who know about HIV/AIDS: a seven-year-old who worried aloud if the illness of the classroom rabbit was caused by HIV; the five-year-old whose toy ambulance was speeding to a hospital carrying someone suffering from AIDS; a six-year-old warning a classmate not to pick up a stick in the park because injection drug users go there at night and the stick might carry HIV; eight-year-olds using AIDS as the label of choice when they wanted to ostracize someone on the playground at recess.

HIV is part of daily life and should be treated as such in schools. Failing to talk with young children about AIDS engenders the belief that it is a mystery, a taboo subject that teachers cannot or will not address. Successful prevention requires greater familiarity with the disease, not increased fear. Fear leads to paralysis and hysteria; familiarity can be the basis of reasoned responses. Such familiarity demands an examination of the ways that social stereotypes function to distance us from others. Stereotypes stigmatize some even as they perpetuate risky myths that can affect anyone – only self-identified gay men have sex with men, only homosexual men engage in anal intercourse, only the poor use injection drugs, all people with HIV appear sick.

To be meaningful HIV/AIDS information shouldn't be held for the science lessons at age ten or health class at age twelve when it may be removed from students' immediate questions. Nor can adults avoid their own complicity in discrimination by permitting children to use AIDS, if only in their games, as a means to exclude someone from the social arena. Like gender, race, sexual orientation, and disability, AIDS must be treated as an issue of equity in schools.

Nevertheless, the second assumption of many curricula is that HIV/AIDS is a phenomenon to be located within the confines of the health curriculum. But diseases are constituted through dynamic interactions of biomedical, economic, psychosocial, and political factors. Understanding the meanings of any illness involves far more than identifying a causal agent and a medical remedy. From this perspective HIV/AIDS lends itself as a subject for current events and social studies classes. HIV/AIDS raises provocative questions about access to prevention education, health care and new drug therapies for many people across the globe, the ethics of confidentiality, and the conduct of scientific research. There is a growing body of novels, plays, and poetry emerging in response to this disease, and they provide opportunities to introduce HIV/AIDS into humanities classes. An increasing number of story books for younger children have appeared and more and more artists, musicians, and dancers are addressing HIV/AIDS in their work. The curriculum should include the richness of all these imaginative reconstructions as they offer alternative routes to understanding the disease.

In effect, children would be best served if the assumptions underlying the curriculum in place were inverted. First, rather than creating elaborate instructional guides based on a logical sequence of facts, it would be more effective to ground the curriculum in the issues that children themselves find problematic. Second, our very definition of the disease needs to be re-examined in such a way as to permit its multiple ramifications to emerge across the disciplines. This is not to deny the importance of explicit prevention messages but to underscore the less visible interconnectedness of our social institutions.

listening to young children

Like psychologists and activists seeking to prevent HIV infection in gay men, adults working with children often have difficulty facing their clients' real lives. This reluctance was evident to me when the director of Project Healthy Choices talked to my college faculty meeting about her work. The most affecting parts of this talk were the words and pictures of the seven-year-olds themselves. A picture of two boys, two massive trees and a football, bears the following inscription across the top, 'He haves AIDS. We play together. I am his friend.' Initially the artist had written 'We have AIDS' but later crossed out the 'We' and substituted 'He'. In classrooms where four and five children may have lost a close relative to the disease, such an error is understandable.

But HIV is not the only or most immediate threat to survival that these inner city children face. Their drawings provide a sense of the larger context in which our AIDS education efforts sometimes take place and remind us that our conversations must reflect the real experiences and concerns of children. For example, seeking to grasp the connections among more visible forms of violence and the less obvious but equally devastating effects of drugs and alcohol, another child draws two stick figures pointing huge guns at one another. The figures are small in comparison to the space, and across the top two-thirds of the page, the teacher has recorded these words:

> Drugs are terrible. Guns are bad things. Drugs are weapons. Smoking is not good for your lungs. Guns and smoke are the same thing like killing someone. They are the same like drinking beer. Someone drinks and they kill themselves one day. People drink so much when they are very disappointed.

The most unsettling picture contains no words. The upper two thirds of the paper is covered by a sky drawn with large blue marker strokes and dotted with four simple inverted-V-shaped birds. In the upper left-hand corner a large, bright yellow sun has its nose, eyes, and mouth drawn in black. The lower third of the page contains rolling green hills and two trees on either side. Scattered across the ground is a mix of objects, including clearly identifiable syringes and beer cans. The child describes the scene with the following words:

> This is the sun wearing sunglasses, and the sun is trying not to see the drugs. These are all beer can and drugs and dead birds dying, and the grass is dying and the sun is dying and trying to keep everything alive, and the trees are dying and the leave are falling down and dying.

Although each of these pictures is subject to many interpretations, it was the awed silence among the adults that drew my attention at our faculty meeting. Finally one dismayed person exclaimed, 'Is there no joy in these children's lives?' I don't know the answer to this question nor the best response to my colleague's evident despair. I do know that if we turn away from the children's painful and confusing experiences, then we turn away from the possibility of relief as well. Classrooms are places in which children should feel comfortable exploring a full range of emotions including authentic moments of distress and pleasure. We are fully engaged as learners only when the curriculum is responsive to the material contexts of our lives. It is through such engagement that we realize our freedom and our humanity.

To accept that children live in a world where they come to learn about HIV/AIDS, drugs, and community violence at a far earlier age than most of us would prefer does not mean we are participating in the denial of childhood. But it does mean we need to create classrooms in which children can feel safe to examine these issues. And it does mean that adults will have to take responsibility for the changing nature of childhood – from the growth of electronic information sources, parental pressure for achievement and the increasing isolation of children in age-segregated institutions, to the pervasive violence in young people's lives.[2]

To support the difficult kind of listening required of adults in schools, community-based AIDS educators and activists will have to work collaboratively with progressive early childhood educators who are questioning the traditional reliance on child development as the basis of curriculum planning. Stage theories of development emphasize the differences rather than commonalities between children and adults, causing us to underestimate children's knowledge of their social worlds and overestimate our ability to protect them.[3] Given the stressful lives of contemporary children, it is important to recognize their competencies and resiliency as well as their developmental vulnerabilities and deficiencies. Like the American psychiatrist Robert Coles, we need to listen to the moral energy coursing through the stories of children living in poverty, as they question and reflect upon their experiences. These stories can tell us how children resist despair, claim dignity in dehumanizing situations, and create redemptive moments out of sorrow.

Preparing classroom teachers to integrate HIV/AIDS into the curriculum is a complex process. Although some teachers first come to learn about the disease in the context of their professional lives, they quickly recognize that it will soon seep into conversations with their own children, affect attitudes toward friends and family, and change lifelong behaviours. It may even challenge their sense of safety in the workplace. Because of these personal concerns and because HIV/AIDS moves previously silenced subjects such as sex and death into classrooms, schools must allot sufficient time for staff development. Teachers who have placed other equity issues high on their own agendas will have less difficulty integrating HIV/AIDS into the ongoing curriculum. For these teachers have already created environments in which human differences are discussed and valued.

HIV/AIDS education for democratic citizenship

At first sight school-based AIDS education for children appears to be very different from community-based HIV prevention for adults. A map of health education including individual behavioural change, self-empowerment, and collective action models allows us to see the similarities. Although early safer sex organizing was an innovative, grass roots process, many of the first large-scale prevention programmes in the gay community – the '800 Men Project' sponsored by New York City's Gay Men's Health Crisis in 1985 or the STOP AIDS Project begun in San Francisco during the early years of the epidemic – were based on individual behaviour change or self-empowerment models. Like school curricula relying on direct instruction or preprogrammed exercises, they assumed that increased information about HIV transmission, or the practice of specific skills, would result in a decrease of high risk behaviours. But the narrow, fragmented focus of information and skill-based programmes ignores the integrated ways that adults experience the world. Nor do they recognize the multiple, overlapping and at times conflicting social identities that inform our actions. HIV/AIDS prevention programmes send a conservative political message when they fail to address the socially constructed nature of the epidemic and need for social action.

For children, the more popular, skill-based approaches are built on the understanding that the lack of a positive self-image is the biggest factor preventing healthy decisions. In the United States, nationally distributed curricula such as 'Project Charlie' and 'Growing Healthy' are being described as panaceas to a wide variety of problems including high school dropout rates, lowered academic performance, widespread alcohol and substance abuse and teenage pregnancy. As in similar programmes designed to improve adult productivity in the workplace, the focus on changes in self-perception and interpersonal skills masks material barriers to real equity and autonomy. Self-esteem has become a popular buzz word for efforts to promote better psychological adjustment to the political status quo.

But as progressive educators from John Dewey to Paulo Freire have long asserted, students learn most effectively when in the midst of meaningful activities. A curriculum that attempts, in a few brief lessons, to teach students how to make critical decisions cannot make up for years of education that have denied them the right to become autonomous, self-determining learners. Friday afternoon 'magic circles' to build self-esteem or Monday morning rehearsals of refusal skills divert our attention from the realities of contemporary children who too seldom have the opportunity to make meaningful choices, follow through on them, and reflect on their consequences.

Both individual behaviour change and self-empowerment models are based on the instrumentalist assumption that behaviour can be isolated, analyzed and understood apart from the socio-economic context in which it occurs. In contrast to 'self-empowerment' models that are limited to quasi-therapeutic strategies to foster self-insight and communication, the collective action model also directs participants to critical assessment of the larger society. Including the need for information and communicative skills, the collective action approach encourages organizing to transform the social institutions that inform individual behaviour.[4] Preventing the transmission of HIV involves not only learning about condoms and negotiating safer sex; it also means developing tools of political analysis, a commitment to social change, and an ethic of caring and responsibility. Shifting our attention from HIV prevention narrowly defined as a means of behavioural control to AIDS education with a broader focus that reflects children's real lives involves three strategies.

First, AIDS education needs to begin with the youngest children and permeate the curriculum in order to break down the taboos with which it is associated and to make the subject a more comfortable one for discussion. Second, our schools should provide safe spaces where children can tell all the stories that make their worlds meaningful. Isak Dinesen wisely reminds us, 'All sorrows can be borne if you put them into a story, or tell a story about them.' Listening to these stories, we can confirm for children the important connections between their lives outside school and the work that takes place within its walls. Academic skills are tools that enable children to deepen and extend their understanding of the things that matter to them – the births and deaths of family members, the comings and going of significant people, the decay and reconstruction of local communities. The classroom can be a workshop in which children learn to recreate their experiences in words and pictures, dance and drama.

Third, as children tell about their worlds, we must also create opportunities for them to respond actively to the discomforting as well as the familiar. There is something to be learned, after all, from the neighbourhood clinic that tends to the needs of HIV-positive children, from the shelter on the corner that feeds and houses the homeless, and from the community organization down the block fighting substance abuse. There are also learning opportunities – professionals to be interviewed, letters to be written to those who determine policy, even immediate gestures of caring to be made. When children learn to make an impact on their environment, no matter how small, they begin to recognize themselves as agents of change. In addition to sophisticated science and advanced technology, prevention of diseases like HIV/AIDS requires the determination of informed citizens ready to resist all forms of social injustice.

Just as effective sexuality education is based on an entire school experience that encourages decision-making, problem-solving, and self-worth, successful HIV/AIDS education is built on a continuing appreciation of equity and pluralism in society. Educators must take an active role in bringing the full spectrum of human difference to the classroom, acknowledging the ways that these have become sources of conflict and domination as well as the ways that they enrich and form the basis of participatory democracy.

The history of HIV teaches us about the power and creativity that reside in a collective response to social problems as well as about individual pain and suffering. The lessons also tell about the limits of science and the importance of human vision, the frailty of the body and the strength of the spirit, the need to nurture the imagination even as we build our powers of rational analysis. Finally, the AIDS curriculum may be more about life than about death, more about health than about illness, more about the body politic than the body physical.

notes

1. These questions and the drawings described further on come from the work of Project Healthy Choices reported in *Stories from East Harlem*, New York, Bank Street College of Education, 1995. All the themes outlined in this essay receive extended treatment in Jonathan G. Silin, *Sex, Death and the Education of Children: Our Passion for Ignorance in the Age of AIDS*, New York, Teachers College Press, 1995.
2. See Allison James and James Prout, eds, *Constructing and Reconstructing Childhood*, London, The Falmer Press, 1992; Martin Woodhead, Paul Light, Ronnie Carr (eds), *Growing up in a Changing Society*, London, Routledge, 1991.
3. On the limits of developmental theory see Maurice Merleau-Ponty, *The Primacy of Perception*, Evanston, IL: Northwestern University Press, 1964; J. Henriquez, W. Hollway, C. Urwin, V. Walkerdine, *Changing the Subject: Psychology, Social Regulation and Subjectivity*, New York, Methuen, 1984; Elly Singer, *Child-care and the Psychology of Development*, London, Routledge, 1992. On changes in early childhood education see Shirley Kessler and Beth Swadener, *Reconceptualizing the Early Childhood Curriculum*, New York, Teachers College Press, 1992.
4. See Hilary Homans and Peter Aggleton, 'Health Education, HIV Infection and AIDS', in P. Aggleton, H. Homans (eds), *Social Aspects of AIDS*, London, The Falmer Press, 1988. For programs reflective of this approach see Kathy Boudin, 'Participatory Literacy Education Behind Bars: AIDS Opens the Doors.' *Harvard Educational Review*, *63* (2), 207–232 1993; Kevin Cranston, 'HIV Education for Gay, Lesbian, and Bisexual Youth: Personal Risk, Personal Power and The Community of Conscience' in K. Karbeck (ed), *Coming Out of the Classroom Closet*, New York, Haworth, 1992; H. Gasch, M. Poulson, R. Fullilove, M. Fullilove, 'Shaping AIDS Education and Prevention Programs for African Americans Amidst Community Decline', *Journal of Negro Education*, *60* (1), 85–96, 1991.

diaspora and globalization

African communities living with HIV in Britain

inequality and injustice

Dorothy Mukasa

> Groups whose language, religion, customs, family structures and so on are most different from the white majority norm will experience the most disadvantage and exclusion
>
> Tariq Modood[1]

introduction

Africa is a continent of fifty countries, and within each country exist numerous tribes, cultures, traditions, languages and histories. According to the 1991 census, 212,000 people living in Britain describe themselves as being of African origin.[2] The vast majority of these are well established and assimilated into the British way of life, having lived in Britain for one, two or more generations. However, there is an identifiable group of African communities, centred within the four Thames regions of London particularly, who have lived in Britain less than fifteen years. These include refugees, asylum seekers, visitors and students.[3] They have an extremely high prevalence of HIV infection and they are my focus.

Over the last ten years, the experience of Africans living with HIV/AIDS in Britain is that of a gradual reduction in overt discrimination as more covert, in the main institutional, discrimination and injustice have become apparent.

Africans most highly affected by HIV are often those who have been in Britain less than ten to fifteen years, coming from African countries with high rates of heterosexual HIV infection. A recent study of twelve HIV/GUM (genito urinary medicine) clinics in London found that the five most affected African communities were originally from Uganda (54 per cent), Zambia (10 per cent), Zimbabwe (6 per cent), Zaire (5 per cent) and Kenya (4 per cent).[4] The January 1996 Communicable Diseases Report (Public Health Laboratory Service) states that 'Most HIV infections and AIDS cases due to heterosexual exposure are thought to have been acquired abroad, usually in a country where sexual intercourse between men and women is the major route of HIV transmission.'[5]

African communities affected by HIV often have unresolved immigration issues and a lack of clarity about what health and social services they are entitled to, living in London's densely populated inner city areas. Many have applied for refugee or political asylum status and are usually affected by anxiety (often due to family separation in the haste to leave their country of origin), stress and depression. There are often language and literacy problems and, typical of newly arrived communities, they are suspicious of the majority white population generally. Others may be highly qualified but unable to find employment in keeping with their training.[6] This group of African communities is disproportionately affected by poverty, deprivation, unemployment and bad housing. Their barriers to accessing health and social services need to be highlighted and contrasted against the needs of other population groups (gay men, injecting drug users) also highly affected by HIV in Britain.

insensitivity and inequality – the obligatory HIV test

Insensitivity and lack of respect for people's culture, language, beliefs and lifestyle is as effective a barrier to service access as overt racial discrimination. Many families affected by HIV do not have English as a first or second language. Many Africans have French as a second or third language. The problems of literal translation from one language to another are well documented; much is often lost in interpretation, people will have a different meaning for the same word. The persistent lack of professional interpretation and translation facilities raises grave doubts about establishment commitment to equal access to statutory sector services by people whose first language is not English. Gross injustices have occurred because of the lack of translation services for Africans in Britain. African community organizations need to be invested in and trained to meet this need. Unfortunately, however, health commissioners give low priority to applications for funding submitted by African community organizations seeking to increase access to health services and to train community members as qualified counsellors, able to deal with issues of culture and language.

Pregnant African women have suffered at the hands of medical professionals over many years, with many being coerced or manipulated into taking HIV tests without their full consent, or with consent based on inadequate information.[7] The need to protect the foetus from avoidable infection from its mother is undeniable – and indeed there may be only a limited time within which infection avoidance procedures can be taken. However, there is an overriding issue of human rights for women to understand and consent to what is being done to their bodies in hospitals, and why.

Anecdotal reports in East London state that many women do not understand the difference between named and anonymous sero-surveys, thinking that they would in fact be told of an HIV positive test result when participating in anonymous sero-surveys. As dictated by institutional good practice, all these women are given a full and frank discussion by qualified (mainly white, middle class) counsellors before the HIV test takes place.[8] Why is it then that so many African women are not made to understand that some blood tests are in fact for the benefit of public health monitoring, rather than for the benefit of the expectant mother?

Health care professionals in hospitals are very keen to test the blood of African patients, the excuse often being that they are trying to eliminate the possibility of HIV infection from their investigations. However, lip service is paid to the need for appropriate or adequate counselling for people who test HIV-positive. This is a major community concern. Culturally appropriate counselling is especially important if English is a second or third language for patients who also come from a different culture. African patients need an objective counsellor who has a clear idea of the cultural and social implications of an HIV-positive test result, in order to help people adopt appropriate ways of living positively with the virus. The counsellor should have some understanding or empathy with the impact of the illness on the immediate and extended family, clan, tribe and society in Britain.

On top of the major stresses of beginning a new life in a foreign land, an HIV-positive test can be the straw that breaks the camel's back. Thus inadequate or inappropriate counselling can have severe consequences. It has certainly led to much family break-up, especially amongst discordant couples and within that group, where the man is HIV-negative and the woman HIV-positive. Following an HIV-positive test result many families isolate themselves from friends, family and support networks, seeking services only at times of complete crisis.

Bad counselling has also led to many deaths and killings within families – suicide, attempted killing of the whole family, or slaughter of the partner blamed for bringing the virus into the family. Given the severe trauma precipitated by an HIV-positive diagnosis, to many Africans in Britain the diagnosis can often seem of more benefit and relevance to the health care professional (who now does not have to carry out further primary investigation tests) than to have any positive health outcome for the patient and his/her family.

counselling in times of loss

Certain African communities are currently disproportionately affected by multiple bereavement, and communities understandably feel besieged by enormous problems. Appropriate counselling remains unavailable to most families. Many African men have lost wives to HIV or AIDS, and now find themselves in the role of primary carer of several small children, and thus require support to develop parenting skills. They need information and guidance to help access health and social services for themselves and for their children. Rarely, however, is this help available.

Many African children from families affected by HIV develop behavioural, psychological and mental health problems as a result of multiple bereavement in the family. All this creates and further feeds into the cycle of deprivation. More culturally appropriate professional help is needed for children.

'tell the children'

Many parents are put under great pressure by professionals to inform their children of the parent's HIV status, or indeed the child's own HIV status. Women especially regularly complain that once children have been told, these same professionals are not there to support the child's new emotional needs and insecurities about the future. One mother and her daughter went through a traumatic time, after her daughter was told of her (mother's) HIV status. The little girl did not want her mother out of her sight, refused to go to school in case Mama died whilst she was away. The child began to sleep in her mother's bed and regularly awoke at night to open her mother's eyelids to see whether she was still alive.

Once children have been told of HIV in the family, parents spend the rest of their lives wondering whether the children have inappropriately shared this information with others in the school playground or amongst neighbours. When this has occurred it has often led to harassment and ostracization and a need for re-housing, creating even more turmoil for the family.

Health and social care professionals often talk about the rights of children, but do not also address the parent's right to be in control, the parent's need to cope at a difficult time. Acknowledging and respecting these needs and rights is particularly important for recent immigrants who are trying to understand the new 'system', language and culture around them.

African cultures, British laws: the individual vs. the family and the community[9]

People in many ethnic minority communities, in Britain and in Africa, do not see themselves as individuals in any autonomous sense. Rather they see themselves as part of their communities, identifying with their tribe, clan, elders, extended family and prioritizing the needs of the community and extended family over individual personal needs. Understood in these terms, HIV frequently affects, not the individual in isolation, but that individual as they interrelate with their extended family and their community.

Health and Social Services in Britain tend to address the individual, and encourage individual decision-making, which can have unfortunate repercussions. This is particularly evident in times of long-term illness, death and planning for the care of children in families affected by HIV. The matrilineal system (as found in parts of Ghana) is better suited to British family laws and the rights of women to bring up their children and determine their future. In patrilineal communities, however, the mother of the children has little cultural right to plan for their future. It is only the children's father's side that can make plans. Many times this has been ignored by social workers, and on the death of the mother, child care plans she was persuaded to make crumble, as the patrilineal system takes over. Decisions about the most appropriate relative(s) to take on primary responsibility for the children of the deceased family member are made within the paternal family and depend on issues such as seniority, financial and social ability, other family responsibilities, strategic place in the family tree, etc. Extended family relatives have been known to arrive, often from abroad, to take on their traditional responsibilities and ensure the children return to the 'web' of the extended family.

non-Western naming and identity systems[10]

There is a need for a better understanding of non-Western naming systems by health care professionals and social workers. The idea of a family name that is inherited by all members of a 'nuclear' family is a very Western concept. In many parts of Africa one is given a clan name, to be used as a second name. These clan names form people's true second names. Women do not lose their clan names on marriage. The children, husband and wife will all have different second names, recognized by tribe and clan. In some parts of Ethiopia a child takes their father's first name as a second name. In some parts of Ghana, the matrilineal system requires that a child takes his or her mother's maiden name.

Family naming systems have been the source of confusion for many British social workers, who on the death of parents have doubted relatives of children because 'their surnames are not the same'. Africans forced to adopt the Western style naming system end up with two identities, one recognized by their community members and the other for the convenience of Western bureaucracy. This has led some Africans to be double counted in statistics and other monitoring exercises and people have been accused of using false names. These experiences are true of other non-Western cultures living in the West, like some traditional Chinese naming systems.

the extended family system[11]

The African extended family system often puts different emphasis on relationships and certain distinctions between close relatives are discouraged. In many African cultures no distinction is made between a sister and a female cousin or a brother and a male cousin. Both one's father and one's father's brother would be referred to as 'father', and the mother and all her sisters would be referred to as 'mother' (not aunt). Keeping close relatives undifferentiated in several African cultures is seen as a sign of a good upbringing.

However, there are interpretation and cultural difficulties in dealing with social and health workers in Britain, when one refers to two mothers, or three fathers. These simple confusions can become serious disagreements when clients insist, quite justifiably, that a child's 'other fathers' or 'other mothers' have culturally equal rights and responsibilities to the biological parent in bringing that child up. Indeed the combination of African naming systems with little differentiation between close relatives leaves many social workers daunted about working with African families affected by HIV. This has led to social workers being less effective about having adequate child care plans for children when parents become increasingly ill.

The Children Act 1989[12]

The Children Act 1989 makes clear that children are best brought up within their own families, steeped in their own cultures, practising their own religions, speaking their own languages. Yet when African parents die of HIV/AIDS few have appropriate child care plans for their children, despite a one or two-year involvement with a social worker. This situation means that African children (without swift intervention from the extended family) often end up in Local Authority care unnecessarily – being fostered, adopted or being placed in residential homes. Urgent investment is needed to train more African social workers to prevent such situations.

Long-term illness, death and bereavement, for African families are often the times when the extended family structure is most badly missed. Informal carers are coping with extremely heavy demands, and inevitably, with no support and supervision, are quickly burning out. Recently-arrived Africans have had to come to grips with the culture shock of the hospice, respite and palliative care. Hospice practices such as the 'withdrawal of food' (stopping a patient's supply of food or liquids) in anticipation of death have left many culturally numbed at a difficult time. In many African cultures, carer behaviour in anticipation of death is very different. Carers do not succumb to the inevitability of death, and it is appropriate behaviour to feed and give liquids to the sick until they die. '*Asiika obulamu tassa mukono*' (Luganda) – one does not rest in the fight to avert death. Unfortunately, hospice practices generally go unexplained to African patients, leaving both patients and their families angry and confused at a most difficult time.

Another great concern for African communities affected by terminal illness is the lack of (establishment) understanding of the cultural importance of issues related to the circumstances of death, bereavement rituals, disposal of the body in the UK or repatriation to the country of origin. Cremation is alien in the majority of African cultures. The mechanics of the extended family system are such that one's life and death are a matter of concern for many in the family tree. It is not only honourable for one to be buried in one's ancestral burial ground, but one's life story is incomplete if one is not – the final chapter is left unfinished. One may become an unhappy and 'wandering spirit' if one is abandoned in a foreign land. If a body (from the family tree) is missing from the ancestral burial ground, this may bar certain traditional and religious ceremonies requiring the blessing of the ancestors. Burial in the ancestral burial ground erases uncertainty about the actual death of a person. So burial abroad is strongly resisted by all concerned. Yet it is expensive for Africans in Britain, most of whom are on low incomes, to pay the average cost of £2,000 to repatriate a body to Africa.[13]

who is best placed to carry out effective HIV prevention?

Over the past ten to fifteen years of this epidemic, far too many Africans in Britain have become infected with HIV – for lack of effective primary prevention. Many in turn have lived and died of their infection with little secondary or tertiary prevention, even though the Department of Health has allocated considerably more funds to HIV prevention than to HIV treatment and care services. This rapid increase in infection rates amongst long identified sub-Saharan communities is a cause for embarrassment within the establishment. In its policy guidance on Health Promotion, 'An Evolving Strategy', the Department of Health now prioritizes 'people diagnosed with HIV and AIDS' and 'women who have male sexual partners in vulnerable groups'.[14] One would expect such protocol to prioritize the development of effective HIV prevention campaigns specifically targeting African communities living in London. To date there has been no comprehensive HIV prevention strategy targeting the small cluster of African communities in the four Thames regions of London where the vast majority of infection is. There is virtually no prevention directly targeted to African women, teenagers and young adults. Whilst public officials claim innocent oversight, thousands are tacitly condemned to further HIV infection, as the Communicable Disease Review figures annually indicate.

There are certain factors and practices influencing sex and sexuality in African cultures that could only be effectively tackled by communities themselves. If we look at the demography of African populations we find they are very young, the majority of populations being below the age of forty.[15] Patrilineal and matrilineal social structures in African culture have a great impact on the esteem of women or men and heavily influence decision-making processes. Such structures will affect the success or otherwise of any health promotion campaigns. Polygamy is practised in many parts of Africa and polygamous behaviour in Britain needs to be addressed. Male and female circumcision is practised in many parts of Africa, some attributed to religion, but the majority of circumcision to cultural practice.[16] These are issues that are best addressed by African communities themselves. The enormous diversity of African communities means that only people familiar with the specifics of a given community's cultural codes can realistically affect sexual behaviour. Communities need to be supported in this work by local health authorities, to assist them to design and implement their own campaigns which acknowledge the complexity and specificity of sexual attitudes and practices.

In despair at their predicament, many community members find solace in religion. Unfortunately, ignorance and misinformation exist in some religious circles, and hope in faith-healing as a cure for HIV infection is encouraged. People are urged to come off their medication with disastrous consequences for their medical prognosis. Concern is further heightened by the advent of drug resistant tuberculosis. Tuberculosis is the most predominant AIDS-defining illness amongst Africans living in Britain.

Although these concerns have been brought to the attention of the statutory sector, few expect African communities to be funded to avert the impending crisis. No doubt a two-year study, conducted by non-Africans will first be necessary to ascertain whether there is in fact a problem. In the meantime Africans will continue to die in terrible and ever-increasing numbers.

the power of exclusion – any excuse not to fund[17]

The Department of Health, Local and Health Authorities (the establishment) know the limitations of African community-based organizations. Typically they are small, with weak management and organizational structures. Although greatly under-resourced, they bear the burden of being all things to all people in their communities. They attempt to assist people's access to information about health and social services, housing, employment, benefits advice, immigration referrals, and education. They also fulfil the social function of bringing a community together to counter isolation in a foreign land. No single community group could possibly take on all these tasks efficiently. When African community groups apply for HIV prevention funds, they almost invariably receive only the most token assistance. They are given just enough to let them continue their operations, but certainly not enough to enable infrastructural development or to increase their operational capacities.

In the financial year 1996/7, as a result of the increased epidemic amongst Africans, the Department of Health set aside £250,000 for targeted HIV prevention with African communities. Desperate as they are for funds, African communities were not officially told of the availability of this £250,000. In its defence for 'non-action' the Department of Health said they did not know how to access African communities (fifteen years into the epidemic!). The Department of Health had, therefore, commissioned The HIV Project (a white gay organization, with no experience of direct HIV prevention work or work with African communities), at a cost of £20,000, to inform them how best to spend the (now) £230,000. As one of the many local government Commissioners (for HIV social services and HIV prevention) in London, I frequently attend funders' meetings and on average, where typically a white organization would attract £30,000 for HIV prevention work, an African organization conducting outreach to a similarly affected, similarly sized community, would be lucky to attract £3,000. Most jobs advertised for working specifically with African communities are part-time or on short-term contracts of six to twelve months at most.

Exclusion and racism have crept into the government's commissioning process – keeping off the agenda the HIV epidemic amongst Africans in Britain. The authorities claim they do not fund African community groups because they are small and poorly organized. This rationalist dissimulation of racism crumbles when one points out that no organization emerging from a relatively poor community would have a large and organized infrastructure without statutory support.

The National Health Service and Community Care Act 1990[18] requires health and local authorities to support community organizations which provide the most appropriate services to vulnerable, 'hard to reach' groups ('The enabling statutory sector'). If organizational and management infrastructures are lacking in African community organizations, and if developing such infrastructures would make these organizations more viable and effective, then that is precisely where money should be invested.

systematic policy of exclusion – unnecessary anthropological research

We already know more than enough to commission and provide appropriate effective, community-designed and community-led, HIV prevention and services for African communities affected by HIV in Britain. Nevertheless, even as they invest virtually nothing in actual prevention or services, health and local authorities continue to spend tens of thousands of pounds funding behavioural study upon behavioural study, survey upon survey, 'assessing' the impact of HIV upon African immigrant communities. On average, each study receives over £20,000 per year. Whilst funding applications from African community organizations for appropriate relevant services are turned down left and right by funders, tens of thousands of pounds are awarded to research and consultancy firms to provide completely redundant information. Recommendations of these studies and surveys are never implemented by health or local authorities who commission them. Research is almost always conducted and managed by non-Africans. By contrast, research examining AIDS in relation to gay men is carried out by gay men as a matter of principle, and as such tends to service gay men's needs because the researchers have a vested interest in stopping the epidemic from further ravaging their community.

The University of London's Institute of Education, King's College Hospital, Focus Consultancy, the King's Fund and The HIV Project are among the institutions that have been awarded contracts to study HIV in African communities living in the four Thames regions of London. Numerous surveys are funded and conducted at local level. The contracts vary in size and geographical coverage, but they all have a similar brief: to anthropologically study Africans' behaviour in relation to HIV transmission in London. Unnecessary research at the expense of appropriate prevention work and services betrays the most vile and deadly systemic racism. Funders tell community groups that no services will be planned until the researchers compile the results of the latest survey. Indeed, it is patently unclear how anthropological profiles of Africans in Britain (rather than in Africa) could increase access to health and social services in Britain. However much culture influences lifestyle, attitudes and behaviour – indeed because lifestyle's influence is so great – the most efficient way to increase access to health and social services is to involve the communities themselves, as equal partners, in service planning, development and provision.[19] Instead of this obviously effective solution, the authorities have thought it better to train completely uninitiated non-Africans from scratch (paying them to research African cultures).

Newly trained non-Africans are entrusted to design and provide services – if there is any money left after the research is complete. As is often the case, the research is either never completed, not published, or (more telling) the recommendations are never effected. Thus the real work is never funded. The actual, if not the intended, effect of funding research rather than community HIV prevention or service provision is deadly: to pay non-Africans to do unnecessary research (unnecessary because the knowledge already exists in earlier research and in the details of Africans' lived experiences) whilst doing little to save African lives.

some ways forward

Insensitivity and lack of respect for people's culture, language, beliefs and lifestyle is as effective a barrier to service access as overt racial discrimination.

Authorities must invest in developing African organizations to meet the very great need for professional interpretation and translation facilities.

More investment should go into training African social workers and counsellors to provide culturally-appropriate HIV counselling, especially after a positive HIV test result. Sensitive family counselling is required at times of death and bereavement.

In circumstances where there is tension between African cultures and British laws, HIV workers need to be more sensitive to the dilemmas and needs of the various African communities, especially around African family law and naming systems.

The variables determining sexual behaviour change lie within communities themselves. They do not lie in government bureaucracy. Africans are best placed to deal with issues such as polygamous behaviour, circumcision, patrilineal and matrilineal social structures. Thus rather than give up on the very possibility of effective African community-based HIV prevention on the basis of organizations' lack of infrastructure, health and local authorities should invest in community groups to be more effective in the fight against HIV transmission.

There is already more than adequate information on behaviour patterns of the few African communities in London. It is time to begin commissioning appropriate health promotion and social services. Unnecessary anthropological research in lieu of investment in African organizations is nothing short of racism. No other highly affected group has been so over-researched with so little new information or action resulting from the effort.

references

1. Tariq Modood, *Racial Equality – Colour, Culture and Justice*, The Commission on Social Justice, 1993.
2. Office of Population Census and Surveys, 1991 British Census.
3. Department of Health AIDS Action Group Portfolio Paper on HIV and Ethnic Minorities, 1992.
4. J. Del Amo, A. Petruckevitch, A. Phillips et al., 'Spectrum of AIDS Defining Conditions in Africans in London', in *AIDS Care*, November 1996.
5. Public Health Laboratory Service, 'CDR Review', 5 January 1996.
6. Health and Ethnicity Programme NE & NW Thames Regional Health Authorities, 'Refugees and The National Health Service', (Ghada Karmi), 1992.
7. Department of Health, Unlinked Anonymous HIV Prevalence Monitoring Programme, 1994.
8. Department of Health, 'Guidelines for Pre-Test Discusion on HIV Testing', 1996.
9. African Issues Group, 'Learning from African Families', The Local Government Management Board 1995.
10. ibid.
11. ibid.
12. Children Act 1989, HMSO, London.
13. London Ecumenical AIDS Forum, 'HIV, The Church and African Communities in London', February 1993.
14. UK Health Departments, 'HIV & AIDS Health Promotion: An Evolving Strategy', 1996.

15. Population Secretariat, 'National Population Policy for Sustainable Development', Uganda 1995.

16. Bernadette P.A. Olowo-Freers, Thomas G. Barton, *In Pursuit of Fulfillment: Studies of Cultural Diversity and Sexual Behaviour in Uganda*, 1993.

17. Stephen Lukes, *Power: A Radical View*, 1985.

18. National Health Service and Community Care Act 1990, HMSO.

19. Dima Abdulrahim, NE & NW Thames Regional Health Authorities, 'Working with Diversity, HIV Prevention and Black and Minority Ethnic Communities', 1991.

official knowledges

the free market, identity formation, sexuality and race in the HIV/AIDS sector

Chetan Bhatt and Robert Lee

introduction

A key area of recent political activism, both in the UK and the US, has concerned how issues of 'difference' and multiculturalism are made integral to broader radical projects. Is it feasible to link together within a universal project the various particular claims of difference based on 'race', ethnicity, sexuality and gender? Is it possible to have a pluralist multiculturalism or are we left with a multiculturalism that is based simply on different, frequently antagonistic groups making non-negotiable and hermetically sealed claims about their difference from others? How are these claims integrated? How do we negotiate sameness and difference? These broader debates involving universalism and particularism relate directly and forcefully to the issue of AIDS. In both the UK and the US, issues of 'race', sexuality and gender have considerably shaped the responses from and against groups affected by HIV. In the UK, and especially in London, issues of 'race', culture and sexuality have been foregrounded in the development of HIV/AIDS prevention and treatment and care policy and services.

Importantly, there have been a set of quite complex and persistent conflicts both between and within discourses of 'race', culture and sexuality within the HIV/AIDS sector. In the mid-1990s, this was illustrated by events in several voluntary sector HIV/AIDS prevention and care service organizations (ASOs) which involved imputed differences of interest between black and white client groups that are identified in epidemiology as at high risk of HIV infection. The dispute at the Body Positive (BP) Centre between the management of the centre and the BP Women's group, the conflict at London Lighthouse about the imposition of 'acceptable' dress codes for gay men and the tensions at the Terrence Higgins Trust in relation to a research project involving black gay men have each revolved around (real or manufactured, explicit or metonymic) antagonisms between gay men and African or other black heterosexuals, or between white and black gay men. The quite severe and persistent disagreements in the HIV/AIDS sector between the positions adopted around male homosexual identity by some black ASOs compared to the hermetic gay identity focus of white ASOs is another illustration of this process. Much sharper antagonisms have occurred in various health authorities and health promotion units across London involving resource allocation to gay men versus resources targeted at African or other black communities. The recent policy thrust to target HIV prevention work at groups epidemiologically identified as at high risk of HIV infection (primarily gay and bisexual men, African communities and injecting drug users) has also been the source of tensions involving race and sexuality, this time reflected in competitiveness around increasingly scarce funds.

This essay examines some of these areas involving race and sexuality through an exploration of some of the highly complex links between sociological and epidemiological knowledge production, public health policy formulation and political identity claims. These areas of knowledge production and identity formation may seem to be purely academic debates that are irrelevant to the urgent task of fighting the spread of HIV and fighting for better medical treatment and health and social care for people with HIV infection. However, in this essay, we critically explore the absolute political centrality and pertinence of these themes to the way HIV prevention policy is directly developed and implemented. In particular, we emphasize how both liberal and absolutist ideas of social, cultural and pseudo-anthropological 'difference' have been in some way central to the development of HIV prevention work. Ideas of 'difference' have been sustained through a distinctive combination of free-market competitiveness, sociological knowledges preoccupied with alterity, the re-configuration of institutional knowledges involving race, gender and sexuality, and the unleashing of a selective ethnic and sexual identity politics within the HIV/AIDS sector. Three main examples of political knowledge production involving 'race' and sexuality are examined: aspects of the re-gaying debate and its consequences for work relating to other, mainly black heterosexual HIV epidemics; the manufacture of ethnically exclusive forms of homosexual sexual identity that have formed the project of some black ASOs; and the impact of HIV infection on UK African communities and the pan-European dimensions to this.

manufacturing 'difference': national and global

Debates about social identity and difference have in innumerable direct and subtle ways been central to the configuration of the HIV/AIDS commissioning, public health, health promotion, National Health Service (NHS) Trust or voluntary provider sector. It is axiomatic that no HIV/AIDS work can proceed without integrally embracing or at the very least being informed by the political and ideological discourses that have been created by the progressive social movements, in particular the gay movement. Conversely, public health discipline also needs to create normative identity constituencies (such as 'African refugees'), and 'anthropological' and sociological knowledges about them for health promotion purposes.

Paradoxically, the recognition in public health policy of the existence of social movements or constituencies that were previously officially marginalized in health and social policy and in formal politics occurred during a period of momentous change in British politics that was presided over by an avowedly right-wing government. That neo-Conservative change is usually seen to represent a rehearsal of nineteenth-century economic liberalism combined with a social authoritarian agenda in the areas of welfare provision, poverty, crime, law and order, the family, sexuality, nationalism and black immigration. Importantly, and again paradoxically if viewed from within an unreconstructed socialist gaze, the virtual explosion of so many identity-based organizations in just the limited field of the HIV/AIDS provider sector has a link with the kind of economic determinism – the ideology of the free market – that has created the NHS reforms.[1] The shape of HIV/AIDS primary prevention activities, at least until recently, has not been a simple reflection of the existence of a devastating epidemic that has affected some minority communities and groups but has also been determined by other concerns, explored later, that have become emergent through the mechanism of the internal market but which often have little to do with practical HIV prevention or treatment and care.

The changes wrought in the British polity and economy are integrally linked to a different phenomenon that is also virtually coextensive with the spread and impact of HIV in Britain and elsewhere: globalization. The responses to globalization by the British state have been seen as resulting in the kinds of political shifts engendered by New Right political thinking, particularly in relation to a racially-informed national identity and nationalism and a barely-disguised xenophobia in relation to European identity formation. Absolutely central to the British government's interventions in the debate on European identity formation and in its attempt to shore up a barbaric and inhumane nationalism at home has been the issue of black refugees and asylum seekers, mainly those from Africa and Asia.

There is a 'contradictory' or dialectical relation between an exclusivist British nationalism, or a Fortress Europe that is lapped by the seas it shares with the African continent, and an overarching globalization of economic, political and cultural relations across nation-states and civil societies.

This tension between reinvigorated European (or rather British, French and German) nationalism and deepening globalization may seem completely removed or irrelevant to the more limited question of developing of HIV/AIDS health and social services in the UK. However, it is necessary to recognize the wider issues and paradoxes of globalization. Globalization has been central to the social, political and cultural organization of Western and to a significant extent non-Western gay communities. It is also the condition not simply for the trajectories of the HIV epidemic worldwide but also for the shape of the epidemic in gay communities as well as in the self-similar gay community's political and ideological responses to HIV.

Globalization is also central to the impact of HIV and AIDS on the numerically second largest group in the UK currently affected by the epidemic: black refugees and migrants, mainly from eastern and south-eastern African countries. The post-war period has witnessed some of the largest events of global mass human migration ever recorded. The national and international movements of refugees from central Europe, Africa and Asia are aspects of a similar globalizing tendency. The issue of HIV among black refugees is not at all recent. People from black refugee communities were among the first groups to be identified in the very early 1980s as suffering from what came to be known as AIDS. Some of the early heterosexual AIDS cases were identified among African migrants and refugees in Belgium (and indeed black refugees from Haiti living in Miami.) For several countries where either civil war or local ethnic conflict is established or on-going, HIV infection has gained a foothold among some populations, especially populations that have fled conflict and have been subjected to inhumane and brutal treatment, including the systematic rape of women, by the neighbouring country or by various government or opposition militias, army factions or local ethnic/clan militias. Consequently, small populations, especially those escaping conflict, may have a very high rate of HIV seroprevalence in a country or region of low(er) overall seroprevalence. Some recognition of the global impact of HIV needs to be central to local health and social policy and service development. Put differently, and rather bluntly, a military excursion into a small village in northern Uganda which has relatively high incidence or prevalence of HIV infection in comparison with surrounding villages can directly and substantially affect the shape of the HIV epidemic in Southwark, Haringey or Newham. The mobility patterns of a small number of Somali or Eritrean refugees who are forced to flee into and then out of Kenya or the Sudan can substantially affect the characteristics of the HIV epidemic in Camden or Westminster. Indeed, the impact of globalization is codified in official epidemiological and sociological knowledges about HIV in ways that are politically consequential for the way the HIV epidemic in the UK, and strategies to combat it, are understood.

HIV, African communities and European identity formation

Most Western European countries have reported the impact of HIV on African communities living within those nations. In particular, France, Italy, the Netherlands, Norway, Denmark, Belgium and Germany, ex-colonial powers that have had major connections with African countries or which previously had relatively liberal policies on asylum and immigration, have reported significant numbers of HIV cases in relation to African communities. This issue is intensely politically charged, since the reconfiguration of European political identity has been integrally combined with increasingly repressive racist immigration and asylum legislation. The legal changes across Europe linked to the Schengen proposals and the TREVI agreements have resulted in a 'normalization' of asylum and immigration legislation by European member states in repressive directions. The need to draw attention to the plight of African people with HIV in Europe, and the importance of vocalizing politically their needs and demands has been undertaken under the shadow of a quite real and violent racist backlash against Africans by racist thugs or racial-populist politicians. The vicious and unprecedented anti-African 'pogroms' in Germany during 1992 and 1993, considered unthinkable in post-war Western Europe, and the systematic brutal attacks against African refugee and student hostels in Germany, France, Italy, Belgium and numerous European countries throughout the period of the 1980s and 1990s is testament to the depth of European racist activism. The level of anti-African racism in Europe should not be underestimated.

HIV/AIDS has been a significant factor for many of these racist formations and has informed both national-popular politics and policy involving African migrants, refugees, asylum seekers, settlers and EC nationals. For example, the Norwegian Health Department held a press conference in July 1996 to issue a warning to the white population against having sex with Africans. Of 244 Africans in Norway found to be HIV-positive, almost a hundred were, after diagnosis, immediately deported or denied residence permits and had to return to the countries they had sought refuge from. In Switzerland, an African HIV-positive man was imprisoned in the summer of 1996 after a white sexual partner became HIV-positive, a repetition of similar incidents which have occurred in other European countries.[2]

The UK has not seen this extent of active racist mobilization against Africans. However, several factors, some of which strikingly parallel the de-gaying of the HIV epidemic, have been instrumental in either minimizing the issue of HIV on African communities or removing it from planning and service development arenas. The impact of HIV/AIDS on some UK African communities has been officially known about since at least the mid-1980s, and the knowledge that

African communities were a major national group affected by HIV has existed in the HIV/AIDS sector since at least the late-1980s. Yet important opportunities for work with African communities were consistently evaded.

Both the Department of Health and the Health Education Authority (HEA) were repeatedly approached in the late 1980s and early 1990s with practical, inexpensive and feasible proposals for HIV primary and secondary prevention projects with African communities but did not respond effectively during a period when they could have made a significant and effective intervention. One contribution of the Department of Health in the early 1990s was a notice to immigration and port authorities that gave immigration control officers powers to detain and question individuals who 'looked like' they had AIDS and had arrived in Britain. This was almost certainly directed at African refugees, asylum seekers and migrants (and perhaps betrayed the knowledge that was held about the impact of HIV on UK African communities). Officials could refuse entry clearance if the person could not demonstrate that they could pay for AIDS treatment and care services. This notice may have been practically ineffectual and was probably the outcome of a battle between politically constrained liberal health officials and more reactionary Home Office and ministerial tendencies. However, it does illustrate a clear link between HIV, Africans and immigration in government thinking, a link that can still be readily exploited for populist purposes.

However, liberal responses were also constrained in other ways that worked against service provision to African communities. The generic 'everyone is at risk' scenario, based to some extent on overblown epidemiological projections about the risk to the (white) UK heterosexual population, is an obvious factor. Additionally, official liberal responses have been wary of drawing attention to African communities in the context of some of the most inhumane regulations seen in Britain and which the Conservative government has seen fit to introduce against black refugees and asylum seekers.[3] Similarly, many liberal health officials were concerned about the stigmatizing of African communities for fear of drawing protests from UK black groups and from various African embassies, High Commissions and exile groups.

The black political configuration in HIV/AIDS work during the early 1980s and into the 1990s was dominated by a need to oppose 'the Africa hypothesis' about the origin of the human immunodeficiency viruses, and to a significant extent this worked against the need to organize practical services for black people with HIV infection. Some of the black and anti-racist responses were based on the belief that by incorporating African communities under the general rubric of 'black' those communities would be protected from stigmatization and discrimination. However, much anti-racist or multiculturalist HIV/AIDS work failed to engage in any practical projects with black gay men, African communities or with other black groups that had been identified as at serious risk of HIV infection. In other ways, the focus on anti-racism, equal opportunities and a bland multiculturalism within several statutory and voluntary HIV/AIDS agencies resulted in efforts being put into black and ethnic minority communities generally rather than black groups identified in the epidemiological data as at risk of HIV infection. For example, an unreconstructed feminist focus on 'women' selectively ignored the epidemiological data that most women with HIV in the UK were black African women, just as the anti-racist focus on 'black and ethnic minorities' ignored the data that most black people with HIV in the UK were either African heterosexuals or Caribbean, Asian, African and South-East Asian gay men. The intervention of new social movement politics involving feminism and 'race' occurred in a field where there were often intense disjunctions between the interests of the groups directly affected by HIV and the political ideologies which, at a different level, claimed to represent and articulate them.

One final barrier to the development of work with African communities has been the general socio-economic and political position that those communities have found themselves in. There has been no strategic attempt to develop an African service provider infrastructure, such as exists for gay men, nor do those communities have the kinds of cultural or political capital that are considered valid by the HIV/AIDS sector (such as luminaries, powerful community stakeholders, politicians and lobbyists or a cultural infrastructure that is recognized as important and valuable). It would be fair to say that African communities are often looked at within the HIV/AIDS sector with a significant and consistent degree of prejudice and antipathy based on a vast and shifting repertoire of racialized stereotypes. Commissioners find it easy to find problems in African groups and reasons for not resourcing them, though in actuality problems (when they have existed) have been minute in comparison with any that have affected virtually every single mainstream HIV/AIDS voluntary sector organization that currently exists. Two very different orientations appear to exist in the sector about how African organizations and all other organizations are assessed, monitored and evaluated.

a selective globalization

A 'commonsense' British nationalism about black immigration is deep and has informed some ostensibly progressive HIV/AIDS tendencies. It is important not to misrepresent this situation, because there have been a few celebrated examples of African heterosexual and white gay political syncretism, coalition-building and knowledge sharing. Additionally, there are further extremely complex differences in mainstream attitudes towards the impact of the HIV epidemic among gay men and among African families, men, women and children in ways that can selectively work against either constituency. However, neo-Conservative anti-gay pro-family ideology has stopped short of embracing African families. Conservative immigration legislation has little moral difficulty in keeping black families separated, a factor which has substantially affected the organization of humane social care and support for African men and women and children with AIDS, especially in situations of severe physical, mental or terminal illness, and in the care of babies and children whose parents have died.

Some otherwise avowedly globalized progressive responses to the HIV epidemic have also reproduced rather regressive forms of British nationalism which seem to suggest that there are acceptable and unacceptable 'globalizations' of the HIV epidemic. For example, while explicitly embracing experiences from the European, Australian, Canadian and American dimensions of the HIV epidemic and their relevance for (the possible epidemiology of HIV among) gay men in the UK, some writers have nevertheless complained that the global heterosexual epidemic is used to de-gay AIDS in the UK:

> It is all very well . . . to refer to the global epidemic, but most of us only live on one part of the planet. Whilst we clearly need to get resources to developing countries, it never fails to amaze me how such arguments are used as if they justified the wholesale neglect of differing local needs in the developed world.[4]

There is little fear of a gush of funds (or even sympathy) from the 'First World' to the 'Third' at the wholesale expense of those with HIV in the overdeveloped countries. However, the existence of these views is of interest because it elides how selective appropriations of the global epidemic and selective oppositions, repeatedly enforced, between gay men and the undifferentiated category of 'the heterosexual' as enemy, can lead to an inhumane ethical orientation towards those predominantly black heterosexuals in the UK living with HIV disease. While gay men are right to protest about the 'heterosexualization' of the HIV epidemic, the reality is that until very recently virtually no work, no funds, no Department of Health or Health Education Authority policy initiatives, no mainstream ASO initiatives, no governmental education projects and no grassroots (for example, MESMAC-type) national initiatives have been directed towards *those* heterosexuals with AIDS. The call for redirecting work towards gay men and *away from* heterosexuals can significantly evade the quite urgent necessity of doing more work with heterosexual communities in the UK from Africa. There have also been extraordinarily severe and virtually unique political and economic constraints on African people with HIV infection in the UK (and throughout Europe) in their ability to forge a militant political voice that can challenge the mainstream HIV/AIDS sector at an institutional level or can effectively and forcefully articulate the impact of the epidemic on their communities.[5] It can appear that anger against the heterosexualization of the epidemic has as one of its consequences a lack of concern about the needs of one of the most marginalized and repressed communities to exist in post-war Western Europe.

The impact and circumstances of the HIV epidemic in European black refugee communities is not easily comprehensible in social movement understandings of either race or sexuality or indeed through the institutional binary mechanisms of purchaser-provider that ostensibly guarantee an effective response to the epidemic. The existing paradigms involving anti-racism and black liberation, race relations sociology, health promotion and those developed around sexuality and sexual knowledges do not provide adequate tools to comprehend the complexity of the issues that are involved in effective and sustained HIV prevention and health promotion work with black refugee groups. With extremely few exceptions, mainstream anti-racism or black politics has barely begun to address the politics of the refugee experience unless it is simply to reduce it to the grammar of racism and anti-racism, or to some nominal taxonomy of 'anti-imperialism'. In the field of HIV/AIDS service provision, this has sometimes constituted a major diversion away from the need to develop effective services for African communities or other black communities at risk of HIV infection. For example, one London-based black HIV/AIDS organization used the corporate slogan: '*Self-determination* based on needs, rights and access to services' (emphasis added).[6] 'The use of the trope of national liberation against colonialism to articulate the need for state institutions to provide HIV health services to black communities may seem curious. However, it represents a significantly different agenda on 'race' (broadly speaking a corporatist black nationalism) that seems incapable of articulating the difficult and complex needs and issues, including those of self and collective empowerment, that are important in the impact of HIV on black communities.

Central to these various areas in policy development is a heavy stress on identity politics and (ethnic, sexual or 'anthropological') difference, with virtually no emphasis being placed on commonality, shared experience, coalition-building or on the difficult issue of how competitively framed group interests can (and will have to) co-exist within the same institutional service providing sector. Put differently, gay men, African communities and other groups will use the same health promotion and treatment and care centres and services in a situation where their interests are otherwise framed as politically and economically opposed.

gay anthropologies, positivist enumeration and anti-pluralist agendas

The re-gaying AIDS debate that occurred in Britain during the early 1990s is extremely important in its consequences and travels well beyond its official containment in terms of the need to reverse the contemptible situation of severely limited funds allocated by district health authorities and the former London regional health authorities for local HIV prevention work with gay men. There is a broader discontentment in the HIV/AIDS sector that needs more direct and politicized articulation. Much of this concerns the extensive misuse of ring-fenced HIV primary prevention funding for generic health promotion capital and revenue expenditure that has little to do with HIV prevention work with any community. Equally important is the reduction in AIDS treatment and care budgets (and the consequent impact on the availability and use of viral load tests, protease inhibitor drugs and triple combination therapy). There have been several situations of sympathetic health commissioners having to protect local AIDS budgets against the encroachments from public health and finance departments and health promotion managers who are keen to utilize AIDS monies for generic health care and health promotion. Indeed, consideration of this issue may explain the bewilderment among both gay and African groups about 'where the prevention and care money is going'.

However, the re-gaying debate is important for other reasons. There is for example a different perspective on grassroots gay involvement in this health crisis from its very early days that would modify the more vanguardist claims of recent re-gaying tendencies. Equally tendentious are the claims of marginalization which led up to the burst of the re-gaying tendency 'into' the sector. Virtually all the leading personalities in the re-gaying tendency were embedded in and almost canonical in the HIV/AIDS sector despite the claims, enunciated often enough, of marginalization, discrimination and homophobia. The re-gaying tendency is best seen as primarily an institutional response from within the HIV/AIDS voluntary and health authority sector which was itself gay-dominated in terms of personnel and professional culture, rather than a simple reflection of grassroots gay anger about the lack of district-based HIV prevention initiatives, though the latter now constitutes the documented history and knowledge about how the tendency arose. There is another issue that requires further discussion, which is about how it came to be that an HIV sector dominated by gay personnel was placed in a position where it could not forcefully articulate the needs of gay men in HIV primary prevention work until the early 1990s. While there was considerable official political marginalization of gay men's work, as well as the ideological thrust to 'de-gay' or universalize the epidemic, we are not sure these factors explain the more complex relation between the development and changes in official HIV/AIDS policy, the formation of a strong gay institutional-career framework[7] and the marginalization of gay men's health promotion need.[8]

Critically important to the emergence of the re-gaying tendency were already established and conducive institutional mechanisms of contracting, funding and administration. For example, Gay Men Fighting AIDS (GMFA) was to emerge in a burst of kinetic energy and immediately received funding from a regional health authority, followed (rightly) by immense project funding from a coalition of London commissioners. Its initial official legitimation was based on a nominal research project that investigated the amount of HIV primary prevention project work with gay men undertaken by district health authorities (though the research could not examine what direct or indirect work or funding went into HIV/AIDS service provision and health education for gay men in primary and secondary prevention areas throughout the HIV/AIDS sector as a whole). However, the demand that district health authorities have to direct HIV work with local gay men was an extremely important and novel democratizing demand of health institutions that were increasingly centralized and perhaps even more formally undemocratic than before the onset of the NHS reforms. Against this tendency, gay communities were articulated as legitimate local citizen-groups that integrally matter in the development of local welfare and health policy.

Interestingly enough, for groups on the relative margins of the HIV/AIDS prevention and treatment and care sector, it was the established belief in the late-1980s that they were receiving little funding since it was all going to or for gay men's work. Indeed, it was the belief that the dominant HIV/AIDS prevention and treatment and care work undertaken was so integrally informed by knowledges, models and professional cultures developed through gay men's work that it was considered a constant struggle to register demands from other groups affected by the virus, in particular African communities. The strong perception was that gay men's work and gay men's agendas were normative in the voluntary and (to some extent) health authority sector and it was all other work that was marginalized.

Some of the tendencies opposed (and which still continue to be opposed) to the prioritization of gay men's needs were informed by a particularly insidious homophobia that naturalized gay men as deserving of or responsible for their HIV infections. Oppositions to work with gay men were also based on various rehearsals of familial or identity politics and of agendas that had little relevance or consequence for HIV work. Some of this included generic as well as sexual health promotion work with various categories, such as 'children', 'young people', 'the elderly', 'women', 'people with learning difficulties', 'people with disabilities', and 'black and ethnic minority communities'. Much of this could not be justified on epidemiological grounds, or in terms of broader HIV prevention need. Similarly, some of this work was based on a spurious equivalence generated between local authority equal opportunities victimist discourse and HIV prevention need, as if the latter could be derived from the former. The tragedy of the normative equal opportunities approach was that it missed entirely several extremely important groups within Britain's black and ethnic minority communities that had established and well-defined needs in terms of HIV prevention, treatment and care. The kinds of broad anti-racist and equal opportunities rubrics adopted were often too blunt to initiate the level of targeting that was required.

Conversely, much of the criticism of HIV prevention policy or expenditure made by some gay men was directed at HIV prevention work in black and ethnic minority communities. This may not have been the intention of those who have argued for re-gaying AIDS, but an important consequence of the re-gaying strategy at frontline service level (in health promotion units and in the voluntary sector) was a wholesale attack on multiculturalist, black and anti-racist approaches. These critiques took various forms. The crude versions, often articulated in health promotion services and ASOs, included views of the type: 'Asian women are never going to get infected – why bother doing any work with them?' or even 'Too much money is being spent on Africans'. The more sophisticated versions attacked 'political correctness' and bemoaned AIDS money or prevention efforts being deployed to deal with 'inner-city problems', 'immigration', 'social ills', 'women and children', 'cultural issues', 'racism', 'language', 'translation' (all, incidentally, factors that are imperative in HIV work with African communities). Importantly, oppositions were manufactured that prioritized gay men's work against work with black or women's groups (though, again, most of the work of both the latter groups would have been with African communities). Similarly, the critique of the category of 'men who have sex with men' (MWHSWM, a public health category developed to acknowledge 'non-gay identified' homosexuals and bisexuals) was often a critique primarily of work with putative 'men who have sex with men' from Asian and Caribbean communities. MWHSWM, while often not acknowledged as such, was itself an heavily ethnicized signifier that marked non-white ethnicity. While MWHSWM itself sustained various pseudo-anthropologies and fictive 'commonsense knowledges' about the organization of sex in black communities that could be constructively challenged, its replacement with the category 'gay/bisexual' can be interpreted as a dismissal of work with men from black and ethnic minority groups and an evasion of the differences in, and meanings of (homo)sexual organization across different cultures.

These various strands involving race and ethnicity are important because they shaped the parameters of the political competitiveness at the grassroots that followed in the wake of the re-gaying debate. Importantly, much of this was rehearsed as between ostensibly progressive social identity groups (gays, women, blacks) rather than between different groups reflected in epidemiological categories as affected by HIV. There is an important overlap between epidemiological categories and social identity ones, but their difference allowed a space for other debates involving gay identity and race to emerge, some of it irrelevant to practical HIV prevention work.

In the discussion that follows, we look at some of the positive and negative ways in which the re-gaying strategy unfolded in frontline practice during the early 1990s. It is necessary to forcefully argue the case that national and local strategies have to prioritize funding for and work with gay and bisexual men and that this has to be the main priority in any HIV prevention strategy, alongside work with African communities and other groups. Similarly, the contributions of Gay Men Fighting AIDS (GMFA) have been necessary and instrumental in repoliticizing the often apologetic approach to work with gay men that existed previously. In particular, GMFA's literature and its strategic approach to community mobilization and peer- (or volunteer-) led services, which has often been criticized by commissioning agencies, is one of the more effective methodological approaches in HIV prevention work and is based on valid foundational principles.

However, there is a difference between acknowledging this and accepting the claims to complete representation and vanguardism that have been equally important to the GMFA project. The market mechanisms that are the condition for GMFA as well as all other organizations have created a situation in which embattled organizations are compelled to compete against each other rather than work with each other. Part of this process has entailed the flourishing of absolutist claims involving efficacy, moral, political and ethical authority, leadership, representation and ownership, as well as the creation of immense expectations that would be difficult for any organization to meet or sustain in practice in the longer term. GMFA, like other organizations, is faced with an overwhelming 'burden of representation', some of it self-generated, of each and all gay interests and constituencies. Moreover, the commissioning process virtually demands the articulation of authoritative and authentic representation of the totality of a social movement or constituency as a condition of funding. This has meant that only one gay HIV primary prevention organization exists to work on a pan-London basis, rather than the wide and diverse range of gay organizations that should be developed and funded. The contracting and market environment has also created the situation, within some frontline services, of instinctive and automatic equivalences between identity claims, epidemiological proportions and funding measures. Epidemiology has to be foundational in HIV prevention resource allocation (and in health promotion discipline generally.) What has been problematic is the shift from arguing the case for funding for gay men and black men and women to political identity claims from these constituencies directed against each other.

Numerical measures of funding and epidemiology were central to the re-gaying demands and were based on a linear formulaic scale: that local expenditure on HIV primary prevention work should directly reflect (variously, national or local) epidemiological data. A common and typical demand was that seventy to eighty per cent of HIV prevention and health education expenditure should be directed towards gay men since cases of AIDS or prevalence or incidence of HIV infection among gay men made up similar proportions of total AIDS or HIV seropositive diagnoses. This demand on its own may be considered problematic if it reduced the nature, quality and outcome of work with gay men to a funding measure. However, it elides several other factors in which race becomes increasingly pertinent.

Positivist social science has significantly expanded in the HIV/AIDS social research field and probably constitutes the dominant paradigm for policy and service development in health promotion areas. The emergence of broad quasi-positivist tendencies within health promotion education and intervention has been complemented with the (effectively) rational choice theory models used to determine both the shapes and the outcomes of those interventions. Some version of rational choice theory seems inevitable in a field now so dependent on 'free' or managed market economic foundations. Consequently, health promotion intervention is increasingly reduced to a model metaphorically derived from double-blind clinical trials methodology or from epidemiology. Similarly, the efficacy of health interventions is deemed to be determinable through rational-bureaucratic, numerical outcome-based, and apparently measurable factors.

We do not dispute the validity and necessity of numerically-based research, and more broadly the importance of a critical realist approach that embraces empirical investigation and analysis. However, it is necessary to have a critical perspective on reductionist approaches to the kinds of diverse and contingent factors that would be involved in affiliation with a sexual identity or in cultural encounters, sexual desire and sexual fantasy.[9] The dominance of positivist science in health promotion seems to suggest a rationalized response to a situation of fragmentation and chaos in a health sector that is expected to produce enumerated hard truths from an assessment of highly complex social phenomena that refuse to easily yield such certainties. This tendency in recent health promotion methodology may be seen as a late modern response to the perceived failures of traditional health promotion discipline, especially when faced with the immediacy of an urgent health crisis in a situation of deep, chaotic and market-led health service reorganization.[10] In this view, the rationalized, technocratic and positivist response exudes a mask of authority and competence behind which lies a deeply political organic crisis in health and social services provision. It should not be surprising that AIDS has become, in numerous ways, the political conductor of this crisis.

The use of solely empiricist approaches has other important consequences in which both race and sexuality are pertinent. Any approach that recognized inequalities in health and health service provision would need to consider the health needs of the most socio-economically or politically marginalized groups. Health promotion work with those groups would have to include qualitative research approaches and strategies of community involvement and community development, and would involve the use of innovative techniques in community mobilization. For many such communities, as the case of health need in refugee populations has shown, solely positivist approaches in health promotion may miss them entirely. There is a more explicitly political agenda within much health promotion discipline in which Conservative ideological impulses, especially those associated with the measurement of service provision in an ostensibly 'consumer-led' market place and a denial of class and socio-economic factors, have increasingly become a 'scientific commonsense'. The emphasis in health promotion on numerical outcome measures, cost-effectiveness, quality markers, consumer satisfaction surveys, empiricist forms of needs 'assessment' and so forth may have beneficial consequences, but by and large, these are yet to be fully demonstrated.

The stress on positivist numerical methods within health promotion has been reflected in re-gaying efforts. This is an interesting phenomenon, since an appeal to positivist science is used as a marker for the validity of gay interventions that are otherwise celebrated as value-loaded and dependent on politicized interpretation of personal and collective narratives.[11] Positivist science has also been misapplied within an overarching aim to defend a monolithic and unfractured conception of gay identity that is untroubled by more complex issues of race, ethnicity or bisexuality. GMFA, for example, has been embroiled in numerous antagonisms around the extent to which black gay men 'identify as gay'. Much of this seems to have hinged on GMFA's keenness to exploit surveys, numerical methods and tests for statistical significance, which have tended to produce 'ethnicity' data that rather than being used to explore issues that may be relevant to black gay and bisexual men sought almost exclusively to prove that there was no evidence that black men 'did not identify as gay'. GMFA's unclear approach to issues of race and ethnicity extends to the value labels it uses for categorizing ethnicity variables in which 'White British' is opposed to 'Black' (but not 'Black-British'), 'Asian' and so forth.[12] Virtually all black people in Britain have British nationality (i.e. are British). Similarly, the majority of black people in the UK were born in the UK. In using the trope of 'British nationality' exclusively for whites, GMFA reproduced unwittingly the conception that blacks are not British (and by implication do not belong here), an issue that has indeed been at the core of black political labour since the 1950s.

The quasi-positivist tendency in much recent gay-led HIV health promotion work is also problematic in its own terms because it assumes the absolute validity of often selective epidemiological categorization, and an evasion of other factors that subvert the idea that the actual complexities of health need can be read off only from published epidemiological proportions.[13] For example, the social care and primary and secondary prevention needs of poor, recently arrived African groups that have no developed infrastructure, let alone a consolidated network of fully operational provider units that can compete on an equalized playing field with other established organizations, would require greater resource allocation than that determined by epidemiological ratios. The level playing-field of optimally-defined rational choice and opportunity is a necessary precondition in any rational free market, even one that is managed or structured through funding ratios.

However, there are other complexities in the epidemiological data itself. In referring to these it is not our intention to minimize the case for further or more funding for work with gay men (the opposite is our view). However, we want to highlight how selective enumeration has become an important, often sole legitimating factor for gay men's work in a way that, if the complexities of the data are not addressed, the issue of resource allocation can (and indeed has) become framed against the needs of African groups. Cumulative data from 1985 to the end of March 1996 shows that 72 per cent of AIDS cases (9,079) and 61 per cent of cases of HIV-1 infection (16,303) are associated with sex between men. Thirteen per cent of AIDS cases (1,526) and 15 per cent of HIV-1 infections (3,996) are associated with sex between men and women where exposure is presumed to have occurred abroad or where there was mother to infant transmission. African people make up the great majority of cases in the latter two exposure categories. If trends in reports of HIV-1 infection over time are considered, then the exposure category 'sex between men' varied from about 65 per cent of all HIV-1 positive cases in the period 1987–1990, decreasing to about 57 per cent of all HIV-1 positive cases in the period 1993–94 (though data from the most recent years suffers from reporting delays). Cases involving 'partners from pattern II countries' varied from 5–12 per cent in the period 1987–1990, increasing to about 18 per cent in the period 1993–1994. Longitudinal trends show a decrease in the percentage of HIV-1 infections among gay men as a percentage of all HIV-1 reports but an increase in the percentage of HIV-1 reports among African communities as a percentage of all HIV-1 reports. In the PHLS Collaborative Laboratory Study[14] of HIV-1 antibody prevalence, the cumulative HIV seropositivity among gay/bisexual men and 'men who lived in or visited Africa' is virtually the same (8.3 and 8.2 per cent respectively), but increases to 13.3 per cent for 'women who lived in or visited Africa'. The latter is the highest seropositivity rate among all the exposure subcategories in the Collaborative Laboratory Study. The seropositivity rate is very similar in the Collaborative Laboratory Study among gay and African men and is the highest among African women. Only about 12–17 per cent of cases of HIV-1 infection among African women in the UK is thought to be recognized, in comparison with about 74 per cent among gay men.[15] If unidentified infection is taken into account, the figures for heterosexual sex where exposure is presumed to have occurred abroad increase to about 28 per cent of HIV-1 cases.[16] Research in London has confirmed that African people tend to present late for testing and treatment and care services in comparison with other groups. Consequently, while gay men constitute the vast majority of cases of HIV infection and AIDS, the way that national epidemiological proportions can be rhetorically employed in district health authorities (typically, expenditure has to exactly reflect national epidemiological proportions) cannot unproblematically reflect changing patterns, seropositivity rates, unidentified infection, longitudinal changes or the problems, particularly relevant to African communities, of late seropositive diagnosis and late clinical presentation.

Similarly, the way the epidemiological data in the UK is hierarchically categorized can underestimate the actual extent of HIV-1 transmission that is occurring in the UK within African communities. Indeed, the extent to which HIV-1 infection affecting those communities did occur abroad or in the UK is not easily knowable since African people presenting for HIV testing would, if found to be seropositive, be far more likely to be placed in the epidemiological category of heterosexual, 'exposure abroad'. (Conversely, there is no epidemiological subcategory of exposure abroad for gay men.)

The epidemiological exposure subcategory of heterosexual exposure abroad is a pragmatic classification developed to make sense of the situation, increasingly obvious from the mid-1980s onwards, of increasing numbers of Africans, mainly recently arrived refugees, testing seropositive. However, it has had the 'commonsense' effect of displacing the need for HIV primary prevention work with African communities in the UK. The classification applies to African people as if they are still permanently elsewhere, do not have sexual lives in Britain, do not have unsafe sex if they are HIV seropositive, or if they do their partners are probably infected anyway. In some important sense, the discourses involving African communities evolve out of a commonsense view of British nationalism in which Africans do not belong here and if they are here their lives or the lives of their sexual partners do not matter. It is similarly striking that so few UK HIV/AIDS political commentators, cultural critics, or political activists have discussed the issue of HIV in UK African communities. However, one important consequence of re-gaying efforts has been to place needs-led targeting firmly on the agenda. This factor has also more recently become instrumental in focusing resources towards work with African communities. This, together with increased and targeted resources for work with gay men and injecting drug users, is a reflection of a clearer understanding of the UK HIV epidemic in the 1990s. Nevertheless, it seems imperative that epidemiological proportions do not become permanently reified as markers of need. It is just as important that careful epidemiological surveillance of other groups continues and that pointers, signals and tendencies in local as well as national data, however small, are reflected in actual health promotion and treatment and care interventions. There is an extremely difficult tension between consolidating health education policies involving some groups and balancing this against the risk that in other groups where no health interventions are taking place, new infections are.

ethnic absolutism, sexuality and the problems of cultural difference

If the impact of HIV among gay men, African refugee groups, injecting drug users and other groups represents an immense tragedy, then consideration of the dominant debates involving ethnicity and sexuality in the HIV/AIDS sector rapidly takes us into the realms of the absurd. This section looks at how some pseudo-sociological knowledges about homosexuality have been reproduced through the prism of ethnicity within the HIV/AIDS sector, and managed by a service provision, commissioning and funding process that is keen to celebrate an unthreatening, uncritical kind of multiculturalism, especially one that self-consciously provides an exotic edge to discussions about homosexual difference. The main focus of this section is an examination of the neo-orientalist obfuscation around sexuality, race and sexual identity that has constituted a major part of The Naz Foundation's[17] (hereafter TNF) work. The reason for doing so is not to single out the Foundation in particular but to highlight its work as an illustrative example of broader cultural absolutist tendencies in much race as well as sexuality related work. Virtually all the themes of culture, ethnicity and difference in TNF's work are reproduced widely in the HIV sector and constitute a quite formidable 'commonsense' among numerous health professionals. Similarly, the issue of political, cultural and ethnic absolutism is going to be a significant factor in HIV prevention work with African communities and will require careful understanding and management. Much depends in the coming years on developing a critical understanding of claims to authenticity and absolute cultural and ethnic difference in HIV prevention and care work.

TNF's policy aims are constructed on the lack of recognition of the needs of South Asian communities around HIV education and the support needs of South Asians living with HIV disease. Those needs have to be officially recognized and resourced. Indeed, one of the most important contributions that TNF has made, against the grain of epidemiology-led evidence-based practice, has been to educate the sector about the global dimensions of the epidemic and the complexities of sexual affiliation in different cultures, as well as asserting the importance of pride in sexual difference within South Asian communities. Similarly, if health education interventions aimed at a general or local population do not reflect or are inaccessible to certain communities then those interventions have been limited or are ethnocentric. There are strong and important ethical arguments in which equity and accessibility have to be a necessary and essential component of any health education strategy – the alternative is to regress back to period of the 1950s and 1960s when the dominant health and social welfare philosophy was as a crude assimilationism backed up by resonant ideas of white or British supremacy. The challenge has been to balance epidemiology with equity and accessibility. More importantly, about 180 South and South-East Asian people in the UK are known at the time of writing to have (had) AIDS[18] and the number with HIV infection must be much higher (though it is difficult to estimate how much higher – the characteristics of AIDS epidemiology in Asian communities is dependent on several factors related to both homosexual and heterosexual exposure, both in the UK and in several countries abroad). It is inexcusable to deny Asians appropriate, specialist services, social support and care from their peers, or to deny them the choice of services that reflect their needs as Asian people. Major parts of India (predominantly urban but some rural centres in Maharashtra and Gujarat, Tamil Nadu and Manipur) are acknowledged to be, alongside Thailand and Burma, the epicenters for the next wave of the HIV pandemic, possibly causing more devastation than has already occurred in Africa. It would be foolish to ignore the potential relevance in the UK of the major HIV epidemics in South and South East Asia, the Caribbean and West Africa. The complex patterns of travel, migration and settlement between areas of high prevalence in these countries and the UK are substantially different from the mobility patterns relevant to recent refugees from East, and to some extent, West Africa, and will require significant and directed HIV prevention strategies involving visiting and travelling groups.

However, TNF's project extends beyond the need to recognize South Asians in HIV service provision. It is worth examining its recovery of South Asian, Muslim and other identities, as well as its views about language, culture and alterity, since these are certain to emerge in work with other black communities. TNF's formulation of these issues has been elementary and rhetorical, but (probably unknowingly) relies on older well-established paradigms, in particular those views of culture and alterity that were a consequence of the Romantic reaction to Enlightenment. TNF also reflects the turn to cultural absolutism or cultural incommensurability ('incompatibility') that has been a major feature of black political discourse during the 1980s and 1990s, both in the UK and the USA. In particular, TNF reproduces in a liberal form virtually all the tropes of cultural absolutism that are also found in tendencies that range from black cultural nationalism and Afrocentricity to the kinds of religious-cultural and nationalist absolutism that have come to dominate South Asian politics. The obsession within these projects with rehearsing particularist ethnic differences, especially those differences mobilized against what are perceived to be 'Western' tropes of reason, humanism and universalism can disguise the debt that is actually owed to some of the most obnoxious strands of Western Enlightenment, Romanticism and, indeed, colonial discourse. The Naz Foundation's project is as deeply Western as 'the West' it ostensibly attacks and claims to distance itself from.

The Foundation's thesis is an elementary and familiar one: in some fundamental way, Western and South Asian discourses, cultures, languages, and constitutive world-views are incommensurable; as a result, Western and South Asian organizations of sex, homosexuality sexual identity, identity itself, gender relations and family are radically incommensurable. One consequence of this is that Western discourses have little or no applicability in the organization of sexual, family, identity and community relations in UK South Asian communities or in the Sub-continent. One other aspect, probably the starting point for TNF's other deliberations, is that gay (or lesbian) identity is a Western concept which South Asian men (or women) in or outside the UK would not identify with. TNF has also preoccupied itself with a selective excavation of ancient Indian anthropologies and archaeologies to demonstrate the existence of same-sex relations in South Asian history or antiquity. Finally, TNF has provided contents for what it views as South Asian cultures. This is a rather essentialist set of 'psycho-dynamics' which it claims exists and indeed defines those cultures.

One can appreciate the political necessity of South Asian lesbians and gay men reinventing antiquity in the contemporary in order to legitimize a present identity. (This is as true of Western gay men and lesbians who wish to celebrate Plato and Sappho.) The astonishing ancient temple carvings at Khajuraho which depict various polymorphous sexual acts, including homosexuality, or the numerous androgynous representations of Shiva, or the powerful representations of Durga and Kali, may assist in the important recovery of a sexual tradition and sexual history in which homosexuality was not despised. However, the fact of this history in itself cannot explain why male homosexuality in India or Pakistan in any form is a criminal offence under their penal codes technically punishable by up to life imprisonment (and/or a hundred lashes in Pakistan).

TNF has derived its thesis on sexual incommensurability from its selective view of language and a rather limited focus on words:

> We . . . assume that the names and words we use in our languages reflect a commonality in all languages, that what we describe and experience through our own language has direct correlation with other languages, other cultures. *This is not true.*(emphasis in original)[19]

Incommensurability (incompatibility) claims such as these often accompany absolute cultural relativism, and are easily shown to be problematic. If, for example, one discovers an 'incompatibility' in meaning between two cultures, then there is no incompatibility there, or at the very least one has begun to translate one culture's meanings into another. Put differently, if one finds that a linguistic sign from one culture is not directly translatable into a sign from another culture, then one has identified, described and comprehended in *both* languages the nature of the difference in the meanings of *both* signs, and hence already translated them or at least begun the process of deeper translation. Similarly, if radical incommensurabilities exist between sexual practices and identities in South Asian and

Western cultures, how is it that we are able to talk about this in English and explain in English what this 'incommensurability' is? (English is indeed the linguistic medium for virtually all of TNF's deliberations about the untranslability of South Asian languages and cultures.) Similarly, if 'Western' discourse will always be faced with such an incorrigibility that exists in the organization of South Asian cultural relations, or indeed its languages, how were the Rig Veda and the Upanishads, all preoccupied in some way with extraordinarily difficult metaphysical concepts of ineffability, identity and the Sublime, ever translated out of archaic Sanskrit?

There are deeper political problems with taking this kind of view of culture and cultural authenticity. Its antecedents are firmly Western and definitive of the pre-Enlightenment views of official or high culture, of 'culture' as 'cultivation', and of Romanticist oppositions between the desirable primitive state and the undesirable forms of civilization, reason and knowledge. The Naz Foundation, like numerous other contemporary Afro-Asian tendencies, essentially reproduces a paradigm that privileges 'high', as opposed to vernacular, 'lived' or syncretic South Asian cultures. TNF is similarly preoccupied with a cultural reification and reduction. South Asian cultures, in this sense, are acknowledged to be in opposition to the forms of reason, humanism and knowledge that are associated with the West. Culture, in this view, is equivalent to alterity and not amenable to the kinds of rationalist ('Western') methods of comprehension. Indeed, in extreme versions of cultural absolutism, the idea of epistemology is itself 'Western' and cultural mystique is the only authentic nativist possibility.

TNF also undertakes another culturalist turn in which South Asians are their culture. This is comprehended virtually entirely in TNF's work through a selective 'anthropology' and a 'psycho-dynamics' of 'public and private, visibility, honour and shame'. 'Psycho-dynamics' of course immediately invokes a (Western, modernist) Freudian trope. The shame-honour binary is particularly important for TNF, and its 'dynamic' means that 'we have to' deny the existence of sexual transgression, domestic violence and so forth. The shame-honour binary is actually a classical Orientalist trope and is frequently used by Western writers to describe Middle-Eastern cultures as if it could explain the totality of both their histories and their configurations of nation-state and civil society.

TNF's description of South Asian homosexual organization and the consequent relation between this and HIV prevention has been the basis of its most robust interventions in the HIV/AIDS sector. TNF has consistently argued that South Asian men who have sex with men 'do not identify as gay', or even homosexual, the latter being Western concepts that are inapplicable to South Asian regulations of sexuality. Its virtual opposite is the GMFA position – that black and Asian homosexual men 'do identify as gay', the added implication being that if they do not, then they ought to. This particular opposition exceeds both organizations and is central to the way debates and interventions involving ethnicity and homosexuality have been structured in the HIV/AIDS sector. Both these positions can appear to be trapped in an instrumentalist view of individual or collective identity as nothing more than a possessive object. However, there is a normative quality to TNF's position which appears to want to deny the validity or political importance of gay identity *as such*, or of the necessity of developing strong, proud and confident lesbian and gay identities, whatever one's ethnicity. Prior to the HIV epidemic, this may have been a luxury. In the situation of the devastating HIV epidemic among gay men, it is a reprehensible position for any organization to promote.

Some of the anthropological knowledges that TNF has promoted about gay identity are not inconsequential. TNF indeed ran into an illustrative dispute with a South Asian lesbian and gay organization, Shakti, after the latter had complained that TNF distributed condoms that were unsuitable for gay sex. TNF remained insistent that the distribution of condoms suitable for heterosexual sex reflected the culturally authentic sexual practices of South Asian gays who attended Shakti events. The condom packets, Milan ke Raat, distributed at an avowedly lesbian and gay event pictured an Asian heterosexual couple in romantic repose.

There are important issues about the organization of homosexual relations in black (and white) communities that cannot be contained in the unfractured categories of gay identity that GMFA, for example, insist upon. Gay identity itself does not form the limits of nor can it contain homosexual experience. Both the present writers, for example, have been involved in the social care and advocacy of South Asian men with AIDS whose affiliation to the commercial or informal gay scenes was non-existent and whose mode of homosexual organization was entirely based with South Asian communities and did not even include knowledge of or attendance at Shakti or similar events. In several such cases, one or both of the partners has remained unmarried. However, there is nothing 'non-Western' about these forms of homosexual organization, nor is there an essence to South Asian cultures that only permits these forms to exist. There is additionally a way in which the displacement of these men into some putative non-Western cultural category can become an insidious apologia for homophobia. However, these examples do illustrate a complexity that needs to be registered in HIV prevention work with homosexual men. An ethical anti-racist lesbian and gay liberationist discourse would ultimately be more effective and validating for these men (and for lesbian women) than a depoliticized acknowledgement of their existence as cultural 'others'.

It is as important to register and celebrate the traditions of black lesbian and gay affiliation that do exist and which have, by and large, remained separate from the mainstream commercial gay scene. The first ever black homosexual organizations in the UK (in 1980) explicitly identified with the tradition of gay and lesbian liberation. Similarly, there has been a severely underdocumented tradition of black gay social and sexual organization in the UK that has included, variously, Pearls in Brixton in the 1970s, the Union Tavern in Camberwell, the Sombrero nightclub in Kensington, the Lift, Bad at the Sound Shaft, Thursdays at the Market Tavern, and in more recent years Pressure Zone at the Vox, Shakti, Kali, Queer Nation, and the People of Colour events at Pride. There is a substantial tradition of black lesbian social and sexual organization. There is also something akin to a virtually hegemonic tradition of black gay cultural, political, film, musical and intellectual production, both in the UK and the US. The enormous diversity of these cultural-political spaces subvert the simplicity of knowledges about ethnic homosexualities that The Naz Foundation has created and suggest a deeply complex affiliation with and affirmation of gay identity. This can involve the use of existing gay commercial and informal scenes and the creation of separate cultural and social spaces, as well as numerous hybrid patterns of intra- and cross-ethnic sexual mixing that are far removed from fixed ideas of black-white, Western-non-Western binaries.

conclusion

The recent emphasis on targeted resource allocation and project development with communities known to be at risk represents an important paradigm shift in HIV prevention work that has taken several years to reach full acknowledgement. However, it has the potential to represent a forbidding emphasis on political and 'anthropological' separation, absolutist ideas of difference, and the consolidation of deeper particularist tendencies that will not necessarily be comfortable with the universal approach that is essential in commissioning and providing the same health services to diverse and unrelated groups. The emphasis on targeting does not remove conflicts involving race, ethnicity, gender and sexuality but may well deepen them.

These areas unsurprisingly reflect a broader philosophical and political debate about universalism and particularism, or about pluralist versus particularist orientations towards multiculturalism and social diversity. These factors are extremely important in understanding the refugee experience, itself a consequence of civil wars and severe national, ethnic, clan, 'tribal' and political conflicts. The refugee experience is intensely political on a number of different fronts along which many of the factors described above are rehearsed sharply. Authoritarian identity claims, cultural absolutism and claims about ethnic, 'tribal' and linguistic incommensurability have emerged as significant factors in work with refugee communities. The rather absurd though sometimes severe rehearsal of ethnic ('tribal') conflict in HIV/AIDS provider organizations has been significantly aided by a commissioning process that is keen to see groups display and magnify their differences and compete on the basis of authentic cultural representation. Conversely, important non-'tribalist', feminist, secular and democratic groups have emerged in facing the impact of HIV infection on African communities. An essential aspect of this work will have to be an approach that stresses the more universal values and ethics of rights, diversity and solidarity, challenge, support and care, rather than those of market aggression, competitiveness, difference, separation and self-seeking. There is ample scope here for stressing universalist approaches in commissioning and service delivery that fully recognize diverse and specialized services but are not solely obsessed with throwing money at each claim to sexual and ethnic difference.

notes

We would like to thank Jeffrey Weeks and Stephen Cross for comments on an earlier draft, though neither of them are responsible for or in agreement with all arguments.

1. Briefly, the NHS reforms were inaugurated under the Thatcher administration and meant a substantial shift away from free and equitable health care provision for all regardless of income and based entirely on state-managed health care to a situation of health care

based on an internal free market of commissioners and providers, a massive encouragement of private health care providers (and insurers) to compete with previously state-managed health services, an ideological emphasis on health care as a strategy of consumption choice (rather than a right) and an overarching belief that internal market competition would both reduce NHS costs and result in the best health service to consumers. This strategy is increasingly viewed as a disaster for UK health services. Both AIDS treatment and care and prevention services are subject to the same set of reforms, manifested especially in competition between ASOs for commissioner contracts.

2. *Migrants against AIDS/HIV*, 4 August 1996.
3. These include the Asylum Act which received royal assent in July 1996, the severe changes to social security benefit regulations for asylum seekers from February 1996 and the restricted rights in housing for homeless refugees and asylum seekers enforced from 1993.
4. S. Watney quoted in E. King, *Safety in numbers*, London, Cassell, 1993.
5. Each refugee, or person granted extended leave to remain in the UK, receives a letter from the Home Office stating that they cannot engage in political activities. While there is scope for reinterpreting this in the situation of HIV infection, its effect can be to prevent any mobilization around rights and access.
6. Bhan, *Assessment and Case Management: HIV and Black Communities*, London, BHAN, 1995.
7. One of the most striking comparisons is with the formation of a black institutional career framework following the burst of post-Scarman funding following the urban riots of 1980–1981 from (the former) Greater London Council, (the former) Inner London Education Authority and local authorities, as well as Urban Aid and section 11 funding. Virtually the same critiques made by gay men of bureaucratization, professionalization, depoliticization (or rather selective politicization) and the ignorance of the needs and interests of the broader social and political movement were made of this process in the 1980s.
   See P. Gilroy, *There Ain't No Black in the Union Jack: The Cultural Politics of 'Race' and Nation*, London, Hutchinson, 1987.
8. See E. King, op.cit.; V. Berridge, *AIDS in the UK: The Making of Policy, 1981–1994*, Oxford, OUP, 1996; See also J. Weeks et al., 'Community Responses to HIV/AIDS: The "Degaying" and "Regaying" of AIDS' in J. Weeks & J. Holland (eds) *Sexual Cultures: Communities, Values and Intimacy*, Basingstoke, Macmillan, 1996; and S. Garfield, *The End of Innocence: Britain in the Time of AIDS*, London & Boston, Faber, 1994.
9. See S. Watney, ' "Risk", research and modernity' in P. Aggleton, G. Hart and P. Davies, *AIDS: Responses, Interventions and Care*, London & New

York, Falmer, 1991; See also P. Davies, et al., *Sex, Gay Men and AIDS*, London & New York, Falmer, 1993.

10. S. Nettleton & R. Bunton, 'Sociological critiques of health promotion' in R. Bunton, S. Nettleton & R. Burrows, *The Sociology of Health Promotion: Critical Analyses of Consumption, Lifestyle and Risk*, London, Routledge, 1995.

11. King's argument illustrates how epidemiology and positivist social science can be used to the benefit of groups facing official neglect and discrimination. While from a strictly empiricist gaze, it would seem odd that virtually every piece of positivist research cited has in effect corroborated every nuance, detail and twist and turn of gay liberationist ideology that has been important during the epidemic, it is the interpretative and political use of positivist research which is essential.

12. GMFA Heath Project report, Summer 1994; GMFA Stop AIDS London (S.A.L.) Files Advertisement 1996; GMFA postal questionnaires, 1994.

13. If health need could be read off simply and only from epidemiology, the extent of health service expenditure on AIDS could be criticized in relation to the health needs involving cervical cancer, heart disease and lung cancer. Indeed, one consequence of targeting HIV expenditure is that overall HIV expenditure will become reduced.

14. Data from the PHLS Collaborative Laboratory Study is based on HIV serotesting at (currently) sixteen centres and needs to be interpreted with considerable care. The seropositivity data from the study is variable across the different centres, and the overall data is highly sensitive to changing testing patterns (such as changes in the numbers from different probable exposure categories being offered, going forward for, and accepting HIV testing).

15. Unlinked anonymous HIV prevalence monitoring programme: England & Wales – data to the end of 1993, Report from the Unlinked Anonymous hiv Surveys Steering Group (Chairman Dr Eileen Rubery, Department of Health), Department of Health, 1995.

16. ibid.

17. The discussion below focuses on the earlier work of what is now The Naz Foundation. This is entirely different from the new Naz Project, formed from the summer of 1996, and which represents a different organizational and service philosophy. The latter is not the subject of the critique which is undertaken.

18. CDSC AIDS/HIV Quarterly Surveillance Tables 31, Data to end March 1996, Table 26. Of 179 people with or who had AIDS and were classified since 1985 under the (unhelpful and non-standard) category 'Asian/Oriental', 108 were gay men and 51 were heterosexuals probably exposed abroad.

19. The Naz Project, *Contexts: Race, Culture and Sexuality*, London, The Naz Project, 1994.

queer peregrinations[1]

Cindy Patton

Researchers believe that the virus was present in isolated population groups years before the epidemic began. Then the situation changed: people moved more often and travelled more; they settled in big cities; and lifestyles changed, including patterns of sexual behaviour. It became easier for HIV to spread, through sexual intercourse and contaminated blood. As the virus spread, the isolated disease already existing became a new epidemic. (Global Program on AIDS 1989: 6)

Although this account has become commonplace, closer examination reveals complex, even incompatible ideas about disease and its translocation. Crisscrossing temporal and geographic metaphors, the account vacillates between the *story* of a virus and a *description* of bodies who might disperse it. 'The virus' is first described as lodged in a timeless and immobile *place*: grounded in an 'isolated population' until modernity stepped in to inscribe time and a mania for travel. 'Now', people move and change, carrying with them the dangerous combination of their new sexual practices and their contaminated blood. Miraculously (inevitably?), an epidemic ensued. Modernity catapulted the virus which had once lived peacefully among unnamed 'population groups' into an epidemic of history-changing proportions.

This travelogue version of HIV's dispersion was easier to

swallow than the part of the story we did not yet know, or could not bring ourselves to believe: that arrogant and grotesquely unethical blood banking practices dispersed HIV-infected blood among haemophiliacs in France and God knows where else.[2] It was preferable to blame modern sexuality than the equally modern capital interests in medicine which fuelled the epidemic in places where no one went anywhere at all.

I want to suggest here that this basic 'explanation' is accepted as fact because it employs widely recognizable ideas that are woven into two medical disciplines and have framed popular beliefs about disease and migration for a century. The sketchiness of the account allows for a plethora of more detailed versions of the story. The central roles are anonymous, allowing reporters and international health policy analysts to enliven their accounts with 'real people', to 'put a face on AIDS'. Almost *anyone* can be implicated as the problematic mobile body. A Canadian airline steward or jetsetting gay tourist, an African truck driver or the rural woman who now sells him sex on the edges of the city, a male migrant laborer who crosses national borders to feed his family, the soldier who defends his country or invades another: these are the vivid characters alleged to bring HIV from Africa, from Haiti, from anywhere but 'here'.

But despite the common tactic of placing infection in the body of an Other, the US media and international policy discourse define the geography of disease differently and rely on structurally different concepts of how disease moves. These differences have a great deal in common with the narrative tropes of epidemiology and of tropical medicine, which, in turn propose different solutions to pathology. The US media and epidemiology share the fantasy of eradicating AIDS, while international policy and tropical medicine hold out hope for immunity. These disease teleologies enable and promote multiple, often conflicting institutional strategies of control, which finally have enormous if unpredictable consequences for the people who are governed by them.

This essay is one of several in a project that contemplates

the incoherences between three bodies of discourse about the HIV pandemic: 1) the national US discourse about its own epidemic, as observed in the US media 2) the discourse about the pandemic as a global phenomenon, as exemplified by documents from the World Health Organization and other non-governmental, transnational organizations, and 3) the Euro-American discourse about the AIDS epidemic in so-called developing countries, evident in the media and in the general outline of international research projects.[3]

The US national discourse about AIDS is the apotheosis of what Foucault described in his many accounts of the rise of modernist knowledge: his 'empirico-transcendental doublet' takes itself as both the object of inquiry and the subject of knowledge,[4] much as the Centers for Disease Control studies the public it both represents and protects. The discourse of the World Health Organization and other Euro-American transnational non-government organizations depends on a kinder, gentler form of knowledge. Territorially divested but very much nationally interested, post-colonial positivist science extracts 'local knowledge' from those who become subject to 'cooperative' policies and programmes developed after translation into 'scientific knowledge' and retranslation into local vernacular. Finally, the discourse *about* AIDS in the developing world covertly acknowledges places outside the first world authorial centre. But these places become a projective screen or laboratory for performing ideological or real (vaccine trials?) procedures that solve the master countries' internal epidemic or absolve their responsibility for the devastation occurring *outside* the collective Euro-American borders.

Although the analysis here is somewhat abstract, my concerns are not disinvested. The ongoing and excessive influence of post-colonial powers over their former or current client states coupled with the reconsolidation of systems of medical control under the sign of AIDS call for urgent, but thoughtful intervention. AIDS science, as it trickles down through policy and media, substantially informs popular interpretations of the epidemic, shaping the experience of those directly affected and forming the moral logic which determines the popular acceptability of policing in fact or through resource distribution. In addition, the narratives of scientific progress, which emphasize the coherence and additive nature of scientific research, help rationalize discriminatory policy and continued pursuit of unwarrantedly narrow research questions. In relating specific documents of the AIDS epidemic to larger, abstract medical logics and suggesting that neither research paradigms nor the various levels of policy and representation are logically coherent, I hope to indicate the relations of power which several forms of AIDS discourse secure.

tropical medicine and epidemiology: competing colonialisms

Many of the concepts in what in the West are called tropical medicine and epidemiology developed as crucial parts of nineteenth and early twentieth century colonial expansion. Tropical medicine, obviously, from its very name, dealt with the problems Euro-Americans encountered in their local occupations, merging empirical science with the fantasy of the colony. As Bruno Latour has suggested, the displacement of the scientific laboratory from the academy to the field was crucial to the 'discovery' of aetiologic agents.[5] Not only did displacement literally produce the isolated research conditions necessary to finally establishing germ theory, but it provided the colonial imaginary with a series of metonymically linked spaces: the colony of scientists in the client state colony studying the colony of germs on the surface of the agar plate. This cemented a homological turn of mind which could justify colonial power as an extension of the emerging modern will-to-control through positive science.

Tropical medicine wedded imperial notions of health and geography to the bourgeois notion of the domestic as a space within a space (the public). Colonial movement is bidirectional along a single axis, movement into the constructed domestic space of the colony is always accompanied by nostalgia for 'going home'. Tropical medicine relies on a diasporal imaginary of displacement and return which presumes that local diseases do not affect indigenous people in the same way that they affect the Euro-American occupier. A tropical disease is always proper to a place, to *there*, but only operates *as disease* when it afflicts people from *here*. Pathogens in a locale are of interest to researchers only when they present as disease in the colonist's body. The colonist's ailing body is not the victim of his or her dislocation, but a hero in the story of conquering the tropics. Tropical disease is contained by virtue of already being *there*, in the 'tropics': even if he (sic) could not always get well, the colonist could always go home.

Critically, the very idea of tropical medicine rests on the ability to reliably separate an indigenous population perceived to be physically hearty but biologically inferior from a colonizing population believed to be biologically superior even while subject to the tropical illnesses. Sustaining this medical paradox requires perpetually refilling the category, 'exotic ailment'. Tropical medicine grows out of and supports the idea that the First World body is the proper gauge of health: the Third World is the location of disease, even while its occupants are not the subjects of tropical medicine. Tropical medicine *points* to a map that already hierarchizes bodies, placing Europeans and European health at the pinnacle.

Epidemiology, on the other hand, is performative: it invents concepts and its object of study as it goes. By separating pathogens from the body, epidemiology enables itself to declare 'disease' from some but not all conjunctures of body/pathogen. Less concerned than tropical medicine to detail the diseases which may befall the Euro-American body in a place, epidemiology visualizes the place of the body in the temporal sequence called 'epidemic'. It is no longer the body fighting disease which is heroic, but epidemiology, the 'disease detective', which alone has the power to visualize and disrupt the 'natural history' of germs' vectorial movement.

An 'epidemic' is more cases than expected, a deceptively simple definition which hides the messy truth that declaring an epidemic depends on cultural perceptions about who is likely to be sick and to what degree. Epidemiology reverses tropical medicine's concern with who may fall sick by removing disease from the natural environment and placing it in the body. Instead of viewing tropical inhabitants as more or less immune to the diseases which surround them, *indigene* are now themselves the location of disease, reservoirs or carriers, poverty is no longer 'natural' but an assault on the middle class. Epidemiology defines the boundaries of a disease by constituting a category of subject ('risk group'), an imagined community produced through vectors which epidemiology simulates as though discovered. Bodies are at once subject to and perpetrators of pathology, both 'sick' and reservoirs or carriers in the larger network of disease.

Pathology is visualized against a background state of health, and this background definition of health becomes the ideological lynch pin, the very condition of possibility for panoptic epidemiology. Health is not an objective external standard applied to all bodies, but a convenient definition that prioritizes the well-being of those with power. If the colonial homology could mask the medical crimes of transporting disease *to* the colony, epidemiology could hide the crimes of class-tiered health care delivery, not through naming disease, but by constituting the background definition of health in relation to the concerns of the enfranchised. Changes in health status only mattered if those at risk were considered important in the first place.

An 'epidemic' is vectorial, movement is always outward from the centre. Migratory sites of pathology can at any time be linked. Each new locale becomes a new centre capable of projecting its vectorial links with yet more periphery, which in turn become new centres. Links are multidirectional; it makes no sense to speak of diaspora or return, only of vectorial logic.

If in theory anyone could be a vector, epidemiology's statistical procedures 'discovered' that some bodies were more likely than others to carry (transport/harbour) disease. Bereft of a stable *place* of pathology, epidemiology must constantly construct and correlate populations and subpopulations in order to make epidemics visible.

vectors as community

The recognition of a change which triggers the epidemiological establishment is usually presumed to be a change in pathogens or in the interaction between disease pools. But the crucial, unspoken part of the AIDS story is the background change in social attitudes about expected health, critical not only in the initial identification of the epidemic but in setting the *terms* of subsequent discourse about HIV and AIDS. By 1981, when the new medical syndrome was identified, the decade old-gay liberation movement had gone a great distance in establishing itself as a civil entity ('minority') and had won increased tolerance from the mental and physical health care establishments. Health care providers were increasingly sensitive both to the 'normality' and to the special needs of gay clients. At least in large urban gay ghettos, openly gay people could come to the attention of openly gay or sympathetic health care professionals. The resistive visibility which enabled rapid collective response by gay men (and their lesbian collaborators) became a tool of epidemiological surveillance: the idea of vectors was nestled into the protective perimeter of 'community'.

The concept of the 'healthy homosexual', combined with the refiguration of gay people as a 'community', turned gay men's collectivities into an agar plate. Intra-gay community transmission was viewed as multidirectional, pure vectors limited by the boundary of community. Unlike women and heterosexual men, gay men were not considered 'partners of' other men: HIV circulated freely within the gay community. However, if such men had a female 'partner' the media banished him from the gay community, now viewed as something like a colony. Bisexual men *went to* the dense spaces of homosexuality and *returned from* it, to the heterosexual home, infected with HIV.

Popular press writers in the US went to great lengths to simultaneously alert heterosexual women to their potential risk of contracting HIV, while denying a *place* within the space of heterosexuality for the man who had contracted HIV from another man. The bisexual man was variously described in the US popular media as 'a bogeyman . . . cloaked in myth and his own secretiveness;'[6] 'men [who] may be dangerous to your health;'[7] 'the invisible men . . . without a national organization or sexual agenda;'[8] the man who might 'live in towns, cities or suburbs and . . . look and dress like everybody else' while 'playing straight with you.'[9]

The authors set out with epidemiology's description of risk groups – homosexual men and female 'partners of' – but they resort to tropical medical conceptions when faced with placing 'the man in your life who has a man in his life'.[10] The switch to tropical narratives enables the homosexual risk of these men to be contained in a specific local: 'Bisexual men and male drug users do have one thing in common, besides their AIDS risk: geography'.[11]

But literal geography only anchors the trope of displacement. Rabinowitz's 'The Secret Sharer: One Woman Confronts Her Homosexual Husband's Death From AIDS' spatializes the Dr Jekyll and Mr Hyde narrative.[12] The now-possibly-infected-wife says, 'I married a very different person' and the writer takes pains to distinguish between the husband's localized homosexual life ('In the bathhouses, Alex marched around exhibiting himself') and his despatialized straight life ('everywhere else, he was the quintessential straight, sometimes homophobic male'). In relation to the 'general population', who live in the generalized 'everywhere else', homosexuality – and with it, HIV – is proper to, endemic in, the imagined place of gay community: bathhouses in cities like New York.

These switches occur because the writers refuse to follow through with the vectorial logic which would acknowledge straight men's risk of homosexual transmission, either directly, as when engaging in queer acts, or indirectly, through acknowledging that their women might have been engaging in straight acts with queer men. Instead, men who have sex with men, as the World Health Organization's Global Program on AIDS now calls them, are reinserted into the endocolonial version of the gay community.

queer bodies, invisible sex

The pressure to contain the AIDS epidemic, and the hope that patterns of spread would be roughly the same worldwide legitimated ethnographic inquiry into sex between men.[13] While this work has extended the range of knowledge about same-sex affectional bonds, the underlying agenda of control and the obvious reluctance to let go of comfortable Eurocentric sexual categories and ideologies have resulted in confusion between 'gay' 'men' and same sex practitioners who go under other names (or no name at all). Euro-American homosexualities are both implicated in and comprise the Other to homosexualities in other parts of the world. Colonial expansion mingled forms of same sex union which operated with different symbolic meanings. But unlike homosexuality at home, which was thought to result from decadence in the upper classes – *over* civilization – homosexualities found in the colonies were perceived to be *un*civilized. Colonial administrators outlawed varieties of traditional homosexual marriage or legal partnership that got in the way of tidy management and Christian missionaries turned special scorn on homosexual practices.[14]

It was unlikely, only a few decades later, that postcolonial governments were going to acknowledge social patterns which had once been used to demonstrate their inferiority.

By the 1980s, disavowal of indigenous homosexualities was articulated *in terms of* the Euro-American 'gay lifestyle' that had become increasingly visible, in part because of media coverage about and international scientific exchange during the AIDS epidemic. Implicating this already stereotyped Euro-American post-industrial homosexuality as the motor of the epidemic enabled developing country governments to ignore the potential for epidemics among other kinds of homosexual social-symbolic formations in their countries.

A representative of the South African Ministry of Mines made a strange reading of an ethnography of male relations in the mines which suggested that while men formed long-lasting domestic and sexual bonds, sex between men had not usually included anal intercourse.[15] Instead of promoting male miners' sexuality as a model of safe sex, the minister concluded that the miners were not appropriate subjects of prevention discourse aimed at homosexuals: they did not engage in 'real sex'.

Citing such work on miners and migratory sexual relations, social constructionist social sciencists were able to get the WHO/GPA to chose and normalize the term 'men who have sex with men', a conceptual move away from Euro-American notions that grounded homosexuality in psychic processes and made queer bodies amenable to organization into an identity and community. But while the term 'men who have sex with men' made it possible for a few HIV educators to work closely and sensitively with local homosexualities, safe sex discourse and WHO policy still insisted on a fixed link between sexual identity and practices of pleasure. To the extent that it tries to hail appropriate (if closeted) subjects to convert to condom use, safe sex discourse – coming as it does on the heels of international media coverage which sensationalizes homosexual sex and connects it with a specific image of the 'gay' man – collaborates in constructing intercourse as both the *sine qua non* and principal danger of sex. This has narrowed the (safe) sexual imaginary available to Euro-American gay men, and produced a tendency, even in the most savvy projects, to accidentally produce the Westernized, urbanized sexual subject among men who have sex with men in other cultures.

Once men who have sex with men are located, it frequently turns out that they in fact do not, or only under some circumstances, engage in anal intercourse with other men: they *already* practise safe sex, but not as such. Thus, in order to promote maintenance of the already safe cultural norms, the Westernized notions of unsafe sex must be introduced. This is difficult to do in a colonial context without suggesting that intercourse, the now-distinguishing preoccupation of urban Western gay discourse, is the 'real' form of homosexuality. Paradoxically, at least in current practice, Western safe sex programmes directed toward 'men who have sex with men' must introduce unprotected intercourse in order to discourage its practice. The inadequacy of a behavioural intervention designed with vectoral, *democratic* concepts of movement in mind and the practices and mores of the actual men who might be its 'target' is nowhere clearer than when the men described by these different frameworks meet.

Western homosexuals are understood to be members of an epidemiological category until they arrive in the developing world. To the extent that they are a vector between North and South, the possibility of HIV transmission is understood as operating in one direction. Thus, the 'Western gay' is believed to arrive and hire the non-gay (heterosexually identified) man who has sex with men, who provides a domestic service – sex.

Haitian researchers have accumulated evidence, through analysis of Haitian blood samples going back over a decade, which they believe shows that the AIDS virus arrived in Haiti with [gay] North American tourists: 'The neighbouring country of the Dominican Republic, another favoured holiday destination for homosexual men from the United States, has seen a similar shift from homosexual to heterosexual transmission.'[16] This tourist version of colonial relations makes the American gay man (a deviant in his homeland) the bearer of disease to the colony, but, as I will detail in the last section, the epidemic produced is not among indigenous 'homosexuals', but among *hetero*sexuals. The hurtling queer body goes ballistic in the tropics, producing abroad the heterosexual epidemic feared at home.

real work, straight sex

The semantic moves from homosexual to gay to men who have sex with men track sophisticated changes in concepts about male sexuality: from gender of object of affection to social identity to specificity of practice. The pressures of the epidemic did not produce a parallel reconsideration of bartered straight sex. But if the shifts in queer nomenclature kept relapsing to already-inscribed notions about Western homosexuality, it was unclear whether or how the co-existence of terms prostitute/prostitution, sex worker/sex work was problematic. While deconstructing the traditional negative associations with prostitution, and signalling the labour issues involved, the term 'sex work' retains a Eurocentric bias. Rooted in a Marxist feminism that attempts to shift debate about bartered sex away from issues of morality and on to issues of labour, the term sex work, at least as it is used in discussions of global HIV policy, promotes capitalist concepts of market and economy.

Like the versions of gay male community work in the West, which attempt to achieve safe sex conformity by strengthening individual identity and identification with an oppositional community, organizing women as sex workers attempts to construct a notion of identity – as a worker – for individuals engaging in symbolically and practically disparate erotic episodes. Promoting the idea that bartering domestic services, including sex, is work requires introducing capitalist concepts of the split between domesticity and labour into cultures where such divisions of labour are not fully established or have resulted from the mixed motives post-colonial development plans.

Like the hyper-production of anal intercourse necessary to Western safe sex ideology, using the term 'sex work' requires introducing the very morality activists hoped to overcome. Sex must be *privatized* in order to make it public as formal work. Even if wages are due for housework,[17] paid-for-sex appears to be a commodified substitute for what properly happens at home.

'Sex work' does not seem to reflect the experience of these informal sector traders in developing nations and probably also misunderstands the role and nature of sex trade in Europe and the US. Renegotiation of domestic and sexual relations in countries experiencing intensive economic reorganization and massive, gender-linked migrations is extremely complex. For most men and women, trading sex and domestic favours is not a profession, but a transient activity that occurs alongside domestic relations, or a cyclical activity used to amass capital alongside economically sanctioned jobs. In the Cameroon and other parts of West Africa, for example, rural women migrated to the cities throughout the twentieth century, and commonly own small beer houses or food stands which they capitalize through periodic sale of 'sexual favors'. Alternatively, especially in Southern Africa where mining has resulted in massive and cyclical migration of men from the countryside, women and sometimes men, who live near mining camps sell homecooked meals and wash clothes, supplementing these cottage industries through trading sex with favourite customers. In the major cities of East Africa, where the massive migrations of the immediate post-colonial period have stabilized, there is a large class of 'free' (unmarried) women working in clerical or other low level non-domestic jobs. These women supplement their wages by trading companionship or sex for consumer goods, a practice known in Senegal as 'going out'.

The women who most clearly fit the Western model of professional sex work receive the most attention in global AIDS discourse, but largely to constitute them as the growing 'reservoir' of HIV infection in an accelerating epidemic among heterosexual men and their families. Like gay communities in the West, geographic areas (parts of cities, sometimes whole countries) where prostitution is thought to occur are treated as colonies with an endemic disease to which single or migratory men go, only to bring HIV back to their proper or future wives.

imaginary diasporas

Policy-makers or newspaper writers switch between logics when they describe the epidemic. Switching is not capricious or illogical but a symptom of the need to make sense of the epidemic in terms of existing power structures and ideologies. Observing when writers switch from vectorial to diasporal logic helps make sense of confusing accounts by revealing the larger investments in the privileges that accrue from maintaining controlling the explanation of world events. For example, many of the first AIDS cases diagnosed in Asia were among haemophiliac men, but this did not challenge the travel narratives that insisted that Western homosexuals had imported HIV to Asia. The Director-General of the Department of Health of the Taiwan Provincial Government described the trajectory of HIV as it made its way to his country:

> AIDS has been identified only within the past ten years in central Africa; from there it quickly spread to Haiti and then to the US and to Europe. It came very late to Taiwan: in December 1984 an American transiting Taiwan was found to have full-blown AIDS. This triggered our first major concern over the fatal disease. However a rapid increase in the number of AIDS patients locally, the spread of the disease to other parts of Taiwan, development of AIDS among HIV carriers in haemophiliacs, the diversification of risk groups – all have followed the same pattern seen in Western countries and throughout the world.[18]

But while the Director-General describes the epidemiological pattern of HIV as identical to that in the rest of the world, colleagues provide considerable detail about indigenous homosexuality in order to construct even the 'tabooed' practices in Taiwan as yet different from those in the more licentious West.

> According to the statements on the questionnaires, kissing was the most common sexual practice but, after extensive interviewing, male homosexuals often admitted anal intercourse as well . . . None described practices of 'fisting' . . . Low prevalence of HIV-1 was detected in several high risk groups. If the results of the questionnaire and interview are accepted as reliable, homosexual behavior in Taiwan appears to be much less promiscuous than in the western world.[19]

Although cases of HIV and AIDS were described among Asians in the early to mid-1980s, HIV only became visible as a problem *for* Asia when it appeared among sex workers, transforming sex workers from the sexual/tropical home-away-from-home for Westerners into a vector within Asia. Because Asian sexuality was stereotyped as passive, as capable largely of receiving but not passing on HIV, early low incidence figures were interpreted within the tropical medical framework as a kind of immunity rather than an artifact of HIV's late arrival per the epidemiological model. But, by the 1992 International Conference on AIDS in Amsterdam, HIV was represented as a phenomenon now indigenous to Asia – being passed among members of the Asian migrant and under classes. Once 'Asian AIDS' was launched, blame concerning the diasporal relations of migrant Western homosexuals was subordinated to hysteria about heterosexual vectorial transmission. Asia's plight was compared to 'African AIDS', not to the unmarked, but unmistakable queer AIDS which the media suggested formed the centre of the epidemic in white America.[20]

Similarly, a description of the 'heterosexual' epidemic in Haiti separates both American homosexuality and heterosexuality from their cohorts' practices in the tropics:

> While large numbers of tourists visited briefly from cruise

> ships, the majority of those who stayed in Haiti were homosexual men, who paid for sex with local men who had wives or girlfriends and considered themselves heterosexual. First the bisexual men become infected, then their female partners, and now Haiti has a full-scale heterosexual AIDS epidemic on its hands.[21]

Western heterosexuals had the good sense to visit Haiti only briefly from the safety of their cruise ships, but the 'homosexual men' stayed to bring both capitalism and HIV. Queer lucre engenders disease in the tropics because heterosexuality in the colony is premodern. As Ugandan President, Yoweri Museveni, described the inscription of two epochs of sexuality in his country:

> [AIDS] is the result of European influences – European liberalism, which is good in some respects, has brought a lot of permissiveness, which in a backward society is dangerous.[22]

The Haitian denial of local homosexualities (the men only 'consider themselves heterosexual') and the Ugandan president's infantilization of heterosexuality allow HIV to take root 'there', to become endemic. From the local perspective, the epidemic *among* heterosexuals may be vectorial, but from the *global* perspective, HIV's arrival is diasporal. The libertine European or queer colonist *arrives* sick, but, as in the Taiwanese account of the 'original' case of AIDS – a transiting American homosexual – his ailing body is simply 'sent home'.

competing logics, master tropes

I hope I have demonstrated both the solidity of two core logics, and the ease with which writers move between them. The insistent use of concepts of movement, the construction and detachment of ideas of place, enhance the legibility of the more general, but 'scientific' story of the epidemic, which in turn serves as the foundation for the more colourful descriptions of a global disaster. A key reason for switching between the two core logics, I suggested, was the desire to sustain larger cultural narratives about sexuality and secure broader national and transnational interests. In the details of producing a story, writers lose their grip on migrating body-objects that resist the codes scientific discourses try to impose upon them.

I suggested, for example, that Euro-American homosexuals are a 'risk group' as long as transmission is considered a 'community' issue. But the very places gay men occupy are a colony for their bisexual cohorts, even if gay men are themselves colonists from the perspective of the developing country governments who wish to deny homosexualities in their own borders. Homosexuality must be kept out of the domestic space and heterosexualities-for-hire must be maintained as private: homosexuality must not count as real sex, and prostitution must not count as real work.

This peregrination of narrative tropes defies science's view of itself as coherent and belies policy and media writers' belief that they can 'apply' objective knowledge. The AIDS epidemic is a particularly spectacular example of the switching, drifting, *bricoleur* use of supposed disinvested descriptive frames. Though tropical medicine's modes of thinking are clearly critical to understanding these multiple registers of AIDS discourse, the limiting meta-discursive logic is still that of epidemiology, though not because it has any greater scientific explanatory power. Rather, because it can describe place, and especially origin, in concrete spatio-temporal terms called 'natural history', epidemiology meets the internal management and the external image needs of the US, the country at greatest political risk of having to acknowledge its role in creating and sustaining the HIV pandemic.

notes

1. This essay is reprinted, with minor changes, with permission of the University of Minnesota Press and the author. The essay originally appeared in Michael Shapiro and Hayward R. Alker (eds), *Challenging Boundaries* (1996), A note on the essay's title: 'queer' is used both in the sense of queer theory – the recent academic work that hoped to move beyond the apparently more fixed designation of lesbian and gay studies – and in the grandmotherly sense of strange, inexplicable. Peregrinations connotes both travel and wandering – movement that is not entirely predictable over terrain that is not entirely under one's control.
2. Jane Kramer, 'Bad Blood', *The New Yorker,* 11 October 1993.
3. Cindy Patton, *Inventing AIDS,* New York, Routledge, 1990; Cindy Patton, 'From Nation to Family: Containing "African AIDS" ', in Andrew Parker, Doris Somer, and Patricia Yaeger (eds), *Nationalisms and Sexualities,* New York, Routledge, 1992; Cindy Patton, 'Ground Zero: AIDS Education and the Decline of Epidemiology', in Eve Sedgwick and Andrew Parker (eds), *Performance/Performativity,* New York, Routledge, 1994.
4. 'Man, in the analytic of finitude, is a strange empirico-transcendental doublet, since he is a being such that knowledge will be attained in him of what renders all knowledge possible . . . For the threshold of our modernity is situated not by the attempt to apply objective methods to the study of man, but rather by the constitution of an empirico-transcendental doublet which was called *man*'. Michel Foucault, *The Order of Things,* New York, Vintage, 1973, p.318–19.
5. Bruno Latour, *The Pasteurization of France,* Tr. Alan Sheridan and John Law, Cambridge, Harvard University Press, 1988.
6. Jon Nordheimer, 'AIDS Specter for Women: The Bisexual Man', *New York Times,* April 3, 1987.
7. Christopher Norwood, 'AIDS Is Not For Men Only', *Mademoiselle,* September, 1985.
8. Anne Conover Heller, 'Is There a Man in Your Man's Life?' *Mademoiselle,* July, 1987.
9. ibid.
10. ibid.
11. Norwood, op. cit.
12. Dorothy Rabinowitz, 'The Secret Sharer', *The New Yorker,* 26 February, 1990.
13. R. Paul Abrahamson, and Gilbert Herdt, 'The Assessment of Sexual Practices Relevant to the Transmission of AIDS: A Global Perspective', *The Journal of Sex Research,* 27/2, May; 1990.

14. Gil Shepard, 'Rank, Gender, and Homosexuality: Mombasa as a Key to Understanding Sexual Options', in Pat Caplan (ed.) *The Cultural Construction of Sexuality* 1997; Gloria Wekker, 'Matisma and Black Dykes,' *Homosexuality, Which Homosexuality?*, Conference Papers, Social Science, Vol. 2. Amsterdam, Free University, 1987; Saskia Wieringa, 'An Anthropological Critique of Constructionism: Berdache and Butches', in *Homosexuality, Which Homosexuality?* Amsterdam, Schorer, 1989.

15. Alan Whitehead, 'Migrant Labor and AIDS in South Africa', Global Impact of AIDS Conference, London, 8–10 March 1988; Dunbar T. Moody, 'Migrancy and Male Sexuality on South African Gold Mines', *Journal of South African Studies*, 14:2, January, 1988

16. Panos Institute, *AIDS in the Third World*, Philadelphia, New Society Publishers, 1989.

17. The slogan 'wages for housework' and 'wages due lesbians' were used by Marxist feminist organizers in Britain. They stem from a similar analysis, which attempts to signal the labour dimensions of women's activities.

18. Chun-Jean Lee, 'Address', *Human Retroviruses and AIDS*, Proceedings of the Symposium, 11–13 November 1988.

19. Ho-Chin Lee, et al., 'Update: AIDS and HIV-I Infection in Taiwan, 1985–1988', *Human Retroviruses and AIDS*, Proceedings of the Symposium, 11–13 November 1988.

20. Reporters and policy makers use the central, unmarked term 'AIDS' to refer to patterns of incidence which match the early perceptions of the epidemic's target – homosexual men. They use another range of terms – 'African AIDS', 'Third World AIDS' – to indicate *some other* phenonmenon. Thus, 'AIDS', while not overtly designated 'gay AIDS' nevertheless connotes a particular understanding of who is affected in the epidemic – homosexuals. See Patton 1990 and 1992, op. cit.

21. Panos, op. cit., p.88.

22. Panos, op. cit., p.91.

it's a straight world after all

heterosexualizing the pandemic

Meurig Horton

introduction

Michael is a pleasant young man who works for the Gay Men's Health Crisis in New York. He has recently returned from Central and East Africa, where he volunteered for the Peace Corps. As he told me about his travels over dinner, he assured me that the Peace Corps is now 'gay friendly', with an active Lesbian and Gay volunteers' organization. Quickly and skilfully, however, he shifted the conversation to the subject that most interested him: his professional future. He told me that he would like to work in international public health. To this end, he had begun study for a Master's in Public Health (MPH) at one of the more affordable New York universities. He stressed that he wanted to be 'marketable' after graduation, but he was worried. He asked if he'd chosen wisely: 'Would this AIDS thing still be around in a few years or was it going down?'

My first reaction to this discussion with Michael was, unfortunately, a judgmental one. How could he be so stupid? He works in one of the largest AIDS service organizations in the United States. He has direct experience of the epidemic in one of the worst affected areas in the world. He is a gay man living in a city that, according to the latest figures from the Centers for Disease Control, has seen a total of more than 60,000 AIDS cases. Roughly 70 per cent of these cases have been gay and bisexual men. New York is currently home to over 200,000 people with HIV, about one third to one half are gay or bisexual men.[1] How could Michael not understand that working at GMHC is the most important place a gay man concerned about stopping AIDS could possibly work in New York City?

But we must never be too quick to judge in this epidemic. Its long-term fall-out has been both catastrophic and unpredictable for gay men. New York is a city whose symptomatic epidemic is four or five years ahead of Western Europe's. It's a city that has lost almost an entire generation of gay men. If some of these men had been alive to share their experiences with Michael, he might have understood very differently his role in the fight against AIDS.

It seems to me that Michael is entirely the wrong person to judge, for he has been badly let down. The available vocabulary with which he can narrate his own experience of AIDS has been dramatically circumscribed within a banal global rhetoric that literally displaces actual AIDS from the consciousness, and – in the same gesture – erases the very real toll the epidemic has taken on homosexually active men in every region on earth. This displacement is what I'd like to explore.

Without a clear understanding of how AIDS affects gay and other homosexually active men in all its complexity – indeed, without confronting actual epidemics – we run the risk of chasing what Simon Watney has called 'imaginary epidemics.'[2] This metaphor suggests a kind of Virtual AIDS, unfettered by any virological restraint, a synonym for general moral collapse, or for racial, sexual and economic oppression. This imaginary AIDS is completely unconnected to the specificities of communities or practices associated with the transmission of HIV. As the virus is ever more understood as a general infectious presence, the real risks for homosexually active men are displaced. AIDS becomes a frightening, random, and remote risk generalized for everyone, like being held hostage by terrorists, or subject to ultraviolet rays leaking through holes in the ozone layer.

My arguments do not seek to privilege gay men over other communities affected by 'actual' AIDS; rather, they seek to draw attention to the epidemiological, social and cultural specificities of those at risk. After all, these are precisely what's essential for the delivery of meaningful AIDS prevention and treatment services. It's useless to target prevention to 'women' without first determining which women are at risk, where they live, what they do for a living, how they can be most effectively reached, and by what means they are contracting the virus.

At first glance, it seems reasonable enough to discuss the health crisis in terms of a single global epidemic. Thus it would appear that there's one disease, one epidemic, and one intervention: a vaccine or cure, probably discovered in the United States and unavailable in the poorer countries for many years. This model would imply a single and straightforward solution: a system of control and eradication.

There is weighty precedent for this way of thinking in the spectacular earlier twentieth-century successes of public health, especially the eradication of smallpox. Unfortunately, HIV is biologically completely different from Variola (the virus that causes smallpox) and other viruses which have been successfully controlled through public health policy. The unique stigmas, taboos and prejudices which exacerbate epidemics of HIV infection further differentiate AIDS from smallpox and other epidemics met by a concerted global response.

Nevertheless, it was the response to smallpox that provided the model upon which bureaucrats designed the World Health Organization's Global Programme on AIDS. Since January 1996 the United Nations Joint Programme on AIDS (UN AIDS) has replaced the WHO GPA. UN AIDS is sponsored by several major UN agencies, and is intended to broaden the global response to AIDS to incorporate social, political, and developmental institutions.[3]

a global silence on homosexuality

Since the formation of the WHO GPA in 1987 – shortly after Jonathan Mann declared that AIDS is a global 'pandemic' – AIDS has become a singular global society, whose administrators include ministries and committees, judges and politicians, priests and laity.

By identifying a singular pandemic, a globalizing effect has erased the diversity of epidemics throughout the world. The notion of a 'global response' to AIDS has constituted itself through systemic exclusions and routine displacements. It has operated by representing *all* people with AIDS through the identity of *the majority* of people with AIDS. Since the largest epidemics are to be found in sub-Saharan Africa, facts and fantasies about the African epidemic have been taken to apply to all other AIDS epidemics throughout the developing world.

I argue that the 'global response' to AIDS has produced a univocal, heterosexualizing, 'majority rule' rhetoric that renders invisible the millions of homosexually active men in the developing world. The rhetoric is familiar to all: in the West, HIV disproportionately affects gay men, though it is 'spreading' to the general population – especially women; in the third world, HIV is a heterosexual problem, spreading through 'primitive and traditional relations' in African villages and through liaisons between prostitutes and truck drivers in India. Clearly, there is no place in this rhetoric for homosexually active men outside the West, and it positions such men and their homosexual and heterosexual partnerships irrelevant to the broader epidemic. In so doing, it opens the floodgates for millions of what should be regarded as preventable HIV infections.

This 'global' narrative obfuscates a realistic view of the scale of the catastrophe that HIV and AIDS has wrought on homosexually active men in both the West and 'the rest'. A look at the current situation is telling.

By mid-1996, 27.9 million people had been infected with HIV worldwide. Of these, 21.8 million were still alive. Close to 19 million adults and children (86 per cent of the world total) were living with HIV or AIDS in sub-Saharan Africa, and in South and South East Asia. Of the adults, 58 per cent were men, and 42 per cent were women.

UN AIDS stresses that virtually all homosexual transmissions are confined to the Western industrialised nations, and that 80 per cent of HIV transmissions occur heterosexually. Indeed, almost everybody assumes that only in the West does HIV spread largely through homosexual anal intercourse. Yet in Latin America, a vast majority of HIV infections occur among homosexual and bisexual men. Community activists have had to fight tooth and nail against official denial of homosexuality in order to collect and publicize this data. A minister of health from a South American country referred to the homosexual component of his nation's epidemic as '*esta cosita*' ('this little thing'), even though more than 80 per cent of HIV cases there affect homosexual and bisexual men.

The scale of the neglect of homosexual HIV transmission in the Third World becomes apparent when one examines official responses to infected blood supplies. No country has reported more than 10 per cent of HIV/AIDS cases resulting from contaminated blood, and yet everywhere governments have been compelled to ensure a safe blood supply. One cannot imagine any official daring to suggest that infection through blood was too insignificant to warrant a concerted and well-funded response.

A 1996 UN AIDS report 'The Status and Trends of the Global HIV/AIDS Pandemic: Final Report at 11th International Conference on AIDS', organized by UN AIDS, and the Harvard School of Public Health, the AIDS Control and Prevention Project of Family Health International (funded by the United States Agency for International Development, Vancouver, 1996) completely ignores homosexual transmission in Asia and Africa, and emphasizes that in both regions accelerating heterosexual epidemics threaten to undermine economic development and the very fabric of society.[4]

However, no data has ever been collected to support this silence on homosexuality. Before most countries began to compile their own AIDS statistics for the Global Program on AIDS, many countries submitted their raw AIDS data on case reports directly to Geneva, where the World Health Organization and UN AIDS are based. I read through hundreds of reports from Africa, and I never came across a case of homosexual transmission – neither did I come across a case of transmission by transfusion or needle sharing. The questions that may have provided information on non-heterosexual transmissions were either never asked, or were asked in the presence of a religious, civic, or family leader.

With GPA guidance, nations around the world established sentinel surveillance systems as part of their National AIDS Committees prevention planning and evaluation process. The data these systems generate directly inform the kinds of prevention efforts commissioned by the government. The systems typically screen women attending ante-natal care facilities, female prostitutes, and male and female patients at STD clinics. Seldom if ever are attempts made to reach gay and bisexual men, male prostitutes or prisoners. The WHO GPA never compiled epidemiological data according to risk exposure category, which specify modes of HIV transmission, nor do most countries and regions report the data in this way. Of all the WHO's Third World administrative regions, only Latin America – following North American protocol – regularly produces breakdowns of the data by gender and exposure category. This has much to do with the autonomy of the American Regional Office of WHO, which also predates WHO as the Pan American Health Organization (PAHO). This unique history has ensured that the American Regional Office is less subject to the centralizing, globalizing tendencies of WHO.[5]

The GPA's large-scale quantitative sexual behaviour surveys – the Partner Relations Study and The Knowledge Attitudes Beliefs and Practices Studies – were conducted in a large number of sites worldwide in the late 1980s. The majority of African countries refused to ask any questions on homosexual behaviour. Then, somewhere between the study design and the selection of sites, a GPA bureaucrat decided that these questions were 'too culturally sensitive' and should be left as optional. All African sites opted out. The only site in the Third World to ask questions about homosexuality was in Sri Lanka. 32 per cent of men reported having unprotected anal sex with another man. This finding is not straightforward either, due to the framing of the questions, but at least it shows what might happen when you do ask the questions. In the final published report, homosexuality (or the UN AIDS catch phrase, 'men who have sex with men') does not even appear in the index.

Even in the most generalized data, in every country in the world, there are indicators of great numbers of non-heterosexually acquired infections. In every country, HIV is significantly more prevalent among men than women. Given the fact that women are far more easily infected by men than men are by women, one would expect women to be considerably more affected by HIV than men, and not the other way round.

If the data suggest such a great number of male-to-male HIV transmissions outside the West, one has to wonder: whence the silence? Why hasn't there ever been sustained research to determine the source of the surplus of HIV-positive men around the world? One might suspect old-fashioned homophobia and taboo. This certainly plays a part. Nevertheless, it is well known that throughout the Third World, many homosexually active men also have female partners. The effects of ignoring male-to-male transmission in Bombay or Harare do not stop at the boundaries of an expendable gay ghetto, as homophobes in the US or UK might imagine.

I would argue that equally central to the neglect of male-to-male transmission is a set of mutually reinforcing discourses, active both in the West and elsewhere. These discourses are the source of how my friend, the student of public health could believe that AIDS was elsewhere – in

Africa, in African American ghettos, and in Bombay brothels. Michael simply didn't have the tools necessary to understand that rather than 'going down', AIDS was going to be part of his life as a gay man in New York for the foreseeable future.

But this displacement of HIV from the First to the Third World predictably implies the displacement of HIV from homosexuality to heterosexuality – even within Third World countries. Members of Gays and Lesbians of Zimbabwe recently asserted that they are not at risk of HIV because, in Africa, the virus only affects heterosexuals. In India, an outreach team doing prevention work in homosexual public sex venues was told by men that they could not be at risk of acquiring HIV as they did not have sex with female prostitutes.

mythical heterosexuality: the African model

I want to analyze some of the collaborating discourses which effect this displacement of attention from homosexualities of all sorts. Surely, among the most central of these is the majoritarian, commonsensical axioms of public health and a subservient epidemiology.

Certainly, public health and epidemiology are not an objective assemblage of fact. The objects of the discourse (such as 'risk group', 'homosexual', 'drug users', and 'unprotected intercourse') are socially and institutionally constituted through history, and are reified by the discipline of public health itself. (For a discussion of these issues in great detail, see Cindy Patton's essay in this volume.) Those statements recognized by the discourse as 'fact' are understood and interpreted within particular language shared among experts within and between institutions. These institutions have their own histories and cultures that actually shapes the language which they use. Therefore, epidemiological truths are neither neutral nor socially disinvested.

Consensus within peer-reviewed journals becomes Truth, objective and neutral.[6]

Public health's 'official knowledge' constitutes homosexualities as unimportant to the global AIDS epidemic. This has profound effects on prevention work in this population as it acts to de-prioritize targeted work. Cindy Patton contrasts epidemiological to tropical medical models and their roles in the global responses to AIDS. If epidemiology, drawing on a much longer cordon sanitaire, is the industrialized nation's response to the epidemic within, then tropical medicine is the nineteenth-century imperial state's concern with diseases that afflict the colonizer.

Because Africa has always been figured as the 'heart of darkness' within the colonial imagination, tropical medicine quickly acquired an unacknowledged geographical referent: sub-Saharan Africa. I use the term 'Africanizing' for this process whereby a discourse illicitly acquires Africa as geographical referent.

Central to the Africanizing of thinking about epidemics is the wholesale colonial understanding of African life as traditional, ahistorical, and unchanging. Africanized public health and tropical medicine builds its models upon a vision of African social relations informed far less by the diverse realities of contemporary Africa than by an antiquated imperialist ethnography that invented traditions in order to legitimate colonial indirect rule. Africanized public health knows a great deal about disease transmission in the 'traditional' extended families of 'untouched' thatched villages, but very little about urbanization, migrant labour townships, or refugee camps.

For reasons that had more to do with politics than data, the WHO GPA presumed Africa – and from there, the entire Third World (and this is the Africanizing gesture) – to be entirely heterosexual. I don't mean to suggest that African epidemics of HIV and AIDS in Africa are best explained by undisclosed homosexual behaviour. There is a paucity of data on homosexuality in Africa, though more has been collected than is often acknowledged. I merely argue that the absolute predominance of heterosexual HIV transmission in Africa was concluded a priori, without any sense that further enquiry would be in order.

I am not suggesting that the 'heterosexualizing' of global AIDS surveillance involves a manipulation of data. To the contrary, it represents a more or less honest account of the data collected; the problem is the data itself. But it is worth considering how the data with a glaring silence on homosexuality came to be considered definitive proof of a general, worldwide heterosexual epidemic.

There are two parts to this argument. The first argument is simple: the majority of HIV infections have been acquired sexually; the majority of people are self-evidently heterosexual; therefore heterosexual intercourse is the major mode of transmission. Public health officials rarely feel any need to justify this argument, and they are rarely called on to do so. Second, officials point out that the ratio of the number of female cases to the number of male cases has grown closer to 1:1 over time. Remember: were there reliable data on transmission or risk exposure, officials would not need to cite changing gender ratios as 'proof' of a heterosexual epidemic.

Increasing incidence of paediatric infection and new infections among women in Latin America – which first recorded high rates of homosexual transmission – is thought to indicate an increasingly 'African style' (i.e. heterosexual) epidemic. One Brazilian epidemiologist complained bitterly that his work on HIV in Brazil had been misinterpreted as representing an 'African-style heterosexual' epidemic; what he had in fact demonstrated was a continuing epidemic among gay and bisexual men (as the absolute numbers of those infected continued to rise). He argued that widespread male bisexuality and needle-sharing caused the rising numbers of infected women and children.[7]

Although a 1:1 ratio of male to female cases of HIV and AIDS is consistent with a heterosexual epidemic, such parity is also consistent with very different, elaborately interacting, epidemiological patterns. (As noted above, because women are more easily infected with HIV than men, one might imagine in a purely heterosexual epidemic that somewhat more women than men would be infected. This would produce an 'inverted' ratio.) A 1:1 ratio can be explained in many ways other than universal heterosexuality. These include female injection drug use, perinatal transfusion of HIV-infected blood, and male-to-female sexual transmission of HIV among men who are also homosexually active.

And again, even if sex ratios are shifting toward 1:1, the question asked above still stands: if the ratios started at 9:1, then shifted to 5:1, and finally 2:1, what are the men doing that they are acquiring HIV prior to significant infection rates among women?

Having established policy recommendations based on incomplete data collection and inconclusive data analysis, GPA felt the need to defend its system. I was confronted with defensive anxiety just one day prior to my plenary session concerning the impact of HIV on homosexually active men at the Berlin International Conference on AIDS. For my talk, I requested a further breakdown of the data for the Western Pacific Regional Office (WPRO) to see how great a disparity in gender ratios there actually was. This precipitated a stand-up row with a senior GPA epidemiologist who snapped: 'You know the line. Stick to it!' (In fact, men in the Western Pacific appear disproportionately affected by HIV. In the Philippines, for instance, when one corrects for purposive sampling among female prostitutes and 'hospitality girls', the data reveals a decisively gay and bisexual epidemic.[8]

The global displacement of homosexually active men from the epidemiological record is related to the power and prestige of the WHO and the UN, which have become, in many ways, the final arbiter of 'what science knows about AIDS'. In fact, so self-authoritative have UN documents become (see, for instance, 'The Status and Trends of the Global HIV/AIDS Pandemic', prepared for the Eleventh International Conference on AIDS at Vancouver) that they no longer cite any specific studies or raw data when they present sweeping trends – for the whole of Africa or the Western Pacific or Latin America – concerning gender ratios or presumed transmission patterns.[11] It's as if to say: we're the UN; we don't have to . . .

new homosexual responses, new homosexual identities

The callous – and deadly (when HIV prevention efforts are not initiated among homosexually active men) – silence on homosexual transmission has compelled homosexually active men in many countries to organize and lobby for prevention resources on their own behalf. In countries where there is no history of a socially identifiable homosexual identity, new organizations – synthesizing indigenous practices with Western models of visibility and gay identity – have forged new homosexual identities and have emerged in response to the epidemic. In Asia, facing both formal and informal, violent and structural repression and stigmatization, new gay or homosexual identified AIDS prevention campaigns have organized in India, Sri Lanka, Thailand, Malaysia, Indonesia, Hong Kong, Taiwan, Singapore and the Philippines – and with them, new identities.

I differentiate between 'homosexual' and 'gay' in order to open space for the recognition of non-Western homosexualities and sexual identities. It was this same concern which inspired the GPA to introduce the term 'men who have sex with men' (MSM). MSM accommodates the fact that men may be homosexually active but without gay identity. One of the most powerful contributions of lesbian and gay scholarship has been to show that there is no universal transcultural and transhistoric homosexual community, life-style or identity. This scholarship understands 'gay' as a historically constituted social marker, upon which various meanings and associations condense. Thus, 'gay' should be used with caution (if at all) across boundaries of cultural difference.

These important insights should have led to a greater awareness of homosexual behaviour and its potential for HIV transmission in differing cultural settings. It should have encouraged health officials to acknowledge and actively seek out homosexual transmission even where homosexuality is not incorporated into any public identity. It should have led to a larger number of interventions, which were more sensitively designed through greater awareness of different sexual cultures.

Too often, however, this argument has been used as a reason for inaction. Claims that 'gay' is a Western category not applicable to different cultural contexts have been extended to imply that *nothing* learned in education, treatment and care in 'Western' gay and bisexual communities is relevant to the developing world. These arguments are sometimes presented by Third World lesbian and gay organizations worried about a form of cultural imperialism perceived to be present among Western lesbian and gay and AIDS service organizations. But more often, they're articulated by health authorities to obstruct the development of targeted HIV prevention and care for communities they'd rather the international community not know about.

The representation of the broader AIDS 'pandemic' as heterosexual has effectively displaced attention from homosexuals even in countries where they represent the largest number of those infected. We cannot under-estimate how much fodder a UN declaration that AIDS is generally a heterosexual epidemic provides to those who would de-gay HIV prevention and treatment efforts within the First World. We can see how Michael, working for Gay Men's Health Crisis, could see HIV as elsewhere, as not relevant to himself as a gay man. After all, in his own community's organization AIDS is represented as what Simon Watney has called 'an equal opportunities virus'.[9] The result? GMHC has five women working on lesbian transmission, a division devoted to people of colour, another devoted to injection drug users, but until very recently, not a single person conducting education among gay men. While this sort of comparative statement unavoidably sounds competitive, it is in no way intended to be. Indeed, it's a terribly unfortunate effect of the under-funding of meaningfully targeted AIDS prevention and care services that constituencies most devastated by the epidemic should compete with each other for attention and resources.

This over-arching Africanizing, heterosexualizing discourse – and the institutions which produce it – have created a global paradigm so dominant that it has overwritten every national and local response to the epidemic. Surely no nation has been autonomous enough to resist the global model, or to prevent its dissemination to peripheral AIDS prevention and care projects. Thus, any nation's history of response can be written only with reference to this over-arching discourse. By undermining the understanding of particular national or local epidemiological patterns, this composite discourse continues to leave millions of men, women and children at actual risk of acquiring HIV.

Rest assured, the effects of the displacement of homosexuality from actual data, as well as the citation of an imagined Africa, have broader effects in almost every discourse related to AIDS imaginable. The heterosexualizing of global AIDS discourse legitimates de-gaying in the West, as well as the erasure of AIDS from lesbian and gay studies. It leads to and participates in the needless deaths of homosexually active men in the Third World, and it provides rationale for the slogan 'AIDS affects everybody.'

The systematic displacement of homosexualities from official responses to AIDS that largely obscures the scale of the tragedy in our communities results from a set of homophobic constructs that – like a gamelan orchestra – is ever changing but always the same. The on-the-ground voice of this homophobia sounds different in different moments. Sometimes, it's the public health researcher who is categorized as 'campaigning' simply because she requests data about transmission category. At other times, it's a memorandum from a US delegation to UN AIDS demanding that a project not be funded because one of the grant recipients has ties to the International Lesbian and Gay Association demonized by Senator Jesse Helms as a paedophile organization because it included the North American Man Boy Love Association.) At still other times, it's a bureaucrat from the Third World angry that anybody would suggest homosexuality exists in their nation.

The end of this homophobia, like all other homophobia, is violence done to homosexuals. In this case, the violence is structural, quiet and lethal. It's a violence done not only to the homosexual men who are figured as 'expendable', but to their male and female partners, their children, and their friends. It's a violence that betrays other agenda which seriously jeopardize the global institutions safeguarding the public health from doing their purported job. But above all, it's a violence which reminds us that the epidemic cannot be controlled in a climate of taboo and silence, that an open and honest discussion of sexuality, in all its diversity, is the fundamental prerequisite for effective response to AIDS.

notes

1. Centers for Disease Control and Prevention, Atlanta, Ga., 1996.
2. Simon Watney, 'Global AIDS', *Gay Times*, London, March 1995, p.38.
3. See Lisa Garbus, 'The UN Response', in D. Tarantola (ed.) *AIDS And The World: 2*, Oxford University Press, 1996, pp.369–74.
4. For example, see World Health Organization, Special Programme on AIDS, *Progress Report No.2*, November 1987, Geneva.
5. See Simon Watney elsewhere in this collection.
6. See Neil McKenna, *On The Margins: Men Who Have Sex With Men and HIV In The Developing World*, Panos Institute, London, 1996.
7. Herbert Daniel and Richard Parker, *AIDS: Sexuality, Politics And AIDS In Brazil*, London, The Falmer Press, 1993.
8. UNAIDS, 1996.
9. See Simon Watney, 'Signifying AIDS', in P. Buchler and N. Papastergiadis

(eds.) *Random Access: On Crisis And Its Metaphors*, London, Rivers Oram Press, 1995, pp.193–211.

traditions of activism

some transitions in the history of AIDS treatment activism

from therapeutic utopianism to pragmatic praxis

Mark Harrington

This paper focuses on the evolution of AIDS treatment activism in America, and particularly in New York City, where the American epidemic has its epicentre, and where treatment activism originated.

I would like to dedicate this essay to Vito Russo, who was both a cultural and a political activist, whose life work, *The Celluloid Closet*, has recently been released as a film.

the outbreak of AIDS treatment activism

A number of unique historical circumstances contributed to the outbreak of AIDS treatment activism in New York City with the foundation of ACT UP/New York in March 1987.

Before the outbreak of AIDS in 1981, there was an innate American sense of entitlement to certain rights. Middle class gay men certainly felt entitled to these as well. Being middle class, they had not known deprivation. Being gay in the 1970s, many of them felt liberation had been won. Being men, many enjoyed relative economic and social privileges. AIDS undermined these entitlements and revealed that the ostensible liberation of the 1970s was incomplete.

For forty years Americans had lived inside the 'antibiotic

bubble', when it was believed that infectious diseases were on the wane and that antibiotic chemotherapy could quickly be developed for new and emerging infections (as occurred with Legionnaire's disease in the 1970s).

There had been almost two decades of gay and lesbian political mobilization, following the civil rights model, and many experienced gay and lesbian activists were able to join a new movement focusing on AIDS.

There had been six years of ground-breaking AIDS activism, including the foundation and growth of service-providing agencies such as Gay Men's Health Crisis (GMHC) in 1981, the invention and dissemination of safer sex practices, starting with Richard Berkowitz, Michael Callen and Joe Sonnabend's *How to Have Sex in an Epidemic* in 1982; the establishment of the People with AIDS (PWA) self-empowerment movement, including its Denver Principles, released in 1983. The Denver Principles maintained that people with AIDS have the right to participate in every decision-making body affecting people with AIDS (PWAS). ACT UP would set out to turn the Denver Principles into reality within the research world.

The introduction of the HIV antibody test in 1985, and its widespread use by people to determine their serostatus, (who didn't yet know how many antibody-positive persons progressed to AIDS), created a population of thousands of anxious but still healthy individuals who might be able to mobilize around AIDS if there were any reason to do so.

New York City was the epicentre of the AIDS epidemic in the United States. By 1987 over 7,000 cases of AIDS had been reported, half had died, and between 200,000–400,000 were believed to be HIV-positive.

The rapid development and FDA approval of AZT in March 1987 created a new climate of hope about the prospects for treating AIDS, combined with outrage over AZT's $10,000 a year price. Hope and outrage made an inflammatory combination.

Finally, Larry Kramer was in between plays.

the outbreak of AIDS treatment activism (1987–89)

In March 1987, just around the time AZT was licensed, Larry Kramer gave a speech at the Lesbian & Gay Community Center in New York, which led to the formation of ACT UP/New York. Larry said 'power means the willingness to accept responsibility', and those words had a major impact on our initial activism.

ACT UP was devoted to 'direct action to end the AIDS crisis' – and our definition of direct action was an experimental, improvisatory one. Initially, we tried a range of scattershot tactics, without any overall strategy. Large planned demonstrations and smaller spontaneous ones ('zaps') were mounted to problematize AIDS as a public issue, enhance gay and lesbian visibility and vilify political adversaries. Among the elements and targets of ACT UP's initial activism were zaps and demonstrations about gay visibility, AIDS discrimination, drug companies, political leaders, the media, other AIDS organizations. Larry's motto 'drugs into bodies' was often chanted, but there was little organized activism directed towards achieving that goal.

ACT UPs spread like wildfire around the United States. Particularly important chapters were formed in Boston, Chicago, Los Angeles, San Francisco and Washington, D.C. ACT UP drew people into an exciting cultural and political ferment, with a new sense of community, collective power and joy. This went hand-in-hand with a good deal of intolerance to outside figures, including other AIDS organizations.

ACT UP was like a religious movement in the following ways. Our prophet was Larry Kramer. People with AIDS were saints and preachers while alive (Michael Callen, Vito Russo, Ray Navarro) and martyrs after they died. We had conversion experiences (joining ACT UP, going to civil disobedience training) and could achieve spiritual liberation by joining the community, ACT UP, which viewed itself as the elect. Demonstrating and getting arrested were like initiation rites (baptism). We had separate congregations (affinity groups) which competed to carry out the most radical demonstrations. We had our iconography ('SILENCE=DEATH', Gran Fury, Art Positive, 'THE AIDS CRISIS IS NOT OVER', 'READ MY LIPS', 'THE GOVERNMENT HAS BLOOD ON ITS HANDS'). We demonized our enemies (Ronald Reagan, Ed Koch, Stephen Joseph, Anthony Fauci, Ellen Cooper). Even our enemies could be redeemed if they 'converted'; Ellen Cooper went from being an 'ice maiden' to 'Joan of Arc', according to Larry Kramer, who also elevated Anthony Fauci from 'murderer' to 'hero'. Politicians, unlike scientists, were never redeemed. We regarded other AIDS organizations, such as GMHC, with suspicion and sometimes denunciation, as assimilationist sell-outs or as moderates too prone to compromise. The congregation of the elect met each Monday night at the Centre and later at Cooper Union. We read our credo at the start of each meeting: 'ACT UP is a diverse, non-partisan coalition of individuals united in anger and committed to direct action to end the AIDS crisis . . .' and we had our 'Amen!' chant, 'ACT UP! Fight Back! Fight AIDS!' We had our communion, 'drugs into bodies'. We had our messianic hopes: the cure was possible, it was just around the corner, we had to work incessantly to make it come *faster.* As Larry Kramer exhorted us in spring 1990, 'WE MUST MAKE TOMORROW HAPPEN TODAY.'

In the late 1980s, we were in the grip of a therapeutic utopianism in which it did not feel naive to believe that a cure was imminent and, together, we could make it appear.

unleashing power: developing a strategic focus on treatment research (1988–1990)

At the same time, some of us were beginning to develop a more long-term, strategic focus on treatment research, developing a unique form of direct action: treatment activism. Treatment activism would inevitably change the kind of work ACT UP did, but initially this wasn't apparent, because we were still on the outside of the research world. Later, after we'd broken into that world and began to carry responsibilities there, conflicts would arise about whether treatment activism was a legitimate form of direct action at all. ACT UP adapted many activist practices from past movements, and invented still more; treatment activism was an ACT UP invention, without precedent in the civil rights, feminist or gay rights struggles activism.

Some implicit strategies informed my own initial work with ACT UP's Treatment + Data (T+D) Committee in 1988–89. In college, I had studied critical theory, where I had been struck by Michel Foucault's emphasis on two themes. First, that in political activism, it is necessary to master the language of your adversaries and use it to advance your own ends. This we did with medical jargon surrounding clinical trials, drug development and FDA regulation. Second, the necessity to mobilize on a number of fronts and advance whenever a position gives way. We couldn't know in advance which front would give way. Once we had gained a strategic position, we needed to continue occupying it. The work, as we learned, goes on for years. We didn't know, initially, that our campaigns against the US Food & Drug Administration (FDA) and the National Institutes of Health (NIH) would be so successful. Looking back, however, it is obvious that those tactical 'victories' meant we'd have to spend years solidifying the reforms we worked for and overseeing the design, conduct and analysis of clinical trials.

We started out with a number of 'drugs into bodies' access zaps. For example, in the summer of 1988, Peter Staley led an occupation of Kowa, a Japanese shoe importer, which also made dextran sulfate. Kowa was refusing to sell dextran sulfate to Americans with AIDS who flew to Japan to get the drug. The zap was a success, and Kowa relented, but the drug didn't work and ultimately people stopped using it. We weren't very sophisticated yet about *which* drugs we wanted to put into *whose* bodies, and why.

Another concurrent campaign was also led by Peter Staley, organized around trying to lower the price of AZT. This involved over a year of demonstrations, occupation of Burroughs-Wellcome headquarters and the New York Stock Exchange, along with pressure from other sources such as Congress and the press. Ultimately the company buckled and the price of AZT was lowered by 40 per cent. Note, however, that it wasn't ACT UP alone, as we liked to think at the time, but rather ACT UP together with the Waxman Committee in Congress, editorials in *The New York Times* and elsewhere, which worked to induce Burroughs-Wellcome to lower the price.

A third access campaign involved DHPG (ganciclovir), which was still not licensed in 1989, although it was already the standard of care for CMV retinitis. Without DHPG, people with AIDS were going blind. This was the first campaign in which we really did our homework. We demonstrated at the FDA, got the press on the story, and secured an alliance with Anthony Fauci of the NIH to demand widespread access to and early approval of DHPG. Access was granted in March 1989, and full FDA approval followed in June. The DHPG example led directly to the proposals ACT UP put forth that summer for a 'parallel track' for access to new AIDS drugs while they continued to be studied in trials.

Parallel Track, which resulted in the distribution of ddI to nearly 27,000 people with AIDS between 1989 and 1991, was really the product of several converging forces – our FDA demonstration, the deregulatory, pro-drug company agenda of President Bush and his administration, and the experience of the DHPG fiasco.

At the time, we were thrilled that so many PWAs were getting ddI, but we were taking an enormous risk. ddI killed some people from pancreatitis, and could have killed many more, had it been more toxic. It wasn't until 1992 that the drug showed any clinical benefit in controlled trials, and not until 1995 (with the release of ACTG 175) that ddI emerged as a superior first-line antiviral to AZT. Thousands of people could have benefited from this knowledge years earlier if activists had focused their energy on answers as well as on access. With ddI, we were lucky. Some commentators felt, however, that AIDS activists were being used by industry to put a human face on drug deregulation. Ultimately Parallel Track paved the way for Accelerated Approval, an FDA procedure adopted in 1992, under which drugs could be approved for treating AIDS if they demonstrated beneficial effects on a surrogate marker such as CD4 counts or viral load. With Accelerated Approval, even less would be known when drugs were licensed, and there were no strong guarantees that appropriate post-marketing studies would ever be carried out.

After we succeeded in making the FDA more flexible and responsive to the needs of PWAS, we turned our attention to the agency which conducts the great bulk of clinical trials of AIDS drugs, the National Institutes of Health (NIH), the logical next step after FDA. After exposure to the philosophy of Dr Joseph Sonnabend and the Community Research Initiative (CRI), which helped to develop aerosolized pentamidine for PCP prophylaxis, we were concerned that NIH was not conducting enough studies of prophylaxis and treatment for the opportunistic infections. We had a massive demonstration at NIH on 21 May 1990. This was the last time ACT UP conducted a truly unified treatment activist demonstration – for it succeeded in achieving our goals, and by doing so, drew some of us into long-term engagement within the NIH and its AIDS Clinical Trials Group (ACTG). By drawing some of us in, however, others were left out, and tactical conflicts arose over whose style of activism was more legitimate.

Within the ACTG, activists created structures for ongoing community involvement in and power over AIDS treatment research. Activists from around the country, representing a diverse array of communities, sat on all research committees, helping to design protocols and work out problems at trial sites. Pressure from activists and from liberal Congressmen such as Henry Waxman of Los Angeles and Ted Weiss of New York resulted in a whole host of new opportunistic infection (OI) treatment and prevention studies being undertaken. Within a few years a whole new generation of OI drugs had been tested, approved and marketed. Among these anti-OI drugs were aerosolized pentamidine, azithromycin, clarithromycin, fluconazole, foscarnet, ganciclovir (oral and intravenous), itraconazole and rifabutin. The standard of care for HIV disease and AIDS changed radically between 1987 and 1993, and part of this was due to the involvement of treatment activists.

At the same time, progress in treating HIV itself remained agonizingly slow.

despair, dissent & dissolution (1990–93)

After 1990, T+D's tactical successes and its commitment to seeing them through created ideological and tactical stress within ACT UP. We'd won more power within research than other groups within ACT UP had won in other areas, so where was the cure? The inside/outside strategy (demonstrations followed by meetings) began to be questioned. Demonstrations and zaps against drug companies stopped working; both the media and the industry were bored by them. They became expected, a sort of 'dog bites man' story.

Some activists felt that T+D's focus on treatment research distracted from struggles against racism, sexism, homophobia, and capitalism. ACT UP became a victim of its very success, drawing in a multitude of activists whose primary focus was not AIDS.

A relentless tide of death carried away some of the movement's most beloved, charismatic and inspiring leaders and members. AIDS was clearly not yet the 'chronic, manageable disease' we'd hoped in 1987–89 that it might rapidly become.

Some ACT UP factions wanted to disengage from research

meetings and did not want to work with other community groups and activists. The Women's Caucus, for example (largely a group of seronegative white lesbians) interrupted conferences to protest two studies, ACTG 076 and ACTG 175. Rather than propose improvements to those trials, they wanted to 'stop 076' and 'stop 175'. If they had been successful, two of the most dramatic discoveries of the 1990s would never have occurred. Activists can impede research as well as improve it.

By 1991, it seemed we were spending more time fighting other ACT UP members than fighting AIDS. In January 1992, the core of T+D left ACT UP to form TAG, the Treatment Action Group, so that we could focus all our energy on treatment activism.

regrouping, reform & pragmatic rationalism (1993–96)

Initially, it was not clear whether TAG would focus on old-style direct action or new-style treatment activism. Peter Staley dropped a giant condom on Senator Jesse Helms' house. The neighbours were annoyed, but the national media ignored the event and Helms, needless to say, didn't stop his homophobic legislative manoeuvrings. We carried out several drug company zaps against Astra, Dai-Ichi and Roche, but the drug companies didn't budge. It seemed like the old kinds of AIDS activism weren't working.

So we became a think-tank. In spring 1992, TAG commissioned Gregg Gonsalves and me to review the 3,000 AIDS research grants funded by the National Institutes of Health (NIH). We found that no one was overseeing the $800 million AIDS research effort, and that eighteen different institutes were each spending their AIDS money however they wanted. Money, time and lives were being wasted. Our report, released at Amsterdam in July 1992, led to Congressional reforms signed into law by President Clinton in June 1993. For the first time, a powerful Office of AIDS Research (OAR) at NIH would coordinate the AIDS research effort and control the AIDS research budget. Implementing these reforms would take years.

Also in 1993 came what was perhaps the most demoralizing moment in AIDS research, at the Berlin AIDS conference, when the Concorde investigators revealed that early AZT didn't prolong life, and when the investigators of ACTG 155 lied about their study results, claiming that AZT/ddC was superior to AZT when in fact combination therapy, in that study, proved worse. At Berlin, several activists from TAG and GMHC confronted Margaret Fischl, the lead investigator of ACTG 155, calling her analysis 'intent-to-cheat'. For the first time, activists were beginning to demand more stringent studies which would yield more unambiguous results, and scientists were defending studies too small and poorly designed to give PWAS clear guidance about treatment decisions.

Over the next years, some treatment activists began to demand larger, better-controlled studies, carried out in populations at all stages of HIV disease, to determine rapidly whether new anti-HIV drugs were safe and effective. After five years of nucleoside analogue research, we still did not know when people should start therapy, or with what regimen.

In 1994 TAG instigated a nationwide furor by calling on FDA not to grant accelerated approval to Roche's protease inhibitor, saquinavir, until adequate post-marketing studies were underway. Saquinavir had at that point been studied in only 200 patients for six months, and looked, judging by surrogate marker data, to be nearly as ineffective as ddC. TAG was widely attacked for our proposal for a large simple trial which would enroll people with advanced, middle and early disease, and determine within one year whether or not saquinavir added appreciably to the standard of care. Despite the furor, drug companies began to listen. Roche doubled the size of its two pivotal studies. Abbott adopted TAG's proposal for a 'standard of care' control arm, allowing patients in a study of its new protease inhibitor, ritonavir, to take any of the approved antivirals, and proved within six months that ritonavir could half the rate of progression and death in people with under 100 CD4 cells. This led to immediate full approval for ritonavir, based on clear clinical data, a first since the original AZT approval in 1987.

TAG was also working on other aspects of AIDS research. In 1995, the Office of AIDS Research commissioned an expert external scientific evaluation of the entire NIH AIDS research effort, which by now had swelled to $1.3 billion at twenty-four NIH institutes. TAG members and other treatment activists participated in this year-long review, which resulted in a set of recommendations for sweeping reform across the entire NIH AIDS research effort. TAG will spend the next few years seeking to implement these reforms, as well as defending the OAR and the AIDS research budget in Congress.

Treatment activists have won many victories which have extended health and life for thousands of people with HIV, but we have had virtually no impact on AIDS in the developing world, where 80 per cent of the cases occur, and the ultimate goals of a cure and a vaccine remain elusive.

future prospects and provisional principles for treatment activists

AIDS treatment activism is unlike other social change movements because our adversaries are biological as well as social, political, economic and cultural.

- Activists must be flexible tactically but stubborn strategically.
- We must master and appropriate the jargon of science.
- Citizens must have power in setting research priorities and running research programs.
- Activists must, like scientists, 'listen to the data' and change course when new findings make it necessary. Goals and tactics which worked in 1989 will not work in 1996.

- Activists must not only abandon, but actively repudiate, activist dogmas which have become outdated or refuted by new research. Treatment activists must not expect more from science than it can deliver. Science is not magic.
- Clinical studies can be rigorous and answer important questions while remaining flexible, humane, and incorporating the best current standard of care.
- Activists need allies among scientists, the press and in government in order to prevail.
- Unreflective activism can impede scientific progress.
- Activist formations must change along with scientific or historical changes; ACT UP had its time and served a valuable purpose; now there is a need for new formations.
- Activists need a proactive program of policy changes, especially for times when (as in the UK currently) a Conservative government may be about to be replaced by a progressive one.

Some people believe that, with the development of the protease inhibitors, we may be at a turning point in the AIDS epidemic. Is this so? Possibly, from a scientific standpoint. From a public health standpoint, probably not. The drugs won't reach enough people to dent the AIDS toll worldwide in this decade, although they may affect progression and mortality rates in the developed world. Even where people can access these drugs, which we still don't know how to use, the emergence of viral resistance to them is virtually inevitable. They're unduly expensive and their side effects are daunting. No one knows how long the antiviral effect will last.

Ultimately, we'll need immunological interventions as well as antiviral drugs to keep infected people healthy, and we'll need a vaccine to keep the uninfected from infection. These goals are still far off. Even if we're not at the beginning of the end of the AIDS pandemic, however, at least we may be nearing the end of the beginning.

questions for activists / questions about activism

Last year I called Larry Kramer for a peace talk. We haven't spoken for several years. I asked him how his lover was, how his dog was, how his T-cells were. We started talking about whether or not we were at a turning-point in the epidemic, and if so what to do. 'But where are the soldiers?' sighed Larry.

I thought about it. Are activists really like soldiers, where all you have to do is point them in some direction and say, 'Go!'? Even if they were, where *would* we tell them to go, and what to do?

Activists aren't like soldiers. They're a self-selected group of people who feel a calling to do something to intervene.

Activism encompasses a complex variety of phenomena: the mobilization of individuals into new formations centred on some common danger or issue; creating or redefining communities of those affected, individual and community rites of identification, mobilization, activation, intervention and reflection. Each stage in this process poses issues and conflicts for individuals and 'the movement' – issues about unity and diversity, tolerance and cohesion, strategy and tactics, negotiation and resistance, evaluation and stagnation, utopianism and pragmatism, messianism and utilitarianism, all before a background of a constantly changing historical context. So in conclusion I'll pose a series of questions for which there are no unequivocal answers.

What is activism? Who defines it? Are some kinds of activist praxis more authentic than others? Who are activists? Where do we get our legitimacy? Are we elected? Not usually. Sometimes we're hired by community-based organizations which derive their support from community members or foundations; other times we're self-selected volunteers. Other questions proliferate: Are activists 'right' because we 'represent' the 'authentic' community? What if activists disagree? Why do we so often disagree? Why are our civil wars so fratricidal?

Are activist interventions 'experiments' or heroic 'battles' with victories and defeats, heroes and martyrs? If activist interventions are experiments, who interprets the data, and how do you correct course?

Why do some activist subcultures outlive their usefulness and become cults wedded to narrow dogmatic practices? Why are activists so insistent on ideological purity, and so intolerant of differences of opinion?

When and why can activists make tactical alliances with other activists or with sometime adversaries (such as scientists, NIH, press, drug companies, Congress)? What is the difference between compromise and co-optation?

Can prevention activism learn from treatment activism, and vice versa?

Is a treatment (and/or a prevention) activism possible in developing or authoritarian countries?

Information is the very lifeblood of AIDS treatment activism. How can the information pools be broadened, diversified and made more accessible?

Why is there so little effective international mobilization to make AIDS drugs more broadly available throughout the world?

movements, markets and the mainstream

gay activism and assimilation in the age of AIDS

Joshua Oppenheimer

Since the early 1990s, there has been a spectacular decline in American grassroots AIDS and queer activism. And yet, gay men are currently experiencing no respite in the devastation wreaked by the health crisis and at the same time are weathering a massive backlash led by religious zealots and social conservatives. If the struggle against prejudice for the basic prevention, treatment, and civil rights needs of gay men confronting AIDS is a matter of survival, it is also a matter of survival to examine why the grassroots movements which initiated and led that struggle have all but disappeared. With this, we must also examine what political structures (lobbies, charities, and so forth) have replaced grassroots organizations, how these non-grassroots institutions have altered the conditions and goals of AIDS and gay activism, and which social processes and policies reinforce – and foster quiet acceptance of – these transitions.

As scientists develop promising new anti-viral treatments,[1] we are potentially living through a critical moment in the epidemic's history. I would argue that, in the US at least, a concerted, grassroots politics could re-focus gay and lesbian community priorities on the fight for equitable distribution of HIV treatments, and could challenge the counter-productive Centers for Disease Control 'prevention' campaigns which still advocate abstinence and monogamy without providing *any* information about how people can protect themselves from HIV.[2]

Writers and activists such as Urvashi Vaid, Sarah Schulman and Michael Bronski,[3] have made the 'mainstreaming' of gay community politics and identities one of their primary concerns. Each has charted the history of gay and lesbian political movements and has developed powerful arguments about how and why mainstreaming has occurred. I want to contribute to this impressive project with a discussion of gay-identified markets and commercial scenes, and an analysis of how they inflect and influence gay community politics and identities. I want to interrogate the relationships among activist strategies, conceptions of gay identity, and commercial efforts which target the queer community – efforts launched by queer as well as straight-owned firms.

Some prominent gay commentators have argued that direct action's strategy of public embarrassment through demonstrations and 'zaps' won activists access to a mainstream political process, and that once this access was won, grassroots activism was no longer appropriate. Then, the argument goes, direct action was rightly replaced by professional lobbies, think tanks, and charities. Using the access to mainstream politics which the direct action groups won, professional organizations are best poised to follow up the campaigns which the grassroots organizations successfully initiated.[4] This argument relies upon two assumptions which I claim are untenable. First, it assumes that access to mainstream civic and medical institutions is won uniformly and permanently. Second, it assumes that if the lobbies and charities won't offer leadership positions to the activists who initiated the direct action campaign, at least they will in good faith represent the grassroots' interests.

This defence of direct action's decline is merely a complacent apology for the status quo. And the status quo it certainly is: ACT UP chapters across the nation have closed, and membership dwindles in the few groups which remain.

Queer Nation no longer exists at all. Lesbian and gay community centres have closed, one by one, as a result of bankruptcy, mismanagement, withdrawal of statutory support, or lack of interest by lesbians and gay men themselves. Community newspapers like *Gay Community News* and *Fag Rag,* which had explicitly political charters and which invited anybody to submit articles, have all but disappeared.[5] In the remaining political lobbies (such as Human Rights Campaign) and AIDS charities (such as Gay Men's Health Crisis), decisions concerning policy, political priority, and strategy are made by upper management and trustees. In ACT UP, by contrast, projects and campaigns could be initiated by anybody who chose to attend the meetings. Similarly, while *Gay Community News* welcomes submissions from anybody, only hired journalists and commissioned guest writers may contribute to *Out* or *The Advocate*. Organizations committed to street activism, open meetings, and an inside/outside strategy,[6] have been replaced largely by professional office-based bureaucracies where decisions are made from the top down.[7]

The decline of grassroots organizations has a profound effect on the options available to gays and lesbians spending 'time out' in the gay community. Beyond places for organizing against bigotry, activist meetings are public forums for political debate and education. In them, activists discuss what it means to be queer, straight, positive, or negative. Meetings are open, announced on notice boards, in the gay papers and bar rags, and in the more progressive non-gay press. At the start of each meeting, all present are invited to listen to and fully participate in political debate. New activists learn to plan protests, and to strategize extended campaigns. They learn civil disobedience, how to deal with police, and how to support other activists when they're arrested. Older members, some of whom were active in the Gay Liberation Front in the early 1970s, have brought to America's contemporary direct action groups a broader history of gay and lesbian struggle against prejudice.[8] In the streets, activists learn how to gather strength from a collective, and assert stigmatized and hated identities in contested and often hostile public space. Through developing incisive rhetoric and demonstration graphics (what Gran Fury and ACT UP have termed 'demo-graphics'), activists literally inscribe and develop a radical conception of gay identity confronting the devastation of the health crisis. Meetings and protests teach how identities and alliances are subject to change and, from this, a profound awareness of how important it is to adapt strategy to context, especially in confronting an ever-changing epidemic. And, significantly, activists find in direct action organizations networks for support and love to sustain them in the grief and loneliness which inevitably accompanies the mass death of the health crisis. These forums charge no admission fee, and are open to all. Indeed, activist meetings constitute virtually the *only* non-commercial and open-access spaces in which gay men and lesbians congregate as a community with the express purpose of discussing politics, protest, and queer identities in response to homophobia and AIDS.

I don't mean to suggest a rigid distinction between open, grassroots forums and commercial spaces. Of course, bars, baths, bookstores, and clubs do constitute community spaces, and it would be a stunningly humourless gesture of orthodoxy to ignore the central importance of a gay economy of pleasure in the face of the near-continuous grief caused by the epidemic. But while resistance occasionally emerges out of bars and clubs (as in the case of the Stonewall Riot), they have not generally functioned as sites for deliberation about and experimentation with liberatory models of identity and citizenship. Indeed, it's fair to say that the Stonewall Bar was a qualitatively different sort of space from, say, a contemporary West Village bar, insofar as it emerged in and is specific to a different moment in the history of gay and lesbian commerce, policing, and harassment. Subsequently, one cannot easily cite Stonewall as evidence that our contemporary gay American businesses could likewise produce spontaneous activism. Why? Partly because they have other official purposes, and partly because their access is very differently controlled. Simply put, they are not free public spaces designed specifically for political discussion and activism.

The process of activism, of participating in a grassroots movement for social change, has created and re-created public forums for deliberation about proactive strategy. I see these forums as radical pedagogical laboratories for the cultivation of the experimental process of subaltern citizenship: a collective selfhood, forged through practice, always adapting new strategies of resistance to new technologies of oppression. That the radical gay identity of a subaltern community capable of re-imagining social relations outside the normativity of compulsory heterosexuality emerged through activist meetings is hardly a surprise, because the convergence of gay people's status as community and status as a movement for political liberation occurred most markedly in grassroots, open forums.[9]

Similar remarks can be made about the more grassroots and political gay press. In *Culture Clash,* Michael Bronski traces the role grassroots gay and lesbian community papers, from *Fag Rag* to *Gay Community News*, played in the development of a queer political identity. These were the subaltern public spheres necessary for the articulation of a radical response to the epidemic. Like activist groups, they provided at once a liberatory pedagogy, a site for collective recognition and investment, a forum where strategies for resistance could be developed, and a place where a gay identity inseparable from struggle and critique was reified and cultivated.

The wane of grassroots AIDS activism, along with these community newspapers, has depleted the gay community of public forums. But this trend has accompanied and collaborated with two other trends: the mushrooming of gentrified gay commercial scenes and the mainstreaming of the firms in those scenes.

Jeff Yarbrough, former editor of America's principal gay lifestyle and news magazine, *The Advocate*, recently explained to me that the demise of ACT UP and Queer Nation made gay markets far more attractive to non-gay businesses. According to Yarbrough, the American direct action organizations of the late 1980s and early 1990s made the gay community a 'loose cannon' in the eyes of would-be advertisers.[10] Advertisers were fearful that following some particularly brash demonstration, the Christian right would organize a boycott of firms marketing to 'militant homosexuals'.[11] The demise of ACT UP made marketing to gays and lesbians more attractive to big business. In turn, the arrival of big business to gay shopping streets and lifestyle magazines promised far greater income to landlords leasing property on the gay commercial strips, and far greater advertising revenues to gay magazines. To accommodate mainstream advertisers, the lifestyle magazines went glossy and professional, and the community papers, unable to compete, have all but disappeared. This mainstreaming of lesbian and gay markets marks a profoundly significant moment in gay economic life.[12] By 'mainstreaming', I refer to the replacement of gay-identified and owned companies by non-gay (or 'mainstream') firms. However, one of the central arguments of this essay is that this rather technically defined 'mainstreaming' fosters assimilationism and anti-activist sentiment; that is, it fosters mainstreaming in the conventional, political and social senses.

Jeffrey Escoffier has noted four stages in the development of post-war American gay and lesbian economies.[13] First came the mail-order industries and bars that constituted what Escoffier calls the 'closet economy'. Second, after Stonewall, there emerged a more open economy which remained centred on bars, but also included bookstores, bathhouses, newspapers, businesses, and community organisations. Third, there emerged the economy of gay and lesbian neighbourhoods. The development of queer commercial and residential ghettos in America (Escoffier's third stage of queer economic development) has been inseparable from the economic realities of urban gentrification (which reached fever-pitch in the 1980s, especially in gay ghettos such as the West Village in Manhattan, the Castro in San Francisco, and the Dupont Circle area of Washington, D.C.). Gay gentrification, in turn, is inseparable from the emergence of significant numbers of openly gay people with economic security, mobility, and purchasing power. In less urban areas (such as Key West, Northampton, Provincetown, and Fire Island), the development of queer communities can't be understood without an analysis of the economics of tourism, and, in some places, the purchase of land by radical queers and lesbian separatists. To understand the history of these trends, one would have to look not only at those gains made by the gay and lesbian liberation movement which made coming out and migration possible. One would also have to look at which sectors of gay and lesbian communities were represented by the movement according to class, gender, race, and geography. This would account for why certain gay neighbourhoods are more or less apt to be residential, to contain gay-owned or merely 'gay-friendly' businesses. After the formation of gay and lesbian ghettos came what Escoffier understands as the fourth stage in the development of gay and lesbian economies; the AIDS service industries. I would argue that the mainstreaming of the firms on gay commercial strips, as well as those advertising in gay lifestyle magazines, constitutes a fifth stage in American gay economic life.

Like all models, this chronology applies only imperfectly, and is probably specific to the United States. For instance, in London, the most visible 'gay ghetto', Soho, isn't really that at all, since it is largely non-residential. Moreover, its principal shopping street, Old Compton Street, has become a queer centre only over the past four or five years. The establishment of Old Compton Street as a gay centre, the gentrification of this red light district through the opening of more up-scale, non-gay and gay firms (alongside gay businesses we find national restaurant chains catering to a mixed gay/straight clientele), and the departure of most of its working-class residents all occurred roughly simultaneously. This simultaneity means that mainstreaming in

Soho has happened differently from in the US, where it came as the gentrification of a previously less wealthy but already established residential gay ghetto. Perhaps because of this different history, many London gays and lesbians are celebratory about the emergence of such a choice and relatively safe gay space in the heart of the West End. The historical narrative in which mainstreaming follows the emergence of a residential ghetto, and all of the attending consequences which this essay discusses, do not necessarily apply. Similarly – and perhaps owing to the UK's relative lack of a strong Christian right able to threaten meaningful boycott of non-gay firms advertising in a politicized gay press – the monthly glossy *Gay Times* continues to cover direct action politics and run sex adverts, even as it has begun to sell ad space to more non-gay national and international firms.[14]

Since the mainstreaming of gay and lesbian markets – attendant to the decline of grassroots forums – gay commercial strips and lifestyle magazines have offered opportunities for gay identification that, unlike activist meetings, are individualistic and non-participatory. Gay men and lesbians are invited to consume, to contribute funds to a lobby group, but not to organize. Now, if lifestyle magazine readers want to join the gay movement *as it's covered*, they would write a cheque or become a volunteer, not an activist. Surely, while cheque-writing certainly might constitute a contribution to progressive politics, it is no substitute for the performative self-invention experienced by activists in the street. Whether it be an ACT UP's die-in at St Patrick's Cathedral, or the delivery of a recently deceased activist's corpse to the Bush White House, dramatically interrupting a state dinner party, participation in direct action offers the affirming, collective experience of proudly asserting an ethical and political version of a stigmatized identity in the most hostile and contested of spaces. Indeed, if for no other reason, cheque-writing can't be a substitute for participation in direct action because one's ability to participate in the former is limited by one's financial resources. I'd suggest that an underlying function – which doubtless differs from the good intentions – of the non-grassroots movement is to disenfranchise people by masquerading cheque-writing as the fundamental form of political participation.

Moreover, and despite the occasional plea for charitable donations, the vast majority of opportunities for gay identification profiled in the lifestyle magazines are not political. These involve buying certain goods and services, such as the swimsuits featured in the fashion spreads, the 'gay classics' orchestral CDS offered by major music distributors, underwear from Calvin Klein, jeans from Levis, belts from Gap, tops from Benetton, computers from Apple, air tickets from Virgin Atlantic, and vodka from Absolut and, more recently, Stolichnaya. Saved only by a network of friendships and sexual relationships, the gay community teeters at the brink of dissolving into a market. A lonely new identity is consolidated in this process: the gay consumer.[15]

The ever-increasing hegemony of consumption as the principal technique of gay identification produces fertile terrain for social, sexual, and political assimilationism, because consumption is widely figured *in its own discourse* (advertising) as a sign of arrival. The message of many advertisements is, of course, that once you own this or that product, you'll have made it. Implicit in 'making it' is an arrival at some highly legitimated and prized status. What could be a more legitimate point of arrival, for a stigmatized minority, than the status of the dominant? (Isn't this what the discourse of 'equality' is largely about?) And didn't the *entire gay community* 'make it' the moment its lifestyle magazines advertised Saabs and Virgin Atlantic instead of porn videos and gay bed and breakfasts?

Given this identity as consumer, advertising and marketing become fundamental to the construction of a gay lifestyle, because lifestyle is largely determined by the patterns with which people spend money. And while identification through lifestyle consumption in gay commercial scenes is not a novel phenomenon, its rapid growth, its ever-greater inclusion of non-gay purchases, and its accompaniment by the disappearance of activist forums – all these changes have had profound consequences on how homosexuals organize and view political participation and dissent.

With the mainstreaming of American gay markets, the lifestyles syndicated in gay marketplaces and magazines have likewise become more mainstream and assimilated. Gay lifestyles advertised in magazines have come to include more and more goods and services shared with straight people, and gay entrepreneurs – many of whom had embraced activism to protect their livelihoods from homophobic neighbourhood organizations – have been replaced by mainstream, centralized corporations.

Moreover, in order for American editors like Yarbrough to profile their magazines as 'professional' and palatable to mainstream advertisers, they had to remove the sex adverts which had long provided the bulk of revenue for gay publications. (In 1992, *The Advocate* went glossy, and the sex adverts and personals were moved into a new, supplementary publication called *Advocate Men*. *Out* was founded in 1992 as the first gay magazine to rely almost wholly on mainstream advertising.) The removal of sex advertisements rendered the most public and visible gay lifestyles (those advertised in the best-financed lifestyle magazines – *Out* and *The Advocate*) less sexual than they had been. In a community largely defined by sexual differences, this translates into lifestyles less *homo*sexual than before. Overt sex became conspicuously absent from these official public identities, banished, as in heterosexual style magazines, to the private realm of the master bedroom.

All these trends collaborated to produce a syndicated gay lifestyle less political, more assimilated, and less sexually explicit than ever before. In turn, the decreasing explicitness of gay identities created fertile terrain for moralistic censure, articulated from within the gay community, of all homosexualities which do not conform to a model of monogamous life partnership, including those which involve promiscuity, group sex, S/M, and public sex. Thus, when landlords seeking higher property values appealed to local homophobia and misunderstanding about HIV transmission to close bathhouses in San Francisco and, more recently, in New York, they found unlikely allies in gay men (often, for reasons suggested below, powerful community leaders) who themselves rejected promiscuity, and presented this assimilationism as concern for the public health. Advocating monogamy is a counter-productive HIV prevention strategy, not least because it fosters guilt whilst misleading people about how HIV transmission is actually prevented. Ultimately, however, the stigmatizing, even lurid rhetoric of the champions of monogamy belie their alleged concern with HIV, and betray their own self-hatred.

The most stunning example of homophobic diatribe against promiscuity to be articulated by gay men themselves is surely Marshall Kirk and Hunter Madsen's *After the Ball.*[16] The book describes gay promiscuity in relation to AIDS in the most hateful terms:

> Then AIDS yanked aside the curtain [concealing what gay men were doing in cruising areas]. Brochures alerting the public to 'safe sex' practices for the epidemic began to make only too clear what had been going on in darkened corners: gays should stop licking one another's anuses; gays should stop shoving their fists up one another's rectums . . .[17]

And if this isn't clear enough, they shamelessly suggest that one of the epidemic's perks is its tendency to cleanse the gay community of the promiscuous and the perverted.

> AIDS has thinned out the number of eager sexual wantons: there is reason to think that the proportion of sexually restrained gay men has risen dramatically. But this news has not spread among straights. As the old saying goes, a lady's reputation is unlikely to improve.[18]

To clean up gays' self-tarnished image, Kirk and Madsen advocate both a massive public relations campaign and a wholesale revival of 'the traditional gay family'. Not surprisingly, Madsen is an advertising agent on Madison Avenue.

As with all markets, the gay commercial scenes advertise their products by making promises, implicit and explicit, to the consumer. These, in turn, imply and legitimate specific representations of gay history as inseparable from the epidemic. Over the past four or five years, one of these representations in particular appears again and again, encoded in gay-targeted advertisements and implicitly endorsed in much gay commentary and journalism published between 1984 and 1994.[19] This representation understands the early 1970s as a period of gay childhood, the years just before and after the onset of AIDS as a reckless adolescence, and the late 1980s and 1990s as a coming of age. Not only does this narrative reinforce long-standing stereotypes of gay men as irresponsible and childish: by stigmatizing the unrestricted promiscuity of the late 1970s and early 1980s as 'reckless', 'self-indulgent', 'narcissistic', and even 'piggish',[20] it's haunted by the same homophobia that leads so many to blame the gay community's deviance for its epidemic.

Moreover, the mature homosexual is a figure for assimilation. At least since the early days of psychiatry, homosexuality has been represented in various discourses as an arrested state of development. Beyond the old psychoanalytic theory, such discourses include the homophobic stereotype of gay men as immature, and the oft-repeated assertion that 'it's just a phase' that so many gay people hear upon coming out. If homosexual difference is a symptom of immaturity, all one needs to do to 'get over it' is 'to grow up'. AIDS is widely figured in public representation as a disease caused by difference. If among gay men the 'culpable' difference is one of arrested development or immaturity, marketing a lifestyle as maturity is a lucrative business. After all, it amounts to selling assimilation – the erasure of that stunted development that's figured as responsible for AIDS in the first place. It holds out the tantalizing promise of a life without AIDS. Thus, to market maturity as a promised assimilation is to market a false security, a treacherous sense of immunity, a sham vaccine to the antibody negative and a precarious amnesia to the antibody positive.[21]

This, in turn, collaborates with the assimilationism implicit in the consumption of mainstream products as a technique of identification.

The pressure to 'grow up' legitimates, naturalizes, and therefore masks real causes for the disappearance of grassroots activism. The sort of oppositional difference activism affirms is incompatible with coming-of-age into an assimilated – and hence AIDS-free – maturity. As such, marketing with a narrative of maturity fosters real anti-activist attitudes, at a time when grassroots activism and involvement are most needed.

Not only does assimilationism, with its privatization of gay identification – from the taking of public political position to the refuge of private patterns of consumption – make the decline of AIDS activism seem natural. Worse, in a disturbing and ironic reversal, an assimilationist withdrawal from activism comes to seem part of a broader strategy of 'growing up' *to protect* oneself from HIV and AIDS.

Grassroots activism itself has been positioned in and de-legitimated by this narrative of maturity. The argument that grassroots organizations were defunct once they won the community access to mainstream politics denies the continuing need to isolate and embarrass public officials and institutions responsible for stigmatizing PWAS or hijacking meaningful prevention efforts. In doing so, it figures ACT UP and other grassroots organisations as illegitimate, germane to an earlier, younger moment in gay community history. This effort to de-legitimate ACT UP and other grassroots groups has been remarkably plausible since the grassroots never had the infrastructure – or the automatic self-legitimation which comes with that infrastructure – of national gay lobbies.

The most aggressively and visibly marketed lifestyles are distinctively upper class or upper middle class. An economic profile of *The Advocate* readership reveals incomes over $20,000 per year higher than the average gay person.

(Nevertheless, profiles of *The Advocate* readers are often presented by both gay marketing agencies and the religious right to represent the whole gay community. The former have a vested interest in representing the gay community as a profitable target market, while the latter try to present homosexuals people as disproportionately rich and powerful to challenge claims that gay people are an oppressed minority deserving civil rights protection.)

But this does not mean that the lifestyle advertised in gay magazines doesn't pretend to constitute an identity available to all gays and lesbians. For those who cannot afford to lead the lifestyles advertised, the magazines function as organizing spaces for a homosexual American dream, a dream of limitless mobility that discourages class identifications and collective action whilst fostering individual materialism. When sold to the less wealthy, the magazines provoke envy and fantasy to propagate the same moralism and assimilationism of the most affluent lifestyle queens. (Because in the US, virtually everybody identifies as middle class, this process is particularly straightforward.)

In ACT UP, anybody can, in principle, participate in the forging of strategy. Of course, in some ACT UP chapters and affinity groups there remain complex class, race, and gender bias for which the coalition itself cannot be fully held responsible. Those with experience in public speaking, those with access to governmental institutions, those with somewhat flexible schedules, and those with the instilled confidence to lead, tended to speak more than others at meetings, and, not surprisingly, to become leaders. These people in turn tended to be white, male, and upper-middle class. Similarly, after zaps embarrassed an institution into negotiation, those with experience setting policy in such institutions (more often than not also white, male, and upper-middle-class) were the first to initiate and lead the 'inside' strategy of working to negotiate changes in ACT UP's targeted institutions. By contrast, America's professional lobbies tend only to invite major donors to sit on boards. Former Executive Director of the National Gay and Lesbian

Task Force, Urvashi Vaid, writes, 'If you have money or are willing to raise lots of it, you can join any board in the land. If you don't have access to money, then you are asked to be a volunteer, not a decision maker.'[22] This is the predictable and structural consequence of the fact that national lesbian and gay lobbies and foundations survive by major donor fund-raising. However, though not motivated by malice, turning leadership over to people with money has serious consequences: national organizations fighting against homophobia and on behalf of people with or at risk of HIV are directed by and generally serve the interests of the economically most privileged homosexuals. Sometimes, these interests overlap with those of most queers and people with AIDS and HIV, but sometimes they do not. Representationally, however, they easily masquerade as the interests of all gays and lesbians (because the wealthy are the ones who can afford the profiled gay lifestyle, and they inherit from it a class-specific identity which *pretends* to include all gays and lesbians, regardless of class).

The national gay and lesbian movement has neglected economic issues (such as health care reform) on the grounds that national lobbies are dedicated to 'exclusively gay concerns'.[23] But the very notion of 'exclusively gay concerns' divorced from economics presumes wealth, because, for all but the most privileged, one of the principal effects of homophobia and AIDS is to exacerbate economic insecurity – especially in the forms of job discrimination, and increased health insurance premiums. The dire economic positions of PWAS without health insurance is another terrible story. That national political institutions and AIDS organizations did nothing in the struggle for national health care while the gay community weathered an epidemic of unthinkable proportion stands, in the history of American struggles for civil rights, as one of the great failures of a movement to represent its community.

When gay commentators argue that organizations like ACT UP won the gay community access to public health administrators and the mainstream political process, and that once this access was won, grassroots activism ceased to be appropriate, they mask two important points. First, that access was purchased by particular class interests which have used it in the service of those interests. And second, that grassroots action is perhaps the only way gay men and lesbians in the fight against AIDS *without* financial access to lobby policy-makers and politicians can ensure that the access that has been *bought* is used to further their interests as well.

notes

1. See Edward King's important contribution to this volume, 'HIV Prevention and the New Virology'.
2. It's stunning that in 1995, a major CDC 'prevention' campaign was launched in American airports which consisted of posters depicting a bat flying through the broken window of a ruined gothic church. The moon is full, and the text reads, 'Beware of fly-by-night relationships: AIDS.' Even more stunning, perhaps, is the lack of any response by gay and AIDS activists to this public (dis)service campaign.
3. See, for instance, Urvashi Vaid, *Virtual Equality: The Mainstreaming of Gay and Lesbian Liberation*, New York, Anchor/Doubleday, 1995. Sarah Schulman, *My American History: Lesbian and Gay Life During the Reagan/Bush Years*, New York, Routledge, 1994. Michael Bronski, *Culture Clash: The Making of Gay Sensibility*, Boston, South End Press, 1984. And Michael Bronski, *Pleasure Envy: Culture, Backlash, and the Struggle for Gay Freedom* (tentative title), New York, St Martin's, 1997.
4. Unpublished notes from a discussion with editor of *The Advocate*, Jeff Yarbrough, 29 December 1995. This is also implicit in Mark Harrington's discussion of treatment activism, in this volume.
5. *Fag Rag* made a commitment to publish at least one piece by anybody who submitted work, but overtly censored writing which attempted to make over the gay community as 'nice' or acceptable. The magazine had a list of words contributors were not allowed to use. This included 'nice', 'Fire Island', 'ice cream cone' (as in, 'I took his cock down my throat like an *ice cream cone*'), and 'Provincetown' (but reference to the nearby cruising ground, Herring Cove, was actively encouraged). *Gay Community News*, a weekly broadsheet, tended to print every letter received, and virtually every editorial written for the Community Voices

page. Clearly defining itself as 'progressive', it selected articles on the basis of the political importance and originality of argument.

6. 'The Inside/outside strategy' was perfected by ACT UP, and, permitting gross simplification, involves the following: well-publicized demonstrations and protests work, from the *outside*, to force a negotiation with policy-makers responsible for intolerable circumstances; once negotiations begin, we would initiate the *inside* strategy, wherein we would demand access to advise and monitor future policy.

7. Of course, grassroots organizations also have offices. From them, members organize protests, produce leaflets, and coordinate negotiating efforts. The hallmark of what I refer to as 'grassroots' activism is the commitment to policies of open participation. An organization which operates through open meetings differs dramatically from a professional bureaucracy where decisions are made by a paid, executive director and a board of trustees.

8. Now in my early twenties, I have attended more funerals than my ninety-year-old grandfather. In the midst of this intense loss, I am sustained by the history of protest which we join and in which we are immortalized through our activism. I suspect this sense of history and ethical struggle provides similar sustenance for all ACT UP members enduring wave upon wave of loss.

9. This is not quite to say that grassroots organizations are free of exclusion and elitism. See, for example, the discussion below.

10. Unpublished notes from a discussion with Jeff Yarbrough, 29 December 1995.

11. Prophetically, it takes less than a shocking demonstration to provoke boycott. In June 1996, Southern Baptists called a boycott on their old favourite, the Walt Disney Corporation, after it extended health benefits to the partners of its gay employees.

12. Big business's entrée into gay marketing did not fragment urban gay communities. Rather, big, non-gay retailers advertising to the gay community simply replaced Mom and Pop shops and gay-owned stores on gay commercial streets. It would be valuable to show how this has altered property values in the neighbouring residential areas. Where property values were raised, this would restrict who could afford to move into the gay ghettos, which had become chic shopping, dining, and entertainment districts. This may account for the fact that the Castro or West Village is inhabited predominantly by fairly wealthy gay men. I am indebted to Urvashi Vaid for her excellent analysis and summary of Escoffier's remarks (*Virtual Equality*, pp.245–46).

13. Opening remarks, 'Homo/economics Conference'. Center for Lesbian and Gay Studies, City University of New York, New York, May 1994.

14. Moreover, in the UK, several gay papers, such as the *Pink Paper,* were founded in Escoffier's *third stage* of gay economic life: namely, the economy of AIDS. Meurig Horton has pointed out that 'since the Health Education Authority made the decision to carry out safer sex education through advertisements in the gay press, assuming the gay community to be coterminous with the gay press, a guaranteed income from the HEA enabled the financial development, elaboration, and consolidation of otherwise tiny gay papers' (from a letter to the author, 19 August 1996).

15. Urvashi Vaid (*Virtual Equality,* p.246) understands the emergence of the gay consumer to be a fifth stage in the development of gay and lesbian economies.

16. Marshall Kirk and Hunter Madsen, *After the Ball: how America will conquer its fear and hatred of gays in the 90s.* New York, Anchor/ Doubleday, 1989.

17. ibid., p.49.

18. ibid., p.48.

19. Again, no text could provide a more explicit example of this sort of writing than Part III of *After the Ball.*

20. Ibid., p.276.

21. Doubtless most gay consumers will not consciously come to believe themselves 'safer' the more assimilated their lifestyles. However, in a community where fifty per cent of men are HIV positive, it would be naive to imagine that marketing an assimilationist identity as maturity itself and, subsequently, as protection from HIV, doesn't have considerable impact on prevailing community attitudes.

22. *Virtual Equality,* p.270.

23. Indeed, one large not-for-profit gay and lesbian organization (Access Network for Gay and Lesbian Equality) has actively campaigned against universal health care (*Virtual Equality* 46). One of ANGLE's founder-members, David Mixner, was paid tens of thousands of dollars by insurance companies to campaign against single-payer health insurance in Los Angeles, and other ANGLE leaders also have ties to the insurance industry. Ironically, David Mixner is a long-time friend and political ally of Bill Clinton.

white noise

how gay men's activism gets written out of AIDS prevention

Peter Scott

Many people assume that any AIDS-awareness education must be a good thing. However, in this paper I argue that, as far as the gay epidemic is concerned, state-sponsored HIV prevention has done more harm than good.

In the early to mid-1980s, whilst public health agencies completely neglected AIDS education, a grass roots gay AIDS prevention activism had developed and gay men rapidly invented and adopted safer sex. However, from 1986/87 governments began to be concerned about the possibility of a heterosexual epidemic. They threw money at the problem and a vast new HIV prevention industry grew up almost overnight.

The overriding agenda of this new industry was to target heterosexuals (regardless of epidemiology) and persuade them that AIDS was 'not just a gay disease' but, on the contrary, a predominantly heterosexual disease. By sheer weight of numbers this heterosexual agenda quickly dominated most areas of writing and communication about AIDS and HIV. Almost every book, every article, every conference, every paper, every leaflet, every poster, every campaign, every interview emphasized heterosexual risk. All this had harmful side effects for gay men. Firstly, little or no state-funded health education was targeted at gay men. Worse, previously gay non-governmental organizations had to adopt the heterosexual agenda and become 'straight-acting' because that was the only way to get state funding. This process is what is usually described as the de-gaying of AIDS.

Secondly, the heterosexual agenda produced an overwhelming barrage of deafening white noise which drowned out the voices of gay activists and buried the history of gay activism in a mass of heterosexual reports and documents. Thus the achievements of gay grass roots safer sex activism have consistently been obscured, under-rated, ignored or misrepresented. The vast majority of professionals employed in the field were newcomers who were not only unaware of the successes of the early gay activist safer sex movement but also unlikely to even encounter references to that history, because the AIDS industry's heterosexualizing agenda so rapidly swamped everything.

Thus, a story of AIDS written from heterosexual perspectives was internalized by previously gay AIDS organizations, and by gay organizations and the gay press. Many gay men have been deluded into believing that the gay epidemic is more or less over (thanks to the efforts of public health campaigns) and less important than the heterosexual epidemic.

Thirdly, the vast majority of professional experience in HIV prevention has developed in work with heterosexuals. Not surprisingly, therefore, methods of HIV prevention that are heterosexual or even heterosexist or homophobic have thus come to seem merely 'normal' and have been imposed upon what little HIV prevention work there has been for gay men.

In reality, far from passing through the gay population and moving on to other groups, the HIV epidemic continues to grow amongst gay men. A new generation of gay AIDS prevention activists are needed now more than ever. But the net result of this overwhelming heterosexual emphasis has been to obliterate, divert, inhibit or undermine gay men's safer sex activism.

Since 1992 a re-gaying movement has begun to develop. However, any new gay activist faces an onslaught of continuing white noise almost designed to distract or de-activate him. A number of key myths about de-gaying and re-gaying need to be addressed and challenged because they inhibit the revival of the essential gay safer sex activism.

the complacent official version of what happened

HIV prevention is big money. In just a few years a whole new profession has developed with hundreds of HIV prevention projects in the UK alone, dozens of conferences, hundreds of reports, leaflets, brochures, posters, videos; a whole army of HIV prevention workers with hi-tech armaments and extended supply lines. What gay man could be blamed for thinking that this army is well-trained, well-informed, well-supplied, has always been fighting on our side, and that its generals know what they are doing?

But with this state-funded and mobilized army comes an official version of the story of AIDS and HIV which is remarkably similar from country to country. Here is the Swedish version:

> 'Sweden's first case of AIDS was diagnosed in 1982. One year later, scientists were able to identify the virus, HIV, by which AIDS is caused. In the years that followed, an intensive effort was mounted for the prevention of HIV and containment of the epidemic . . . So far the HIV epidemic has spread less rapidly in Sweden than in many other countries . . . Even so, more than 20 new HIV infections are reported every month . . . this country had a long-standing tradition of combating STDs, and the experience thus acquired provided a foundation for HIV prevention . . . An extensive HIV testing programme . . . enables us to keep a close watch on developments and to decide which actions are needed most.'

And here is a British example:

> Nearly ten years on from the first Government campaigns to alert the population to the risks . . . the spread of HIV is at present relatively controlled in the UK but there is no room for complacency . . . rates of reported new infection remain

> high among gay and bisexual men . . . Our only weapon in the fight to prevent HIV from spreading is health promotion, ranging from public education campaigns to . . . other outreach activities . . . Early health promotion efforts have proved effective in slowing (but not stopping) the spread of HIV in the UK . . . Health Promotion for HIV and AIDS in the UK has contributed to the achievement of a lower rate of infection than in a number of other European countries.[1]

In every country the official versions claim that the HIV prevention job has been well done, that resources have been used with maximum care to maximum effect in a timely way, and that there has been a steady, consistent and rational strategy, evolving over time. Supposedly without delay, governments and public health agencies acted rationally, on the best medical and epidemiological advice, to introduce measures such as HIV-antibody testing and mass-media information campaigns. And supposedly, this is what has effectively contained the epidemic. Apparently, there is no history of the epidemic before the first state-funded campaigns. Governments have been anything but complacent, have successfully alerted their populations to the risks and have always targeted gay men with useful information. Indeed, it was the government that warned gay men about the risks, and the epidemic amongst gay men has declined because they heeded those warnings.

Naturally, any gay men still being infected today have only themselves to blame according to this story.

In fact it's all an utterly dishonest account! Three things are principally obscured in these official accounts: the crucial role of gay men's self-help in the early stages of the epidemic, the neglect of gay men by public HIV prevention agencies for the best part of a decade, and the actual obstacles put in the way of gay safer sex education by government policy and public health agencies.

In the official versions the most disturbing and counterproductive things don't get mentioned: for example, the so-called 'mouse-trap anonymity' in Sweden, where those taking the test are guaranteed anonymity unless they test positive. In that case they are forced to register with the state and their sexual partners are required by law to get tested. Or the funding of a quango, Noah's Ark, as a direct and damaging rival to the national gay and lesbian organization, RFSL.[2]

Similarly, the 'Clause 28' legislation in the UK has been used to produce a climate of terror about the so-called 'promotion of homosexuality' which has meant that effective school HIV education for gay men is either absent or trivial. Typically, in a local survey 70.7 per cent of gay men asked about the quality of their sexual information at school said it was non-existent, 24 per cent thought it was poor or very poor and as few as 5 per cent thought it was fairly or very good.[3] The author concluded that 'these ratings may well be a reflection on the omission in school HIV education of relevant information for gays and bisexuals.' The power of legislation to suppress gay-friendly safer sex education is exemplified at its worst by the 1987 Helms Amendment in the US.[4]

More importantly, even when, late in the 1990s, governments have finally begun to realize their mistakes and begun targeting funding towards HIV prevention activities for gay men, there is no acknowledgement that anything was ever amiss. Thus, whilst the British Government's new guidance in *An Evolving Strategy* (UK Health Departments, 1995) belatedly incorporates some of what a small group of re-gaying activists have been arguing for a number of years, the illusion is nevertheless created of an apparently seamless evolution of targeting (encapsulated in the very name of the document) which obliterates the approximately six-to seven-year history of activism and the hard, exhausting, thankless struggle to change the agenda in this direction. In reality, the document represents a complete U-turn.

This disguising of the history of homophobic neglect is not limited to state agencies' publicity. The de-gaying of the Terrence Higgins Trust (the largest AIDS service organization in the UK) provides a classic example. In its own official publicity, it routinely claims to have 'consistently broken new ground' in advocating 'targeted campaigns for those groups most at risk, particularly gay men'.[5] In reality, as Edward King describes, 'from 1987–1991 the Terrence Higgins Trust undertook virtually no new activities targeting gay men.'[6]

Why does this matter? Is it just sour grapes on the part of activists who get no thanks for their efforts? No, the point is that it peddles a cluster of lies: that homophobia has never existed in the response to the AIDS epidemic, that gay men's safer sex education is safe in the hands of heterosexual professionals, that gay activism achieved nothing, wasn't needed in the past, and is certainly not needed in the present or the future. In consequence, gay men's most effective weapon in the fight against AIDS is effectively discredited and disarmed. Simon Watney has explained:

> Historical accounts of AIDS that overlook the achievements of the non-government AIDS service organizations, or treatment activism, or the role of gay men in the statutory sector, amount to nothing more than strategic disinformation.[7]

Examples of this kind of disinformation abound in the mainstream histories of AIDS. For instance, Virginia Berridge ends her history, *AIDS in the UK*: 'In Britain, the immediate threat of an epidemic had ended . . .'[8] This is a conclusion hardly in line with epidemiology or direct experience. It could only come from a perspective where the only thing that really matters is a heterosexual epidemic. As Watney has noted:

> For most heterosexuals in the United Kingdom, HIV is indeed a most remote statistical probability, and this is why they are generally so ill-equipped to understand or comment upon the situation confronting gay men . . .[9]

what really happened – grass roots activism

The reality is quite different, and in almost every respect the opposite of the official story described above. Safer sex was an invention and an achievement of gay community activists and the rapid and widespread adoption of safer sex by gay men in the 1980s was a result of community-initiated grass roots education.[10] And gay men's sexual behaviour changes took place before governments began national education campaigns, even though they later tried to take the credit:

> Contrary to popular wisdom, this unprecedented mass behaviour change owed little or nothing to the actions of governments or others outside the gay community, or to HIV antibody testing, or to the application of theory-based health educational models.[11]

How do we know that this isn't just the wishful thinking of gay activists? There are four sorts of evidence that corroborate the history that we took part in and helped create. Firstly, we know from considering historical epidemiology. In an elegant and wide-ranging literature review Mitchell Cohen has shown how the gay epidemics (whilst staggered in time) in different countries have nevertheless followed a common pattern with recognizable stages: a beginning stage, a peaking stage, a declining stage and a tail.[12]

What is clear is that wherever surveillance data exists, it can be shown that the incidence of HIV transmission amongst gay men fell before governments became involved, before public education campaigns and before the local state-funded AIDS industry was established, and that 'there is no question that change to safer sex is related to a declining incidence of HIV'.[13] Typically, one study summarized it as 'the most rapid and extensive (albeit still incomplete) changes in human behaviour ever observed'.[14] Moreover, academic epidemiologists found conclusive grounds for dating the change before public health campaigns.[15] Tony Coxon writing about the Project Sigma research in the UK (a very large and detailed longitudinal study of gay and bisexual men's behaviour in relation to AIDS) frankly admits:

> Our greatest regret was that we had no resources to investigate

> gay men's response to the threat of AIDS during the period when most change occurred, from 1982 to 1986. It was galling and saddening to have to expend energies in battling continuously for funding in an intensely political environment when we were up and ready to start the much-needed research . . . On the main features of the change which undoubtedly occurred, both we and other studies in the Western world have agreed: the change that occurred, did so before health education or a political response had crystallised.[16]

Secondly, although a remarkably small proportion of academic studies have investigated the effectiveness of HIV prevention interventions, we know from the few studies there have been, that the kinds of intervention that continue to be most effective are those that attempt to harness gay community grass roots peer education.[17] This point should not be lightly under-stated. Whereas no evidence exists for the effectiveness of typical public health promotion activities, there have been a number of controlled trials which demonstrate the effectiveness of activist-led peer education.[18]

Thirdly, we know from studies where gay men have said that they got useful advice or support for learning and sustaining safer sex. To this day, despite the many millions of dollars and pounds spent on AIDS education programmes, there is no evidence that gay men have received substantial useful advice or education from any state-funded campaigns or projects. By contrast, there is evidence that the significant sources of information and support for gay and bisexual men have been the gay press and their gay peers.[19]

Fourthly, we know from comparative national data that the relative magnitude of the epidemic in countries with similar populations can be related to the extent of pre-existing gay community institutions and activism.[20] For instance, France, with much the same size of population as the UK, has an epidemic with four to five times as many gay men infected. And the reason for that can be attributed to the fact that France had much less in the way of gay community organizations and a much smaller gay press in the 1980s than did the UK, and thus a much less developed base for gay community safer sex activism.[21]

the history of de-gaying

The history of the de-gaying of responses to the epidemic has been extensively described and analyzed (Rooney, 1991; King 1993; Watney 1994; Scott 1995).[22] Meurig Horton and Simon Watney show how de-gaying is part of a wider global neglect that succeeds in displacing gay and homosexually active men from all areas of discussion, discourse, research and practice.[23] A spectacular early example of the extent of the de-gaying is provided by 'a public service project of the publishing industry', a widely distributed free book offered as 'a gift from the publishing and book-selling community to the millions of Americans whose energy and compassion will win the battle against AIDS'.[24]

It has suggestions for almost every kind of activism imaginable: talking to children, educating parents, what teachers can do, working with the local school board, action on campus, what clergy can do, a union approach, what journalists can do, what people in the arts can do, taking action in minority communities, and so on . . . But guess what gets completely left out of the book? You guessed it: not a single reference to, or encouragement of, specifically gay safer sex activism.

Another typical example is provided by the annual report of a local AIDS service organization in North London (Brent HIV Centre, 1990) which de-gayed by making vastly exaggerated heterosexual projections of the epidemic. Thus, it claimed that 'based upon current available statistics for increase nationwide and the known client group of the Brent HIV Centre . . . we would expect the numbers of those infected in the Borough to be . . . 90 children, 427 women, 132 gay men, 88 heterosexual men, 228 drug users.'[25] In other words they projected that only about 13 per cent of HIV infections would be amongst gay men. In reality, approximately two thirds of new HIV infection acquired in the UK continues to be amongst gay men.[26]

Finally, a vivid and eloquent example of the continuing power of the de-gaying of the story of AIDS is provided by a recent book purporting to be about the economic and social impact of AIDS in Europe, and sponsored by the UK's National AIDS Trust.[27] Out of its thirty-six chapters, not one focuses upon gay men. The word 'gay' in the index only says 'see homosexual and bisexual men' and when you look that up there are precisely six short references throughout the whole (nearly) four-hundred-page book. The editors assure us in the preface that 'AIDS is predominantly a disease of the young' (defining youth, ludicrously, as people between twenty-five and forty)! This is complete nonsense. Throughout Europe AIDS is still predominantly and overwhelmingly a disease of core target groups: gay men, injecting drug users and immigrants and refugees from sub-Saharan African countries (who were probably infected outside Europe).

Paradoxically, the sheer volume of de-gaying material makes it hard for a newcomer to the field to stumble upon descriptions or analyses of the reality and extent of the de-gaying. The deafening white noise of de-gaying has also hidden the fact of the very existence of that history of de-gaying. Thus, although the magnitude and extreme nature of de-gaying was little short of breath-taking, it took a number of years before gay activists' perspectives were noted in the mainstream AIDS literature. For example, one researcher pointed out that:

> by the early 1990s in California the gay male community accounted for nearly 85% of deaths from AIDS in the state but received only about 8% of state funding for prevention, a pattern that also seems to exist in England . . .[28]

And he warned that:

> the tendency to declare victory in the fight against AIDS and

> then to leave the field has been a disaster for gay male communities.[29]

Indeed, a pioneering survey showed that only 3.5 per cent of local HIV projects throughout the UK were undertaking any substantial HIV prevention work with gay men![30] As if to add insult to injury, the survey itself had been turned down for funding by a number of public health agencies and would not have happened without the work of volunteer gay activists. Such neglect of the very means of demonstrating neglect was true not only of health promotion but even of epidemiological surveillance:

> A profoundly depressing thought is that since funders and policy-makers take the view that gay men have looked after their own salvation, the situation needs no further systematic monitoring, just at the point where it is most needed. 'Re-gaying' is needed not only in the AIDS political and health movement but also in the AIDS research area.[31]

activism written out of history

Kippax et al. have argued that 'the field of HIV/AIDS research was colonized from the start by medical discourse' which produced a 'vocabulary of AIDS-talk' that effectively marginalized the question of social action:

> In policy discourse the process of elision results in categories such as 'behaviour change as an outcome of intervention programs', which effectively deny the agency, and especially the collective agency, of groups who are responding to the epidemic among them . . . The language itself seems very revealing of a prevention strategy that presumes (a) an authoritative, knowledgeable, powerful centre, ready to fire its bullets of information or persuasion at identified targets; and (b) a dispersed, passive ignorant periphery waiting to be fired at.[32]

This medicalization of the story of HIV prevention was not restricted to research alone, but has moulded the mainstream histories of the epidemic. In her book, *The Coming*

Plague, Laurie Garrett is aware that the effectiveness of medical and scientific responses to infectious diseases is undermined by social factors such as poverty and post-colonial militarism. Writing about the Zairian outbreak of Ebola, she records that:

> Everywhere the group [of doctors] went they noticed the people had taken remarkably wise measures to stop the epidemic's spread . . . 'These people have really got their act together,' [one scientist told another], who was also impressed by the steps taken.[33]

Nevertheless, despite this token recognition of community-led disease prevention, the book presents almost all disease prevention through the eyes of heroic doctors and scientists, so-called 'disease cowboys'. Two to three hundred pages of Garrett's book detail the development of the AIDS pandemic, but we look in vain for any mention of the phrase 'safer sex'. It's not even in the index. The nearest index entry is: 'human immunodeficiency virus (HIV), measures to prevent the spread of, 463–77.' And when we look at those pages, what we get is the peddling of a notorious canard:

> 'Studies of gay male behavior in San Francisco showed that crucial to individual protective action, such as consistent use of condoms, was a high level of fear, brought about by witnessing the deterioration and AIDS death of a close friend, relative, or lover . . . on a societal scale it was apparent that few cultures were able to confront AIDS until the death toll had become sufficiently high to have given more than 10 per cent of all adults a firsthand view of the horrendous disease.[34]

As I have discussed above, this is only true from a perspective that ignores all gay communities everywhere in the world. Revealingly, in a book with thousands of references, this *particular* explanation is completely unreferenced (including the supposed studies on which her claims are based). In reality a striking feature of gay men's uptake of safer sex is that it happened before the vast majority of gay men could possibly have known anyone who was openly HIV positive, let alone symptomatic.[35] Amazingly, Garrett cites a report (British Market Research, 1987) which shows that the infamous highest profile 'tombstones' AIDS education campaign of the UK government was less than effective.

> It was a case where most of the elements for success appeared to be in place: top-level political will, resources, national television accessibility, and a heightened media interest. Yet the campaign was eventually judged a failure, as it *succeeded in raising AIDS awareness and fear* but failed to put a dent in public misperceptions about how the virus was transmitted or general disdain for those who carried HIV. [Emphasis added.][36]

Thus, without realising it, she herself contradicts her own explanation of the importance of fear. She then notes that:

> in no country, it seemed, had a government found the secret to preventing further spread of HIV once the epidemic became endemic.[37]

Thus she casually neglects the evidence and dismisses the very possibility of safer sex. For all this she got rave reviews: 'probably the best informed AIDS journalist writing' according to *The Economist*, for example.

Extreme examples of this implicit denial of the very possibility of safer sex abound in the mainstream literature.

> So what can we say to the nomads and the poor? What is their choice? To suffer the viral haemorrhagic fevers such as Ebola and Crimean Congo? Or face the crowded, polluted, violent city teeming with people who spread deadly AIDS?[38]

Similarly in his social dimension of AIDS chapter, Grmek can pronounce: 'No effective prophylaxis exists outside of serologic detection and information campaigns covering risk and prevention'.[39] Grmek has written an influential and otherwise authoritative book which on every other topic is well-referenced and based on firm evidence. What reader will spot that his implicit claim that social action is ineffective is not based on any kind of evidence whatsoever?

activism misrepresented

The majority of official accounts then, have completely written gay activism out of the history of responses to the epidemic. The few exceptions marginalize and misrepresent it. In a widely hyped and award-winning journalistic history, *The End of Innocence*, Garfield, characteristically misrepresents what activists did in the early 1980s. I know this because the source of some of his material is an interview with me:

> When Peter Scott first read about AIDS, it still had a variety of gay-related names. *As part of his job* [my emphasis] he heard about it earlier than in the reports from America in mid-1981 . . .[40]

In reality, it had nothing to do with my profession. I heard about it because I was a volunteer on London Lesbian and Gay Switchboard. The crucial thing obscured in Garfield's inaccurate account is how much the early response to AIDS depended upon gay men acting in an activist, voluntary capacity rather than in any kind of 'professional' capacity. An article could be written about how journalists and historians have misrepresented the results of the debates that took place in London Lesbian and Gay Switchboard in 1983 about what that organization's response should be to the emerging health crisis. Typically, two different authors select partisan and partial sources and recollections which emphasize the 'difficulties the organisation had in adjusting to AIDS' and thus give the misleading impression that the safer sex activists lost the argument and left Switchboard.[41]

The truth was exactly the opposite. So successfully did the safer sex activists win the day that the Switchboard safer sex manual was the precursor for the National AIDS Manual, out of which grew the leading HIV information-producing charity in the UK.[42] For that matter, the UK's National AIDS Helpline, set up in 1987, could not have been staffed without a ready supply of trained and motivated Switchboard volunteers. Unfortunately, alternative gay activists' histories are still only available in a fragmented form. 'For those actively involved in HIV/AIDS work the time has not yet arrived for the writing of history. We have other priorities.'[43]

internalization, de-activation, de-motivation and mis-direction

The effect of the sheer volume of this chorus of de-gayed words, reports, articles, books and workers cannot be overstated. Even a professional historian finds that:

> AIDS is an overwhelming subject, in many ways. Those who attempt to research and document even one country's history are quickly deluged with published material, from cultural analysis through to reports, guide-lines, and working papers. The political and cultural sensitivities of the issue at all levels make academic interpretation a minefield.[44]

As a result it is as difficult for a newcomer to the HIV prevention field to find out about the gay activist perspective, as it is to find the proverbial needle in a haystack. A deafening 'white noise' has been generated by a de-gayed HIV prevention industry which has had the effect of obliterating the voice of gay activism and thus preventing the handing on of gay activist experience from one gay generation to the next. Not surprisingly, then, most gay men, gay organizations and even the gay press have bought into the heterosexual story.

A de-gaying emphasis that was designed to convince heterosexuals that they might also be at risk, ended up convincing gay men that gay men were at no special risk compared to heterosexuals, that they needed no special support and education services specifically targeted towards them, and that safer sex activism was not an important issue for gay men. Many gay and lesbian activists (from areas of gay activism other than the HIV/AIDS field) now falsely believe that there is some sort of 'gay party line' as regards AIDS, summed up in the slogan 'AIDS is not a gay disease: AIDS can affect everyone.' Moreover, many gay men have just assumed that most AIDS organizations were doing what was needed to support gay men, when in reality they'd drifted off course.

A typical example of the power of 'straight-acting' AIDS organizations to promote de-gaying even within the gay press is provided by a fund-raising leaflet inserted in the Summer of 1995 into gay newspapers by London Lighthouse, the largest AIDS hospice in the UK. Its front page screams in very large red capitals: 'HAVE YOU FAILED THE AIDS TEST?' and follows with only two tick-boxes the gay reader might choose between. 'I don't give a toss about people with HIV or AIDS' or 'I would like to take positive action to help'. Turning the page, the reader is again screamed at: 'IT'S NOT JUST A GAY THING'. The message of the leaflet is clear: 'RIBBONS AREN'T ENOUGH. PLEASE DO SOMETHING MORE POSITIVE. DONATE . . .' to generic, straight-acting organizations. The Lighthouse leaflet insinuates that the services that really matter are those for groups other than gay men and that gay men have no useful role to play other than giving money to help support heterosexuals.

It is important to understand that there were good reasons in the 1980s when gay men themselves wanted to buy into the de-gaying of AIDS. For instance, gay human and civil rights were being threatened by AIDS-hysteria and it seemed important to ward off blame and stigmatization by emphasizing heterosexual AIDS. I have described the important reasons why gay men joined in this de-gaying elsewhere,[45] together with its unintended side effect, the marginalization of gay activist experience.

The effect of all this is to deactivate potential gay safer sex activists who can see no role to play. However, even if they get past the white noise telling them that they are not needed, there is a further danger: the danger of applying 'lessons' and working methods derived from heterosexual prevention work and projecting them inappropriately on to safer sex work with gay men.

Ultimately it is not difficult for gay activists to spot the inappropriateness of heterosexual and heterosexist methods. Nevertheless, special vigilance is needed, when planning, designing or carrying out interventions to avoid the inadvertent projection of unstated implicit heterosexual assumptions and methods on to safer sex education with gay men. For example, Walt Odets has eloquently argued that the kind and quality of messages in HIV prevention campaigns in the USA are harmful to sero-negative gay men in a number of ways.[46]

It is not possible in a single article to adequately describe or even summarize all the wrong assumptions, irrelevant targeting and inappropriate methods that have resulted from the de-gaying of AIDS all over the world (both in countries where male-to male transmission accounts for the majority, and also in countries where it accounts for a minority of cases). However, I have already mapped out what planners and designers of HIV prevention projects need to be vigilant about.[47] Similarly, a core 're-gaying curriculum' for would-be gay AIDS activists is described in a forthcoming pocket handbook for new AIDS activists, the *Gay Guerrilla Guide*.[48]

re-gaying and its 'professional' enemies

Gay safer sex activism is needed now more than ever. Since the mid-1980s gay activists have been arguing that

> it is not easy for anyone to sustain changes in their sexual behaviour without substantial support and education services. Sustenance is needed not only for appropriate individual behaviour change but also for the organisations and networks that enable and encourage it. (Such sustenance would involve professional training and resources for gay and

lesbian 'switchboards', gay befriending groups, the gay press and other opinion formers within the gay community.)'[49]

A small group of activists understood that what was needed in 1992, was a new gay 'community mobilization' which adapted the lost methods of the 1980s to the new realities of the '90s, and, above all, was gay-specific again. The founding of a new organization, Gay Men Fighting AIDS, began the reversal of the trend where gay organizations had become progressively more straight-acting, best exemplified by the transformation of New York's Gay Men's Health Crisis into the more closeted GMHC. Central to this community mobilization methodology was the realization that merely targeting gay men with basic, neutral, 'shallow' sloganizing information was useless in helping them change to safer sex or to sustain it in the long term. Moreover, the situations in which gay men have unsafe sex and the reasons for doing so, are multiple, overlapping, complex and deep. All this called for a multi-faceted community mobilization and diffusion programme led by gay activists drawn from all walks of gay life.

Within a short time Gay Men Fighting AIDS had pioneered and developed a whole range of new and adapted activist interventions that had been missing from the HIV prevention field for some years, including in-depth sex workshops, commercial scene zaps and events, SM and bondage safety workshops; cruising work; posters, postcards, surveys, a journal devoted to gay men's issues, gay radio advertisements, a revival of safer sex discussions in the gay press, and even (extraordinarily for the UK) prize-winning television advertisements explicitly addressed to gay men, and many other activities designed to get gay men to acknowledge the reality of continuing unsafe sex and to consider personal strategies for dealing with temptation.[50]

In the UK at least, re-gaying is now firmly on the agenda. The mere existence of a new national gay HIV organization, founded in 1992, revolutionized the whole climate, so that even the British government has now begun to come round to the (diluted) re-gaying agenda (described above) and quite a few dedicated gay men's projects have been established in towns throughout the UK. However, the battle to match HIV prevention resources to epidemiological risk has not been won, but has only just begun. Is it surprising, given the long period of huge investment in de-gaying that there is just as much white noise being generated about re-gaying?

Some of the key myths are: that re-gaying has successfully been completed, that it's had enough time to prove itself; that it's been sufficiently resourced and gay men are now getting a fair share of HIV prevention resources; that ordinary gay volunteers are only capable of unsophisticated HIV prevention activities; that re-gaying is only about 'jobs for the boys' and that re-gaying is about selfishly caring for gay lives whilst endangering innocent heterosexuals, 'men who have sex with men', women, and everyone else . . .

For instance, Berridge concludes that the re-gaying movement has hidden, dysfunctional, trivial motives:

> behind the fight to re-establish gay men's needs as central to health-education strategies were other issues. There was a desire to recapture the spirit of what was becoming seen almost as 'the good old days'.[51]

In support of this theory she offers nothing more substantial than her own intuitions and an unnamed source, a single 'volunteer at the Terrence Higgins Trust'. An example of anti-re-gaying drawn from the other end of the spectrum is provided by a recent article in the gay press about 'whether re-gaying is working or not' which asked why re-gaying hadn't stopped all HIV transmission amongst gay men yet, as if it could possibly have done so within two years of its having started.[52]

Elsewhere the same researcher is quoted as saying 'there is no evidence to suggest that the involvement of gay men in the development of campaigns for gay men had resulted in any improved outcomes'.[53] The truth is exactly the opposite. The only effectiveness evidence we have after fifteen years of international research is that 'community members, rather than outsiders, usually know their communities best and often know what is needed to create successful HIV prevention programs'.[54]

Just as Ron Stall warned what a disaster for gay male communities 'the tendency to declare victory in the fight against AIDS and then to leave the field'[55] had been, so too, I would warn against the tendency to declare prematurely that re-gaying has failed, even as we are still making the case for it. In reality, it has only just begun, has managed with extremely limited resources, and has had to work within the context of the 'white noise'.

notes

1. Swedish extract: National Institute of Public Health (1995) 'STD and HIV Prevention in Sweden', Sweden, National Institute of Public Health (Folkhalsoinstitutet); British extract: UK Health Departments, 'HIV and AIDS Health Promotion: An Evolving Strategy', London, Department of Health.
2. S. Watney, 'Safer Sex as Community Practice' in P. Aggleton, P. Davies and G. Hart (eds), *AIDS: Individual, Cultural and Policy Dimensions*, London, The Falmer Press, 1990.
3. G. Turner, 'The Health Needs of Gay and Bisexual Men in Southampton and South West Hampshire', Southampton Gay Men's Health Project, 1995.
4. E. King, *Safety in Numbers*, London, Cassell, 1993.
5. 'Community HIV and AIDS Prevention Strategy' (CHAPS), a disseminated but unpublished report produced as part of a tendering application pack by the Terrence Higgins Trust, London.
6. King, op. cit., pp.208–15.
7. S. Watney, *Practices of Freedom: Selected Writings on HIV/AIDS*, London, Rivers Oram Press, 1994.
8. V. Berridge, *AIDS in the UK: The Making of Policy, 1981–1994*, Oxford University Press, 1996.
9. S. Watney, 'These Waves of Dying Friends: Gay Men, AIDS and Multiple Loss' in P. Horne and R. Lewis, Outlooks: *Lesbian and Gay Sexualities and Visual Cultures*, London, Routledge, 1996.

10. See P. Scott (ed.), *National AIDS Manual*, London, Nam Publications, 1988; Watney 1990, op. cit.; M. Rooney and P. Scott, 'Working Where the Risks Are' in B. Evans, S. Sandberg and I. Watson (eds), *Working Where the Risks Are*, London, Health Education Authority, 1991; P. Scott, *A No-Nonsense guide: Commissioning HIV Prevention Services for Gay and Bisexual Men*, London, Health Education Authority, 1995, (Chapter 5).

11. King 1993, op. cit., Chapter 2.

12. M. Cohen, 'Changing to Safer Sex: Personality, Logic and Habit' in P. Aggleton, G. Hart and P. Davies (eds), AIDS: *Responses, Intervention and Care*, London, The Falmer Press, 1991.

13. ibid.

14. J. Joseph et al., 'Are There Psychological Costs Associated with Changes in Behaviour to Reduce AIDS Risk?' in V. May, G. Albee and S. Schneider (eds), *Primary Prevention of AIDS*, London, Sage, 1989.

15. B. Evans et al., 'Trends in Sexual Behaviour and Risk Factors for HIV Infection Among Homosexual Men, 1984–87', *BMJ*, 1989, p. 298.

16. A. Coxon, *Between the Sheets: Sexual Diaries and Gay Men's Sex in the Era of AIDS*, London, Cassell, 1996.

17. A. Oakley, S. Oliver and G. Peersman, 'Review of Effectiveness of Health Promotion Interventions for Men Who Have Sex With Men', The Epi Centre, Social Science Research Unit, Institute of Education, University of London, 1995.

18. J. Kelly, *Changing HIV Risk Behavior: Practical Strategies*, New York, The Guilford Press, 1995; S. Kippax, R. Connell, G. Dowsett and J. Crawford, *Sustaining Safe Sex: Gay Communities Respond to AIDS*, London, The Falmer Press, 1993; Ronald O. Valdiserri et al., 'AIDS Prevention in Homosexual and Bisexual Men: Results of a Randomized Trial Evaluating Two Risk Reduction Interventions', *AIDS*, Vol. 2, No. 1, pp. 21–26, January 1989; T. Myers et al. 'HIV, Substance Use and Related Behaviour of Gay and Bisexual Men: An examination of the Talking Sex Project cohort,' *British Journal of Addiction*, Vol. 87, Part 2, pp. 207–14, 1992.

19. P. Davies, F. Hickson, A. Hunt and P. Weatherburn, *Sex, Gay Men and AIDS*, London, The Falmer Press, 1993; Turner, op. cit.; P. Scott, 'Moving Targets: An Assessment of the Needs of Gay Men and of Bisexual Men in Relation to HIV Prevention in Enfield and Haringey', a report published by Enfield and Haringey Health Authority, London, 1996.

20. Watney 1994, Chapter 25, op. cit.; H. Moerkerk and P. Aggleton, 'AIDS Prevention Strategies in Europe: a Comparison and Critical Analysis' in P. Aggleton et al., (eds), *AIDS: Individual, Cultural and Policy Dimensions*, London, The Falmer Press, 1990.

21. See essays by Edmund White and Larys Frogier in this volume.

22. Rooney and Scott, op. cit.; King, op. cit.; Watney 1994, op. cit.; Scott 1995, op. cit.

23. See essays by Meurig Horton and Simon Watney in this volume.

24. S. Alyson (ed.) *You CAN Do Something About AIDS*, The Stop AIDS Project, Boston, 1988.

25. Brent HIV Centre, Annual Report, London Borough of Brent, 1990.

26. K. Alcorn, *AIDS Reference Manual*, 19th Edition, January 1996, London, NAM Publications.

27. D. Fitzsimons, V. Hardy and K. Tolley (eds), *The Economic and Social Impact of AIDS in Europe*, London, Cassell, 1995.

28. R. Stall, 'How To Lose the Fight Against AIDS Among Gay Men: Declare Victory and Leave the Field' (editorial), *BMJ*, 1994, pp. 309, 685–6.

29. ibid.

30. E. King, M. Rooney and P. Scott, 'HIV Prevention for Gay Men: A Survey of Initiatives in the UK', North west Thames Regional Health Authority, London, 1992.

31. Coxon, op. cit.

32. Kippax et al., op cit.

33. L. Garrett, *The Coming Plague: Newly Emerging Diseases in a World Out of Balance*, Harmondsworth, Penguin, 1994.

34. ibid., p.474.

35. King 1993, op. cit.

36. Garrett, op. cit.

37. ibid.

38. B. McGormick and S. Fischer-Hoch, *The Virus Hunters*, London, Bloomsbury, 1996.

39. M. Grmek, *History of AIDS: Emergence and Origin of a Modern Pandemic*, Princeton, New Jersey, Princeton University Press, 1990.

40. S. Garfield, *The End of Innocence: Britain in the Time of AIDS*, London, Faber, 1994.

41. ibid., pp.27–32; Berridge, op. cit., pp.17–20.

42. Scott 1988, op. cit.

43. Watney 1994, op cit., Chapter 30.

44. Berridge, op. cit.

45. Scott 1995, op. cit., Chapter 4.

46. W. Odets, 'AIDS Education and Harm Reduction for Gay Men:

Psychological Approaches for the Twenty-first Century,' AIDS & Public Policy Journal, 1994, 9(1): pp. 3–15.

47. Scott 1995, op. cit.

48. P. Scott, *The Gay Guerrilla Guide: Gay Men Fighting AIDS*, London, Cassell, forthcoming in 1997.

49. King et al., 1992, op. cit.

50. M. Dockrell et al., 'Stop AIDS London 2 Year Report', a report produced for funders by Gay Men Fighting AIDS, London, 1995.

51. Berridge op. cit, p.273.

52. F. Hickson, 'Unsafe Sex Goes On', *The Pink Paper*, 20 October 1995.

53. S. Browning, 'Behaviourally Bisexual Men in the UK: Another Population to Prioritise?' *HIV Seminar Notes*, No. 7, February 1996, London, The HIV Project.

54. Kelly, op. cit.

55. Stall, op. cit.

red lights

a brief history of sex work activism in the age of AIDS

Cheryl Overs

This essay is dedicated to my great friend and fellow activist, Danny Cockerline, who died recently. Danny and I used to have really heated arguments about 'whore politics' as well as tons of laughs. One of our favourite laughs was bemoaning the motley crew which passes for the sex workers' rights movement. We may not have the skills or political savvy of other social movements. But then on the rare occasions I can look around a room at 'us' I am overjoyed by this unlikely group of activists. Amateurish it may be, but the movement is nothing if not authentic and therein lies its strength.

The 'movement' consists of a few individuals, several health promotion projects, scattered social welfare initiatives, and a handful of small organizations. Members rarely keep in touch, let alone engage in the discourse normally associated with political activism. Any attempt to map out or document projects and goals is random. As I reflect on my twenty years as a sex workers' rights activist I am aware that my perceptions are subjective and selective. No unifying or authoritative moment has marked the sex workers' rights movement, which means that anyone is free to create its history and define its ideologies, and they do. I was saddened recently to read a book by a feminist academic about a sex workers' rights movement which I barely recognized.[1]

When I was seventeen, I worked in a massage parlour in Melbourne, Australia, for the bat of an eyelid, before I realized that operating a massage parlour was a much better idea than working in one. I began a brothel co-op across the road from the university. The staff were students, and I soon became one, which was very convenient. The brothel was long-lived, highly successful and absolutely problem-free. I rarely discuss the brothel these days because it doesn't ring true: no 'pimps', no violent inter-brothel rivalry, no police hassles and, best of all, no social workers.

Like all small business people, we wanted to advance our own interests and those of the sector. Since the central issue affecting the sex industry was its illegality, the obvious thing to do was to form a group to lobby for decriminalization.

The public or collective issues for any sex workers' organization were the same there and then as they are anywhere else today, and have been in the past: vulnerability to violence and arrest, sub-standard working conditions including low pay and health risks, and exclusion from civil and social institutions and systems. Issues for individual sex workers have also been fairly constant across time and space. As the impact of the stigma of selling sex reaches into almost all aspects of sex workers' lives, sex worker organizations invariably function as support or self-help groups as well as lobby groups, and our first group in mid-1970s Melbourne was no exception.

Resources of all kinds were scarce and we were pretty bereft of ideology. Predictably we adopted most of our philosophy, strategies, and what I now know as 'corporate image', from a crumpled sheet of paper which someone had collected from the English Collective of Prostitutes while on a trip to London. 'No Bad Women, Just Bad Laws' was our mantra, and socialist feminism was our guiding light. The Australian Prostitutes' Collective was open for business.

The road to legalized sex work in the state of Victoria was relatively straightforward and our collective became primarily a technical advisor in the process of legal reform.

We didn't see that at the time, because we were immersed in political discussion. In retrospect, I think we fulfilled the advisory role relatively well because, after all, we knew a lot about the sex industry.

From my Australian perspective, it seemed as if the modern sex workers' rights movement began in the UK, the USA and their anglophone outposts in the mid-1970s. At this time in Melbourne, a church was occupied by prostitutes, and an important book about prostitutes' rights by Claude Jaget was published.[2] Like the ECP's flier, the book espoused an intoxicatingly straightforward Marxist analysis of international capitalism, characterized by patriarchal notions about women's work remaining unpaid in order for the ruling classes to impose poverty, and therefore prostitution, on women. According to this analysis, prostitution is inherently demeaning, an institution created for and by men, into which women are forced, or pushed, depending on your theoretical want. Those who deny this at best have false consciousness, and at worst are collaborators. The short-term 'solution' is wages for housework, with the long-term goal the collapse of international capitalism.

This account of prostitution is fatally flawed for two reasons. Firstly and absurdly, it barely gives sex a mention. This calls to mind Brownmiller's hasty conclusion that rape is 'about' power, not sex, an influential notion in the discourse of early 1970s feminism which helped justify discussions about the desexualization of prostitution. Secondly, socialist feminism, in common with most theories of sex work, attempts to explain prostitution by placing supply rather than demand at the centre of the analysis. To this day I become annoyed and astonished each time I hear the ridiculous and frequently asked question, 'Why does a woman sell sex?' What could be more obvious an answer than, 'Because people buy it'? The search for the pathology of the prostitute is both fruitless and insulting. Perhaps a more important question is, why are the questions framed in this way? The role of social 'science' is increasingly being questioned – albeit by social scientists. However, social scientists still show no sign of doing the one thing they could do to support sex workers, which is to go away!

However, for better or worse, throughout the late 1970s and early 1980s, the sex workers' rights movement operated within the existing feminist movement. The alliance was not comfortable. Sex workers themselves were usually excluded from feminist activism except in the traditional role as compliant testifiers in support of arguments about male oppression, male violence and state oppression in the face of poverty and single parenting. The task of orchestrating 'women's response' and the agenda for action was reserved for others.

You don't have to be on first name terms with too many hookers to know that all this far-fetched politicizing doesn't have a lot to do with what prostitutes actually think. In my experience, sex workers almost universally reject accounts of their occupations which desexualize the work and identify the sex worker as a victim, or worse, a symptom, of male domination, capitalism or anything else. Outside my laughably atypical brothel you wouldn't have found too many feminist prostitutes raging against the capitalist patriarchy between punters! Although you would have then, and still will today, find plenty of talk of poverty and probably 'male oppression', if not in those words. Of course the same can be said for the supermarket, factory and the dole office, but those are not the places in which sexual puritanism stalks its prey.

Another matter which should have been self-evident to feminist 'supporters' is that sex workers, like any workers, are not likely to be impressed by an ideology which aims to abolish their occupation, regardless of whether that coincides with the end of 'women's poverty' or not. In one of British feminism's more nauseating moments, our supportive friends claimed to oppose the institution of prostitution but to support the prostitute. Sound familiar?

In the US, feminist theories of prostitution at least acknowledged – if only to disparage – the sexual element of prostitution (perhaps because, as is often the case in

American political discourse, there was no discussion of class or economics). Discussions of sexuality and prostitution generally were articulated within the terms of Catherine McKinnon and Andrea Dworkin's anti-sex feminism. Their spin on the subject was that male sexuality is excessive, inherently violent and socially determined. Male sexuality, the argument went, inevitably conflicts with female sexuality, which is presented as loving, nurturing, and not for sale. Once again, this theory is blatantly at odds with the word on the street, despite ever-present highly edited testimonies from selected prostitutes in support of the proposition.

It is important to note that many sex workers who testified as 'prostituted women' have since joined the sex workers' rights movement, and tell chilling stories of having been manipulated by feminist puritans. In more recent times, anti-sex crusaders have turned their attentions to the so-called third world. The testimonials of prostitutes are no longer needed. Here, the prostitutes can be represented as 'children' or, even more conveniently, they need not speak at all since they often don't speak English. Even more appalling is the breathtaking display of racism in which middle class, anglophone women from the developing world are accepted as the testimonial voice for the sex workers, presumably since being the same colour as the sex workers is good enough.

As time passed it became apparent that a political and social movement for sex workers should consist primarily of sex workers themselves. The presence of the prostitute as true speaker, rather than as testifier to the speech of another, has been an important or even revolutionary development. It was the Californian sex workers' rights movement that first called for this empowerment and agency. This may be why most sex workers' rights organizations ignore their socialist feminist forerunners and locate Margot St James of COYOTE (Call Off Your Old Tired Ethics), San Francisco as the founder of the modern movement. The St James-led US movement was invigorating in comparison with the twee approach of the English, French and others, who claimed that it was too dangerous for sex workers to reveal themselves in social action.

Regardless of the obvious bravery of Margot St James, who wisely chose not to clarify the scope of her involvement in sex work, the sex worker speaking for herself does not constitute any particular political direction unless one considers demanding the repeal of anti-prostitution laws a political position, which I do not.

It is impossible to overstate the importance of demanding repeal of anti-prostitution laws in the US. Repeal quite rightly remains the primary focus of the US movement. The American laws are probably the worst in any democracy. Prostitution itself is an offence in the United States. By contrast, in most other industrialized democracies, and for that matter post-colonial countries, only prostitution-related activities are illegal. So it's logical to argue that the US anti-prostitution law should be abolished simply because people should have the right to have consensual sex with whomever they like, under whatever circumstances, as long as their actions do not adversely affect others. This is a straightforward question of civil liberties.

This argument has motivated a whole series of 'civil libertarian' arguments about sex work. All of them maintain that sex work should not be regulated by any laws at all – a scenario manipulatively and misleadingly conflated with 'decriminalization'. Civil libertarianism is not a fertile basis for progressive political action. In the sex workers' rights movement, and I suspect in others too, grounding one's ideology in civil liberties can create bankrupt pseudo alliances with, for example, free market economy libertarians. I was horrified recently to read a far right, libertarian discourse in *Whorezine* – a San Francisco mag for hipster whores.

> Bad management is a problem in every industry. But I think lousy managers end up with what they deserve – a second rate shop staffed by second rate people . . . The market is not

> only efficient, it can be surprisingly just . . . if you are working for a terrible madam you are creating a market for her terrible behaviour.[3]

Ross Perot couldn't have put it better!

The American civil liberties message – 'We have the right to sell sex, we are not hurting anyone' – went nowhere fast. All that the puritan feminists and the religious right needed to do was to name the hurt and produce the victim. This of course is a well practised routine – the testimonial again. Self-evident accusations that anti-prostitution laws are inequitable and sexist are also easily answered by increasing criminal actions against the client and sex industry entrepreneurs and service staff. This is a scenario currently being played out to 'fight' sex tourism in South East Asia.

The sexual politics of the American civil libertarians were certainly more positive than those of the English Prostitutes' Collective. Liberal, heterosexual slap and tickle tolerance is how I think of the sexual politics of the early US prostitutes' rights movement – the stuff of wife swapping and naughty weekends as opposed to the sexual austerity of the British Leninists.

American audiences are easy to work. Movement organizers may have felt that daytime TV viewers would marvel at brazen escort girls who seem just like normal women, and then accept arguments for decriminalization. However, history shows that they weren't so easily convinced. Pleas for decriminalization simply weren't taken seriously in the face of larger moral concerns. Arguing for no laws or regulations whatsoever was, and is, bound to fail. Liberalism and libertarianism do not produce sufficiently robust policies to translate the empowerment of the talk show/Hookers' Ball circuit to the brutal world of prostitution, complicated as it is by questions of desire, racism, sexism and economic inequity.

By the early 1980s the movement was floundering. The problem was not a lack of opportunities to meet, but rather a lack of strategic vision. We had recently held two World

Whores' Congresses at which sex workers, mainly from rich countries, swapped stories of oppression and demanded repeal of anti-prostitution laws without suggesting how the sex industry might fit into highly regulated commercial life in industrialized countries.

Then suddenly the brutal world of prostitution became a lot more brutal. The new brutality was HIV. And with it came very serious complications for sex workers organizing. Suddenly, the ancient stigma of prostitutes as conduits of disease became one hundred times more ferocious. At the same time, however, HIV made plausible new arguments for decriminalization of prostitution and money for health promotion to save clients from this new and seemingly fatal sexually transmitted disease.

HIV changed the demographics of sex worker activism. It brought those most affected by the virus and its related persecutions – gay men – into the newly focused sex workers' rights movement. Maybe the movement would have developed a workable social ideology without HIV (I wish we could have found out) and without gay men joining the movement. But I doubt it.

Whenever I think of this development I think of my dear friend Danny Cockerline. He wasn't the only gay man to join the movement but he had an enormous effect on it. Indeed, given how small our movement was at that time – before it was swollen by health workers – any one person was a significant percentage of our rank and file!

Danny was a leather queen, porn starlet, stripper and hustler. He was the quintessential proud whore. I remember begging him not to announce the mega truth to fellow passengers on planes and trains who innocently asked what you 'do' for a living. Danny insisted that sex and the politics of pleasure, rather than gender or economics, were at the centre of the sex work question. 'We are not prostituted women' he would say to mock the feminist label (waving his dick to illustrate the point if necessary, or in any way advantageous).

I remember a workshop with a bewildered audience of

European social workers. We were asserting that the source of whore persecution and stigma is not simply sexism, but also those views of sexuality wherein desire is understood as legitimate only when confined to 'true love' within a heterosexual family. As Andrew Hunter of the Australian Prostitutes' Collective said:

> For the gender-based analysis of socialist or liberal feminists to hold out, rent boys and people of transgender have to be relocated as political women, temporarily subject to sexist persecution. This is clearly nonsense. A fundamental change in sexual ideology, one which embraces absolute sexual diversity, is the route to social justice and liberation for the sex worker, the client and the whole rest of society too, as it happens. In such a society people would accept commercial sex as a valid and wholesome option, an integral part of the landscape of sexual diversity.[4]

Implicit in our position was – and still is – the conviction that the current problems associated with sex work can be traced to socially and legally sanctioned persecution and stigmatization. We would stress that our positions are not anti-feminist, acknowledging wholeheartedly that the whore stigma affects women more profoundly than it does men. Nevertheless, our new whore politics was no longer directly derived from orthodox feminism; it was more properly a part of that tradition which might be called the 'queer nation'. Within this tradition, commercial sex could be both valid work and meaningful sexual expression for seller and buyer alike.

Women were as keen as men to reject previous attempts to vindicate working women while condemning their male clients, lovers and bosses. Sex workers at the Prostitutes' Collective in Melbourne were quick to reject the notions of law reform which had followed from both socialist feminist ideology and civil libertarianism. They recognized that if the sex industry is to operate as an industry, 'decriminalization' is implausible and undesirable. Socialist feminists and civil libertarians alike misleadingly called deregulation 'decriminalization', and differentiated it from 'legislation'.

Legislation, they had argued, meant subjugation to state regulation and tax, which would 'make the State a pimp'. What this fails to appreciate is that sex workers are interested in improved working conditions, not misguided dreams.

These arguments bear an offensive subtext: sex work must remain a female-controlled cottage industry, too insignificant to require regulation; to sell sex is such a supreme sacrifice that the victim should at least be able to keep all the money; commercial sex should resemble as much as possible its superior cousin, private sex.

While nobody likes to pay tax, it has been my experience that sex workers are eager to comply with fair regulations similar to those which apply to other business enterprises. Progressive regulation protects sex workers' labour rights and recognizes the sex worker as a full participant in society. Sex workers are concerned with improved working conditions, not utopian dreams of total freedom.

The new alliance with queer movements had practical effects on our political and collective energy. It gave new life to what I referred to at the outset as the support group function of sex workers' organizations. The Prostitutes Collective had a drop-in centre which was soon adorned with images of the new heroine for male and female sex workers alike – Madonna! Her powerful statement about sexuality and control particularly hit home with sex workers who had never accepted the idea that overt and commercialized sexuality indicated victimhood or even vulnerability. For the first time a spontaneous cultural activism sprang up in which male and female sex workers asserted pride and, conveniently, safe sex at the same time.

The sex workers' rights movement has been renewed where it has moved away from simplistic notions of civil liberties and Marxist commentaries on sources of oppression and victimhood. The dual discourses of human/labour rights and sexual politics are meaningful to sex workers and can handle the tough questions. They have enabled us to develop some of the best possible responses to HIV/AIDS and to questions of modern slavery and child prostitution. These theoretical developments have crossed cultural and political boundaries. Emerging sex workers' rights organizations in developing countries testify to the assertion that they are as meaningful in Delhi as they are in Zurich.

And all of that with a bare minimum of resources and solidarity. I sometimes wonder what sex workers could do if they were not systematically deprived of resources by our friends and enemies alike . . . but that's another story.

notes

1. Gail Pheterson, *The Prostitution Prism*, Amsterdam, Amsterdam University Press 1996.
2. Claude Jaget, *Prostitutes Our Lives*, Falling Wall Press, 1978.
3. Tracy Quan of Prostitutes of New York, *Whorzine* 31.
4. Andrew Hunter, *The Sex Industry and Public Policy*, Canberra, Australian Institute of Criminology, 1992.

AIDS awareness and gay culture in France

Edmund White

Since the very beginning of the epidemic, France has had three times more known cases of AIDS than Britain; as of 30 June 1995, France had a cumulative count of 37,000 cases (including 17,200 homo-bisexuals) and Great Britain had 11,051 cases (including 7,923 homo-bisexuals). Since the two countries were hit by the virus at roughly the same time, have about the same size population, and each has a huge capital city where most of the gay population is concentrated, one would not have expected such skewed statistics.

The 6,000-case difference in the gay-bi populations of the two countries begs for an explanation. Many theories spring to mind. For instance, France was one of the last countries in Europe to have an organized AIDS movement directed at gays. Holland, England and Luxembourg had gay AIDS associations by 1982, Germany and Spain by 1983, Denmark and Italy by 1984, but Belgium and France inaugurated their organized struggle only in 1985, followed by Ireland in 1986.

Or one could point out that in the 1980s the AIDS movement in France (unlike the struggle in other countries) counted very few former gay liberationists; almost all the AIDS activists in France first turned to gay political issues only with their commitment to the AIDS struggle. Simultaneous with the advent of AIDS activism in France in the mid-1980s was a corresponding demise of gay activism: something like a rebirth of the old militancy occured only in the early 1990s with the advent of French ACT UP.

Some historians of the phenomenon have tried to blame the extreme right in France or the power of the Catholic Church, but in fact both organisms formulated their anti-gay policies only in 1987 – too late to be a significant factor. A better target is Mitterand's extreme reticence even to mention the disease, much less to implement useful prevention programmes, for if France has always been strong in AIDS research and treatment it has been very weak in prevention.

Part of the blame, surprisingly, can be attributed to gay intellectuals and artists in France; at least their attitudes are emblematic of the response of the more general population. As early as 1982, Michel Foucault, writing under a pseudonym in *Libération*, declared that fear over 'gay cancer' in the United States had caused the American gay press and gay movement leaders to spread slogans 'in favour of monogamy and the couple and on the need to practise sports rather than sex.' As late as 1985 a journalist in *Gai Pied* was declaring that AIDS is 'a sickness of the press', a psychosis invented by sensationalists rather than a genuine problem. In the same year the famous novelist Guy Hocquenghem wrote (also in *Gai Pied*): 'Tobacco causes cancer, we all know that. Have we stopped smoking? Sex causes diseases, should we stop making love? . . . How can we believe in a medical science that discourages us, which announces nothing but catastrophes of contagion, which keeps company only with fear and despair?' The tragic irony, of course, is that both Foucault and Hocquenghem died of AIDS.

The extreme reluctance of the French to recognize the gravity of AIDS and then to campaign against its spread is linked to other national ambiguities that show up in an overview of French attitudes towards gays and literature in particular and towards identity politics in general.

One of the great paradoxes is that France, the country

that produced some of the most renowned pioneer homosexual writers of this century – Marcel Proust, André Gide, Jean Genet, Jean Cocteau – is also today the country that most vigorously rejects the very idea of gay literature. As Didier Eribon, the author of a major biography of the philosopher Michel Foucault (the homosexual author of *The History of Sexuality*) pointed out recently, this response is all of a piece with a more general rejection in France of everything that smacks of a politics based on minorities or the legitimization of feminism.

The French constantly ridicule American-style departments of women's studies or books or courses in the States on African-American or Jewish or Native American literature. An alarmist book like the recent *Une Amérique qui fait peur* by Edward Behr attributes most of America's ills to feminism. Five or six years ago, the French expressed a general alarm about the excesses of political correctness in America and only the celebrated historian François Furet had the wit to point out to his compatriots that the excesses of racism and religious bigotry in the United States far outweigh the dangers of political correctness, which in any event holds sway only on liberal campuses.

Perhaps the most telling contrast between France and the English-speaking world, however, is over the whole question of lesbian and gay literature. In all of France there is only one gay bookstore, Les Mots à la Bouche, which is in Paris. And in 1996 there are only two serious, non-pornographic gay publications, due to a lack of advertising support. When I was interviewed by the (now defunct) French gay literary magazine *Masques* in the early 1980s, I was asked if I considered myself a 'gay writer'. When I said, 'Of course,' the astonished journalist told me I was the first person the magazine had ever interviewed who'd said yes to that question. When an international gay literary conference was held in London in the mid-1980s, several French writers were invited but only one lesbian accepted; all the others indignantly refused.

Despite the fact that so few men in the French media are

out, in fact AIDS was the cause of more than half of all deaths in 1987 of French men in the media, the arts and entertainment.

Or take another example: I recently received the announcement of the upcoming publication of a book about homosexuals in France since 1968; typically, the promotional pamphlet says 'Not at all a history of a "minority" or of a "community" – debatable terms – but rather a skein of individual paths that end up by composing what could be called a "group with a destiny".' Despite this pussy-footing editorial presentation, the book itself, Frédéric Martel's *Le rose et le noir*, is an excellent history of French homosexuals since 1968, and most of the facts at the beginning of this paper were drawn from its pages, even though I strenuously disagree with Martel's neo-conservative conclusions.

American or English or German gays often dismiss the French as simply being 'closeted' – fearful, Catholic, guilt-ridden, conformist. But the curious thing is that the very writers in France who would most strenuously reject the label of 'gay writer' are often those who have been the most explicit and courageous in the presentation of their homosexuality. In 1972 Hocquenhem published in *Le Nouvel Observateur* an article titled 'The Revolution of Homosexuals'. In 1979 Renaud Camus published *Tricks*, a blow-by-blow account, as it were, of his gay sexual adventures; Tony Duvert in *When Jonathan Died* spoke with startling frankness about one of *the* great taboo subjects, man-boy love. And Yves Navarre (who committed suicide in 1994) wrote in *Our Share of Time* about a forty-year-old schoolteacher's love for a much younger man. Yet no gay male writer, with perhaps the sole exception of Dominique Fernandez, would accept the 'gay writer' label, and even Fernandez has argued that the degree of acceptance that gays won in the 1970s had a disastrous, lowering effect on their writing that only the new stigmatization brought about by AIDS might correct. And in any event Fernandez does not want to be 'reduced' to a label.

A cynic might argue that French writers who reject the 'gay' label have been able to stay sufficiently in the mainstream to win lots of honours. Hector Bianciotti may have written about his gay experiences in a seminary, but he is still sufficiently discreet to have been elected a member of the French Academy in 1995. Fernandez won the Prix Médicis in 1974 and the Goncourt in 1982; Yves Navarre won the Goncourt in 1980 and quickly thereafter seemed to be *the* 'homosexual writer' in France, although he angrily rejected this category. What is certain is that these elusive writers have been able to keep a general readership, sell lots of copies and win prizes with their fiction, whereas no clearly labelled gay writer in America or Britain has ever enjoyed a comparable renown or popularity.

The French themselves would argue that their rejection of all ghettoization, far from being a sign of closetedness or cynicism, is in fact coherent with their 'singularity' as a nation. The French believe that a society is not a federation of special interest groups but rather an impartial state that treats each citizen – regardless of his or her gender, sexual orientation, religion or colour – as an abstract, universal individual. For the French any sub-group of citizens is a *diminishment* of human equality. This is a position stated with eloquence and clarity by Mona Ozouf in a recent book, *The Words of Women: An Essay on French Singularity.* Or as the social commentator Michael Pollak has put it, 'In France, specific groups linked together by a shared identity are generally perceived as illegitimate.'

The only problem is that this universality and impartiality doesn't always defend the rights of particular groups. As Ozouf points out, France is the country where women in Europe have the highest level of education; already in 1963, for instance, 43 per cent of French students were women, as opposed to 32 per cent in England and 24 per cent in West Germany. But this academic equality has not been matched with power in the society at large. French women gained the right to vote only after World War II – *after* women in India and Turkey. And even today in France there is a smaller percentage of women in high government posts or in executive positions in business than in any other European country, including Portugal.

Similarly, the lack of community organization among French gays and the lack of political representation have meant that France has been particularly hard hit by AIDS and has responded slowly and tardily to the crisis.

The problem is that the leading French AIDS organization, AIDES, felt that given the national character it could not address itself directly to gays. Daniel Defert, Foucault's surviving partner and the power behind AIDES, recently said, 'In 1984, with 294 known cases in France, there weren't very many activists and those who were ill and mobilized were mostly homosexual. Those who were ill thought that to publicize their AIDS would be a real burden, just as to announce their homosexuality publicly would have been difficult since most of them had not discussed it with the people around them.' When Defert showed the ill members of his organization a poster clearly aimed at the gay community, they rejected it: 'They wanted their image to be respected at the hospital.' As Frédéric Martel puts it, 'What is the best way to fight an epidemic: the American-style identity-politics model and multiculturalism or the (French-style) universalist – or even republican – model?'

In 1987 a splinter group, AFLS, and later ACT UP began to use more militant tactics to reach gays more directly, but by then the numbers were already appalling and a fatalistic mood had set in among French homosexuals.

The French way of looking at homosexuality – or any other special interest group – is defensible; characteristically, the French think that sexuality is a private matter that should not be politicized or even discussed. This discretion – joined to a secularism that approaches atheism – has meant that French gays have not come in for any of the fag-bashing they've had to endure in the States at the hands of red-necks, fascists and Christian fundamentalists. But French individualism – abstract and universal – and a corresponding scorn of identity politics have made France unusually vulnerable to AIDS.

The paradox of the French spirit – boldly outspoken about individual experience but against all communitarianism based on that experience – is best reflected in its literature. France has given the Prix Goncourt to Haitian writer Patrick Chamoiseau – but there is no 'Black Novel' in France. Similarly, movie actress Simone Signoret could publish a novel about Jews in World War II – but there is no 'Jewish Novel' in France. And, most dramatically, so many of the leading French writers of this century have written openly about their homosexuality – but the label 'gay fiction' evokes only a tired smile in Paris.

homosexuals and the AIDS crisis in France

assimilation, denial, activism

Larys Frogier

A book entitled *Le rose et le noir* (The Pink and the Black)[1], which examines the history of homosexuals in France since 1968, was published in the spring of 1996. Its author, Frédéric Martel, is a sociologist, journalist[2], erstwhile chairman of a homosexual student association (Gage) and former Socialist Party delegate. Most dailies and weeklies acclaimed the scientific quality of the book in articles with resounding headlines: '*Sida, les gays en accusation. Les associations d'homosexuels ont-elles contribué à l'extension de la maladie? Un livre explosif l'affirme*' ('AIDS – Gays on trial. Have homosexual organizations helped to spread the disease? An explosive book says they have)[3]; '*Sida: quand les gays se voilaient la face*' (AIDS: when gays looked the other way)[4]; '*Les homosexuels se divisent sur la question du communautarisme*' (Homosexuals divided on the issue of communitarianism)[5]. Favourable reports in the national press were peppered with homophobic asides blaming homosexuals for the spread of HIV, and trying to demonstrate the futility of homosexuals closing ranks in an attempt to defend their rights. Sadly, none of this comes as any surprise. Martel claims to have constructed an objective historical survey by 'casting a critical eye and keeping his distance from the "homosexual debate" '.[6] In actual fact, he has produced a biased, finger-pointing and simplistic view of the complex, multi-faceted history of homosexuals and the AIDS crisis in France. Lacking any real rigour, the book combines anecdotes with historical facts, firsthand reports with personal analyses. As such, it is more akin to a journalistic safari than an historical examination.

Writing in what appears to be a liberal vein, Martel, however, consistently blames and rejects all forms of militancy which endorse, implicitly or explicitly, homosexual visibility. Thus he describes the Stonewall riot as a 'romantic event', playing 'an important part in the collective memory of "homosexual militants", even if its importance has been exaggerated'.[7] Gay Pride, he argues, is something to beware of, not so much because 'it reinforces stereotypes', but because it emphasizes 'the minority to the detriment of the national culture'.[8] (Martel, it should be noted, never clearly defines 'national culture'.) He rejects all forms of activism – such as ACT UP/Paris and AIDES which emerged in the late 1980s – for highlighting the centrality of homosexuality to the AIDS crisis. He concludes by defending the 'right to indifference':

> The homosexual must once again become an individual free of labels or stigma. What is peculiar to him or her is no longer a factor that divides society. Indeed, it's not even a factor that continues to threaten family structure . . . To find a less impossible form of happiness, we must defend the idea, in the name of our individual independence, that the homosexual issue no longer has any meaning or *raison d'être* . . . Despite AIDS, the homosexual can start living. 'Homosexuality' no longer exists.[9]

This polemic denies the very real historical and political issues associated with homosexuality. In France, however, Martel's position is not new or unusual. Rather, it is part and parcel of the universalist ideologies of assimilation and tolerance still vaunted by intellectuals and politicians, left and right-wing alike. These mythologized values are touted even as France is mired in acute racism, flagrant economic injustice, sexual discrimination, and the carnage of AIDS. *Le rose et le noir* is typical of the intellectual conservatism that prevails in France. Such conservatism thwarts the analysis of social, sexual and identity-based difference, dismissing such efforts as communitarian plagiarism of American-style political correctness.

This blind and complacent stance would not have serious consequences were it not for the harm it has caused since the start of the AIDS crisis, and particularly within the current context of a 'return to order'. It relies upon a conception of universal, egalitarian history, whereas the AIDS crisis demonstrates the imperative of dealing with the medical, social, and political specificities of affected individuals and communities.

who's denying whom?

Le rose et le noir reveals the widespread denial of AIDS in the early 1980s by homosexual militants, organizations, and the press. The well-documented analysis of this denial needs to go beyond the facile accusation levelled by Martel at individuals and gay activists. Questions must be asked about the early AIDS campaigns and how they gathered momentum within political institutions and discourse that were ill-prepared to tackle HIV and the social crisis that would stem from it.

The French homosexual population in the early 1980s turned its back on any proper strategy to forge a gay movement. The absence of a movement capable of questioning the historical, cultural, intellectual and political relationships between concepts of homosexuality, identity and difference had serious repercussions. The predominant fear, at that time, was that gay issues would be ghettoized. This fear was apparent both in left-wing, anarchist-style militancy and in the inverse stance of political invisibility, of 'feeling included in society by keeping your mouth shut'.

In academic circles in Northern Europe, Britain, and the United States in the late 1960s there was an emergence of discussion about sex and gender. This was accompanied by (though not caused by) the self-assertion and articulation of homosexual subcultures, and the emergence of many distinct gay communities during the 1970s. These communities facilitated political and community HIV policies from the very beginning of the epidemic. The emerging fight against AIDS problematized the history of the gay movement in the 1970s, as well as the ideological and discursive commitments implicit in liberationist models of community and identity.[10]

In France, the period after May 1968 witnessed the development of positions that were pro-homosexual rights, but which were too disparate to have any real cultural and political clout once the AIDS crisis gathered momentum. They were dominated by a revolutionary left-wing ideology that perceived homosexuality as the individual's total and symbolic liberation from the capitalist system. The robust reflections of Guy Hocquenhem and Jean-Louis Bory on homosexuality inspired the creation in 1971 of the *Front homosexuel d'action revolutionaire* (Homosexual Revolutionary Action Front) (FHAR). The *Front* rejected wholesale any concept of homosexual identity and visibility, and declared that the individual is not the proper subject of politics.[11] Michel Foucault gave interviews about homosexuality and the possibilities of a homosexual culture, but these were, for the most part, confined to American universities and reviews; French institutions were keen to maintain his status as an apolitical intellectual.

It was not until the early 1980s that a precarious communitarian politics began to emerge. 1979 had seen the birth of the *Comité d'urgence anti-répression homosexuelle* (Anti-homosexual Repression Emergency Committee) (CUARH), working on a programme of legal reforms. In the same year, the *Association des Médecins Gais* (Association of Gay Doctors) (AMG) and the magazine *Gai Pied* were founded, followed by other periodicals (*Homophonies*, *Masques*, *Sàmouraï*). However, any coherent structure which embraced community dynamics and pluralism was still in its infancy when the HIV/AIDS crisis was reported, first in biomedical journals and then in the mainstream media.

Attempts were made to offset the effects of discriminatory and sensational language. At that time, suspicion of medicine ran very high indeed. Such scepticism should be seen as an act of defiance in the face of the history of the medicalization of the homosexual individual. It should be understood in the context of the real danger of homosexuals being stigmatized anew in the discourses emerging from the AIDS crisis. Homosexual scepticism of medicine remained heavily influenced by anarchist and left-wing cells which sought universal equality and complete freedom. Indeed, these utopian ideologies thwarted critical thinking about contemporary representations of homosexuality in biomedicine. They also hampered the pragmatic development of militant gay information and support networks to deal with the HIV crisis. Contrary to Martel's criticisms of gay militants in the late 1970s, what merits reproach is the inadequate formulation – by gay community activists – of a comprehensive gay strategy for the fight against AIDS.

While the militants of the 1970s spurned any real involvement in the AIDS crisis, a second form of refusal came to the fore in the early days of the epidemic: the reluctance of the first AIDS organizations to publicly discuss the needs of HIV-infected homosexuals. The early 1980s saw the founding of two service and support groups for AIDS patients, which singlehandedly led the response to the health crisis. In 1983, Patrice Meyer, a doctor and member of the *Association des Médecins Gais* (AMG) founded *Vaincre Le Sida* (Beat AIDS) (VLS). In 1985, Daniel Defert set up the association AIDES, which he modelled on the Gay Men's Health Crisis (GMHC) in New York. By the late 1980s, these two organizations had developed programmes in outreach to people with HIV, primary prevention, care, and treatment research support. They were joined by new organizations (Sida Info Service, Aparts, Arcat-sida). But although VLS and AIDES emerged from the gay population, their initial positions on homosexuality were ambiguous. Eager not to stigmatize homosexuals, the early activities of these associations focused on addressing 'all population groups' in the hope of securing political and economic acknowledgement from the health authorities. Wittingly or not, these activities were part of a consensus which regarded AIDS as a global issue affecting a 'general population'. The many specific factors associated with HIV, in particular where homosexuals and drug addicts were concerned, were thus ignored. In his book *Résister ou disparaître? Les homosexuels face au Sida* (*Resist or Vanish? Homosexuals and AIDS*), Frank Arnal comments:

> AIDES was primarily run by gay men, but did not want to be a homosexual organization . . . This suited the authorities just fine, who, for their part, were happier financing an organization that was a homosexual organization without being one. A perfect alibi for having a clear conscience about homosexuals without upsetting or offending constituents. Misunderstanding, cynicism, or blindness?[12]

It is telling that the socialist government tolerated, and even supported these organizations' denial of the vital needs of HIV-infected gay men. Frédéric Edelmann, then secretary general of AIDES and currently editor of *Le Journal du Sida*, declared:

> In the spring of 1985, I was myself twice received, along with another representative of AIDES, in the office of the Secretary of State for Health, to plead the cause of prevention particularly in relation to the homosexual community, which was the most affected group then as it still is today in France, incidentally. At that time, Great Britain served as an example, because the first prevention campaigns were being launched there, which the French were obviously going to poke fun at . . . Mr Hervé's representative was thoroughly informed about AIDS, and he showed us, both by what he said and by confiding in us, just how much he shared our worries. But he would before long explain to us that after talks with Matignon [the Prime Minister's office] it was impossible to release funding for prevention because, with the election just a year away, the government did not want to give the impression that it was supporting gays.[13]

This incident reveals the left-wing government's deliberate negligence, even after decriminalizing homosexuality in 1982. The consequences, in the AIDS crisis, included failing to publicize condoms until 1988 and banning the distribution of syringes. The French authorities were at that time happier to regard HIV as something unusual that threatened marginal groups rather than treat it as a public health issue. Indeed, 'public health' came to signify only the welfare of the dominant population. Thus, it was not necessary to act in accordance with what is, in traditional public health discourse, called 'general prevention'. Casting a blind eye to 'marginal groups', which were being decimated by HIV, amounted to formulating depictions of 'high-risk groups' 'catching AIDS' as a result of 'immoral practices'. The sensational stereotype of the 'AIDS carrier'[14] enabled the heterosexual population to become assimilated as an ideological entity, as a 'general population' passively watching AIDS wreak havoc on its periphery. Out of this general population came the 'family' unit, seen either as a nucleus safe from the virus, or as an innocent victim. It is in this sense that the French authorities' neglect of AIDS before 1987 was not just a result of biomedical ignorance, but a deliberate act which has had terrible effects on the lives of thousands of people.

So what can be said about these two forms of denial, the one gay militant refusing the reality of AIDS, and the other militantly opposed to any targeted discussion of the relationship between homosexuality and AIDS? These two apparently conflicting positions in fact share a common ideological perspective: the unshakable incompatibility between issues of homosexuality and issues of AIDS. This perspective understands homosexuality as germane to the private lives of autonomous individuals, separated rigidly from social, medical, political and economic rhetoric and realities. It understands AIDS as a matter of health, to be managed by experts. Questions of identity and representation contribute nothing to the specificities of prevention and care. This position is implicit in the arguments of Frédéric Martel, among others, when he questions the validity of public subsidies paid to homosexual organizations: 'Fight against AIDS or fight for the homosexual cause?' he asks in all innocence.[15] More broadly, it recurs in the hackneyed admonitions levelled at gay AIDS activists: 'Why talk about AIDS at a Gay Pride meeting or a debate on homosexuality?' 'AIDS does not affect homosexuals alone. Why talk about homosexuals when you are discussing AIDS?' The statistics which show that homosexuals are disproportionately affected by HIV are enough, on their own, to justify discussing AIDS in any debate on homosexuality, and vice versa.[16] Many intellectuals and AIDS professionals in France do not recognize that AIDS and homosexuality are bound together in multiple systems of visual, cultural, and symbolic representations, in which individuals and groups try to construct and are implicated in a changing matrix of sexual identities. In the light of this, it is necessary for everyone in the fight against AIDS to perceive homosexual identity not in simplistic terms of secrecy and disclosure, being 'out' or being 'closeted', but as systems of representation articulated within economic, medical and social structures, as well as within individual and collective histories. This simple awareness would help to hone pragmatic strategies against HIV infection and heighten resistance to the resulting social crisis.

The universalist and anti-communitarian approach to AIDS and homosexuality had its heyday in 1987, when the Ministry of Health declared AIDS a 'major national issue'.[17] Nevertheless, it is doubtless the case that anti-communitarianism and universalism continue to have a bright future, if only because they are politically expedient, in French political, intellectual, and activist circles.

'AIDS concerns us all' versus 'people are dying of indifference'

The Ministry of Health's declaration opened the way to representations which declared with pride that 'AIDS concerns us all'. All French HIV prevention campaigns have been based on this message. But there is an urgent need to question this message, with its now-famous attendant slogan 'we're all in this together'. We need to ask how this collective, general subject – 'all of us' – erases the specificities of groups affected by HIV, and, within those groups, how the significant differences among approaches to HIV prevention and treatment are blurred. The depiction of AIDS in the 1990s has been marked by tolerance. Sadly, tolerance does not amount to accepting a diverse range of sexual preferences, the many ways the body can be used, and the many different ways of experiencing HIV positivity and illness. Policies based on 'tolerance' are often surreptitiously authoritarian at the best of times. During the AIDS crisis, in France, they have become dramatically repressive.

'We're all in this together' has led the authorities to systematically remove or tone down from prevention campaigns any explicit reference to homosexuality.[18] There are lessons to be drawn from a major campaign launched by the Ministry of Health in the summer of 1995. From the outset, the Ministry of Health was eager to reduce homosexuality to a visual symbol of two pairs of hairy legs. Officials then complained that this image was too prurient, and replaced it with two pairs of men's shoes. Likewise, the authorities have completely erased the existence of infection among intravenous drug users.

'We're all in this together' thus becomes a mantra which speaks only to the silent – and largely uninfected – majority, which takes pity on 'AIDS victims', but which is never outraged by the fact that AIDS primarily affects homosexuals and intravenous drug users and that nothing is being done to prevent this.

Some would argue that French HIV prevention campaigns have been careful not to raise unnecessary alarm in the 'general population', or to ignore 'high-risk groups'. Some may also claim that these 'high-risk groups' have been addressed in targeted prevention campaigns since 1989. But these arguments crumble under the weight of several unanswered – and, by their terms, unanswerable – questions. First, why did the government wait so long to warn 'high-risk groups'? Why does the French government continue to balk at subsidizing overtly homosexual organizations and addict support groups which are best-placed to develop HIV-prevention programmes? Why must the authorities claim to act on behalf of 'high-risk groups' by taking refuge behind the vital but untargeted and generalized programmes of organizations like the *Association des Médecins Gais*, *Santé et Plaisir Gai*, and *Autosupport d'usagers de drogue* (Drug Users Self-Support Group) (ASUD)? Why is the legalization of the open sale of syringes so hard to implement in pharmacies? Why does care and support for HIV-positive drug addicts receive so little attention? Why, in official prevention campaigns, are messages of love and respect confined to heterosexual couples kissing each other on the mouth? Why are homosexuals never represented in these campaigns? Why do these campaigns include images solely of white, urban, middle class couples when those heterosexuals most affected by the epidemic are immigrant groups living in the suburbs? Why are there absolutely no policies in prisons designed to encourage care for people with HIV, safer sexual practices, and the safe use of injected drugs? Why are HIV-positive immigrants from the Third World lacking the right papers expelled, even though they will receive inferior treatment in their home countries?

So far, universalist ideologies of tolerance and assimilation have been a ruse. Or more accurately, they constitute a new means of blinding people to the real problems linked with HIV, and to the possibilities of incisive interventions, articulated across the whole gamut of sexual orientations, in the heterogeneity of racial and sexual identities, and in the complexity of high-risk behaviour patterns. French authorities and intellectuals refuse to articulate publicly the inseparability of the AIDS crisis from homophobic, racial and economic discrimination.

It was within this ambiguous consensus about AIDS, seen as a national issue which 'affects us all', that AIDS activism in France emerged in 1989, with the founding of ACT UP/

Paris by Luc Coulavin, Didier Lestrade and Pascal Loubet. Though inspired by the New York movement set up in 1987 by Larry Kramer, ACT UP/Paris swiftly became an effective and vital force in a uniquely French fight against AIDS. The central leap forward in French AIDS activism was ACT UP's deconstruction of the ubiquitous cliché-ridden political cant which had masked deliberate neglect with entirely ineffective policies and misleading slogans. ACT UP's demonstrations and representations were the first forums in France in which people openly declared that they were HIV-positive and identified with a homosexual history and community. ACT UP also exposed, for the first time, the tensions between social security, treatment, and therapeutic research in which people with HIV are caught.

ACT UP, and the new attitudes which it created, challenged endemic beliefs in the universal equality of care for the ill. ACT UP unquestionably revealed the influence of homosexuality, drug addiction, immigrant status, imprisonment, or involvement in the sex industry on the status and type of care an individual receives. For the first time, in ACT UP actions, zaps and demonstrations, gay men and lesbians directly denounced discrimination against other risk groups.

It is crucial to understand that AIDS activism involved nothing short of a dramatic reconceptualization of French policy toward minorities, health, and social welfare. Activism in the 1980s wasn't easily assimilated to the socialist and productivist ideologies of the left. AIDS activism does not claim to fight for universal values such as truth and equality. The distinction of AIDS activism is its deliberate appropriation and displacement of cultural, political, and economic codes of group representation and management. It hijacks these codes when they endanger lives of individuals and communities. In other respects, AIDS activism emerged from and participated in the formulation of a supportive and proud homosexual community.

By interpellating – naming as a process of constitution and construction – a 'homosexual community', French AIDS activism does not define homosexuals as monolithic, ahistorical or apolitical. Rather, it names individuals who have of their own accord come together at different moments in contemporary history to question and fight attitudes, laws and actions that opposed same-sex partnerships, and the diverse accompanying lifestyles.

That a homosexual community is at the root of a movement to combat AIDS troubles a great many people. The movement is criticized for having turned AIDS into a 'homosexual lobby'. Many reproach the 'excessive' visibility of homosexuals in the fight against AIDS. Apparently, gay visibility frightens the 'general population', making them even more reluctant to concern themselves with AIDS. But as Didier Lestrade and Pascal Loubet have said, the role of the homosexual community in the fight against AIDS is:

> not to latch on to AIDS in order to legitimize a homosexual culture, whose existence is by turns denied and stigmatized, both by some homosexuals themselves, and by people who, when it suits them, react to homosexuality with censure and vitriol. What is at issue is a refusal of the head-in-the-sand policy via a project of self-acknowledgement. Everybody knows the extent to which this policy has encouraged the spread of the virus. Everybody must realize that the success of the fight will require each and every person to recognize his difference and the differences of other people.[19]

The 'general population' and the authorities responsible for managing the French response to AIDS have once and for all had to respond to the claim that to fight AIDS, authorities must work with individuals who openly declare a plural homosexual identity – an identity which has consistently been at once repressed and exploited by the 'public debate' on AIDS.

Many intellectuals are content to construct general arguments about AIDS which are removed from the political and symbolic challenges of the crisis. This rhetoric conveys distorted and discriminatory messages to people living with AIDS. In France, AIDS activists have been criticized for the visual violence of their demonstrations. Such criticisms detract attention from the *very real violence* created and legitimated by rhetoric which appears neutral, well-intentioned and theoretical.

(Translated from the French by Simon Pleasance & Fronza Woods)

notes

1. Frédéric Martel, *Le rose et le noir: les homosexuels en France depuis 1968*, Paris, Seuil, coll. L'Épreuve des faits, 1996.
2. He contributes to *Le Monde*, *Esprit* and to *Le Journal du Sida.*
3. Jacqueline Remy, 'Sida: les gays en accusation', *L'Express*, 4 April 1996, no. 2335, pp.48–50.
4. *Libération*, 2 April 1996.
5. *Le Monde*, 14–15 April 1996, p.10.
6. Martel, *op.cit.*, pp.14–15.
7. ibid., p.24
8. ibid., p.407
9. ibid., p.411
10. For a critical look at structures of community and identity in the United States, and their impact on the AIDS crisis, see Cindy Patton, 'The AIDS Service Industry' in *Inventing AIDS*, New York, Routledge, 1990, pp.5–23.
11. In his book, Martel launches a moralistic criticism of the FHAR. He lambasts the 'sexual debauchery' of their meetings. He fails to make an in-depth ideological critique of the FHAR, or to discuss how its ideological commitments inform its representations of the body, sexual practices, and individual freedom. See also Guy Hocquenghem's book, edited by Bill Marshall: *Guy Hocquenghem, Theorising the Gay Nation*, London, Pluto Press, 1996.
12. Frank Arnal, *Résister ou disparaître? Les homosexuels face au Sida. La prévention de 1982 à 1992*, Paris, L'harmattan, coll. Logiques sociales, 1993, p.71.
13. Frédéric Edelmann, 'Sida, la faute des politiques', *Le Monde*, 12 June 1991.
14. To understand the consequences and extent of these early stereotypes, it is instructive to leaf through magazines depicting AIDS patients with Kaposi's sarcoma. The body covered with KS was early on mythologized as *the* HIV-infected person. Other stereotypical imagery includes homosexuals isolated in their hospital rooms, without friends or families.

For further analysis of stereotypes of people with AIDS, see Simon Watney, 'The Spectacle of AIDS', and 'Photography and AIDS' in *Practices of Freedom: Selected Writings on HIV/AIDS*, Durham, N.C., Duke University Press, 1994. See also Sander L. Gilman, 'Seeing the AIDS Patient' in *Disease and Representation: Images of Illness from Madness to AIDS*, Ithaca, Cornell University Press, 1988, pp.245–72.

15. *Le rose et le noir, op.cit.*, p.409.

16. In 1995, 46,000 AIDS cases were reported: 38 per cent homosexuals, 28.3 per cent drug addicts, 17 per cent heterosexuals, and 14 per cent haemophiliacs.

17. Michèle Barzach, then Minister of Health, justified this declaration by claiming that HIV was now affecting heterosexuals. 'We are embarking on nothing less than a race against time; [. . .] furthermore, in 32 per cent of cases, the people infected are heterosexual, and this figure rises to 43 per cent for new cases in the third quarter of 1986.' In *Le Monde*, 29 November 1986.

18. This process was examined in 1992 in England under the term 'The De-gaying of AIDS'. See Edward King, 'The De-gaying of AIDS' in *Safety in Numbers*, London, Cassell, 1993, pp.169–232.

19. Didier Lestrade, Pascal Loubet, 'L'intégration homosexuelle à l'heure du Sida' in *Lettre du Centre Régional d'information et de Prévention sur le Sida*, May 1990, no 8; the article is included in the appendix of Frank Arnal's book, *Résister ou disparaître? Les homosexuels face au Sida*, op.cit.

wait a minute

Common( )place(s)

Alexander García Düttmann

> *Faux dialogues (serait bon pour le Politique, qui est ratiocination contestatrice sans fin)*
>
> Roland Barthes, *Vita nova*

– Wait a minute. Will activism not always be at odds with thought, precisely because thought must remind the activist of something he seems to be rushing away from?

– Wait a minute. Thought can orientate activism, it can give it a direction without which it would be blind, unable to expose itself to whatever it seeks to transform.

– Wait a minute. Isn't there an activism of thought, too? I don't mean ideas that serve the purposes of activism. I am thinking of the very moment thought is carried away by its own movement and activity. Thought as pure activity: an arrow traversing a space it opens up. Call it an inspiration. Call it an exaggeration. If you become a philosopher, if you bring the experience back to the intelligibility of a justified and justifying discourse, you will have to stop thinking.

– Wait a minute. Are you suggesting that the impact of thought is as blinding as the way in which the virus operates? Maybe philosophy tries to recuperate thought, just as culture attempts to inscribe the virus into recognizable forms and contents. But is the thought of the anarchy of thought not already an institutionalizing one?

– Wait a minute. People die from AIDS. It is not known that they die from thinking. Let's get this straight. Activism is a disrupting intervention in a given context that anticipates a possible political effect. Or it effects the tireless repetition of self-sufficient actions, thus creating a general uncertainty. In both cases an intention or a strategy is involved.

– Wait a minute. How come you can do the right thing and then spoil it by justifying yourself and explaining why you did the right thing?

– Wait a minute. Who says you are doing the right or the wrong thing if your actions cannot be questioned? We will never overcome the sense of discontinuity and fragmentation that results from an increasing specialization if we deprive ourselves of the means to evaluate, to judge or to prescribe possible actions in a field as heterogeneous as the field of so-called AIDS work. The effort of activism is directed at enlightening scientific research and denouncing institutional exclusion, social repression and political ideologies. If it accomplishes its task, activism will also have diminished the resistance to intelligibility. It will have maximized dialogue and debate. To fight the virus and to oppose the obscurantism which acts as its ally we need an intelligent coordination of activities.

– Wait a minute. You won't be capable of measuring up to the (biological, social, political) mobility of the virus if you distinguish between the general coordination of actions or thoughts and the singularity of a single intervention. There is no other coordination than the one achieved in an intervention both blind and lucid. Activism must try to recognize and to seize occasions which by definition escape coordination. That's why the only chance of a conference called *Acting on AIDS* is to create a minefield of secret societies. Short-term allies turning against the chair, queer elements gathering for an unexpected *coup de chance*, the stroke of a paint-brush, the injury of an idea, the violence of an imposition.

– Wait a minute. You are an aesthete, not an activist.

– Give me a break.

voices from the front

soil and salve

a meditation and litany

Michael Bronski

In the dream there is the feel of dirt, shovels hit ground, figures loom and leave dark caresses across the image, noises rumble from the body, stench and retch lurk in the background. 'Bless me father' remains unspoken but the terror remains. Nothing happens, nothing should. It's too late. Too fearful. What judgment could be as final? The wages of living are death; the bone and flesh, breath and movement gone. A murmur persists, nearly inaudible, a tattoo of supplication. Is this comfort or dread, memory or salvation? The soil of the body, the filth of living is complemented by the sound of prayer, the salve of pleasure. The dream ends, the voices persist, the body starts awake.

meditation

Question 190. **What must we do to love God, our neighbor, and ourselves?**

To love God, our neighbor and ourselves we must keep the commandments of God and of the Church, and perform the spiritual and corporal works of mercy.

Question 191. **Which are the chief corporal acts of mercy?**

The chief corporal works of mercy are seven: 1. To feed the hungry. 2. To give drink to the thirsty. 3. To shelter the homeless. 4. To visit the imprisoned. 5. To clothe the naked. 6. To visit the sick. 7. To bury the dead.

From the Baltimore Catechism No.2

And today? When corporeality is all too real and mercy too elusive?

to feed the hungry

Walta is strapped to the hospital bed: head half-shaven, stitches red and flared from the wound that allowed them to run the plastic tube from brain to stomach to drain cerebral fluid. He is panicked, struggling to get up, out; to know who, where he is. Fear of pain replaced by fear of unknowing; terror of death by terror of confusion. I ask repeatedly, hungry for signs: 'do you know where you are,' 'do you know who I am.' A litany of anxiety and hope: 'do you know where you are,' 'do you know who I am.' 'do you know where you are,' 'do you know who I am.' His eyes, uncomprehending, stricken with the impossible: the questions 'where,' 'who,' 'what' meaningless; his body rigid, shaking with unknowing. Finally a calm: the body retreats into limpness. Tears appear and he whispers in answer to the unspoken question: 'fine.'

to give drink to the thirsty

A year before his death: Walta is helped by my sister, visiting from New York, to get to his aerosolized pentamidine appointment at the clinic. Step by step, legs refusing to move as they should, vision skewered, half-shadowed despite the sheer effort of will to walk and see, see and walk as before. Determined not to use a wheelchair until he has to; defeats occur daily, soon enough. They reach the last of the short flight. She encourages: 'That was good, you're doing very well.' A truth whose very evidence brings pain. Walta: 'Oh, Suzanne, I can't even remember what I used to be able to do. When I remember it's worse.' They look at each other, eyes dry; the wetness and comfort of tears superfluous.

to shelter the homeless

I climb into bed: Walta starts in fright. Dreams of terror flood the room, he yells in fear thinking that I am going to hurt him. I reach out my hand, he yells 'help, help, what are you doing?' Arms that once consoled become dangerous, hands that soothed become weapons.

'Help' he yells in bed, 'help' as he struggles to get away from me. 'Help.' The comforts of bed and home, hands and arms are lost in panic, discarded in rage.

to clothe the naked

We are in front of our house: Walta – weak and walking with a cane – and meet a neighbor, a noted photographer. She gasps and cries out 'oh my God, what happened to you?'

The unrehearsed, unadorned emotion jabs like the needle stick I gave myself earlier that day; like the monthly needle in the spine that draws out the fluid flooding and muddling Walta's brain. The illusion of privacy ripped away, the reality of illness exposed. 'What happened to you?' It rests in the chilled October air, suspended without a crutch, a cane, a shred of respect or decency.

to visit the imprisoned

The specialist explains the bronchoscopy: tubes, swabs, lungs, fluid. It is all details and no reality. The words fear, mourning, terror, death, loss, pain are not articulated. 'How do I breathe?' Walta asks after being told of the invasive procedure. 'There is no trouble breathing,' he is told, 'you just relax, you'll be able to breathe.' The breath of the lungs, even diseased lungs, is not the same as the breath of the quickening heartbeat, the tenseness of the hands, the legs, the neck. The brain races, the eyes dart, the pulse rages. The breath comes from the body like air long trapped in a vacuum; with sound and pain, empty and hollow.

to visit the sick

The back is blistered in neat rows: shingles. We both run fingers over the festering. Words go unspoken. Jim is in the hospital; Gerry is just dead. Walta's body is strong, the red, scabbed sores appeared overnight. Rash, hives, sun: to mention alternatives is to imply the reality of the possible: the body has begun to die. The new words go unformed: 'symptomatic.' 'scared,' 'sick,' 'embarrassed,' 'failed,' 'nothing.' Fingers touch skin, pus breaks from sore. The unmentionable seeps into the open; a visitor, uninvited, all too expected.

to bury the dead

The baths: wordless and inevitably mysterious. Walta and I have just met, bodies in the steam, sex, heat that mists about us. Skin and beard, flesh moving and constricting, impulse and instinct join together as if in a dream. The cold, dead night city outside is a grave; the past is gone, we are here now, living and breathing together as if one. The sheer pleasures of flesh and bone, spit and hand seem simple, unpronounced and endless. The body can transcend, the flesh transfigure. For a moment the past, the fear, the outside world, the pain is gone, dead.

litany

Sacred heart of Jesus, broken in sorrow
    pray for us
Bleeding heart of Jesus, wounded by pain
    pray for us
Tormented heart of St Margaret Mary Alacoque
    pray for us
Broken body of St Catherine
    show us the way
St Lawrence, whose body was scorched and burned
    pray for us
St Roche, with lesions and bleeding wounds
    pray for us
St Lucy, sightless and scared

remove us from the shadows
St Fabiola, tender of the dying
grant us rest, give us solace
St Teresa, whose heart was pierced by the knowledge of God
pray for us
St Julian, who lay with lepers and Christ
remove our fear, forgive our terror
St Camillus, rough trade and nurse
bring us joy, grant us peace
St Simon, wracked and transfigured by mortification and pain
pray for us
St Barbara, beautiful and abandoned, despised and spat upon
show us the way
St Januarius, whose miraculous blood cleanses our heart
give us hope, ease our fear
Sts Marcellus and Pentamidine, givers of breath
forgive us our pains
St Ganciclovir, giver of light
forgive us our fear, restore us our sight
Sts Reglan and Fluconazol
cleanse our body, cleanse our fear
Sts Acetylcysteine and Cannabis
show us the way
Sts Amyl and Hashish
Grant us our visions
Sts Mescaline and Soma
allow us our bodies
Sts Morphine and Dexedrine
open our hearts, open our souls
St Psilocybin
forgive us our fear, allow us the ease

let us pray

O God, remove the terrors of fear and remorse from our bodies. Grant us the ease to live with pain and the ability to remember the joy. Let us not forget the smell of sweat, the movement of skin, the taste of salt. With your grace and power force our hearts and bodies open to receive delight and scourge, nurturance and contentment. Transfigure our bodies, transform our lives. Let us use our bodies to their greatest glory. Let us find salvation through their pleasure. Let us find transcendence through their pain.

niche-marketing to people with AIDS

Sarah Schulman

The current trend for new commercial markets to be defined with increased precision intersects serenely with the separation of people with AIDS from the rest of the gay community.

Since the mainstream press has never presented truthful or complex AIDS coverage, the gay press has often been the only arena for layered reporting of AIDS information and experience. However, as the gay press in the US has increasingly lost its oppositionality, magazines like *OUT* have now surpassed the level of falsity in most general interest publications' coverage of AIDS. Since dying homosexuals are more palatable than any other kind for the mainstream press, AIDS mitigated homosexuality enough to allow gay men more social visibility. The emergence of the HIV-positive gay man as an acceptable consumer encouraged mainstream companies to advertise in gay magazines. The magazines, in order to accommodate these new advertisers, began narrowing their parameters determining what kinds of gay people could be represented. This meant less aggressive AIDS coverage, fewer photographs of sick people, less anger towards heterosexuals, and fewer critiques of pharmaceutical industries. While gay magazines still niche-market to people with AIDS, the emergence of separate PWA publications made that marketing easier and more direct. At the same time, the political desire to identify a community of the HIV-infected across sexual, gender, racial and class borders also required the emergence of separate publications whose AIDS coverage would not focus exclusively on infected white gay men. As a result, the development of publications specifically for PWA's created enormous opportunities for niche-marketing to the AIDS consumer.

Dan Mulryan is a senior partner of Mulryan/Nash, a marketing firm that helps large companies reach gay consumers. He has handled accounts for Angels in America and the government of the Netherlands in their efforts to reach gay tourists. 'When you look at a niche group,' Mulryan told me[1], 'you have to ask how that person identifies. People who identify as HIV-positive are an evolving market for consumer goods. Their spending patterns are largely influenced by their HIV status. People with HIV are not going to spend their days worrying about IRA's.[2]'

Sean Strub has lived with AIDS for almost twenty years. He is the founder of *POZ*, a slick glossy magazine for people with AIDS that features celebrity interviews side by side with monthly updates on medicine, science and Strub's own lab work. While *POZ* does take a political position on AIDS research and public policy, it does not use its pages to organize readers into taking action on their own behalf. It is not an activist organization. Instead, it approaches activism through consumerism. By emphasizing which AIDS-related products should be supported and which companies should be pressured, it prefers to foreground the buying power of PWAS as their primary means of political influence.

This approach stems from more than Strub's background as a successful businessman and his belief in a businessman's right to profits. It is also rooted in a deeply held emotional committment to the idea that AIDS is not necessarily terminal. He believes that if people like himself can live with it for almost two decades then AIDS is not a 'death sentence', it is a Lifestyle. And in America, Lifestyle is normalized by the purchase of accoutrements. It is easy to sympathize with Strub's view. The more normalized the lives of people with AIDS are, the more they are viewed as an ongoing, *normal* part of society, the easier their lives will be. The problem, of course, is similar to the homogenization of gay imagery in national magazines: namely that most people with AIDS do not have a lot of discretionary income and cannot participate in the consumerism promoted by AIDS niche-marketing. Indeed, the recent and hopeful pharmaceutical discoveries in treating the disease are not even available to most PWAS. So, how are they going to buy portable infusion pumps and their accompanying fanny packs?

Simultaneously, general interest gay magazines are also proposing a model of normativity as a means to full social integration. The fact that most gay people neither can, want to or should have to fit that model is a growing, yet neglected contradiction. Similarly, protease inhibitors and combination therapies are beginning to cast an artificial shroud of resolution over the AIDS crisis. But, as others have repeatedly pointed out, if a glass of clean water was the cure for AIDS, most infected people in the world would still be unable to access it. As Eric Sawyer, co-founder of Housing Works, said at the Eleventh International Conference on AIDS at Vancouver in 1996, 'Most people with AIDS in the US cannot get their aspirin paid for.' The October 1996 issue of *POZ* revealed that Strub's own treatment currently costs $68,000 per year.

When I talked to him in 1995, Strub was very comfortable with examining the consumer potential of the AIDS market. 'There is an accelerated consuming pattern when people face their own mortality,' he said. 'They tend to have greater liquidity – at least for some time.' *POZ*, consequently, carries the most advertising of the current AIDS publications. With fifty per cent free subscriptions, it appears to be targeting readers with more discretionary income than the newsprint publications *PWA Newsline* or *The Body Positive*, neither of which accept advertising, and have a ninety-five per cent and seventy-five per cent free subscription rate respectively.

POZ, unlike most national gay magazines, does feature

people of color, women and lesbians on the cover regularly. But the entire magazine is couched in gay male sensibility, from its bright, slick design to campy, sexualized language. Most of the contributors are white and gay, unlike writers for *PWA Newsline* and *The Body Positive*. Furthermore, almost all of the ads in *POZ* feature male models who appear to be young and gay with gym bodies. The people featured in the pages of *POZ* do not look sick.

I asked Strub if there is an evolving marketing strategy towards people who, while they are HIV-positive, are at the same time asymptomatic and so would not identify with a magazine featuring models and subjects with physically obvious symptoms. 'The fact is,' Strub told me, 'most people who are HIV-positive do not look sick.' Mulryan agrees: 'People with HIV are living longer without symptoms than ever before.' Stuart Elliot, openly gay advertising columnist for the *New York Times*, supports Strub's position. 'No disease-related advertising features people who look sick,' he said. 'Take hemorrhoids ads for example.' But, clearly hemorrhoids serve a different political and medical role in society than AIDS. The not so hidden message behind a great deal of AIDS advertising is that the profiled products will make you hunky, young and healthy, just like the normal gay people in *Out* magazine. 'I have never believed that AIDS is a hundred per cent fatal,' Strub said. 'Some people are determined to make AIDS look awful and horrible and they're angry if you try anything outside of that image.'

So, just as normalizing advertising to the gay market provides an illusion of acceptance, assimilation and approval for gay male consumers, normalizing advertising in the AIDS markets provides illusions of health, wealth and love to the HIV-infected. This is all achieved without the uncomfortable and unmarketable honest appraisal necessary for the fight against inequity. People with AIDS are no longer to be fought for, they are to be sold to.

Niche-marketing to people with AIDS took its most sinister turn with the advent of the involvement of the Viatical industry. Viaticals are companies that buy an individual's life insurance policy for a percentage of the return, and then cash in the full amount upon the holder's death. Tax free. As gay magazines have had to exclude the sex ads that formerly funded them, in order to attract advertising from major corporations, they've lost the foundation of their funding. This has shifted their financial dependency from ads for phone sex, pornography, massseurs and escort services to those for Viaticals.

In general, the tone of Viatical advertising is fairly transparent. Ads usually show young, white, well-dressed and handsome men, either sitting alone making a troubled decision, or happily playing on the beach. What these depictions hide is that most people use their settlements to pay medical bills and to buy food. Both gay and straight-owned, Viaticals do not generally make a public show of contributing money to community-based projects, and their labor policies (domestic partnership, grief leaves, etc.) are unknown. To date, only one major gay magazine, *Genre*, has done an investigative piece on Viatical companies.

'Everyone realizes that Viatical advertising is gruesome in some ways,' says Mulryan. 'But they do provide a service. Whether it is completely moral is open to discussion.' Mulryan believes that 'whatever the market will bear is ethical'.

Strub, who financed *POZ* on a Viatical settlement, adopts a harsher tone. 'Viatical returns of twenty per cent are average,' he said. 'But many are making excessive returns from thirty to fifty per cent. Considering that life insurance proceeds are not taxable, fifteen to twenty per cent should make an attractive enough lucrative business. Beyond that is usually a symbol of exploitation.' However, at the time of our interview, life insurance companies were beginning to take a newly aggressive role in competition against Viaticals. Strub had just sold a policy to New York Life for ninety-two per cent when the highest Viatical offer he could find was seventy-three per cent.

What Strub could not predict was the impact on Viatical profits of medical advances in the treatment of AIDS. David

Dunlop, gay 'beat' reporter for *The New York Times* reported in July 1996 that 'longer life means lower return' for the Viatical industry. He reported that since the Vancouver AIDS conference at which combination therapies were highly touted, Viatical payments had fallen by five to ten per cent. One company, the San Francisco based Dignity Partners, had ceased processing new applications altogether. 'If treatments are effective in the long term,' Dignity's press release stated, 'the company's results will be adversely affected.' (The name *Dignity* is not only the title of an organization of gay Catholics who seek acceptance from the Church. It is also a coded, euphemistic word like *pride* and *rainbow* that allows companies to attract gay consumers without having to use the words *gay* or *lesbian* which might turn off straight customers or scare away closeted ones.) In the first half of 1996, Dignity's stock traded at $14.50 a share. After Vancouver, it dropped to $3.28.

'Alzheimer's is another market that is fairly plausible,' said Brian Pardo, chairman of Life Partners and a supporter of anti-gay conservatives in Texas legislative races. His is but one of the sixty Viatical companies, mostly straight-owned, currently buying $500 million worth of policies from people with AIDS annually. So, while Viaticals enter the market territory created by other terminal illnesses, policy holders with AIDS may be stranded. Ironically, many people with AIDS need the income from cashing in their insurance policies in order to purchase these hopefully life-sustaining treatments. Given the lack of subsidized medical treatment in the US, a Viatical company's refusal to make a purchase could, in and of itself, bring the holder to a quicker death.

So, while living longer may hurt the Viatical industry, longer life for people with AIDS can mean larger profits for firms selling other kinds of AIDS-related products. For example, Strub was an early investor in the home-testing kit. 'The home HIV test kit that we are developing is going to transform the epidemic,' he told me early on in the approval process. 'It will double the numbers of people who know they are positive.' Strub believes that there are currently more people who don't know that they are positive than those who do. Therefore, the home-testing kit will significantly increase his target market – HIV-positive asymptomatics who are ready to liquidify their assets. The message that new protease inhibitors are most effective with early diagnosis further stimulates the home-testing market. This adds another category of AIDS consumer to the roster. We have already shown that symptomatic HIV/AIDS and asymptomatic HIV/AIDS have different buying patterns that have been identified by marketeers. But we can now add people who think they might have HIV infection as a new consumer in the AIDS marketplace. These people will purchase home-testing kits. If they remain negative they may continue to purchase home-testing kits. If they are positive they will move over into the asymptomatic related spending and buying patterns.

The kits were finally approved in May 1996 and by July, Johnson and Johnson, a major American corporation, was involved in a protracted court fight over their ownership and distribution rights. The kits were originally developed in the 1980s and sold to Johnson and Johnson in 1993. The inventor, Elliot Millenson, is a major donor to Newt Gingrich, the anti-gay Republican leader of the House of Representatives. The kits are called *Confide*, which again is harmonious with the discreet names favoured by gay businesses and gay bars like Secrets and Whispers.

In some ways, the most painful and complex element of niche-marketing to people with AIDS is the role of gay people ourselves in making possible such overt profiteering off our own experiences of illnesses, abandonment by our families, and insecurities about our place in American society. After all, the illusion of normality without the fact of normality is the sinister centerpiece of niche-marketing to people with AIDS. It is very seductive for gay people to confuse the presence of limited gay images in advertising with some kind of social equity, but it is entirely illusory. There is no corollary between appearing in advertising and attaining real social or political power. We want our recognition by marketeers, gay or straight, to be synonymous with a broad social recognition of our realities but, in truth, it has the contrary effect. Cynical niche-marketing to people with AIDS, as it is currently disconnected from the broad needs of people with AIDS, is a destructive and painful manifestation of how truly vulnerable gay people and people with AIDS are.

And when commodification obstructs the progress of the rest of the community, profiting from it is an act of domination. If this understanding was the ethical basis of our investigations we would not have this kind of wholesale erasure as the gap between those who are represented and those who are ignored increases dramatically. And if those who most resemble the dominant culture opposed these deceptive practices, it would be far more difficult for the mainstream to represent us falsely as a mirror of their own most destructive urges.

notes

1. I interviewed Dan Mulryan and also Brian Pardo, Stuart Elliot in 1994, and Sean Strub in 1995 in preparation for a piece published in the Annual Lambda Book Report, 1995.
2. IRAs are private retirement pensions.

the nature of AIDS-related discrimination

Jonathan Grimshaw

This essay examines, from the perspective of a person with HIV, the causes of HIV-related discrimination, the forms of HIV-related discrimination and how HIV-related discrimination affects the health and well-being of those discriminated against and, indirectly, societies.

the causes of HIV-related discrimination

When AIDS first came to public attention, shortly after the first cases were identified in 1981, it was a new disease, its origin was unknown as was its means of transmission. It was incurable and appeared to be invariably fatal. The rapid escalation in the number of cases suggested that the disease was easily spread.

In the absence of scientific and rational explanations for AIDS, lay or 'folk' beliefs about the causes and origins of disease came to the fore. Four such beliefs have been observed to be particularly prominent in public discourse about AIDS:[1]

endogenous: the belief that an individual has some innate characteristic or flaw that causes them to have disease (the identification of all the initial cases amongst gay men led to suggestions that homosexuality 'caused' AIDS).

exogenous: the belief that disease lurks opportunistically in the external environment, 'waiting to pounce'; this is linked to ancient beliefs that diseases spread like a miasma through the air, beyond human control.

personal responsibility: the belief that a person's behaviour makes it acceptable or appropriate that they should become diseased. In the context of HIV, this underlies distinctions between 'innocent' victims, such as children, and 'guilty' victims, such as gay men, injecting drug-users, prostitutes and the sexually promiscuous.

retributionist: the belief that actions which infringe supposedly fundamental moral values are likely to bring about divine retribution. AIDS was considered by some to be divine retribution for transgression against certain biblical proscriptions on homosexuality and promiscuity.

The potency of these beliefs, the fear that AIDS could spread easily, and the obstacles to the formulation of rational discourse about a disease which challenged social taboos on sex, disability and death, made it inevitable that social responses to people with AIDS would be characterized by prejudice (literally 'forming judgments without proper information') and discrimination. Even the most extreme forms of discrimination, ranging from refusal to provide medical treatment to verbal and physical abuse, could, in this climate, find justification not only on the grounds of self-protection from disease but also adherence to fundamental moral values.

Some social responses to people with AIDS echoed medieval reactions to disease. In Barcelona, all efforts to open a home for people with AIDS were met with political refusals and violent protests from the population. In the Netherlands the opening of accommodation – in a former monastery – for drug users with AIDS in the Jordaan district of Amsterdam had to be abandoned because of hostile demonstrations; the local residents threatened to set fire to the monastery.[2] In the United Kingdom, a senior policeman memorably described people with AIDS as 'swirling around in a cesspit of their own making'.[3]

American people with AIDS have been treated in the following ways:

> (The) removal of a teacher with AIDS from teaching duties; refusal to rent an apartment to male homosexuals for fear of AIDS; firebombing of the home of haemophiliac children who tested positive for HIV; refusal by doctors and health care workers to treat people with or suspected of having AIDS; refusal of co-workers of a person with AIDS (PWA) to use a truck driven by the PWA; filing of a charge of attempted murder against a PWA who spat at police; requiring a PWA to wear a mask in a courtroom; denial to children with AIDS of access to schools; threatening to evict a physician who treated homosexuals; boycotting of a public school after a child with AIDS was allowed to attend; firing of homosexuals who displayed cold symptoms or rashes; refusal of paramedics to treat a heart attack victim for fear he had AIDS; refusal by police to drive a PWA to hospital; police demands for rubber masks and gloves when dealing with gays; refusal to hire Haitians, and urging of funeral directors not to embalm the bodies of persons with AIDS.[4]

Although a rational, scientific explanation for the cause of AIDS and the means of transmission was soon established (the discovery of HIV as the viral cause of AIDS was announced in April 1984), and many countries from the mid-1980s have conducted large-scale public information campaigns giving 'the facts' about HIV and AIDS, the disease remains perhaps irrevocably stigmatized. Public education campaigns have undoubtedly had a significant impact on prejudice, but such is the persistence of discrimination in social, economic, political and cultural responses to HIV and AIDS that prejudice has come to be recognized as a third 'epidemic' in its own right, in addition to those of HIV infection and AIDS.[5]

the forms of HIV-related discrimination

Because legal definitions of discrimination vary between countries, a common international standard against which to judge whether actions, measures or behaviours in relation to HIV are discriminatory is that of universal human rights.

The rights conferred in various international treaties and conventions provide a conceptual framework for assessing whether policies or actions restricting the rights and freedoms of individuals in order to protect others from HIV and AIDS are justifiable. Where such measures or actions are not justifiable, they could be considered, from the perspective of international human rights law, to be discriminatory. This was the basis for an assessment of HIV-related discrimination published recently in the United Kingdom.[6]

A comparative study on discrimination against persons with HIV or AIDS in twelve member states of the Council of Europe[7] discusses HIV-related discrimination under fifteen policy/area headings. The main concerns raised in both the UK and Council of Europe studies are:

epidemiology

- Compulsion to undergo HIV testing.
- HIV testing as a condition for admission to certain occupations.
- Compulsory treatment.
- Conditions placed on the personal behaviour of those infected; isolation of patients.

confidentiality

- Disclosure of medical information without consent.
- Disclosure of HIV status in the media.
- The unnecessary circulation of personal HIV status information in hospitals and for administrative purposes in other settings.

- Unnecessary collection of data on people with HIV (e.g. police files).
- Disclosure of a person's HIV status by a public authority to private individuals or organizations.
- Unnecessary disclosure of HIV status to prison authorities and within prison settings (sometimes arising from the failure to follow policy in practice).

criminal law

- Criminalization of HIV transmission.

family law

- Denial of right of access of an HIV-infected parent to their child.
- Problems in arranging foster care and adoption for HIV-infected children.
- Compulsory HIV testing of adopted children.
- Refusal of medical authorities to carry out artificial insemination of a parent who has HIV.
- Pressure on pregnant HIV-infected women to have abortions.

social security

- Disadvantage to HIV-infected people arising from the structure of public health insurance systems and in entitlement to invalidity benefits.
- Problems with the administration of social assistance programmes (resulting in people with AIDS dying before assistance was made available) or having to prove permanency of incapacity before assistance was provided (incapacity can be episodic in HIV disease).
- Level of benefits insufficient to meet basic needs.

private insurance

- Threat to confidentiality in the process of applying for insurance.
- Refusal of private insurers to take responsibility for costs arising from HIV and AIDS.
- Disadvantage to those perceived to be at risk as a result of higher premium rates.

aliens

- Compulsory testing of nationals on return from a period spent abroad.
- Negative HIV status as pre-condition for issue of residence permits.
- Expulsion of non-nationals for HIV-related reasons.
- Compulsory testing of asylum-seekers and granting of asylum dependent on the result.
- Compulsory testing of students from abroad and permits for entry and residence dependent on negative status.
- Certification of HIV-negativity of non-nationals as a pre-condition of obtaining work.

employment

- Dismissal from work or inappropriate changes in post as a result of HIV infection and AIDS.
- Avoidance or rejection of people with HIV or AIDS by colleagues or customers (potentially leading to dismissal as a result of disruption to the business).
- Pressure from employers on suspected HIV-infected employees to undergo HIV tests.

civil public service

- Compulsory testing of recruits for public service.

housing law

- Public sector housing on favourable terms made available to people with AIDS but not to those with HIV.
- Provision of public housing for people with AIDS and HIV that is inadequate for their needs.
- Protests in neighbourhoods at (or preventing) the opening of residential schemes for people with HIV.
- Refusal to grant leases to people with AIDS or HIV.
- Abusive notices to quit served on people with HIV or AIDS.
- People with HIV or AIDS experiencing abuse and harassment from neighbours and landlords.

education

- Refusal of admission of HIV-infected children to schools.
- Ostracism or rejection of children with HIV at the instigation of parents of other children.
- Provisions allowing parents to withdraw children from sex education classes (thus depriving them of education about HIV and sexual health).
- Confusion about the legitimacy of HIV and sexual health education in the context of legal restrictions on education about homosexuality.

medical sector

- Routine and clandestine HIV testing of patient.
- Pressure for routine testing of medical staff.
- Pressure for the HIV status of health care staff to be made known (to the public or to their employers).
- Refusal of medical or dental treatment to people with HIV or AIDS.
- Exaggerated and inappropriate infection control

procedures in medical settings (often involving the loss of confidentiality).

AIDS in prisons

- Routine screening of prisoners
- Prisoners refusing to be tested treated as though they are HIV-infected.
- Isolation and segregation of HIV-infected prisoners.
- Lower levels of medical care for HIV-infected prisoners compared to the level of care available outside prisons.
- Restrictions on HIV-prevention methods (e.g. non-availability of condoms).

armed forces

- Compulsory HIV testing on certain categories of recruits and units.
- HIV status being used as grounds for detailed enquiry into whether a subject is gay or a drug-user (which could result in dismissal).

social sphere

- Social exclusion.
- Prohibition of access to public places (e.g. swimming pools).
- Incitement to hatred (e.g. through stigmatization in the media).
- Dual discrimination against 'risk groups' (i.e. homosexuals, prostitutes, drug addicts, haemophiliacs, persons belonging to ethnic minorities).

Some of these forms of discrimination occur in only one country surveyed, others in several.

The Council of Europe and UK surveys also examine anti-discrimination measures. In appraising these measures, the Council of Europe survey notes that, with the exception of France, no country (among Council of Europe members) has introduced legislation dealing specifically with health-related, particularly AIDS-related, discrimination.

> Everywhere else, protection remains patchy, being confined to isolated measures of limited scope (employment, medicine, processing of health-related data, etc); these guarantees . . . seem to be the result, not of any overall thinking on the problems raised by discrimination, but of a desire to attend to the most urgent matters first.[8]

Some countries have brought HIV and AIDS within the scope of legislation protecting people with disabilities from discrimination. In the United States, people with HIV and AIDS are effectively given protection under the Americans with Disabilities Act (1990), although the Act does not explicitly mention discrimination against individuals with HIV or AIDS. The Act has been praised for extending protection to people wrongly perceived as having the disability as well as those who in fact suffer from the disability. The United Kingdom Disability Discrimination Act (1995) also offers protection for people with HIV and AIDS, although its provisions are more limited than the American Act and it does not extend protection to people 'perceived' to be disabled.

The Council of Europe Survey notes that the protection from discrimination provided by rights conferred in international human rights conventions is 'minimal' because none of them refer specifically to discrimination on health grounds, or because they have not been incorporated into domestic legal systems or 'appropriate supervision machinery is lacking'.[9] The survey concludes that 'existing mechanisms [for protection from discrimination] are by no means suited to the distinctive features of discrimination on health grounds'.[10]

There are compelling disincentives for those affected by HIV-related discrimination to seek redress through legal processes:

- The slowness and inflexibility of procedures, sometimes outlasting the lifespan of the claimant.

- Cost.
- The risk of additional discrimination arising from public disclosure of their identity.
- Stress, affecting not only quality of life but also progression of disease.

The Council of Europe survey also notes 'an almost universal failure to recognize the various associations defending the interests of AIDS victims and HIV-positive persons as having capacity to take legal proceedings'.[11]

Accounts by people with HIV and AIDS suggest that they experience discriminatory behaviour most often at the level of personal social interaction in the form of rejection or ostracism by partners, families, friends, and colleagues at work. It is recognized that governments can't directly regulate private relations; public education about HIV and AIDS has been seen as the most effective way of changing social attitudes to AIDS, serving as an antidote to discrimination at the personal level.[12]

In the United Kingdom however, where there has been major government investment in public education on HIV and AIDS (a 1986 AIDS public education campaign was 'the largest public health campaign ever mounted'[13]), it was possible for a woman who had discovered in 1995 that she was HIV-infected, having been deceived as to his status by her HIV-positive boyfriend, to write:

> . . . he will no doubt deceive again and all because HIV is loaded with such shame and repulsion, because he feared rejection in his relationship and society, because we fail to help people come to terms with HIV and AIDS . . .
>
> I have done nothing wrong except make love with someone I trusted and for that I'm to be shunned and isolated . . . I desperately want people to treat this illness like any other, otherwise my story will happen again and again, and parents will have to live in shame and disgrace about how their child died, and some wonderful people will live and die alone, all because of ignorance.[14]

how HIV and AIDS-related discrimination affects individuals and societies

The psycho-social, material and physiological effects on people with HIV or AIDS may include:

- Earlier progression to disease and death as a result either of denial of access to medical care and treatment or reluctance to seek testing and treatment (there is increasing evidence that early intervention – i.e. before symptoms appear – with prophylactic treatments can delay the onset of illness and prolong life).
- Earlier progression to disease and death as a result of being placed in circumstances detrimental to health such as poor housing (or homelessness), poverty and poor nutrition (good nutrition is therapeutically important for people with AIDS).
- Physical assault and harassment.
- Significant loss of quality of life due to loss of income and financial security, social and emotional isolation and loss of emotional and physical intimacy.
- Loss of privacy.
- Increased risk of psychological harm – stress, depression, anxiety and contemplating suicide.
- Loss of self-esteem, leading to lack of motivation to pursue or adopt behaviours which promote or maintain personal health and which protect the health of others (e.g. adoption of 'safer' sexual practices).

In addition, as has been shown above, HIV and AIDS-related discrimination may result in loss or infringement of basic human rights such as freedom of movement, education and the right to marry and found a family.

Some of these effects may also be experienced by those associated with HIV-infected people, such as partners, family members, friends, care-givers and members of 'risk groups'.

In many societies the 'risk-groups' are those who are

> already disadvantaged . . . and particularly vulnerable to

> infection as they have limited or no access to HIV/AIDS-related education, prevention and health-care programmes. Such groups include women, children, minorities, migrants, indigenous peoples, men having sex with men, commercial sex workers and injecting drug users.[15]

It is now recognized that

> prevention of (HIV) transmission depends on people coming forward to learn how to avoid infection, how to practice safe sex, and how and why they should act responsibly. Coercive measures, such as mandatory testing, lack of confidentiality and segregation, drive people away from prevention education and health-care services and subvert this process of behavioural change . . . Thus, the discrimination and stigma associated with HIV/AIDS both infringe on the rights and dignity of those infected and pose a serious public health threat to society.[16]

Additional indirect harms to society occur through the loss of the economic and social productivity of people incapacitated through HIV disease (or prevented from working or otherwise contributing to society because of discrimination) and the costs of welfare, care and treatment for ever-growing numbers of people with HIV disease. It could also be argued that a further harm arises through the disincentives to people affected by HIV seeking protection from, or redress for, discrimination through the law. The perception that one is excluded from the protection of the law, or that access to the law is unequal, undermines respect for law.

conclusion

The realization that HIV-related discrimination is a 'serious public health threat to society' and that health and human rights are, in the context of HIV and AIDS, inextricably entwined, is a major advance. But this diagnosis begs the question of a remedy. Most problems in the field of human rights arise when there is a conflict between the wishes of an individual to pursue his or her own interests, and the claims of other members of the same society to restrict that pursuit because it would harm *their* interests.[17] The human rights of people with certain diseases have traditionally been restricted to protect public health. HIV has shown that, in public health terms, restriction of the human rights of infected people can be counter-productive; it has also shown how deeply entrenched is the instinct to restrict those rights.

Unfortunately, as has been shown, while human rights may exist in international law, the machinery for upholding them at national level is limited and often, for people with HIV and AIDS, inaccessible. Even where legal remedies for discrimination are available, they offer little protection against prejudice and stigma experienced at the personal level in social or family interactions. Public education campaigns have an impact on discrimination at this level, but they are not sufficient to eliminate it.

Elimination of prejudice and stigma may, however, be a utopian goal and there is evidence that progress can be made. Although HIV-related discrimination may, like HIV itself, be incurable, it can be treated. A 1995 study in Scotland, for example, found that 'the public's avowed attitudes to HIV are not as punitive or stigmatizing as those infected believe them to be'.[18] This should provide an incentive for continued political activism in and on behalf of communities affected by HIV for enlightened legislation, improved access to the law and public education as components of a strategy to combat HIV-related discrimination.

It will, however, be critically important to monitor the impact of anti-discrimination measures. As the author of the Scotland study remarks, 'previous studies have tended to highlight the views of the illiberal minority rather than the liberal majority'. Discrimination has become synonymous with HIV: part of the 'folklore' of AIDS. It would be a cruel irony if, in failing to observe evidence of its own success, anti-discrimination activism were to perpetuate a fear of discrimination that was out of all proportion to the incidence of discriminatory behaviour. Such a fear, itself a form of prejudice, would be as harmful to public health as discrimination itself.

(This is an amended version of a paper originally prepared in December 1995 for a Working Group on Legal Services for Discrimination in AIDS and HIV Cases, funded by the European Union.)

notes

1. Homans, Aggleton & Warwick, 'Learning about AIDS', Health Education Authority/Avert, London, 1987.

2. These examples are quoted in 'Comparative study of discrimination against persons with HIV or AIDS' by the Swiss Institute of Comparative Law under the auspices of the Council of Europe, Strasbourg, 1993.

3. James Anderton, Chief Constable of Manchester, in a speech to a national conference of police officers called to discuss measures to protect police forces from occupational exposure to HIV. *The Guardian*, 18 December 1986.

4. Watt, 'HIV/AIDS in the USA and the UK: Similar problems, different solutions'. Paper presented to the EU Working Group on Legal Services for Discrimination in AIDS and HIV Cases, London, May 1996.

5. Statement at the World Health Assembly by Dr Jonathan Mann, then Director of the World Health Organization's Global Programme on AIDS, 5 May 1987.

6. J. Glasson, 'Luxury or Necessity? HIV and Human Rights: A Policy Overview', UK Forum on HIV and Human Rights, London, 1995.

7. 'Comparative study of discrimination against persons with HIV or AIDS' by the Swiss Institute of Comparative Law under the auspices of the Council of Europe, Strasbourg, 1993.

8. ibid., p.489.

9. ibid., p.489.

10. ibid., p.490.

11. ibid., p.490.

12,13. 'AIDS. Monitoring response to the public education campaign February 1986 – February 1987', Department of Health and Social Security and the Welsh Office, London, HMSO, 1987.

14. In *The Guardian*, London, 30 November 1995.

15. Paragraph 13, 'Report of the Secretary General on international and domestic measures taken to protect human rights and prevent discrimination in the context of HIV/AIDS', United Nations Economic & Social Council, 22 December 1994,

16. ibid., para 15.

17. Paul Sieghart, 'AIDS & Human Rights, A UK Perspective', BMA Foundation for AIDS, London, 1989.

18. Gill Green, 'Attitudes towards people with HIV: Are they as stigmatizing as people with HIV perceive them to be?', MRC Medical Sociology Unit, Glasgow, 1995.

a land of silence

political, cultural and artistic responses to AIDS in Spain

Juan Vicente Aliaga

The statistics that lie behind the AIDS epidemic in Spain leave no room for doubt. By the end of September 1996, 41,598 cases of AIDS had been reported; 52.4 per cent had died.[1] Twelve thousand Spanish prison inmates, just over a quarter of the entire jail population, are HIV-positive. The number of HIV-positive cases had reached 120,000.[2] Spain has a higher number of HIV cases per inhabitant than any other European country; it has also borne the greatest proportional increase in cases since 1994. Of the total number of AIDS cases reported in Europe, Spain occupies second place, after France. In fact these numbers have been contested by certain non-governmental organizations (NGOs) as being inaccurate and conservative.[3] If the NGOs are correct, it means that the magnitude of the crisis is even greater than reported, further exposing the disastrous prevention policies of the Ministry of Health, which until the Spring of 1996 was in the hands of PSOE (Spanish Socialist Workers' Party). A poll conducted by the University of Santiago de Compostela among 7,580 teenagers concluded that 75 per cent of adolescents are barely informed about AIDS, and half do not use condoms.[4] If we add the shortage of condoms and their price (higher than in most other European countries) to the lack of information about HIV prevention, the results are disheartening indeed.

The fact that Francisco Parras, Director of the National

AIDS Plan, appointed by PSOE and kept in post by the right-wing Popular Party, announced in 1994 that he would subsidize the price of condoms during the three summer months (apparently Spaniards are more lusty in the festival season!) could only be taken as a surrealist act of buffoonery. Moreover, there is no proof that this measure was actually carried out. The increasing number of HIV transmissions among young people is in stark contrast with data published by the Spanish press agency, EFE: 'The Spanish condom market is second among developed nations, beaten only by Japan: every potential consumer in Spain uses ten condoms per year.'[5] Something is amiss here. Should we infer that Spaniards acquire prophylactics but do not – or cannot – use them? Or that people have anal or vaginal intercourse ten times a year on average, and that the rest of their sexual activity is unprotected? When customers (a diverse group of men and women) were asked by Telecinco TV whether they felt embarrassed about buying condoms in pharmacies and supermarkets, most said they didn't – with easy confidence.[6] If the high cost of condoms is not a disincentive, and if Spaniards are as lacking in modesty as this survey suggests, how can we explain the continued high levels of HIV transmission? Indeed, what are the predominant means and patterns of HIV infection in Spain?

In June 1996, data gathered since 1981 revealed that 64 per cent of HIV cases corresponded to unsafe injection drug use, 14.6 per cent to unprotected heterosexual intercourse, and 16 per cent to unprotected homosexual and bisexual activity. The rest were recipients of blood transfusions and hemoderivatives. Regarding paediatric AIDS, the most recent data claims 667 HIV-positive children, a number greater than any other European Union country. The principal road to infection is through the unsafe use of injecting drug equipment. Sexual activity is a secondary means of infection. In data studied by the Ministry of Health there are no indications of transmission via unprotected lesbian sex.

Despite the crisis of HIV infection among injecting drug users, neither governmental nor regional governing bodies have launched a single campaign directed at this group. And although needles have been sold in pharmacies in the Basque region since 1989, the rest of Spain has been slow to develop any initiatives at all. A small-scale needle exchange programme took place in Valencia in 1993, 1994 and 1995. Vans equipped for needle exchange were based in areas frequented by drug users. This project was organized by the Valencia Anti-AIDS Citizens Committee in cooperation with the NGO, Médicos del Mundo, who were funded by the socialist-controlled Ministerio de Asuntos Sociales (Ministry of Social Affairs). A similar project, where drug users could obtain a kit containing needles, cotton, condoms, and AIDS prevention and treatment information, has been implemented in Santander, Palma de Mallorca, and Alcalá de Henares in Madrid. A needle exchange programme is planned to start in Barcelona in December 1996.

The AIDS crisis in Spain needs to be understood within the complex and often chaotic socio-political environment of the early 1980s. The fascists, soundly defeated in the socialist victory of 1982, refused to acknowledge this defeat. Their refusal manifested itself in the attempted coup d'état orchestrated by Lieutenant Coronel Antonio Tejero on 23 February 1981 and was the death rattle of the military extreme right wing. The socialist victory was a cause for celebration, leading to an initial widespread burst of euphoria. However, the government of Felipe González had a paradoxical lulling effect on those who had so boldly opposed the Franco regime. Before long, PSOE had departed from its original political principles, and had weathered a number of confrontations, with the leftist trade unions most notably, all of which engendered a mood known at the time as 'the disillusionment'. This mood of political apathy prevailed, despite – or perhaps because of – the encouraging economic effects of Spain's incorporation into the Common Market in 1985, and the media's infatuation with the 'beautiful people', the bankers, business people, magistrates and legislators who supposedly embodied the values of the new Spain. The glamorous lifestyles flaunted by the 'beautiful people' struck a sour note with many Spanish people, revealing the chasm between the realities and the ideals of democratic socialism.

As the 1980s got underway, a growing sense of discord and disillusionment set in. The transforming solutions and 'new ethics' expected from the government encountered a series of setbacks. High-profile cases of nepotism, corruption and charges of State-run terrorism, raised serious doubts about the virtues of Felipe González's governments. It was within this mood of anxiety and disenchantment that the first news of AIDS arrived.

The first reactions to AIDS in the Spanish media were similar to those in most Western countries, though reports were fewer in number.[7] All were characterized by the dual messages of panic and sensationalism and confused medical information, taken mainly from American scientific studies.[8]

The gay community, suffering from malevolent popular associations of AIDS with homosexuality, reacted by attacking the unsound principles and prejudices of scientific 'truth'. In the Basque gay publication, *Gay Hotsa*, Héctor Anabitarte took things one stage further: 'It is clear that the combined horrors of prejudice, the law and religion are not enough to combat homosexuality. Now science has taken the lead, not only of considering homosexuality a pathology, a deviation or detention of normal processes, but also of promoting the view that intense homosexual activity itself creates deficiencies.'[9]

Although it seems commonplace to refer to the habitual Spanish tolerance of homosexuality, Spain has not been exempt from repressive legislation. Together with a group of articles on the Penal and Military Codes, the unfortunate Law of Danger and Social Rehabilitation (LPRS), which was approved on 4 August 1970, five years before Franco's death, punished the following: public scandal, corruption of minors, and attacks on moral decency, shame and 'good manners'. Among people assumed to be a danger to the

State, Article 3 cites 'those who perform acts of homosexuality'.

Several articles of the LPRS were repealed through an urgent procedure in January 1979, following PSOE's proposal which was a response to lobbying by gays, lesbians and other sympathetic parties. But it was not until 1983 that article 431 of the Penal Code (concerning public scandal) was partially modified. The crime of 'public scandal' and 'unusual and obscene conduct' was still in effect as late as 23 October 1986 when two lesbians, Arantxa and Esther, were arrested for kissing outside the State Security Headquarters in Madrid.

If such homophobic aggression was exercised late in the 1980s, who can be surprised by the wariness of gay organizations which, in 1983, perceived 'the bad faith and thinly disguised homophobia throughout the media that seeks to relate homosexuality to horrific diseases.'[10] This fear must not, however, conceal the dangerously erroneous advice given by certain gay groups: 'try to avoid sexual contact with anyone who gives you the slightest reason to suspect a venereal disease. A quick examination of your partner may reveal signs that he or she has not noticed.'[11] The foolishness of such recommendations is obvious. Withholding vital preventative data about the use of condoms had grave consequences for public health. Missing the target so, in a defence against puritan attacks, captures the disorientation of gay militancy of the time.

Not until 1987 were practical measures taken to encourage gay men to stop seeing AIDS as an anti-homosexual phenomenon and to regard it as a serious, but preventable, risk. Contributing factors to the slowness of this move include: the scant consciousness of a gay identity among Spanish homosexuals; the dispersal of any gay activism that did exist throughout multiple regions and nationalities; an overall lack of activist coordination; the wear and tear of personality clashes; the eagerness of some gay leaders to land the starring role; and the counterproductive creation of rival factions in the gay community. Linked to this is the false sense of complete freedom, accompanied by political apathy, of so many gay men, who felt immune from harm within the security of the gay commercial scene.

Thus did the celebrated 'tolerance' of Spanish society have paradoxically damaging results. Tolerance is not the same as accepting the full facts of gayness. Tolerance can in fact exacerbate gay invisibility, under the guise of protecting privacy. In countries like the US and Great Britain where anti-gay laws have been more explicit and, at times, brutal, gays and lesbians have fought hard to defend their visibility and identities. In relation to AIDS, tolerance masquerades as acceptance. The renowned poet, Jaime Gil de Biedma, whose homosexuality was known by his relatives, as well as by readers who could read between the lines, kept his AIDS condition silent right up until his death in 1990. According to the writer Ana María Moix, 'Perhaps he did not make it public because his mother, for whom he had an enormous amount of affection and respect, was still alive. But I believe that he was simply ashamed of disease, not because it was AIDS. He would have done the same had it been cancer. I remember him saying, "I really go to the dogs when I'm sick, I don't want to see anyone or anyone to see me." '[12]

The apparent inability of drug addicts to organize politically or socially, along with the disillusionment of the heterosexual population, added to this political paralysis. There had been a deafening silence around AIDS for many years, and from silence spring lethal consequences. Fearful of abuse and stigma, homosexuals seemed intent on fleeing reality. For many people, contracting HIV meant chaos and confusion, in which their very lives and lifestyles were suspect.

The first Anti-AIDS Citizens' Committees emerged in 1984. Despite their misguided activities in the early 1980s, we should not ignore their efforts. Made up of gays, lesbians and heterosexuals, the Anti-AIDS Citizens' Committees were legally recognized in 1986, and were to initiate a series of campaigns with the message that AIDS is of concern to everyone, a similar message to those found in advertisements from the Ministry of Health.

Trailing initiatives from other Western countries, the Ministry of Health conceived its first prevention campaign in 1987. Brief TV 'spots' showed little dolls and grotesque puppets which, jumping around and emitting infantile sounds, explained what caused AIDS, and what did not: the play on words between the name of the syndrome (SIDA) and the two syllables uttered with little shrieks – *Si da* (it strikes), *No da* (it doesn't strike) – bordered on the ridiculous. The next institutional campaigns emphasized the general implications of the disease. Up until 1 December 1995 only one campaign provoked an outcry. This was an ad which promoted the use of the condom with the endearing double imperative, 'Póntelo, pónselo' (Put it on yourself, put it on him). In the foreground was a rolled condom underneath an array of sexually transmitted diseases including gonorrhoea, condylomas, and AIDS. The Episcopal Confederation reacted violently, demanding legal action, arguing that the promotion of latex encouraged sexual contact.

As I have already noted, not a single governmental campaign has ever targeted injecting drug users. The small-scale, under-funded campaigns of the Basque authorities directed at injecting drug users only underline the paucity of prevention efforts nationwide.

Overall, the Ministry of Health's campaigns have been scant on explanations, pusillanimous with direct language, and directed at a general population which is, by implication, heterosexual. Within this context we must ask, what representations of AIDS has Spain generated since the 1980s? Until 1985, when the anthropologist Alberto Cardín announced that he was HIV-positive, the silence about AIDS was practically absolute among the Spanish intelligentsia. Cardín, one of Spain's very few openly gay theoreticians, published two texts. The first bore the ominous title, *SIDA: Maldición bíblica o enfermedad letal?* (AIDS: Biblical curse or lethal disease?, 1985); the second was entitled *SIDA:*

Enfoques alternativos (AIDS: Alternative views, 1991). In the prologue to the second book, having attacked the supposed expertise of the medical profession, Cardín addresses homosexuals, for whom the transition from a cult of the body as an instrument of pure pleasure, to a new conception of a body in pain and in need of care could be problematic.[13] Aside from Cardín, who was relatively neglected during his lifetime, the impoverished bibliography on AIDS in Spain is shocking. A 1990 article by Vicente Molina Foix documented the large literature generated by AIDS in the Anglo-Saxon and French worlds, and the limited literary response to the epidemic in Spanish. What are the reasons for this critical vacuum? The fragile status and tradition of the Spanish essay? The perception of AIDS as an individual problem? The fear of associating oneself with such a loaded subject?

Pepe Espaliu, an artist from Córdoba, broke the silence once more with his Carrying Project. In 1992 the artist was carried through the streets of San Sebastián and Madrid by successive pairs of supporters who linked hands beneath him.[14] The transportation of the AIDS-stricken artist became a metaphor for solidarity with the sick, clearly showing that human contact with an AIDS sufferer was not synonymous with danger. Making the symbolic gesture of showing his sores, just as Joseph Beuys had done in *Zeige deine Wunde* (Show Your Sores, 1976), Espaliu highlighted the social dimension of art, fleeing the formalist self-absorption which informs so much contemporary culture. In Madrid his route traversed Parliament and the Reina Sofía Museum, figuratively linking politics with aesthetics.

The success of Espaliu's work can be seen in the many variations of the carrying that were subsequently orchestrated by people outside the art world. For example, a carrying performed by groups of people with AIDS in Barcelona circled the city's male 'model prison' where so many people with AIDS were incarcerated. In conjunction with a performance in Pamplona, Espaliu manufactured pieces of iron, inspired by the discovery of photographs of sedan chairs which had been used by members of the eighteenth-century Spanish nobility. Espaliu's sedan chairs were at once funeral urn, sealed boxes, protective armour, and psychic shelter. They convey the paradoxical lives of people with AIDS. Forced into hiding from fear of attack and discrimination, the crudeness of the sick body may have offered a *via meditatio* through which to consider, free of theatricality, carnivalesque, and mock repentance, the foundations of human relations, and even a more serene vision of existence. The power of Espaliu's late works lies in its reconciliation of the pleasures of extreme sado-masochistic sexuality with the knowledge that such *jouissance* may lead to danger and harm. His holistic conception of the body, life and death, shows a debt to the Sufi poet, Yalal al-Din Rumi (1207–1273).[15]

In Spanish art taking AIDS as its theme, there is a before and an after Espaliu. The Carrying Society, a group created in San Sebastián, spurred on by Josu Sarasua and especially by Jorge González, continued the spirit of Espaliu's projects until recently. One of their most successful projects involved tape-recording the testimonies of people living with AIDS. *Como una antorcha* (Like a torch, 1995) privileged the voices of people with AIDS and the ears that hear them. The installation revolved around a circle of chairs in which the viewer felt drawn to sit. On one of the chairs was seated a loud speaker, emitting, without interruption, the different testimonies of people with AIDS. A naked bulb hanging above the circle of chairs projected a torch-like light. This was an emotionally-charged offering of the privacy of the sick to a public audience. The disembodied voices made the emotional impact of those testimonies particularly acute.

On a different plane, and not unlike the combative texts and graphics of New York's Gran Fury, the diverse works of the Valencian artist, Pepe Miralles, underscore the failures of the government, the exploitative practices of pharmaceutical companies, and the public's ignorance about AIDS. In one of his most effective installations, *Etnografía de una enfermedad social* (Ethnography of a social disease), which considers different parts of a single person's body, as if that individual body symbolises *all* bodies, he gathers the belongings of a friend who has died of AIDS and scatters them among the antiquities of Madrid's Museum of Anthropology. The cabinets throughout the Museum, in rooms dedicated to different continents, are occupied by the relics and remains – photographs, packets and bottles of pills, letters – of the dead man. Through the scattering of the private throughout a public museum, Miralles powerfully yet simply conveys the sense that AIDS penetrates and modifies all cultures.

In the fight against AIDS, most Spanish artists have limited themselves to donating a few pieces of work to AIDS charities. Pepe Espaliu commented in 1993 that even the so-called 'political-social' artists did not confront AIDS, accusing them of being unable to make art for a public arena, despite their claims. In Espaliu's view, it is easy for artists to adopt an ironic or critical stance, but this kind of 'cool' attitude does little to compel spectators' attention.

The first exhibition in Spain with AIDS as its focus took place in Santiago de Compostela in 1994, some six years after the first AIDS-related shows in the States. Curated by Juan de Nieves, the show was entitled SIDA, *Pronunciamento e Acción* (AIDS, Statements and Action). The artists represented two main responses to AIDS: the first, exemplified by Pepe Espaliu, Javier Codesal and Jesús Martínez Oliva, combine elaborate metaphors of the body, pain and bereavement; the second, epitomized by Pepe Miralles, the Carrying Society and Alejandra Orejas, invoke blunter, more direct messages.

Alejandra Orejas, one of the few women artists to have explored this subject, had already died from AIDS-related diseases when the exhibition opened. Her work (photographs on back-lit brass boxes) is striking and disturbing. At a time in Spain when the faces of people with AIDS were still hidden, Orejas dared to show men and women with visible signs of the disease. She stressed that AIDS should not stop people having sex. In her series, *Sexo y Sida y Sexo y . . .* (Sex and AIDS and Sex and . . .), 1989, she showed the intermingling of male and female bodies engrossed in passionate sexual activity, next to a picture of a person with AIDS. The message was ambiguous. Did she want to suggest that voyeurism was the only form of safe sex permitted for people with AIDS? Was she illustrating the point that people with AIDS feel desire? It is hard to say whether the apparently healthy bodies appearing in Orejas' photographs belong to people with AIDS or not. Does it really matter? What counts in these bold representations is that bodies are reinvested with pleasure.

The Aragonese artist, Javier Codesal, is also concerned with the relationship between appearances, health, disease and the body. In a time when many people were unclear about the distinction between being HIV-positive and having AIDS, Codesal embarked on a quest to find a handsome HIV-positive man. He failed in Madrid: nobody wanted to pose naked for him; so he went to Barcelona. The resulting project, entitled *Días de Sida* (Days of AIDS) was finally presented in a gallery in Madrid in 1993. The man from Barcelona is depicted in a large, classically framed photograph next to an older man in a composition resonant of a Renaissance *Pieta*. The long-term HIV sufferer appears about to fall but is tenderly held and protected by the older man. This image underlines the false security in thinking that unprotected sex with a healthy-looking person is safe. It also stresses the importance of compassion and care within homosexual imagery. The religious poses of the figures, and art historical iconography, give it a sacred air.

Sexuality as metaphor also distinguishes the work of Jesús Martínez Oliva, an artist from Murcia. In Santiago, Martínez Oliva devised an installation (*Untitled, 1994*) comprised of various mattresses which he arranged vertically and horizontally on the floor to form a kind of tunnel. Placed in the middle of the exhibition space, the 'tunnel' forced spectators to walk alongside it if they wanted to cross the room. Discarded from an old boarding school, the worn mattresses evoked the tribulations of sex for young people in the age of AIDS. Despite the trouble of crossing the tunnel, there was a way through and a way out.

Blatant sexual imagery figures in a number of art works focused on AIDS. Pepe Espaliu was insistent about the sexual content of his work. An untitled collage/drawing on paper of 1993 combined an erect penis, a hand bearing evidence of ejaculation, and a scrotum pierced by nails. A metal ring adorns the penis's head. In the lower half of the picture is an inverted flower with thorns. This piece fuses the pleasures and pains of gay sado-masochistic sex with the safety of masturbation. What does the flower represent? Suffering? Torment? Beauty?

Spanish art which takes AIDS as its theme is as dispersed and scattered as the political and social responses to AIDS itself have been. The huge impact of Espaliu's Carrying Project is remembered and mourned. Occasionally, an individual initiative re-ignites consciousness of the magnitude of AIDS: Pepe Miralles, an HIV-negative artist who has been working on the subject of AIDS for five years, organized an exhibition in Jávea, Alicante, called *Pensar la SIDA* (Thinking on AIDS) in 1996. But no institution, art centre, or museum has dedicated space to artistic responses to AIDS.[16] Curators, directors, magazine editors and artists alike continue to be suspicious of an art that combines aesthetics with social commitment. The AIDS crisis is in danger of being engulfed once more in silence.

Translated from the Spanish by Vincent Martin

notes

1. *El País*, 6 November 1996
2. *Ajoblanco* 84, April 1996, p. 21.
3. Ricardo Llamas, *Construyendo Sidentidades. Estudios desde el corazón de una pandemia* (Constructing AIDentities. Studies from the heart of a pandemic), Madrid, *Siglo* XXI, 1995, p. x.
4. *El País*, 16 February 1996, p. 30.

5. *Levante* (Valencia), 5 July 1996.

6. 'Telediario' [TV news]. Telecinco, 5 July 1996.

7. See Alberto Mira, '*Esta noche SIDA. Comentarios a algunos tratamientos del SIDA en prensa y televisión* [AIDS tonight. Commentaries on press and TV treatment of AIDS], *De amor y rabia. Acerca del arte y el SIDA* [On love and rage. About art and AIDS], ed. Juan Vicente Aliaga and José Miguel G. Cortés, Valencia: Universidad Politécnica de Valencia, 1993, p. 146 ff.

8. For example, 'El Cáncer que ataca a los gays' [The cancer that attacks gays], *Interviu* 335, October 1982. The macabre commonplaces of this text are analyzed by José Miguel G. Cortés in 'A Alberto Cardín. In memoriam', *De amor y rabia*, p. 70.

9. *Gay Hotsa* 18, 1983. Also cited in a study by Ricardo Llamas and Fefa Vila, *Spain. The Passion for Life. Una Historia del movimiento de lesbianas y gais en el Estado Español* [A history of the gay and lesbian movement in the Spanish State], p. 14. This text will form part of a compilation to be published by Laertes (Barcelona), provisionally entitled *ConCIENCIA de un singular deseo: Estudios gays y lesbianos en España* [ConSCIENCE of a particular desire: Gay and lesbian studies in Spain], ed. Xosé M. Buxán Bran.

10. *Gay Hotsa* 19, 1983.

11. *Gay Hosta* 27, 1985.

12. *Panorama* 278, 21 September 1992, 14.

13. Following Baudrillard, Paul Julian Smith strings together a hypothetical interpretation of the visualization of AIDS in Spain which departs from the concept of fatality. See 'Fatal Strategies: The Representation of AIDS in the Spanish State', *Vision Machines, Cinema, Literature and Sexuality in Spain and Cuba, 1983–1993*, London, Verso, 1996, pp. 101–27.

14. The first 'carrying' was performed on 26 September 1992 in San Sebastián; the second in Madrid on 1 December of the same year.

15. Rumi's thought pervades Espaliu's final installation, *El nido*, The nest. Here we also find remnants of Duchamp and of the dances of the dervishes. *El nido* is a reflection on the bodily dispossession produced by AIDS. For just as birds pluck their own feathers in order to make nests for their young, so the AIDS patient sees the body erode at the same time that they surrender to themselves in the act of solidarity, struggle and love. See the catalogue, *Sonsbeek 93*, ed. Jan Brand, Catelijne de Muynck, and Valerie Smith, Ghent, Snoeck Ducaju & Zoon, 1993, pp. 114–18, 130, 238–53.

16. Following the Vancouver summit, the magazine *Interviu*, known for

promoting irresponsible sensationalism, published a hyperbolic article which called attention to claims made by HIV-positive Spaniards that general practitioners in Spain were not sufficiently prepared to treat AIDS. The article also mentioned the unbearable situation of HIV-positive prisoners with terminal conditions and the criticism by AIDS activists and HIV-positive gays of the catastrophic public measures taken to combat the pandemic. See Nuria Varela and Mony Padura, '*No podemos con el SIDA*' (We can't beat AIDS). *Interviu* 1005 (5–21 July 1996), pp. 26–20.

Gary Fisher in your pocket

Eve Kosofsky Sedgwick

walking

In my fatigue, and my beer stupor, I still moved more effectively than the living . . . one dead foot before the other, dead hands pocketed, in fists around my keys and around some change (not enough for anything – not even sugar) so nothing would rattle or chink. I walked as steadily up the hills as down them, not a robot, not even inhuman, because I felt the pull in my calves (would have to rub them when I finally stopped) and then I felt the threat of gravity, several times, but not for several moments after any step taken, indeed well into the next step. Dead foot in front of dead foot – it registered late with me or not at all, and never once like the most basic mathematics (like it might for a kid, or a carpenter, or a blind man) – I couldn't keep count to keep distance to save my life; at best I detected a rhythm, a groin-level sinus-thing, strains of a song I'd heard. Probably Schooly D, because that's where I was walking from. That's where I'd seen him, the white man I was returning to (but soon to be waiting for) and that's where I'd left him after the crowd had changed from half black to half empty and mostly white, slam-dancing (though rather politely) to some local darlings. Left him, cause he was the only thing to keep me there and I was afraid he would notice how I watched him, like he was the only man in the world and I was the only woman.

But I never was a woman, and I never was white, never even pretended to be a little, the way he could pretend some blackness, bobbing his head and throwing his fist to fight-the-power that he actually was, that most of those on the floor who grabbed up the posters and the 12-inch cards and cassette tapes of 'Am I Black Enough For You?' actually were, while the black people, us who looked like black people, chilled in the dark corners – overwhelmed by it all, or def-fer than it all. I knew that this man understood the very margins of a history that had brought him to this borrowed outrage, brought him to it so cleanly, so thoroughly, with such conviction that if I hadn't met him before and didn't know a side of him so fantastically white – the very horrific myth of white – I could have sworn he was a mix with at least one parent at stake, (or, perhaps a mixer, with one, two, maybe several children to defend) or even better, a white man with a black sympathy so single-minded it bordered on psychotic – indeed, his conviction dwarfed the fashionable and startled the mighty rapper himself; Schooly-school had to slap hands with him twice to drain off his charge, had to look him in the eye when he called the collective audience his fag and groped himself – 'this is my weapon and you want it, you actually paid for it – hit it!'

I knew better, or differently, or at least more about this particular white person, and I had to make sure that he noticed me enough to turn away, to laugh in gestures too wide with his friends, to drink and smoke and churn his strong body with an oblivion too complete to be unconscious – enough to turn away but enough to remember why, and then enough to fuel his occasional but great rotations about the room, eyes like beacons into every crevice, till they touched me and registered nothing. Nothing – but like the notch in a ring, something he had to finger over and over again, till it felt familiar, though I think he recognized me instantly as I had recognized him. Good sex, like hate and love, (and violations of their integrity) seldom calls for a reacquainting of the parties (unless it's an orgy). But if I'd left my stoop then when he failed to see me, and walked up to him (instead of half an hour later walking out of the club, away from him) we would have been friends, even brothers in the battle against the powers-that-be for all of half an hour. He never would (would never) have returned to the scene of our first meeting, like I knew now he must – for having not seen me, but having detected an important lack of something he had to be certain of what he was already sure of.

So I knew before the show was over, before I was halfway up the hill, well into the mist shrouded park and aware of being out of breath and cold and so tired, and allowing all those little discouragements (from which I'd walked so steadily away) to finally graze me – I knew he was following me. First in his thoughts, then in a curious stride, angered, even gimped towards his sexual vengeance – a violence of near-consent or of no-consent but his own which overpowered mine in the court of the park – and nothing of such maladies ever went further than the park; the most casual remark of it went unheard, the most fervent cries got drowned in laughter or jeers. He would have his way with me in doubles because I had dared him in his own house, had threatened to call his politic 'fashion' when it wasn't that at all, when it was actually stronger than any young militant black man's of some education who thought he could fight power with words or with borrowed money and still have white friends, stronger than any white woman's who, while she knew oppressions by names and remained sensitive to even the as yet nameless sources, had to endure a revitalization of the myths that made her so knowledgable and sensitive to begin with, like a fast child in a slow class, she only has to be careful not to separate the myth as it comes from the black rapper from the proprietary caress of her white lover who tells her to shut up and dance to it.

Gary Cornell Fisher III (he dropped the middle name and roman numeral in his twenties) was born in Bristol, Pennsylvania, on 19 June, 1961, to Cornell and Virginia Fisher. The first child in an army family that relocated frequently, he lived in Phoenix, El Paso, Dusseldorf, Virginia, and North Carolina before graduating from Pine Forest Senior High School in Fayetteville, N.C., in 1979. He grew up with three younger sisters, Leslie, Luchina, and Crystal. The family never had much money, and Fisher supported himself – mainly by working in restaurants and, later, catering – from the age of eighteen, when he entered college at the University of North Carolina at Chapel Hill.

As an undergraduate at Chapel Hill from 1979–83, Fisher majored in English and took several creative writing classes. In his early career fantasies he was a multimedia superstar (or, briefly, a lawyer). While he remained passionate about a vast range of popular music, he seems in college to have come to a settled understanding of himself as a writer. From that time on, his notebooks show an incessant and profuse activity of drafting and redrafting stories and (especially in college) poems. Discovering Southern literature, especially the fiction of Faulkner and O'Connor, seems to have given him decisive access to the development of his own style.

It was also in college that Fisher began to describe himself as gay and sought out his first sexual experiences, all with men. Judging from his journals, the issue of being gay, in itself, seems not to have been an especially fraught one for him, though he did suffer in these years from unrequited erotic obsessions, discouragement and loneliness. Although he wasn't out in his daily life of classes, work, and straight friends, he danced avidly at nearby gay bars and felt comfortable there. He also had his first experiences of anonymous sex, in two men's rooms at the UNC library, and a relationship with a somewhat older man living nearby who remained an important figure for him throughout his life. His college years coincided with the beginning of the AIDS epidemic, and it was probably as a college undergraduate that he became infected with the virus.

In 1983 Fisher moved to San Francisco without any particular plan for the future; after a discouraging series of temporary jobs, in 1984 he entered the graduate programme in English at Berkeley. Continuing to live in San Francisco and commute across the bay, he did well in graduate school, was admitted to the Ph.D. programme after three semesters, became a gifted teacher of composition and of American and African-American literature, and developed strong friendships with a few other graduate students. Several of the faculty who taught him recognized the encounter with an unusual talent. But despite the support and flexibility of a few of his professors, the mesh between the graduate programme and Fisher's real aptitudes and ambitions was strained. At the time of his death, ten years into the programme, he was still enrolled but hadn't yet taken his orals and didn't have a realistic plan for doing so. His identity as a graduate student and teacher was important to him – and not only because of things like insurance, though increasingly for such reasons – but the reading and writing that meant most to him were hardly oriented toward that career path.

One aspect of being a graduate student that seems to have been transformative for Fisher was the access, in classes and especially among his friends, to a sustained and speculative conversation about race. His journals suggest that Fisher's willingness to be reflective about race had always before encountered a withering wall of static: the realization that, brought up on army bases surrounded by many white families, attending predominantly white schools, and sharing values that he didn't readily associate with African-American culture, his own identification as black could hardly be a settled or simple thing. To see that unsettled and unsimple were constitutive conditions – rather than prohibitive ones – for thinking about race and racism was probably the single event that most galvanized the writing and perception of his last decade. Along with interpretive and artistic power, however, this development also opened him to new experiences of anger and pain.

The realization that he might have HIV infection came early to Fisher and deepened gradually. Over many years he shared the knowledge with very few even of his close friends, until less than a year before his death when an acute health breakdown necessitated a long, frightening hospitalization. At that point Doug Sebesta, the one nearby friend in whom he had confided and who had assumed virtually singlehanded responsibility for his care, encouraged him to start letting other friends and family members know what was going on. Once the secrecy about his illness was over he savoured the company and care of many people who loved him. Despite the identification with death and the dead that he had been exploring in his journals, Fisher maintained from that point on an extraordinarily aggressive fight against the deterioration of his health. He demanded heroic measures from his doctors and himself through several crises; and until only a few days before his death it was clear that to die was the very last thing he had in mind. His father, from whom he had been estranged since his mother's death six years before, was in touch with him toward the end and was about to visit when Gary Fisher died on 22 February 1994, in the company of his sister Luchina, at the age of thirty-two.

From a letter to one of Gary's sisters, not long after their mother's death:

I can't think straight anymore. Everything blurs and shifts on me when I try to think straight. Of course I need glasses, but it's more than that. I don't sleep and I've been eating strangely – lots of cheeseburgers – and it's more than that. I dealt with death, mom's death, on a level I've never touched before and couldn't approximate again.

Understand me: she was (in the hospital) the ugliest sight and the most fulfilling sight that I have ever witnessed. Not just her, but everything she stood for, everything she was to me, in some sense, all of me, shrivelled there flitting in and out of knowing me and bleeding away through plastic tubes. I was gored deeply and winced with a funny, almost sexual, almost dead (touching dead) sort of electricity everytime I told myself that she was going to die.

New York is your reality. Mom dying is mine. Dad becoming a nigger is mine. Shit on the sidewalk is mine . . . This all sounds much too negative and it's worse than what I mean. At the peak of an understanding that I no longer know (and seem to be seeking w/some indirect urgency) I knew what it was like to die. I didn't go all the way, but there was a moment in the hospital where I thought I could change places with her. I'm not being noble. I mean, I thought it would be me in there and I would give her this shell. And not because I thought I owed it to her. But because I was her.

My rebellion was her rebellion. We could never fight right because she was never sure which side to take. I was a fool for shifting sides, always finding the side she wouldn't take, because, more than you know, more than I knew, mom and I were the same person. Difference is she let him fuck her; emphasis on let. I never did. Extrapolate.

I never fucked mom. It wasn't on my agenda. Freud fucked up with me, fucked up doubly because – I wouldn't let dad rape me either – he couldn't break whatever it is that I held up against his authority. Couldn't whip it out, couldn't send the message even through mom. I was a hard knot mainly because I refused to fight. Not docileness, but a brooding, stubborn refusal. The ultimate slap was to let it loose that I'd let some other man, not my dad, have me . . .

In the spring of 1987, as a visiting professor at the University of California, Berkeley, I taught a graduate class in gay/lesbian literature – I think I called it 'Across Genders, Across Sexualities' – in which Gary Fisher was a student. There were too many students enrolled to fit around the seminar table, and I can still picture Gary habitually sitting on the floor, almost always silent, just by the door. I noticed him early because he was the only African-American student in a class where issues of race were going to be fairly salient, and I worried that he would feel pressured to speak or to withdraw – scrutinized, resentful, or claimed, or just lonely. I also worried about the pressure of his actual or imagined judgments of the substance of these discussions – and how those might impinge on my teaching. (And I had assigned my students to keep journals for the semester, so I knew even a silent judgment would impinge eventually, for better or worse.)

Gary's demeanour during the first few weeks of class neither alarmed nor reassured me. His was a light and sweet, but oddly formidable presence: his station by the door and his silence seemed to make him a kind of allegory for the liminal. Several times he missed classes. I didn't know then, though now that I've been immersed in his papers I do, that his note-taking when he did attend classes was meticulous verging on mechanical, maybe in proportion to how alienated he felt from a given course: mercifully, his detailed record of this one sports some lapses and relaxations. It was an edgy seminar in general – I think it was the first explicitly gay one offered in that department – and because of his silence and his absences I couldn't be sure whether Gary was quite *in* it. I knew he had a beautiful smile, infrequently used in this setting, and a reserve whose specific gravity might not have been as palpable to himself as it was to those around him. Really I wasn't sure whether he was a serious student or a flake, or fake.

The seminar began in January, and things continued in this way until a day in March when Gary turned up for the first time at my office hours. I can't remember much about our conversation except the stark double twist of it. He handed me his class journal. And apologized for missing so many classes, but – he hadn't told this to other people, so would I please not do so either? – he was dealing with a lot of ill health; in fact with ARC.

It wasn't commonplace back then, at least it hadn't happened to me before, to hear from young people that the futures they look forward to are so modest in duration.

I think it was as soon as he left my office that I opened his journal and started to read the entries and, it turned out, stories ('Tawny' and 'Red Cream Soda') and notes and photocopied collages gathered in it. If the news of grave illness in our students sat strangely, at least 'back then,' in any teacher's ear, the news of genius is something else. Now, as I write, in front of me again are my dippy handwritten sentences from the bottom of the last page of the first half of Gary's journal: beginning,

Generally, what I most get from this journal is that you're a

> pretty sensational writer. Are you doing anything about this, intensively? Are you taking it seriously, in terms of your time & plans? There are so many sentences in here that are just right. The journal form seems not a bad one for you, but some of the dialogic/operatic effects of 'Tawny' go, in *their* way, much beyond it . . .

It wasn't that Gary's journal was especially forgiving about the aspects of the seminar that had been worrying me. He'd written, for instance,

> *2/2 Not thrilled by the class discussion Friday. Race is up front in both stories and yet . . . and yet race like homosexuality has sort of a hyper-presence in the graduate student mind and needn't be talked about. [. . .] Did we even get close to the line of absence that not mentioning it creates? I couldn't find any shape, any form of where it might have been, not even a discussion on victim/victimizer or martyrdom; it just wasn't there, and I didn't say anything because I thought this was charity, and talking to it would have been as crude as flinging coins back at a sidewalk philanthropist.*

I identified with, as I was envious of, the excitement of realizing one could put a sting like that in a paragraph's tail – which didn't, either, soothe the hurt of being at the other end of it. Of course, I wasn't sure what response I was supposed to make, or had it in me to, to the claims of either real vocation or encroaching fatality (let alone both). I could tell that Gary was shy – at least with me – and I, shy with almost anyone, was only more so with him.

It didn't help a bit that I was already an old hand at the same strategy he'd adopted for dealing with the rage that concomited with his talent and identity. He put the rage naked on paper, then half-shielded the paper from sight with the smokescreen of a deprecating or even puppyishly ingratiating persona. I recognized the strategy too well – and knew the dimensions of his luminous sweetness too little – to find his rather beatific manner at all relaxing in those days.

As for his writing talent, I understood it through the image of, say, two creative people let loose in an art studio, only one of whom, maybe not even the one more visibly gifted, would find the place more absorbing on the fifth day or the fiftieth than on the first. To say that someone has found an art: doesn't it mean that they have learned, not just to solve problems in the medium, but to formulate new problems in it – whether soluble or not – that would be worth solving? This ability, this generative autotelic habit, was so unmistakably established in Gary's writing that the leaps that didn't work were almost more thrillingly instructive than the ones that did. 'What if I could just – ?' is the formal question the author seems, all but rejoicing, always to blurt out; in this way readers experience how powerful new desires are born and shared.

And because this deepest kind of talent resides in the learning process more than in the writing process of a given moment, Gary's mutilated career offers no such consoling possibility as that he had already accomplished the best writing he would be capable of. It is certain that he had not.

After that seminar was over, I returned to the east coast and it got harder to stay in touch with Gary. We'd had some nice, feather-light and feather-soft talks in Berkeley, but neither in conversation nor writing had we developed much of an idiom for friendship. And since there was nothing remotely apprentice-like about Gary's writing, I couldn't tender teacherly observations on the bottoms of those stories forever. (For that matter, Gary quickly reverted to his maddening habit of promising for months to put stories in the mail *that very day.*) I had it in mind – and I think he did too – to make sure we wouldn't lose each other. But I'm not sure we could have avoided it without the wonderful fortune of having, in Eric Peterson, a mutual friend so affectionate and patient that the thread of contact, however finely spun, was never irremediably distant from our fingers.

Even so, it wasn't until after I was diagnosed with breast cancer in 1991 that we began to get real. A note from Gary a few months later, when I was in the middle of chemotherapy:

Can't figure out exactly why I haven't called; unless it's fear of your pain, fear of my own and fear that I'll fumble-up in talking about it. I've been able to write about it with real depth of feeling, I think. (The last sentence is no indication of this.) So, I'll exorcise some pain/fear on paper here and then I'll be able to call. Make sense?

x

There it is, exorcised. You didn't think I really wanted to waste a nice card on all that, did you? I've met a nice guy – Sherman's his name and he reads. He describes himself this way so I'll respect it now. He works at a bookstore because he can read vast amounts at a discount. He has a beard and a dab of hair beneath his lip (what's that called?), all of it dark. This is all I know about him – though, surprisingly, we met at a sex club. I'm anticipating something physical after we've accomplished [the ritual] three meals (breakfast on Friday) and talked about dying-too-soon. I'm not sure but I suspect he's positive too. He talks about various illnesses. depressions, lethargies and odd humours with too much ease. And I suspect a great many men at the sex clubs . . .

I'm living with two straight people – I mean really straight. I wonder if they'd recognize human anatomy when they see two men fucking. They know I'm gay, but I think they deal on a conceptual level – so of course I've said nothing about my condition. I've said nothing to Eric as well though he might suspect. Sympathy is difficult, sorrow impossible to handle right now so I don't tell Eric though he's probably my dearest friend. I might regret this later; there must be a richness in battling an illness with friends (seems so obvious I must be looking at it wrong, must have misspelled something, must have). I'm saving Eric, I guess, for when I need . . . I'm still too healthy . . .

I had a small battle with KS *recently. The kimo made me ill, even at such low dosages. I can't imagine . . . I guess I need to talk to you.*

– Fucking flags everywhere!

– I have a batch of stories for you.

– Haven't started your book but I LOVE *having it . . . want to wallow in it.*

Absolute love

. . . G

How abruptly this note restructured, for me, the space of

Gary's and my relationship. I'd been aware of not knowing much about his life, but assumed it was because, simply, I didn't *know* him – I'd assumed there were circles of companionship and intimacy far interior to the loose, light holding of our attenuated contact. It was true Gary had said to me, four years earlier, that he wasn't telling people about his illness. But I'd assumed, especially as time went on, that he meant authority-figures and strangers, not friends. I'd assumed that being an active, out gay man in San Francisco meant belonging to a community of people dealing with HIV.[1] And I'd assumed, the several times Eric had set up dates for the three of us and Gary had missed them because of measles, upset stomach, or fatigue – and Eric never seemed surprised – I'd certainly assumed Eric was interpreting them through the same grid of HIV-related anxiety that I was.

In a way, then, I was learning that I was much closer to Gary than I'd thought. But by the same stroke I was learning that to be close to Gary must be a strange, perhaps a fractured or fracturing thing. Waiting behind the revelation that he hadn't told Eric about his illness was the realization that his closest friend must know him as someone who just naturally didn't show up half the time; who naturally dropped out of one's life for long periods. Aspects of Gary that I had before imagined in terms of a more or less concentric, consolidating selfhood and privacy – his passion as a writer, his sexual life, his complex understanding of racism, for example, along with his friendships and his relation to illness – I now saw might coexist as far sharper, less integrated shards of personality, history, and desire.

Gary and I saw each other next in December of 1991. We revelled in a long exchange of war stories at a bar in the Castro, and I finally felt we were finding our feet with each other, and some ground to put them on. At least, the particular awe or shyness that can separate the healthy from the ill no longer kept us apart. I remember describing to Gary what I'd experienced as the overwhelming trauma of half a year of chemotherapy-induced baldness – a narcissistic insult, of no medical significance whatever, that had so completely flooded my psychic defenses that, for the whole duration of the treatment, almost every hour of consciousness had remained an exhausting task.

Gary said, yes, this was what it felt like for him to have KS lesions on his arms. Nobody else ever saw them: he always wore long-sleeved shirts. But alone, he said, in his apartment, he would spend hours, sometimes whole days of months, paralyzed in front of his mirror, incredulous, unable – also unable to stop trying – to constitute there a recognizable self. Impaled by the stigma.

After Gary's death I recounted this conversation to one of his sisters. She said: I think that's how Gary experienced being black, too.

From Gary's journal:

> *. . . Last night I went to BUENA VISTA park and pigged out on half a dozen men (was it that many?). Three of the men came in my mouth and I drank it. That's a horrible two minutes after the climax, or rather the 2nd of the two minutes as the guilt and gorge rise in us both. Why am I jeopardizing my life for an ounce, no a teaspoon of . . . I don't even know what it is? If I described it in the glowing terms I'm tempted to or in the transcendent way so many others have used, I'd know too well, too easily. It's the essence, the reduction of another man's pleasures, desires, maybe his hopes and his dreams, and I want it more keenly when I don't know the man, when he's a big man or a man with a big cock. Loss of control in him and in me. I want some token of that kind of contact, an abandon that forgets all the bullshit that destroys daytime relations, particularly where race difference becomes involved. Yeah, we are one and at the same time so far apart, so caught up in ourselves that the danger of each other cannot intrude. That's the point when it comes. But I'm conscious at these times; I'm not coming; I'm not delirious – just possessed, possessed for him, an extension of him like a hand . . .*

A letter to someone Gary had met through a personals ad:

> *. . . Dear Master Park,*

> *Here's that letter you wanted. I'm laying here sideways in the bed with* Slavery Defended *opened to about midway, sampling the arguments and thinking about how good it felt to serve. Not that it matters, but I enjoyed Thursday immensely, particularly the sleaze and humiliation of some of it. Ultimately my service depends on the strength of my attention, hence my addiction to those things that I enjoy.*
>
> *My pain is high on your list of pleasures and I do like giving in to your desires, but some of the more grueling extended tortures stick in my mind and make me hesitant to call or answer your calls. Master Crandall and others use the pain more sparingly . . . Honestly the pain frightens me and brings me out of the stupor I need to be in in order to be a subservient slave. I need some pain but the extended periods seem to drive the desire to serve out of me – all I can do is soberly register the craziness of what I'm doing.*
>
> *The racial humiliation is a huge turn on. I enjoy being your nigger, your property and worshipping not just you, but your whiteness.*

'What is this fantasy that cuts across all of me, racial, intellectual, moral, spiritual, sexual . . .?' Gary asked his journal in 1987, and continued, 'I hope Carl is rougher than he seems and calls me boy and etc.' A lot of things were happening at once for Gary Fisher in the few years after he moved to San Francisco, and there's no easy way of tracing the feedback loops by which the transformations of his sexual practice, political consciousness, literary vocation, theoretical interests, and relation to illness and death were making one another happen. What seems clear is that exposure to the varied sexual vernaculars of San Francisco catalyzed for him a project of sexual representation that – visionary, mundane, ungraceful, and sublime – was frightening even to him in its ambition and intensity. It was a project, not in the first place of representing sex, but of stretching every boundary of what sex can represent.

'Representation' is no straightforward matter, especially in the vicinity of sex; witness the starkness of Gary's metamorphoses between the supersubtle exegete of a hermeneutic of anti-racist suspicion, on the one hand, and on the other – in the sexualized space of Buena Vista Park in the small hours – the black man whose pleasure in offering service is incomplete unless he can induce some white man to call him 'nigger' and seem to mean it. The sexuality in these journals is prismatic, analytic. Under the pressure of a stringent demand of *sexual* relevance, *sexual* excitation or pleasure, it bends and differentiates the elements of its culture.

In doing so, it is partly responding to a long, speculative tradition of sadomasochistic exploration in which the representational limits of sexuality are never presumed, always experimental. Over the past fifteen years, there has been a need – and an opportunity – to defend SM as a sexual minority movement within the context of American intolerance of all sexual variety. Both mainstream and feminist anti-SM propaganda have refused to perceive any complexity at all in what they see as the completely continuous relation between SM violence and violence tout court. This has resulted, reactively, in a public self-presentation of SM that emphasizes the *dis*linkages between the social realities of power and violence, on the one hand, and the sexualized representation of power and violence, on the other; that emphasizes, too, the crisp way in which SM play can explicitate and therefore manage issues of power, consent, and safety that often remain dangerously obscured in more conventional sexual relations.

It is true that these hygienic dislinkages are among the representational possibilities put into play by sadomasochism. For many people, they may be the most important, exciting, or enabling ones, and their articulation is by now a staple of what might be called 'official' SM culture. What remains underarticulated outside of fiction, though, is the richness of experimental and experiential meaning in these scenes when they are understood as neither simply continuous with, nor simply dislinked from the relations and histories that surround and embed them. Which also means that, as in Gary Fisher's stories and journals, the ontologies of power, consent, and safety may be anything but simplified in the representational field of such a sexuality. If not simplified, however, the issues are treated in another way: they are powerfully dramatized, embodied, and borne witness to.

For instance, there is a sturdy anecdotal tradition that many people who do SM are survivors of sexual trauma or abuse. The anti-SM movement has a victim-discrediting use for this lore: it makes sense to them that people too abject or damaged to stay out of harmful situations would seek out abusive treatment in this realm, as well. In their view, the mimetic aspect of SM guarantees that no new meanings, feelings, or selves may ever emerge through its practice. One can view both trauma and mimesis less rigidly, though; there are people – Gary Fisher was one – for whom the only way out is through. Suppose, as Gary seems to suppose, the sadomasochistic scene to occur on a performative axis that extends from political theatre to religious ritual; an axis that spans, as well, the scenes of psychotherapy and other dramaturgically abreactive healing traditions. According to this understanding, the SM scene might offer a self-propelled, demotic way – independent of experts and institutions – to perform some of the representational functions that, for instance, in *Trauma and Recovery* Judith Lewis Herman assigns to the trauma therapist: the detailed, phenomenologically rich reconstruction of the fragments of traumatic memory; claiming and exercise of the power to re-experience and transform that memory and to take control of the time and rhythm of entering, exploring, and leaving the space of it; and having its power, and one's experience of it, acknowledged and witnessed by others.[2] (I don't, by the way, offer this comparison with the anaphrodisiac intent of making sex sound as respectable as therapy; both are potent, body-implicating, and time-bending representational projects.)

The fierce beam of history that propelled Gary Fisher's sexual imagination was evidently less that of individual trauma than of a more collective violence and loss. All the more was it a trauma that he couldn't otherwise make present to himself, a violence that his culture offered him the most impoverished means for realizing and hence for mourning. Like others gone before him, he forged a concrete, robust bodily desire in the image of historical dispossession, humiliation, compulsion, and denegation, among other things. Probably any sexuality is a matter of sorting, displacing, reassigning singleness or plurality, literality or figurativeness to a very limited number of sites and signifiers. Tenderness (here brief, contingent, illuminating); a small repertoire of organs, orifices and bodily products; holding, guiding, forcing; 'your' pleasure and 'my', different and often nonsynchronous pleasure; infinite specificities of flavour, shape, and smell; the galvanized, the paralyzed; the hungry, impartial, desiring regard in which ugliness may be held as intimately as beauty, and age as youth: these are among the elements here splayed through the crystal of anonymity. And while for another person, or at another place or time, it might have been true that fatality played no very necessary role among these elements of a sexuality, for this person at this time and place it too was central, the need to give a face – or many faces – to a fate.

> . . . KS. *I'm so thoroughly occupied . . . with this occurrence, with these purple fingerprints all over my arms and thighs, that I feel it's dishonest to write about anything unless I include this. It's totally changed the way I live, the way I dress, the way I move, the places I go, the activities I join. On a sunny day I'd rather stay indoors: because I no longer wear T-shirts or short sleeve tops. I've folded them all and put them on a shelf out of sight (and mind, as they used to torture me). I feel most comfortable in a long sleeve white shirt. No one questions its appropriateness even on the hottest day. I would probably invest in more of them if I didn't maintain some small hope that this malady will end. God, then to be left alone with a closet full of long sleeve white shirts would be the torture; or don't I invest in more of them because I'm running out of energy for this charade, I'm anticipating death before the need for more white shirts so why waste the money. My thoughts probably run the line between these positions too.*
>
> *I keep thinking this is a game, so simple that I'm losing for thinking too much, too far ahead, too fast and too broad, for thinking while I should be sleeping – the remedy, I honestly*

believe (sometimes, on occasion), is in my head, in a simple compartment, within a simple room, within a simple building that I can see from here, not far along a path so broad and so bright that I've been following it without knowing all along. The single key to building, room and compartment is free and available to me like the toilet key at a filling station on a rural route where few travel and now fewer (if any two ever did) stop, and nobody, not another soul, has ever yet had to use the facility there, so when you ask for the key note that strange pride and juvenile delight in the station attendant's eyes and as he places it warmly in your palm, covering your hand with both his, and again he's to show you where to go, offers to check your oil and water and to do your windows while you enjoy the facilities . . . and yet again, as he asks you in utter rural route innocence, if everything came out all right. No, he hasn't even noticed that you're black or remembered that he's white and that you two are half a continent away from the reconciliation of big cities . . .

Somehow the mesh between you two is too simple, and perhaps too big for such doubts. All those anxieties and inhibitions, restrictions and recriminations those time-honored and blood-cherished hatreds and passions, those myths, histories and great churning philosophers of difference) pass right through. You leave them in the starchy water when your situation gets drained . . .

. . . I want to write about KS. *I haven't really written about what I look like now. I have a new skin. I have a new identity. They are not the same, but they do on occasion converge, even eclipse one another. First it's odd to be writing so specifically about things so specific when the largeness of my situation is what impresses me. I want to write large. Don't I want to write large? Can I get to the large through an analysis of these many small things? So I want to talk about* KS. *This film ['And the Band Played On'] keeps using* KS *as the tell-tale sign, the first indication, the marker, the scarlet letter. I thought* KS *was rare, even among* AIDS *survivors.*

The spots, the lesions, patches – they are so random, (Even the name is slippery. What should I call these things, individually I mean. One KS. *Look, there's a* KS. *I have a* KS *on my hand, under my thumb.) They refuse a common shape or texture or size and they sprout-spring-develop-appear unpredictably, time and location. (Backtrack: even the action of the disease is slippery.) Some are clustered; some are island-like. Some are small – just dots. Some are large, sprawling, giraffe-like.*

I'm looking at my arm and I don't trust what I just said. There is a geometry to this, a poetry too. If I didn't know it was cancer and AIDS *I'd say my arm – my right arm – is interesting, attractive.*

The spots are grayish, purplish, a light eggplant, mauve – a combination . . .

I'm that sick.

I could die that soon.

Why does my hope seem so long and so broad, a great big room full of possibilities, future light and death is a broken bulb there in the center of it. A conundrum! Does the dark of the bulb matter to the room? Are there windows and is it daylight? Can a room full of this light rejuvenate the bulb, fix it, change it? How much light does it take to change a light bulb?

40 million people will have it by the end of the decade.

I'm in good company. I'm in plenty of company. I'm less afraid. It's a big big room and it's full of everybody's hope I'm sure.

In April of 1993, Gary wrote me,

I want to compile my book this spring (this fucking month!). Would you, could you, might you write an introduction – any peculiarly related thing you want to say – oh, and no rush, I can attach it later. I just really want to be attached to you on this.

Of course I said yes – not because I thought mine would be the perfect aegis for his stories to appear under; not for that matter because I thought they needed any aegis but their own – but because I wanted to do anything that would encourage Gary to get them published and out there and read, ideally during his own life.

I was always underestimating the diffidence that kept Gary from circulating his work, though, and after his health gave out that spring and summer, it slowly came to be understood between us that the book would probably be posthumous; that I would take responsibility for getting it published; that it might include journals, notebooks, even letters as well as stories. We both liked the idea of offering people who hadn't known him or his writing, as well as the few who had, a sort of 'portable Gary' – hence the title we agreed on.

Since Gary's death, I along with other people have had a

lot of second thoughts about calling the book *Gary in your Pocket*. After much consultation, I even chose an alternate title, *Soul Releasing*, from one of his poems. As one of the manuscript's readers put it, *Gary in your Pocket* risks sounding 'in some wise trivializing'. In metaphor, it seems to make Gary small, appropriable; in so doing, it may be all too resonant in the context of the posthumous publication of an African-American writer, mediated by a an older, Euro-American editor and friend, from the press of a mostly white, Southern university. Gary and I were both very conscious of a history of white patronage and patronization of African-American writers, the tonalities of which neither of us had any wish to reproduce. Sexuality was a place where Gary was interested in dramatizing the historical violences and expropriations of racism; friendship, authorship, and publication, by contrast, was not.

Yet, whether well- or ill-advisedly, *Gary in your Pocket* has insisted on remaining the title of that volume. Its Whitmanian intimacy has, perhaps unexpectedly, come to feel more powerful rather than more dubious since Gary's death. The indignity, the promiscuity of book publication – of an individual spirit held often mute in a closed box that anyone can buy and put in their pocket – answers eerily to the indignity of death; but also to the survivor's yearning for a potent, condensed, sometimes cryptic form of access to the person who would otherwise be lost. But, as in Whitman, it is also publication that allows the dead to continue to resist, differ, and turn away from the living.

> Or if you will, thrusting me beneath your clothing,
> Where I may feel the throbs of your heart or rest upon your hip,
> Carry me when you go forth over land or sea;
> For thus merely touching you is enough, is best,
> And thus touching you would I silently sleep and be carried eternally.
>
> But these leaves conning you con at peril,
> For these leaves and me you will not understand,

> They will elude you at first and still more afterward, I will certainly elude you,
> Even while you should think you had unquestionably caught me, behold!
> Already you see I have escaped from you.

The few times when I saw Gary delirious in the hospital, the things he said wouldn't make much sense, but no fever or confusion could burn out the princeliness of that sentence structure. Once when he wanted us to leave the room so he could (as he fantasied) get up and walk to the bathroom in his short hospital gown, he murmured, 'I am about to ask you to perform a task as delicate in conception as it is arduous in execution.' Nor did he cease conferring the beatific smile. The hours we spent in this fragmentary fellowship, holding and being held, always reminded me of the gentle, imperious deathbed dictations of Henry James, sometimes in the person of Napoleon, sometimes in his own:

> Our admirable father keeps up the pitch. He is the dearest of men. I should have liked above all things seeing our sister pulling her head through the crown . . .

> Invoke more than one kind presence, several could help, and many would – but it is all better too much left than too much done. I never dreamed of such duties as laid upon me. This sore throaty condition is the last I ever invoked for the purpose.[3]

Perseveration of a voice worn to the very warp and woof of its syntax: experiencing this, I recognized the good sense of the psychoanalyst Christopher Bollas, when he decided in his writing to render 'id' as *idiom*, and to describe a self as 'a kind of "spirit" of place, unique to the strange aesthetic of an idiom':[4]

> The idiom that gives form to any human character is not a latent content of meaning but an aesthetic in personality . . . Being a character, then, means bringing along with one's articulating idiom those inner presences – or spirits – that we all contain, now and then transferring them to a receptive

> place in the other . . . Although it is difficult to witness how one person 'moves through' the other, like a ghost moving through the internal objects in the room of the other's mind, we know it is of profound significance, even though exceptionally difficult to describe.

If an idiom is like a syntax – at least, if it is for some people – then to be inhabited like this will be familiar to those who sometimes fall asleep reading, and then dream their own mental semantics into the sentence structure of the author. The time of immersion in *Gary in Your Pocket* has brought me many such experiences. Almost every night of it I have dreamed, not *of* Gary, but *as* him – have moved through one and another world clothed in the restless, elastic skin of his beautiful idiom. I don't know whether this has been more a way of mourning or of failing to mourn; of growing steeped in, or of refusing the news of his death. One thing I couldn't doubt: for all its imposing reserve and however truncated, Gary's is an idiom that longs to traverse and be held in the minds of many people who never knew him in another form.

notes

1. I think I was underestimating the redoubled silencing effect that the stigma of HIV may have for, specifically, African-American men. Marlon Riggs discussed this eloquently in 'Letter to the Dead' (*Thing*, Fall 1992, pp.40–44).
2. Judith Lewis Herman, M.D., *Trauma and Recovery*, New York, Basic Books, 1992).
3. Leon Edel, ed., *Henry James Letters*, Cambridge, Mass.: Harvard Univ. Press, Belknap Press, 1984, 4 vols., 4, pp.811–12.
4. Christopher Bollas, *Being a Character: Psychoanalysis and Self Experience*, New York, Hill and Wang, 1992.

deliverance

introduction, foreword, description and selected text

Ron Athey

Nothing is pure. Everything becomes either self-destructive, the moment of redemption, or a God-awful parody, depending on which day of the week it occurs. In this humdrum, bleak state of mind, I find myself writing a piece called *Deliverance*. By description, deliverance is the fulfillment of epiphany, it's the day spoken of by prophets, the day of freedom from suffering for that sorry ass son of a bitch, Job. Or an eagerly awaited day, like the Second Coming. There's also the movie *Deliverance*, where, while snaggle-toothed hillbillies rape a straight man (Ned Beatty), they tell him to 'squeal like a pig'. He is 'saved', or at least vindicated, by either Burt Reynolds or Jon Voight, but that's beside the point. The point is that the violation of the asshole itself – sodomy – is (understandably) the root of so many fears.

In *Deliverance*, the Ron Athey & Co. piece, this fear is engineered throughout, the asshole produces hidden treasures, is receiving and expelling enemas, and for the finale is taken on a double-headed dildo ride with a friend while reading a story. With a predictable literal-mindedness, a man asked me during a post-performance discussion if indeed, since these performances were taken from my own life, did I read books while being anally penetrated.

In my performance material, I am guilty of enhancing my history, situation and surroundings into a perfectly depicted apocalypse, or at least a more visual atrocity. Knowing a few ever-simple realities of life, I probably do this out of disappointment for there not really being hellfire and brimstone, for my Aunt Vena not really bearing the second coming of Christ, as was prophesied. It's a stretch to call the delusions of fanatical religion, glamorous. Not to say that living my adult life through a time of AIDS has been disappointing as far as a drama goes; it's taken very little work for me to parallel my experiences with the jewelled doomsday prophecies from the Book of Revelations.

As an adult homosexual, I've started to come out of my self-obsessed daze, and realize how many aspects of my lifestyle I take for granted. I've always more or less ignored society's contempt towards us homosexuals, and still don't think of people as being my straight friends, or my gay friends. I read Derek Jarman's *At Your Own Risk: A Saint's Testament*, which I quite enjoyed, but there were certain points in the book – particularly his history of British queer rights – where I thought, 'Why is he spending so much time going over legislation? This book could be an advertisement for OutRage!' But *A Saint's Testament* was equally filled with profound one-liners like, 'I was writing in the dark, angrily.' There's no political agenda in facing the dark. I always find comfort that others are also left with nothing to do but fight their way through the dark places.

Like myself, writing inventories of my life, early on trying to keep a grip on my visions even though the nightmarish realities of drug addiction and violent suicidal depressions almost finished me off. In my thirties, it became nights of debauched sexual conquests and self-loathing. I had hoped it was all just teen angst that carried into my twenties, but as middle age sets in my bones, I'm still struggling with demons. I am becoming more gentrified, finding comforting niches for myself. If this is a consolation prize for the American Dream, somebody kill me. Though I swore I never would, for the past few years I've taken to calling myself an Artiste.

It's only out of justification, I'm apologizing for myself to the world, 'What I am doing is important and purposeful because it is art. Though it may offend you, please be patient with the experimental rough edges of my work.' I suppose it was more work trying to defy labels, and much easier to take on such an ambiguous title. People want an answer they know, even if it doesn't mean a thing to them. To some extent, I only pretended to let the system suck me in. Saying 'fuck you' to everything began to sound trite, and I didn't want to be the eternal, rebellious, punk-ass motherfucker.

As far as state-of-the-art, raging fuck you's are concerned, David Wojnarowicz did it with finesse, clarity, and conviction. He had a righteous anger, really, the only kind that works. His writings cut through me, rile me up, make me feel pathetic, and lonely. In comparison, I hate my writing. Wishy-washy and hypocritical, I avoid moralizing. Because in the big picture, I don't know what's right or wrong, I don't think that way. I can bc annoyingly and dishonestly existential about all of life's injustices. I've always tried to write my way into discovering and dealing with the truth. Contrary to my bold images, I think it's telling how tolerant and well-mannered I behave in most situations.

Sometimes I question the meaning of my performance work, I'm still not exactly sure what the reasons are to keep doing it. And though their reasons would vary, I'm not sure my cast of nine could tell you either. Why the fucking bloodbath? The shit? The vomit? All performed on a well-lit stage so that, hopefully, no details will be missed. To take a stab at it, using these bodily functions, assisted by the voice, words, and sound, I'm testifying. I'm wanting people to endure these real experiences, and grasp the ideas behind them. I'm sure it's because I'm damaged, but I want it to be heard: that I was raised in the realm of God, channelled spirits in an un-Christian-like manner, and walked away daring to be the world's only atheist. In my destruction, I barely survived drug addiction, then recovered and became innocent, like an injured child.

That I think I'm somebody because I was into punk and

Goth and industrial music. And once without my Bible, I read Genet and Smith and Gide and Sartre and Camus and Burroughs. And Tennessee Williams, Truman Capote and Flannery O'Connor. And later, Wojnarowicz and Cooper and Jarman. That I adored Pasolini, Fellini and Fassbinder. I was trying to find something worthy to believe in, or at least to educate myself into an acceptable reality. I could see up front it was not going to be pretty, but it was already laid out for me. It finally came down to finding living people I could relate to, and new obsessions. Body piercings became my kink. Tattoos saved my life. Modern Primitives became a new religion, which, quickly turned into a clown show.

a foreword to *deliverance*

Deliverance (premièred December '95) is the third major performance piece I've done. I jokingly call this trilogy the holy torture trinity. The first two, *Martyrs & Saints* ('92–'93) and *4 Scenes In A Harsh Life* ('93–'96), were very different, but they overlapped in theme and structure.

Martyrs & Saints is a meditation that was fuelled by rage and grief I felt in the early '90s, tackling the ambiance created by the AIDS catastrophe, and tying it into my inheritance, a grandiose martyr complex (this was all my Jesus-freak family could afford to leave me with). It was a hodge-podge of short vignettes. My reaction over the death of David Wojnarowicz inspired *Scene I: A Nurses Penance*; the death of my beloved Okie drag-queen Cliff Diller, who was like a best girlfriend and a son to me, offered not only the meditative preset, 'A New Blood Cure', but supplied the set with his memorial pyramid. It was a structure he hallucinated on that last morphine drip. At the time, I wasn't so focused on the effect of my childhood religious training, but it's all there looming in the background, fleshing out the rest of the piece with 'Surgical Stigmata' and 'The Casting Out'. I was aware that using Christian images seemed too obvious, but they were the images that I've been affected by for my whole lifetime. They are heartfelt. They seem inexhaustible because they are archetypal, yet in my adult years, I've watched Jesus and Elvis become parallel kitsch. So fuck Jesus if his image had lost its impact. I studied books that contained stories about the lives of the saints to enrich the iconography for the piece, and, in doing so, added much to my own vocabulary. I was already involved in technical kink (procedures commonly used in proper sadomasochism groups), which I borrowed from for the first scene, where three nurses perform invasive genital procedures simultaneously on three patients. The piece unfolded like stations of the cross, each scene fluctuating between chaotic action and contrived setup. The set was lit with blinding bald bulbs (operating room) and sepia toned gels (to give the effect of old religious paintings), and tons of special spot lights. A shameless drama queen, *Martyrs & Saints* ended with myself as St Sebastian martyred in a Zen garden. I learned only recently that devotees would often pray to St Sebastian in times of plague.

4 Scenes In A Harsh Life takes place in contemporary situations, either autobiographical, or based on real-life observations. In some ways, it is the classic Modern Primitive piece, with the right amount of scarification, piercing, and a tribal dance scene. Where *Martyrs & Saints* may have at points been shrill, in *4 Scenes* I had to strive to drop the judgments, and really take a look at working class sexism, drug addiction, suicidal depression, prophetic dream images, Pentecostal evangelism, leather daddy/boy role-playing, and for a finale, a non-traditional lesbian three-way white wedding. In a sick way, I viewed all these states, habits or obsessions, as personal mantras. One's spirit pulse. They can be judged as destructive, perverse, tragic, violent, silly or ecstatic, that's the point. Underneath the judgment is the essence, the reason why a man spends six hours in a strip bar. The reason a woman channels the voice of God and travels the world, performing. The miracle of dreaming my tattoos were finished and I was levitating, which led me to finish tattooing my body. The need for a grown man to be another man's little baby bear. These scenarios lent themselves for perfect tableau vivant, each with their own set, cast and costumes; then once allowed to breathe and talk, they would eventually. I found the pulse in each scene: in attempting this, I found the answer I've been looking for to explain my childhood: the arrogance of being chosen by God, and the pain of active self-destruction. I was already in touch with the fact that my life probably wouldn't have been so extreme if I had been loved, privileged, and guided in a more coherent direction, but when I get told *4 Scenes* contains too much suffering, what can I say? What comes to mind is the voice of Patti Smith, testifying: 'Those who have suffered know suffering.'

In making *Deliverance*, I started at a difficult point; I was in transition with my belief system and wasn't sure I could still call myself an atheist. I had stubbornly held on to this title with pride. After nine years of HIV seropositivity, I was still mortified by the idea of dying young, especially due to an ugly, AIDS-related illness. Even today, some days I remain aloof, but metaphorically, I still hear the clock ticking. I'm hyper-aware that I'm dying; and worse, I feel guilty because I don't take good care of my health, frantic because I haven't realized all of my goals and find myself getting further and further away from being able to accept love in my life. In my frenzy to be alive and heard, I'm afraid I may not really be experiencing my life.

It is not my intention to find God through *Deliverance*. It started as both a challenge and a search for acceptance. And hopefully, theatrically, a chance to mature and develop. I looked at the origins of theatre: the Greek tragedies, and their setting. That they were performed as an act of pagan worship. I have also been working with monologue coaches to gain control of my voice. And collaborating with different choreographers who are teaching me about beautiful movement. For a 'perfectly awkward' person, this is a challenge. I still feel conviction to use blood, though it seems to be in different ways. Apparently, judging from a couple of scenes in *Deliverance*, I feel drawn to use the asshole more than ever, particularly mine. In *Deliverance*, every scene has a continual polarization of filth and glitz. Gorgeous movement in the dirt. Strings of pearls and shit. Cleansing rinses and smelly herbs. Castrated sinner and Holy Eunuch. Santeria Queens and Penitents.

Krishna orange or fake-tanned muscle queens? Reinfection or sexual freedom? Death and decomposition or death and reincarnation? *Deliverance* – more so than *4 Scenes* – is about AIDS, and the possiblility of miracles and direct evidence of debauchery. It all takes place on a psychic plane, the stage. *Deliverance* has taken The Almighty Apocalypse by the reins, and is riding it into the ground. If I'm wrong, and *Deliverance* is a crime against nature, I hope it means I have to appear before God wearing a cheap costume-jewellery crown upon my head, and half a double-headed dildo hanging out of my ass.

deliverance: outline and selected text

preset and scene I

Deliverance opens with a vision, of a black Buddha (Darryl Carlton) bathed in golden light, sitting still on top of the set, on scaffolding. The scene is supposed to be the Philippines, in a psychic surgery hut. Within the hut are three surgeons, played by butch women. The two matching surgeons wearing? (Cross and Pigpen) place the third, the Healer (Julie Tolentino) in the dirt. The healer (whose persona is modelled after a Trickster God) abstractly moves her body through the dirt, 'burying herself deeper into the ground'. A portal of light opens up, and the three sick men enter. A visual lifted from butoh, the three gray men (Athey, Billy Diggs and Brian Murphy) walk bent over, carrying heavy loads of crutches on their back, moving the circle like three decrepit hands on a clock.

voiceover (excerpt)

Once, long ago, I defied the inevitable consequences of my illness but it's become a never-ending tribulation
I seek your guidance,
deliver me, deliver me

As of my own beliefs,
I say I believe in nothing but life itself,
and yet on this quest to heal my body
I've drank the water from Lourdes
I've eaten the dirt and
I've been rubbed in dirt from New Mexico
I've been prayed over
and had those hands lain upon me
At first I was a sensible man,
I was medicated, infused
but my fall to ideopathicthrombosietapenia
was cause to have my spleen removed
I am feeble, full of shame, and my mantras are cynical
But here, could I have ever imagined such a beautiful place to die?
Could I ever have imagined such a beautiful place?

II. Each surgeon takes a sick man, to the sides of the hut, and restrains him with flesh hooks in a standing up position. I am taken to the bed inside the hut and washed. Jewellery is pulled out of my asshole, I have been given an enema, and when I am expelling it I am gagged, causing me to vomit. I am laid on my back and my limbs are held straight up and out by flesh hooks and rope. I am 'castrated' with steel surgical staples, much the way a queen tucks with tape. The other two sick men have also been washed and castrated.

III. I re-emerge, naked and humble. Above me is the Buddha, now appearing as God Himself. I take position, standing close to His feet.

the eunuch confesses

(confession based on a Yom Kippur service)

The voice of God (indented) is inspired from my experience of active prophecy: 'Verily, verily, I say unto thee' always precedes direct prophecies from God or Jesus. Quotes on the eunuch are modified from Isaiah 56:3–5:

> And let not the eunuch say: Behold I am a dry tree.
> For thus saith the Lord to the eunuchs: They that shall keep my sabbaths, and shall choose the things that please me, and shall hold fast my covenant: I will give to them in my house, and within my walls, a place, and a name better than sons and daughters: I will give them an everlasting name which shall never perish.

The voice of the eunuch is based on a service of Yom Kippur – the xxx of atonement – the eunuch has personally taken on the sin of the world.
The Eunuch Confesses

> Verily, verily, I say unto thee, Let not the eunuch say:
> I am a dry tree
> For thus sayith the Lord to the eunuchs:
> I will give them an everlasting name which shall never perish

I have trespassed
I have dealt treacherously
I have robbed
I have spoken slander
I have acted perversely
and I have wrought wickedness

> He who hath wrought wickedness, hath done wrong
> he shall have both testicles removed, this is the law of the land
> still, I give you an everlasting name

I have been presumptuous
I have done violence
I have framed lies
I have counselled evil
and I have spoken falsely

He who speaketh falsely against God as thou hast spoken
shall succumb unto a penectomy, it is written
still, I give you an everlasting name

I have scoffed
I have revolted
I have provoked
I have rebelled
I have committed iniquity
and I have transgressed

He who transgresses against the laws of man
invents the path of his own destruction
still, I give you an everlasting name, verily I sayith unto thee

I have oppressed
I have been obstinate
I have done wickedly
I have corrupted
I have committed abomination
I have gone astray
I have led others astray

IV. God drops a beautiful velvet cape – previously worn and made famous by none other than Leigh Bowery – over the eunuch's head. Overacting and poncing about, Miss Eunuch works every hideous moment of the monologue, the demented shrill voice of Alessandro Moreschi (the only known recordings of a castrato, done at the Vatican in 1902) playing in the background.

the eunuch emerges

This life plays out like a relentless Tragedy
Thrice I've watched death approach, and narrowly survived
In response, my whole being seems to continually bask in the splendour of rebirth
These healings are little more than a masking,
for horrors thinly veiled in salvation

Quite heavy talk for an atheist
though really, by nature I'm quite superstitious
in practice, I sidestep around curses, jinxes, karma and symbols of bad luck

reasoning to myself that it's better to be safe than sorry
perhaps I turn simple fucking irony
into complex strategies of psychic warfare

Whose idea was it for me to be completely castrated?
step right up – welcome to sexual judgment day
why didn't they sew my asshole shut while they were at it
and cut off my chewy, luscious nipples
perhaps this is my payback

According to some, I had become scum of the earth
moving from man to man, fuck to fuck
thriving on fornication
spreading and enhancing my disease
abandoning my humanity for sexuality
using random flesh as a replacement for love

That is until the disease took away my sex drive
and the surgeons cut away my organs
I feel caught in a cycle of penance
I keep paying and paying and paying a price

If I could picture a simple universe
where the gods rule earth from up above,
if they would lay their eyes upon my sorry ass and throw me a little
forgiveness my way
I would walk forth and take position as a royal and holy eunuch

Eunuch #2 (as he snatches microphone away): Oh my God, you're so fucking deluded!

V. After another 'healing', the show takes a strange reality twist. In the beginning, the sick men were all grey, now they have been anointed an exaggerated fake suntan colour.

VI. Loud, blaring disco music comes up, the two tanned eunuchs, in a very posed manner, are kissing, then take several turns to rim the other one. Out comes a double-headed dildo, once that's down the hatch and in place, I begin reading the following from paper:

Rod'n'Bob: a post AIDS boy-boy show

'I'm going to read you a story about my relationship with choreographer Mehmet Sander, and a conversation we had upon meeting.

'We met one Saturday for a paper I was writing. Mehmet showed me videos of his dance. Then we talked for over two hours about, you know, pseudo-intellectual body theory discussion – wherein he compared his precise face forward falls, militaristic repetitions and body-slamming, to my body piercing, cuttings, and public enemas. After that, we talked about SM, raunchy sex, and the fact that we both have been HIV positive for nine years. He asked if I knew Rudy, a mutual friend who had recently died of AIDS. Mehmet told me he used to go over to Rudy's house, he would shove his cock up Rudy's ass, and shoot a big infected load inside the already infected Rudy. I acted shocked, but had to admit that I had done the same thing with other HIV positive men.

'After a few more turns of telling debauched stories, the conversation had sunk pretty low. Talk changed to speculations on our health, and theories about reinfection; how we were both trying to stop rimming assholes because of bacterial infections, hepatitis, and whatever else is going on in someone's shit. We had to stop saying, "yeah boy, come sit on daddy's face". We attained an immediate intimacy through bragging about our destructive sexual conquests, and were now getting vulnerable with each other about our HIV disease.

'We talked about the gay community's "new morality", the conservative climate we interpreted as a backlash of the sexual revolution and AIDS. We bagged on tired muscle queens, and the new homo fascist body aesthetic, and their ultimate representatives, the former Mr Universe, Bob Paris and his blond husband, Rod Jackson, who are now known collectively as Rod'n'Bob Jackson-Paris.

'We both agreed the most sickening aspect of Rod'n'Bob is their gay-couple-of-the-year publicity campaign. Every magazine interview went on at length about their teenage girl-like-romance, how they were in love and will always be together. First bodybuilding champion Bob Paris comes "out" to be with Rod, the precious couple get married and hyphenate their surnames. All the while heavy marketing: Flawless, the workout book written by Bob, exercises modelled by Rod; Straight From the Heart, a hardback account of their fairy-tale romance, then the coffee table books of their nude photos by famous homo photographers Herb Ritts and Tom Bianchi, since which they have been on a non-stop book-signing tour.

'Other than being fascinated by their steroid pumped, orangey, fake-tanned bodies, you can tell in all these photos that they have been neutered. It's definitely gone way beyond imagining how small their testicles have shrunk from shooting steroids.

'I said to Mehmet, "We should do a duet called Rod'n'Bob."

' "Fuck yeah man. Are you going to be Rod or Bob?' " he asked, sort of coy.

'For some reason I felt put on the spot. I suspected he was using this opportunity to confront my butch topman reputation (we were both wearing keys on the left and a cockring around the wrist.) I blatantly sized up his dark Turkish looks, and replied curtly, but demurely, "I'm the fucking blonde, I'll be Rod."

'So in admitting that I was the blonde, I would have to "sacrifice" and take bottom. I thought, I don't want a big infected load shot up my butt. Yet I started to say – against my will of course – "why don't you go ahead and shoot your sick spunk up my fucking nasty hole." A split second inner dilemma about being re-infected stifled the impulse. Instead, vaguely out of context, I said, "I'm not ready to die next year."

'He smiled crookedly at me as if I was a gym queen with medium-length feathered blonde hair and a toothpaste commercial smile. "Neither am I," he said.

'This is Rod'n'Bob: A Post AIDS Boy-Boy Show.'

Throughout the reading, we change position from doggy style to missionary, the dildo always penetrating us both. Buddha comes back and severs the dildo, face fucks us with our respective half. Since writing this piece, it has been announced that Rod and Bob are no longer a couple, and that, in fact they hadn't been for some time. There is speculation that they covered up their separation to keep up sales on their various books. It's funny to do that scene with Brian Murphy, as he is my ex-lover from five years ago. At the time, you could say we were sort of fantasized as the Rod and Bob of the piercing set.

VII. VIII. & IX. Buddha changes character, ties on her new trophies to her belt, and does the solo 'Shiva Penis Dance'. Lights up and we're in the morgue, all three sick men hanging from their ankles on slatboards. The surgeons are in their mortician mode, everything covered in black, even their faces. They drain the bodies and close the straps on the body bags. The ankles are released, the bodies slid into formation. The surgeons reappear as widows, and after they are through with burying the bodies, are finally able to show emotion. They stretch their bodies over the burial mounds, pull the pins from their brow, and cry blood.

As a performer in *Deliverance*, I'm flooded with a sense of accomplishment each night when I get hung up by my ankles. My active performing is finished. Still, I try to be good at acting dead, trying hard not to twitch or cough or sneeze. I stay in the moment, it's too early to start reflecting on how the piece went. As the writer of *Deliverance*, I feel very exposed, not sure if anyone could relate to the piece, if anyone could get over our injuries, or if anyone gave a fuck at all. Then I feel the straps of the black canvas body bag wrap over my head and around my body. They are bound, tightly. I quickly re-position my arms when I feel my ankles release, hoping my head doesn't hit the ground too hard. As the dirt is being shovelled on me, I begin to feel the sadness of the scene. The idea of the women grieving over our deaths breaks my heart, makes me feel numb in a strange way. I know that on each side of Theresa this same scene is going on with Cross and Pigpen, but I can't imagine what it looks like happening simulaneously. The heavy dirt is making the air thin in my bag, my breathing speeds up, becomes faster and shallower and I start to panic, but I have to surrender to the situation. I feel Theresa sit on my feet, her hands running through the dirt on top of me. I think it's over, I hear muffled clapping. I feel Theresa get up and minutes seem to go by. If the audience is waiting for us, the girls will dig us up, so we can take a raggedy bow together. If the audience is leaving, we have to wait in the ground, even though the air is getting thinner, so as not to disrupt the setting. There is a certain honour to be maintained in staying true to the piece.

the photo

Edmund White

(During the conference at the ICA on AIDS I felt, from something someone said, that there was, even in this gathering, an assumed prejudice against the way people with AIDS look, especially towards the end of their lives. Perhaps because I belong to that Stonewall Generation that redefined homosexuality itself as something good and beautiful, perhaps because I've tried to continue in that tradition by fighting ageism in the gay community and by always being open about my HIV status, I've never accepted the idea that PWAs are 'ugly' or 'pathetic'. The discussion reminded me of this piece that I'd written earlier for a Key West newspaper on National AIDS Awareness Day).

In January 1994 when I was in Key West with my lover, Hubert Sorin, we had drinks with Rollie McKenna and she took his picture. Rollie, of course, is one of the great portraitists of writers, and she's been around long enough to have done pictures of some of our finest poets and novelists both when they were young and old; only she can give concrete proof of the old adage that we're given the face we have before forty and we earn the face we have afterwards.

We were sitting around with James Merrill, J.D. McClatchy and other friends. Hubert was very ill and had only two more months to live (he died on 17 March in Morocco, a place he favoured because, like Florida, it offered the warmth he craved). At Rollie's that evening, however, he was peculiarly peaceful. For days he'd scarcely been out of the house we'd rented on Elizabeth Street; his only pleasure was the hot tub, which heated and massaged his poor, wracked body. But that evening he wanted to go out and I called up the bicycle rickshaw man, a young Englishman with a sunny nature and a sweet, understanding spirit. He conveyed us the short distance to Rollie's. Hubert brought along his camera, which surprised me slightly; I'd never seen him take pictures at social gatherings before.

Perhaps he was so exhausted that he feared not being able to follow (or to contribute to) a conversation in English (he was French, and though his English was excellent he'd acquired it late and it sometimes gave out when he was tired). Or perhaps, since he knew the end was close, he wanted to commit to the memory of colour on paper the image of dear friends. To be sure, he was an architect and illustrator and he always felt most at home when armed with a pencil or crayon or, in this case, a lens.

Rollie took a snapshot of Hubert as he was fiddling with his camera. He's wearing a three-day beard (a noticeable effect in his case since his beard grew in fast and black). He's tan, although he'd spent so much time in bed and he'd sat out in the garden only a few minutes, but towards the end of his life he seemed to tan with eerie rapidity, perhaps because all the medications he was taking or his compromised pancreas made him strangely susceptible to the sun. I know that just before he died the Moroccans all thought he was a countryman and would address him in Arabic, which surprised Hubert. He's also wearing his favourite blue jean jacket (only I knew how many layers of clothing he had under it in order to give himself a semblance of substance).

But the most remarkable thing is his expression, one of sweet concentration, at once an absorption in the camera in his hands and an almost saintly look of abstraction, as though all objects now must necessarily seem arbitrary, interchangeable, faintly amusing.

Now that he's dead I often look at this picture. Hubert liked it very much, too. Before Rollie sent it to us, framed and inscribed, a few days after her party, Hubert bitterly disliked all images of himself. He'd been such a handsome young man (he was only thirty-two when he died) and he'd always been very *coquet* about his looks, as the French say – which in the French language and culture is a permissible form of vanity, one invariably remarked on with smiling approval. He'd never had much money but he always took great care of his clothes and even when he was feeling desperately ill he could still get himself up so that he looked extremely elegant. Despite this elegance (even his sobersides doctor remarked on it), Hubert hated any new photograph, sure evidence of his rapid and disastrous decline. In his last year he went from weighing 155 pounds to 105.

Rollie's picture changed all that. Suddenly he could see a new beauty in his face. I'd always seen it because I loved him and admired him and treasured every moment with him and because I knew how handsome he'd been when I first met him five years earlier. But I, too, was impressed by the sweetness of Rollie's picture. Hubert said, 'That shows the difference between a real artist like Rollie and all the amateurs. She was just taking pictures casually with the same kind of camera most people have, and yet she chose the right moment, the right light, the right setting, the right distance, the right mood.'

After Hubert died I put Rollie's portrait of Hubert on our mantlepiece in Paris. Hubert's brother Julien was with me and he said, 'Oh, I don't like to remember Hubert looking like that. You have so many pictures of him when he was healthy and handsome, why do you have to display that one so prominently?'

Julien is one of the people I love the most in all the world. He's just two years older than Hubert, he's gay and Hubert adored him (he dedicated the book *Our Paris: Sketches from Memory* – which I wrote and he illustrated – to his brother). Julien has exactly the same deep voice and laugh Hubert had and the same elaborate, seventeenth century way of speaking French. Hubert and I relied constantly on Julien during the last year of his life and whenever I had to travel away from Paris for a few days Julien would instantly fly up from Nice to stay with Hubert. Julien helped me make all the funeral arrangements and he handled all the necessary forms for recovering Hubert's body from Morocco (not an easy matter at all). Julien and his lover, who've been together fifteen years, did everything humanly possible to sustain us during Hubert's long and difficult illness. And now that he's dead they call me constantly. Julien and I are often surprised that we're going through the same stage of grief at the same rate, often moving from one level of sorrow down to a deeper one on the very same day, even the same hour.

But I simply couldn't agree with him about the picture. In fact I was offended by his confidence in airing such a strong opinion. Maybe because I'm positive and he's negative, maybe because I'm as fat as Hubert was skinny and Julien is a dedicated bodybuilder at the peak of physical perfection, but for whatever reason I resented the insolence of his health.

Then the next day when I went to my shrink for a session, I burst into tears while discussing the photo. I said, 'Maybe I'm crazy but I think Hubert was more beautiful at the end than he was when I first met him. Five years ago of course he made heads turn, he was the elegant young Parisian, he was manly and graceful and wonderfully polite – that uniquely French combination of virility and elegance. But he *earned* that face that Rollie found. Before, he looked like dozens of cute guys, but there, at the end, he had an etched, lined, starved beauty that he'd *achieved* and I'm proud of it and of him.'

The shrink pointed out that these feelings were connected to my reluctance to lose weight, go back to the gym and get the grey out of my hair. 'You and Hubert went through a lot and it changed your looks. If you were to put up a pretty picture of Hubert – or if you were to go back to looking like a clone – it would be a way of denying that experience. We gay people sometimes go through the most horrendous things with a rare heroism – and then when it's all over we repackage ourselves and put ourselves back on the market as though nothing ever happened.'

Of course I went back to Julien and I told him all that and he humoured me by pretending to agree with me because he could see how much it meant to me. Perhaps he's just indulging me, but I know that I don't want to throw a cloth over that rare photo Rollie took on one of the last sixty days Hubert was to have on earth.

contributors

Juan Vicente Aliaga lives and works in Valencia, where he is a Lecturer at the Faculty of Fine Arts. He is co-editor of *Arte Conceptual Revisado* (Conceptual Art Revisited, 1990), *De amor y rabia. Acerca del arte y el Sida* (On Love and Rage. Art and AIDS, 1993), and *Identidad y diferencia. Sobre la cultura gay en España* (Identity and Difference. On Gay Culture in Spain, 1996). A curator and art critic, he writes regularly for *Artforum* and *frieze*.

Ron Athey is an internationally-acclaimed performance artist. His trilogy, *Deliverance*, confronts AIDS and loss, martyrdom and apocalypse, ritual and oblivion, in visually and viscerally stunning form.

Chetan Bhatt is involved in several HIV/AIDS social care and advocacy projects.

Michael Bronski is a long-time AIDS and gay activist. His books include *Culture Clash: The making of gay sensibility*, and he is the editor of *Flashpoint: Gay male sexual writing* and *Taking Liberties: Gay male perspectives on politics and culture*. His essays have appeared in more than twenty-five anthologies, and in numerous magazines. His book, *The Pleasure Impulse: Culture, backlash, and the struggle for gay freedom* is forthcoming from St Martin's Press

Alexander García Düttmann is a philosopher. Born in Barcelona, he lives in London and Sydney. He is the author of *The Memory of Thought: An essay on Heidegger and Adorno; At Odds With AIDS*; and *Between Cultures: Tensions in the struggle for recognition*.

Larys Frogier is an AIDS activist and art critic. He teaches contemporary art history at the University of Rennes. He has written on AIDS activism and has published work on contemporary artists including Nan Goldin, Felix Gonzalez-Torres, Robert Mapplethorpe and Kiki Smith.

Sander Gilman is Professor of German at the University of Chicago and Head of the Modern Language Association. He is author/editor of over fifty books, including *Images of Health and Illness* and *A History of the Jewish Body*.

Robin Gorna is the Director of Health Promotion at the Terrence Higgins Trust, with which she has been associated since 1986. She is author of *Vamps, Virgins and Victims: How Can Women Fight AIDS?* (Cassell, London, 1996).

Jonathan Grimshaw co-founded, in 1985, Body Positive, the first self-help group in the United Kingdom for people with HIV. He has been a leading figure in the development of community-based responses to HIV and has advised national and Government bodies on AIDS policy. He co-wrote the UK Declaration of the Rights of People with HIV and AIDS and is a founding member of the UK Forum on HIV and Human Rights.

Mark Harrington studied critical theory, film and photography at Harvard University. He joined ACT UP/New York in 1988 where he was among the leaders of the Treatment + Data Committee (T+D), which spearheaded successful campaigns including those against the FDA for more flexibility and expanded access to AIDS drugs, and against the NIH to demand the full participation of activists and people with HIV in AIDS research. He authored many of ACT UP's key publications. In 1990 he discovered he was HIV-positive. In 1992 he left ACT UP to help found TAG, the Treatment Action Group. In 1994, legislation based on *AIDS Research at the NIH: A Critical Review*, which he co-authored, was signed into law by President Clinton; this resulted in a restructuring and streamlining of *NIH AIDS* research under a strong Office of AIDS Research. He is working on a book on AIDS treatment activism.

Meurig Horton has been active in AIDS organizing since 1985. From 1989–1995 he was an officer of the World Health Organisation Global Program on AIDS in Geneva working with community-based groups in the developing world on prevention and care initiatives and strengthening community groups' capacity to respond to the epidemic. He has published widely on HIV prevention, research, sexuality and human rights and is doing a PhD at the London School of Hygiene and Tropical Medicine.

Edward King is the author of *Safety in Numbers* (1993) which documents the history of gay safer sex initiatives and the harmful effects of the degaying of AIDS, and, with Chris Markham, *Rubber Up! Every gay man's guide to condoms*. He was the Terrence Higgins Trust's first gay men's health education officer, co-founded the education and campaigning group, Gay Men Fighting AIDS, and serves on the board of the gay HIV prevention charity, Rubberstuffers. He works for the *National AIDS Manual* as editor of AIDS Treatment Update and the HIV and AIDS Treatments Directory. His writing can be found on the Internet at http://www.users.dircon.co.uk/~eking/.

Robert Lee is HIV programme manager for Enfield and Haringey Health Authority, London, and has been involved in various HIV/AIDS organizations and prevention activities in the UK, the USA, France and the Caribbean.

Dorothy Mukasa is the HIV Planning and Development Officer for the London Borough of Tower Hamlets in London. She is responsible for policy development, commissioning HIV social services provision as well as joint commissioning (with the East London and City Health Authority), of HIV prevention for people with HIV in Tower Hamlets. Dorothy was one of the founders of the Uganda AIDS Action Fund in 1987, and is author of their report, *The Fight Against AIDS in Uganda – An Insight* (1989). Between 1992 and 1994 she was seconded to work for the Department of Health, Communicable Diseases Branch as Ethnic Minorities Advisor HIV/AIDS. Dorothy has written many papers and addressed numerous conferences on HIV and African communities in Britain. As an active member of her community in London, she is a member of, and advisor to, several Ugandan community based organizations. She is studying for an MSC in Public Policy at London University.

Walt Odets is a clinical psychologist in private practice in Berkeley, California. He is author of *AIDS Education and Harm Reduction for Gay Men: Psychological Approaches for the 21st Century* and *Why We Stopped Doing Primary Prevention for Gay Men in 1985*; of two chapters for *Therapists on the Front Line: Psychotherapy with gay men in the age of AIDS*; and a book, *In The Shadow of the Epidemic: Being HIV negative in the age of AIDS*. A member of the AIDS Task Force of the Gay and Lesbian Medical Association, he has spoken frequently on education and prevention for gay men including two of the eleven International Conferences on AIDS, conferences of the American Psychological Association, American Psychiatric Association, the National Gay and Lesbian Task Force, the National AIDS update and the National Gay and Lesbian Health Conference.

Cheryl Overs has worked in the prostitutes' rights area for almost twenty years. She ran a brothel and studied law in Melbourne, Australia, where she was one of the founders of the Australian Prostitutes' Collective. Since moving to Europe in 1989 she has worked as a consultant to health services working with sex workers. In 1991 she was one of the founders of an international information and human rights advocacy network of organizations working with sex workers and sex worker groups. She is currently coordinator of the International Network of Sex Work Projects.

Cindy Patton teaches lesbian and gay studies at the Graduate Institute of the Liberal Arts at Emory University in Atlanta, Georgia. She is the author of many works on activism and social aspects of the AIDS pandemic, including: *Sex and Germs: The politics of AIDS; Inventing AIDS; Last Served: Gendering the HIV Pandemic and Fatal Advice.*

Tim Rhodes is Research Fellow at The Centre for Research on Drugs and Health Behaviour, University of London, where he is undertaking ethnographic studies into drug use, risk perception and behaviour change among injecting drug users, people living with HIV infection and their sexual partners. He is also involved in cross-national studies of drug use in developing countries and the development of community-based HIV prevention interventions. His publications include: *Risk, Intervention and Change* (1994) and (with Richard Hartnoll) *AIDS, Drugs and Prevention: Perspectives on Individual and Community Action* (1996).

Sarah Schulman is the author of nine books, including the novel, *Rat Bohemia*, a collection of essays, *My American History*, and a new novel, *Shimmer* (Avon). She is a founder member of ACT UP and a co-founder of the Lesbian Avengers. She is currently collaborating with Tina Landau and Michael Kone on a musical theatre epic about McCarthyism, *Innocent Ancestors*.

Peter Scott is a Founder of the *National AIDS Manual*, Gay Men Fighting AIDS and the London Lesbian and Gay Switchboard.

Eve Kosofsky Sedgwick is the Newman Ivey White Professor of English at Duke University, North Carolina. Her books include *Between Men: English literature and male homosocial desire; Epistemology of the Closet; Tendencies; Fat Art, Thin Art*, and several edited volumes including *Gary In Your Pocket: Stories and Notebooks on Gary Fisher* (Duke University Press, 1996).

Jonathan G. Silin is the author of *Sex, Death, and the Education of Children: Our passion for ignorance in the age of AIDS.* Formerly a community-based AIDS educator, he is a member of the Graduate Faculty at Bank Street College of Education, New York.

Paula A. Treichler is a professor at the University of Illinois, Urbana-Champagne, serving on the faculty of the College of Medicine, the Institute of Communications Research, and the Women's Studies Program. Her work on AIDS/HIV has appeared in many journals, including *Cultural Studies, October, Art Forum, Science*, and *Transition*, and in many edited collections. Her book, *How To Have Theory in an Epidemic: Cultural Chronicles of AIDS*, is forthcoming from Duke University Press.

Simon Watney is Director of the Red Hot AIDS Charitable Trust, a London-based funding initiative for international HIV/AIDS education for those at demonstrably high risk of infection. He is also a well-known writer, critic and broadcaster. His most recent book is *Practices of Freedom: Selected Writings on HIV/AIDS*, Rivers Oram Press, London/Duke University Press, Durham NC, USA, 1994.

Edmund White, Chevalier des Arts et Lettres, is an American author who lives in Paris. He has written such novels as *A Boy's Own Story* and *The Beautiful Room is Empty* as well as the biography of Jean Genet, for which he won the National Book Critics Circle Award. His new novel, *The Farewell Symphony*, is about the impact of AIDS on the New York gay community. He is a member of the American Academy of Arts and Letters.